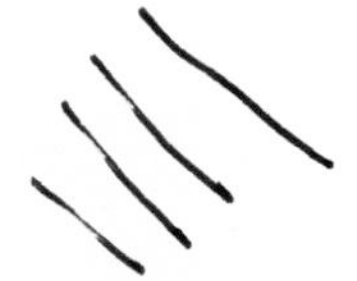

LANGUAGE IDEOLOGIES

OXFORD STUDIES IN ANTHROPOLOGICAL LINGUISTICS
William Bright, *General Editor*

Volumes Published in the Series:

1 Gunter Senft: *Classificatory Particles in Kilivila*
2 Janis B. Nuckolls: *Sounds Like Life: Sound-Symbolic Grammar, Performance, and Cognition in Pastaza Quechua*
3 David B. Kronenfeld: *Plastic Glasses and Church Fathers: Semantic Extension from the Ethnoscience Tradition*
4 Lyle Campbell: *American Indian Languages: The Historical Linguistics of Native America*
5 Chase Hensel: *Telling Our Selves: Ethnicity and Discourse in Southwestern Alaska*
6 Rosaleen Howard-Malverde (ed.): *Creating Context in Andean Cultures*
7 Charles L. Briggs (ed.): *Disorderly Discourse: Narrative, Conflict, and Inequality*
8 Anna Wierzbicka: *Understanding Cultures through Their Key Words: English, Russian, Polish, German, and Japanese*
9 Gerrit J. van Enk and Lourens de Vries: *The Korowai of Irian Jaya: Their Language in Its Cultural Context*
10 Peter Bakker: *A Language of Our Own: The Genesis of Michif, the Mixed Cree-French Language of the Canadian Métis*
11 Gunter Senft: *Referring to Space: Studies in Austronesian and Papuan Languages*
12 David McKnight: *People, Countries, and the Rainbow Serpent: Systems of Classification among the Lardil of Mornington Island*
13 Penelope Gardner-Chloros, Robert B. Le Page, Andrée Tabouret-Keller, and Gabrielle Varro (eds.): *Vernacular Literacy Revisited*
14 Steven Roger Fischer: *Rongorongo, the Easter Island Script: History, Traditions, Text*
15 Richard Feinberg: *Oral Traditions of Anuta, a Polynesian Outlier in the Solomon Islands*
16 Bambi B. Schieffelin, Kathryn A. Woolard, and Paul V. Kroskrity (eds.): *Language Ideologies: Practice and Theory*

LANGUAGE IDEOLOGIES

Practice and Theory

Edited by

BAMBI B. SCHIEFFELIN

KATHRYN A. WOOLARD

PAUL V. KROSKRITY

New York Oxford
OXFORD UNIVERSITY PRESS
1998

Oxford University Press

Oxford New York
Athens Auckland Bangkok Bogota Bombay
Buenos Aires Calcutta Cape Town Dar es Salaam
Delhi Florence Hong Kong Istanbul Karachi
Kuala Lumpur Madras Madrid Melbourne
Mexico City Nairobi Paris Singapore
Taipei Tokyo Toronto Warsaw

and associated companies in
Berlin Ibadan

Published by Oxford University Press, Inc.
198 Madison Avenue, New York, New York 10016

Library of Congress Cataloging-in-Publication Data
Language ideologies : practice and theory / edited by
Bambi B. Schieffelin, Kathryn A. Woolard, and Paul V. Kroskrity.
p. cm. — (Oxford studies in anthropological linguistics; 16)
Includes bibliographical references.
ISBN 0-19-510561-3; ISBN 0-19-510562-1 (pbk.)
1. Language and culture. 2. Ideology. I. Schieffelin, Bambi B.
II. Woolard, Kathryn Ann. III. Kroskrity, Paul V., 1949- .
IV. Series.
P35.L333 1998
400—dc21 97-23336

9 8 7 6 5 4 3 2

Printed in the United States of America
on acid-free paper

PREFACE

Edited volumes, like all texts, have histories, and in this case it is a long one. This book grows out of a full-day symposium on "Language Ideology: Practice and Theory" organized by the present editors, sponsored by the Program Committee of the American Anthropological Association, and held at the Association's annual meeting in Chicago, November 1991. The premise of that symposium was that language ideology stands in dialectical relation with—and thus significantly shapes—social, discursive, and linguistic practices. Not merely an epiphenomenon, but rather a crucial link mediating human acts and institutions, language ideology merited more scholarly attention than it had thus far been given.

In that early attempt to bring an area of inquiry to the attention of the discipline, we adopted a relatively unconstrained sense of "language ideology." We included cultural conceptions not only of language and language variation but also of the nature and purpose of communication, and its role in the life of social collectivities. In order to build toward a general understanding of the cultural variability of language ideologies and their roles in social and linguistic life, the symposium brought together a broad spectrum of anthropologists. Some worked in more traditional societies, others in postindustrial settings; some focused more on linguistic structure, others on social process.

Most of the papers presented in that symposium were expanded and appeared in a special issue of *Pragmatics* on "Language Ideology" (1992, 2:235–453). Since then, language ideology has increasingly coalesced as the focus of scholarly attention. Both the symposium itself and the special journal issue led to a number of conversations and events organized around the proposition that language ideology is a mediating link between social forms and forms of talk. In particular, a number of the authors included here participated in the working group on Language and Nation sponsored by the Center for Transcultural Studies in Chicago (1992–94). That group produced another session at the American Anthropological Association meetings (Washington, D.C., 1993) and a second special issue of *Pragmatics*, "Constructing Languages and Publics," edited by Susan Gal and Kathryn Woolard (1995, 5:129–282). Many of our authors also participated in the Advanced Seminar on Language Ideologies sponsored by the School of American Research in Santa Fe (April 1994) and a related session at the American Anthropological Association meetings (Atlanta, 1994). Paul Kroskrity organized that seminar and session, and has edited the forthcoming volume of papers from them, *Regimes of Language*.

The volume in hand is a fully revised version of the 1992 *Pragmatics* special issue, with contributions reworked and expanded to reflect thoughts developed in those extended discussions and in the advancing literature. This book also reflects repeated (endless, some contributors feared) rounds of commentary and exchange between authors, between authors and editors, and especially between authors of primary articles and authors of the three commentaries. We have difficulty identifying which is the call and which the response in some of the highly collaborative textual artifacts that have resulted. As editors, we found it necessary to break into a lively ongoing dialogue so that it could be aired. Nonetheless, although we have updated, refined, and expanded the volume, we have also tried to retain its original character as the first in a series of exchanges, the foundational collaborative effort in a line of inquiry that we hope will continue.

Over the years of its evolution, many people beyond the immediate authors contributed to this volume. We particularly thank the other participants in the 1991, 1993, and 1994 AAA sessions and in the working group on Language and Nation: Dick Bauman, Don Brenneis, Susan DiGiacomo, Sandro Duranti, David Gegeo, Bill Hanks, Monica Heller, Ben Lee, Hy Van Luong, Jacqueline Urla, Karen Watson-Gegeo, and Mike Willmorth. We are also grateful to the International Pragmatics Association and the editors of *Pragmatics*, to the Center for Transcultural Studies and Ben Lee as its director, to Douglas Schwartz and the School of American Research, to our series editor Bill Bright, to our colleague Rob Moore for all kinds of support, and to David Valentine whose assistance in the proofing stage made all the difference.

Organization of the Volume

This book attempts to reposition the anthropology of language in a research agenda addressing the social-historical processes that link face-to-face communities to national and transnational spheres. The collection is framed by an introduction to language ideology as an area of inquiry. In it, Woolard discusses motivations for, potentials of, and problems with the ideology concept, and she reviews the principal literatures relevant to language ideology. The remaining chapters are organized into three parts, each followed by a commentary (chapters by Michael Silverstein, Susan Philips, and Susan Gal). The three parts highlight by juxtaposition certain aspects of multifaceted papers, which could as easily have been grouped differently. However, the divisions are not simply arbitrary, but rather allow us to bring out certain analytic themes that deserve emphasis.

Part I, "Scope and Force of Dominant Conceptions of Language," focuses on the propensity of particular cultural models to affect linguistic and social behavior, and on the range or scope of social phenomena over which they exert influence. Ideologies that develop in relation to one kind or domain of speech activity can become elaborated as key ideas and play a structuring role in other domains of activity, shaping a variety of institutions and linguistic structures. The exportation of such models from one social group to another is as much a concern as is exportation from one area of human activity and communication to another.

Part II, "Language Ideology in Institutions of Power," continues the examination of the force of specific language beliefs, but narrows the scope to the central role that language ideologies play in the functioning of particular institutions of power such as schooling, the law, or mass media. All of the cases in Part II are drawn from state societies and/or institutions of the state, but it is not our design to limit the investigation of institutional language ideology to such settings.

Part III, "Multiplicity and Contention among Ideologies," reconsiders some of the assumptions that may underpin our emphases in the first two sections. While in looking at the scope and force of ideological tenets we tend to focus on ideologies taken to be dominant, the chapters in the final section emphasize multiplicity, contradiction, and contention among ideologies within particular societies.

Unintended intellectual divides have sometimes emerged between linguistic and sociocultural anthropologists and even among anthropologists of language themselves, whether on grounds separating traditional and complex societies, Western and non-Western, linguistic and social foci, or "macro" and "micro." The topic of language ideology may be one much-needed bridge between work on language structure and language politics, as well as between linguistic and social theory more generally. But more than just a unifying force, we hope that attention to language ideology remains as a fresh and productive reformulation of problems in linguistic and social life.

New York B.B.S.
San Diego K.A.W.
September 1997

CONTENTS

Part II: Language Ideology in Institutions of Power

Part III: Multiplicity and Contention among Ideologies

CONTRIBUTORS

Jan Blommaert received a Ph.D. in African history and philology in 1989 from the University of Ghent, with a thesis on "Kiswahili Political Style." His main areas of interest are pragmatics, political discourse, and intercultural and international communication. He was affiliated with the IPrA Research Center at the University of Antwerp from 1991 to 1997. He is now teaching African linguistics at the University of Ghent.

Charles L. Briggs is professor of ethnic studies at the University of California, San Diego. Having conducted extensive research with Spanish speakers in New Mexico and in eastern Venezuela, he is interested in the discursive construction of social inequality based on concepts of race, ethnicity, gender, and class, particularly in law and medicine.

James Collins is an anthropologist and linguist who teaches in the department of anthropology and the department of reading at the State University of New York at Albany. He has done extensive research on language and education in urban and rural settings and has studied Tolowa language, culture, and social history for more than a decade. His publications include *Understanding Tolowa Histories: Western Hegemonies and Native American Responses* (1998).

Rachelle Charlier Doucet received an M.A. degree from the Center for Latin American and Caribbean Studies at New York University where she is a Ph.D. candidate trained in anthropology and linguistics. Her dissertation research focuses on language ideology and pedagogy in urban elementary schools in Port-au-Prince, Haiti.

Joseph Errington is a professor of anthropology and East Asian languages and literatures at Yale University. His current work, on bilingualism and social change in Indonesia, is titled *Shifting Languages: Interaction and Identity in Javanese Indonesia* (1998).

Susan Gal is professor of anthropology at the University of Chicago. Her research focuses on the political economy of language and the language of politics in European societies. She has written about bilingualism and its historical contexts in *Language Shift* (1979). Other publications deal with language and gender, codeswitching, and the history of Hungarian linguistics. She is currently engaged in a project on the performance of political change in Eastern Europe, and another on the nature of linguistic boundaries with Judith T. Irvine.

Jane H. Hill is Regents' Professor of anthropology and linguistics at the University of Arizona. She specializes in the sociolinguistics of the indigenous languages of the Americas, especially languages of the Uto-Aztecan family. She is currently president of the American Anthropological Association.

Judith T. Irvine is professor of anthropology at Brandeis University. Her research concerns the sociocultural context and political economy of language, with a particular focus on African languages, especially Wolof (Senegal). Her current projects include a study of African linguistics in the era of colonization and (with Susan Gal) an exploration of language ideologies, boundaries, and differentiation.

Paul V. Kroskrity is associate professor of anthropology at the University of California, Los Angeles. He received his Ph.D. from Indiana University and has conducted extensive research in the Arizona Tewa (First Mesa, Hopi Reservation) and Western Mono (Central California) Indian communities. His research interests include language contact, language and identity, verbal art, language renewal, and language in new media applications (e.g., CD ROM). He is the author of *Language, History, and Identity: Ethnolinguistic Studies of the Arizona Tewa* (1993).

Don Kulick is associate professor of anthropology at Stockholm University, Sweden. He has carried out fieldwork in rural Papua New Guinea and in urban Brazil, and his work in linguistic anthropology has focused on language socialization and language shift, and on language and gender. His publications include the monographs *Language Shift and Cultural Reproduction: Socialization, Self, and Syncretism in a Papua New Guinean Village* (1992), and *Practically Women: The Lives, Loves and Work of Brazilian Travesti Prostitutes* (1998).

Elizabeth Mertz is associate professor at Northwestern University School of Law and research fellow at the American Bar Foundation. She received her Ph.D. in anthropology from Duke University and her J.D. from Northwestern University. Her research has focused on the intersection of language, social sciences, and law and on the semiotics of social identity. She is currently coeditor of the journal *Law and Social Inquiry* and a member of the board of trustees and the executive committee of the Law and Society Association.

Susan U. Philips is professor of anthropology at the University of Arizona. She received her Ph.D. in linguistic anthropology from the University of Pennsylvania in 1974. She is the author of *The Invisible Culture: Communication in Classroom and Community on Warm Springs Indian Reservation* (1983/1993) and coeditor of *Language, Gender and Sex in Comparative Perspective* (1987). Her latest book is *Ideology in the Language of Judges* (1998, Oxford University Press). Her most recent research has been on language use in the postcolonial courts of Tonga, a tiny Polynesian nation in the South Pacific.

Bambi B. Schieffelin is professor of anthropology at New York University. A linguistic anthropologist, her research areas include language socialization, discourse analysis, literacy, metalinguistics, and social change. She has carried out ethnographic and sociolinguistic fieldwork with Haitians in New York City and among the Kaluli of Papua New Guinea. She is the author of *The Give and Take of Everyday Life: Language Socialization of Kaluli Children* (1990) and is currently working on a new book, *New Words, New Worlds: Missionization, Literacy and Social Transformation in Kaluli Society.*

Michael Silverstein has been on the faculty of the University of Chicago since 1971 where he is currently the Charles F. Grey Distinguished Service Professor in the departments of anthropology, linguistics, and psychology, and in the Committees on General Studies in the Humanities and on Ideas and Methods. His theoretical and descriptive contributions range from modeling the flow of communicated meanings during verbal interaction to the role of language as a medium and semiotic operator of cultural ideologies. He is involved in long-term study of languages and cultures of indigenous North America and Australia, and he has turned the framework of linguistic anthropology to investigating contemporary American English. With Greg Urban, he has recently brought out the edited volume *Natural Histories of Discourse* (1996).

Debra Spitulnik is an assistant professor in the department of anthropology at Emory University. She works primarily within media studies and sociolinguistics, and her research interests include large-scale discourse processes and the mediation of national communities, the social implications of codeswitching and hybrid languages, and the experience of modernity in Africa.

Jef Verschueren is a research associate of the Belgian National Fund for Scientific Research. He received a Ph.D. in linguistics from the University of California at Berkeley. His main interests are theory formation in pragmatics, metapragmatics, and intercultural and international communication. Publications include *What People Say They Do with Words* (1985), *International News Reporting* (1985), and *Understanding Pragmatics* (1998).

Kathryn A. Woolard is associate professor of sociology at the University of California, San Diego. She received her Ph.D. in anthropology from the University of California, Berkeley. Her previous research has been on bilingualism and language politics in Catalonia and in the United States. She is currently engaged in a comparative study of language ideology in Spain, Mexico, and the United States.

LANGUAGE IDEOLOGIES

1

Introduction

Language Ideology as a Field of Inquiry

KATHRYN A. WOOLARD

As Raymond Williams observed, "a definition of language is always, implicitly or explicitly, a definition of human beings in the world" (1977:21). The essays in this volume examine definitions and conceptions of language in a wide range of settings. They focus on how such defining activity organizes individuals, institutions, and their interrelations. Representations, whether explicit or implicit, that construe the intersection of language and human beings in a social world are what we mean by "language ideology."

There is as much cultural variation in ideas about language and about how communication works as a social process as there is in the very form of language (Bauman 1983:16; Hymes 1974:13–14, 31). However, language ideology is of anthropological importance not simply because of its ethnographic variability but because it is a mediating link between social forms and forms of talk (if I may be forgiven a turn of phrase that emphasizes product over process). As all of the contributions to this volume point out, ideologies of language are not about language alone. Rather, they envision and enact ties of language to identity, to aesthetics, to morality, and to epistemology. Through such linkages, they underpin not only linguistic form and use but also the very notion of the person and the social group, as well as such fundamental social institutions as religious ritual, child socialization, gender relations, the nation-state, schooling, and law.

Although efforts have been made recently to delimit language ideology, there is no single core literature, and there are a number of different emphases. Linguistic or language ideologies have been defined most broadly as "shared bodies of commonsense notions about the nature of language in the world" (Rumsey 1990: 346). With more emphasis on linguistic structure and on the activist nature of ideology (to be discussed later in my essay), Silverstein defines linguistic ideologies as "sets of beliefs about language articulated by users as a rationalization or justification of perceived language structure and use" (1979:193). On the other hand, with a greater emphasis on the social facet, language ideology has been defined as "self-evident ideas and objectives a group holds concerning roles of language in the social experiences of members as they contribute to the expression of the group" (Heath 1989:53) and as "the cultural system of ideas about social and linguistic relationships, together with their loading of moral and political interests" (Irvine 1989:255).

I use the terms "linguistic ideology," "language ideology," and "ideologies of language" interchangeably in this essay, although differences among them can be detected in separate traditions of use and are sometimes evident in the contributions to this volume. At least three scholarly discussions explicitly invoke "linguistic ideology" or "language ideology," sometimes in seeming mutual unawareness. One significant, theoretically coherent body of work originates in linguistic anthropology and concentrates on the relation of "linguistic ideology" to linguistic structures. This literature centers on Michael Silverstein's concept of metapragmatics, which encompasses implicit and explicit commentary on and signaling about language-in-use (Silverstein 1976, 1979, 1981, 1985, 1993).[1] A second focal area is contact between languages or language varieties, and on this topic sociologists of language and educationists, as well as linguists and anthropologists, have offered considerations of "language ideology" (e.g., Heath 1989, 1991; Hornberger 1988a; Sonntag and Pool 1987), "purist ideology" (Hill 1985; Hill and Hill 1980, 1986), and "ideologies of standard(ization)" (Milroy and Milroy 1985). Finally, the recently burgeoning historiography of public discourses on language has produced an explicit focus on "ideologies of language," including the scientific ideologies of professional linguistics (Joseph and Taylor 1990).

Beyond research that explicitly invokes the term "ideology" are countless studies that address cultural conceptions of language, in the guise of metalinguistics, attitudes, prestige, standards, aesthetics, and so on. The field could profit from a rethinking of much of this material within an explicitly social-theoretical frame of ideology analysis.

The point of the comparative study of language ideology is to examine the cultural and historical specificity of construals of language, not to distinguish ideology of language from ideology in other domains of human activity. Exclusion of some cultural conceptualizations because language is not sufficiently focal in them would be an ironic outcome to this attempt to denaturalize our own intellectual tradition's compartmentalization and reification of communicative social practices (see Briggs's and Kulick's chapters for further comment; see also, Lucy 1993a; Mannheim 1986; Rumsey 1990). Our hope is not to restrict vision but to focus the attention of scholars of language on the unavoidable significance of the ideological dimension, as well as to provide firmer linguistic ground for students of ideology and discourse more generally.

In this introductory essay, I first review the general concept of ideology and traditions of its analysis. This is not a comprehensive overview of the immense literature on ideology, rather only a rehearsal of some of its recurrent themes, in order to situate this newly coalescing field of linguistic inquiry and to point out the promise as well as the pitfalls.[2] I then turn to literatures on language ideology in particular, illustrating and reviewing a spectrum of approaches to cultural conceptions of language and of communicative behavior as an enactment of a collective order (Silverstein 1987:1–2). Throughout the discussion I try to situate the chapters of this volume, but I leave the extended discussion of each contribution to the commentaries invited from Michael Silverstein, Susan Philips, and Susan Gal.

What Is Ideology?

The word "ideology" is associated with a confusing tangle of commonsense and semitechnical meanings (Friedrich 1989:300). As Silverstein discusses in his commentary here, the term was first coined at the end of the eighteenth century by the French philosopher Destutt de Tracy, a follower of Condillac who optimistically hoped to develop a science of ideas and their basis in sensation. Destutt de Tracy envisioned this positive science as a branch of zoology, one that not only would allow the complete understanding of the human animal but that might ultimately also serve the Enlightenment project of the rational regulation of society.

The term was soon given its negative connotation in Napoleon's effort to discredit Destutt de Tracy and his colleagues, whose institutional position and work were tied to republicanism. In Napoleon's use, ideology became "mere," and "ideologue" a dismissive epithet for proponents of abstract theories not based in or appropriate to human and political realities.

While Destutt de Tracy's intended meaning of a "science of ideas" has been thoroughly abandoned, and Napoleonic negativism has proved quite enduring, there is still significant variation even among social scientific meanings of the term. As Eagleton says, the word "ideology" is itself a text, woven of a tissue of conceptual strands (1991:1). In contemporary uses, several strands recur with particular salience. Although none of them is universal, and none is untroubled or untroubling, I wish to single out four such recurring strands or themes that are picked up by many if not all of the contributors to this volume.

1. The first common strand is an understanding of ideology as ideational or conceptual, referring to mental phenomena; ideology has to do with consciousness, subjective representations, beliefs, ideas. Like Destutt de Tracy's, some contemporary social scientific uses of the term focus almost entirely on this ideational aspect, and when branding a phenomenon as "ideological," they do not intend the social or critical dimensions that are discussed later in this essay. In the broadest instance, ideology is taken to be the more intellectual constituent of culture, "the basic notions that the members of a society hold about a fairly definite . . . area such as honor, . . . the division of labor" (Friedrich 1989:301)—or, we could propose, language. But even more sharply focused and critical analyses of ideology often share this emphasis on ideation and even explicit verbalization. In the sociologist

Alvin Gouldner's communication-based schema, for example, ideologies are discursive, rationalist "reports about the world" (1976:31), or as J. B. Thompson has put it, "that part of consciousness which can be said" (1984:85).

However, a primarily subjective, mentalist siting is far from a universally accepted, or even the most influential, view of ideology in the past few decades. In much recent theory, ideology is not necessarily conscious, deliberate, or systematically organized thought, or even thought at all; it is behavioral, practical, prereflective, or structural. Signification—or, more simply, meaning—rather than ideation in a mentalist sense is the core phenomenon in these contemporary uses. And even the most material aspects of life are invested with meaning, rife with signification when they are encompassed within the field of human action.

French structuralists and poststructuralists cast ideology not as a matter of consciousness or subjective representations but rather of lived relations, to use Althusser's (1971) formulation. Eagleton characterizes ideology in this sense as "a particular organization of signifying practices which goes to constitute human beings as social subjects, and which produces the lived relations by which such subjects are connected to the dominant relations of production in society" (1991:18). This conception disperses ideology throughout the social order (McCarthy 1994:416) and is recognizably related to Bourdieu's use of "doxa" (as opposed to heterodoxy and orthodoxy), as well as to his notion of habitus (1977). There are also similarities, discussed further in this volume by Susan Philips, to Raymond Williams's (1977) interpretation of Gramsci's idea of hegemony as the "saturation of consciousness" and "structures of feeling." The tension between different sitings of ideology, between subjectively explicit and constructively implicit (immanent) versions, is a recurrent concern of contributors to this volume.

A related dimension of variation is the degree to which ideology is held to be a coherent system of signification. In this volume, Hill follows Eagleton (1991) in expecting an ideology to form a relatively coherent system of meanings. But ideology can be viewed as piecemeal and internally contradictory. (Whether the contradiction lies in the conceptual model of the world or in the world which is accurately modeled is another point of some debate.) Vološinov, for example, does not reserve the term "ideology" for organized systems of signification but writes of the "lowest stratum of behavioral ideology" as one that lacks logic or unity (1973:92). Characterizing ideology as a social process, not a possession, Therborn finds it more like "the cacophony of sounds and signs of a big city street than . . . the text serenely communicating with the solitary reader or the teacher . . . addressing a quiet, domesticated audience" (1980:viii).

2. A second, and the most widely agreed-upon, strand is a conceptualization of ideology as derived from, rooted in, reflective of, or responsive to the experience or interests of a particular social position, even though ideology so often (in some views, always) represents itself as universally true.[3] Unlike the first view, this emphasis on social and experiential origins necessarily denies explanatory independence to ideology. It casts ideology as in some way dependent on the material and practical aspects of human life. The character and degree of that relation of dependency vary across different theories, ranging from a view of the material and ideo-

logical as mutually constituting and dialectical to views of ideology as secondary, entirely contingent, and/or superfluous.

3. The third major strand of ideology, often seen as following from the second, is a direct link to inhabitable positions of power—social, political, economic. Ideology is seen as ideas, discourse, or signifying practices in the service of the struggle to acquire or maintain power. For some (e.g., V. I. Lenin), ideology may be a tool of any protagonist in the contestation of power—that is, it can be "ours" as well as "theirs," subaltern as well as dominant. But in the most restrictive formulations of this connection, ideology is always the tool, property, or practice of dominant social groups; the cultural conceptions and practices of subordinate groups are by definition nonideological. For J. B. Thompson, for example, ideology is signification that is "essentially linked to the process of sustaining asymmetrical relations of power—to maintaining domination . . . by disguising, legitimating, or distorting those relations" (1984:4).[4]

4. A fourth major strand in the text of the ideology concept, closely related but not identical to the third, is precisely the last one pointed to by Thompson: that of distortion, illusion, error, mystification, or rationalization. Such distortion can derive from the defense of interest and power, but that is not the only source recognized. When a theorist's emphasis is on the intellectual rather than the social character of ideology, distortion can be seen to derive from limitations on human perception and cognition, as well.[5]

The Marxist tradition has treated distortion as central to the ideology concept, beginning with Marx and Engels's *The German Ideology*, which took up Napoleon's pejoration of the term to criticize the "Young Hegelian" philosophers. Perhaps the best-known phrasing of ideology as illusion is Engels's description of it as "false consciousness" (see discussion in Eagleton 1991:89). A much quoted metaphor of ideology as distortion is Marx and Engels's *camera obscura*, which produces an upside-down image of the world (Marx and Engels 1989:47.) But it is not only Marxists who hold to this conceptual focus. The sociologist Talcott Parsons, for example, asserted that cognitive distortions are always present in ideologies and that deviation from scientific objectivity (itself selective according to community values), through selectivity and distortion, is an essential criterion of ideology ([1959] 1970:294–295).

To many observers, this concept of error or illusion implies complementary forms of knowledge as truth, as well as a privileged position (often reserved for science) from which such truth is knowable. It is this implication in particular that has led many social theorists, Foucault most influential among them, to eschew the notion of ideology in favor of more encompassing concepts such as "discourse" (1970, 1980). As is well known, Foucault argues that "truth" is constituted only within discourses that sustain and are sustained by power. That is, all truth is constituted by ideology, if ideology is understood to be power-linked discourse.

THE GREAT DIVIDE in studies of ideology lies between the second and third conceptual foci, between neutral and negative values of the term. Uses that focus on power and/or distortion share a fundamental critical stance toward ideology; such uses have been variously labeled critical, negative, particular, pragmatic, or pejorative.[6] More globalizing and intellectualizing approaches apply the term broadly to all cultural conceptual schemata and are noncommittal on the truth value of ideology. These have been discussed as neutral, descriptive, notional, or social scientific conceptions of ideology.[7] Betraying my own linguistic ideology, I have come to suspect that a phonological shibboleth can diagnose where a commentator is at least momentarily positioned on this fundamental intellectual divide. A pronunciation of "idea-ology" ([ay]deology) invokes the ideational and representational, while the pronunciation "id-eology" ([ɪ]deology) places power and interest (the id lurking under thin cover?) at the core of the phenomenon. But arguably, even the most doggedly neutral social-scientific uses are tinged with disapprobation, the truly neutral stance more often encoded by the choice of other labels such as culture, worldview, belief, *mentalité*, and so on.

Among anthropologists, there have been vocal advocates for both the negative and the neutral visions of ideology. Clifford Geertz ([1964] 1973) argued forcefully that social science must eschew negative uses and concern itself not with the truth value of ideologies but rather with the way that they mediate meanings for social purposes. The Marxist anthropologist Maurice Bloch (1985), on the other hand, reserves the term "ideology" for critical uses, indicating systems of representation that mask social processes and legitimate a social order. He advocates retaining a distinction between ideology and everyday cognition, derived from experience in interaction with a culturally constructed environment. John and Jean Comaroff (1991) have also proposed a schema that distinguishes culture on the one hand from more power-charged cultural forms of ideology and hegemony on the other, in a taxonomy that is perhaps most clearly applicable to colonial and other culture contact situations. Susan Philips takes this discussion further in her commentary later in this volume.

Karl Mannheim, a founder of the sociology of knowledge, is one theorist who attempted (albeit ambivalently) to neutralize the negative connotations of the ideology concept. In contrast to a "particular" conception of ideology (the negative one that unmasks or debunks an ideology always seen as the intellectual property of others), Mannheim advocated a "total conception" of ideology, as systems of thought that are socially situated and collectively shared ([1936] 1985). That is, all knowledge, including that of the social analyst, is to be understood as ideological. Mannheimian ideological analysis is fundamentally nonevaluative, indistinguishable from the sociology of knowledge, as it studies the way knowledge systems are influenced by the social and historical circumstances in which they are situated.[8]

J. B. Thompson (1990) criticizes Mannheim's total ideology concept for neglecting power relations, but it might be argued that the approach does not so much neglect power as situate it as one aspect (surely an important and inevitable one) of the social positioning of cultural forms. If by ideology we mean signifying practices that constitute social subjects, surely we should also attend to, for example, affiliation, intimacy, and identity, all of which are complexly imbricated with but not directly and simply equatable to power.[9] This larger intersection of signifying practices with social relations is, I think, what both Heath and Irvine are after in defining cultural conceptualizations of language as ideological when/because they are also politically and morally loaded ideas about social experience, social relationships, and group membership.

To be sure, almost any human act of signification in some respect serves to organize social relations.[10] But this does not necessarily mean that enlarging the focus of the ideology concept beyond signification in service of power necessarily enlarges the term to the point of uselessness. Although it does not distinguish one form of signification from another (almost all signification having an ideological aspect), the concept can still very usefully hold one *facet* of signification to the light, what Mannheim called the "social and activist roots" of thinking and signification (1985:5).

Why Ideology?

We have, then, no easy consensus on the meaning and use of the term in question, "ideology." Given this welter, its invocation in the research program announced in this volume and essay should not be construed as a fierce commitment to terminology. Indeed, the initial choice was as much circumstantial as considered, and there may well be better ones.

Again, there is little point to attempting to legislate a single interpretation of ideology from the range of useful meanings (Eagleton 1991:1). Particularly in a volume whose genesis has constituted a first foray into identifying a field of inquiry, recognition of multiple existing traditions has been essential. Although most contributors' formulations are critical, they explore various dimensions of ideology.

A source of particular interest to most contributors, and of unresolved tension for some (see especially the exchange between Kroskrity and Briggs), is the problem of alternate sitings of ideology. Ideology is variously discovered in linguistic practice itself; in explicit talk about language, that is, metalinguistic or metapragmatic *discourse*; and in the regimentation of language use through more implicit metapragmatics. ("Implicit metapragmatics" means linguistic signaling that is part of the stream of language use in process and that simultaneously indicates how to interpret that language-in-use; see Lucy 1993a and Silverstein 1993 for full discussions, and see also Gumperz's (1982) notion of "contextualization cues.") Irvine insists and carefully demonstrates that linguistic ideology must be treated as distinct from and not just implicit in and discoverable from linguistic structure and practice. In the comparative study of honorification, she argues, only by looking at the patterning of linguistic structure, usage, and ideology can cross-linguistic similarities and thus the core of the phenomenon be revealed. Kroskrity argues that a focus on overt ideological contestation should not lead us to lose sight of ideology as doxa, naturalized dominant ideologies that rarely rise to discursive consciousness. Blommaert and Verschueren similarly argue for a methodology that emphasizes the unsaid, the unexpressed assumptions that implicitly frame a text and enable its coherence. Briggs, in contrast, suggests that such an emphasis not only privileges the analyst's perspective but may contribute to the analyst's unintended collusion in reifying the perspective of only a sector of a community.

Some contributors simultaneously examine ideology on more than one level: Spitulnik compares language ideologies that are embodied by the practices of radio broadcasting in Zambia with explicit language ideologies discoverable in discourse about these practices. Mertz, too, looks at ideology as it breaks through multiple layers of language use, from implicit metapragmatic indicators to explicit metapragmatic regimentation. Philips contrasts the degree of explicitness of ideology in the different chapters she discusses and, not unlike Briggs, raises questions about the privilege of reading out ideology as implicated in discourse data. Silverstein identifies institutionalized and interaction rituals as particularly productive (because privileged and value-setting) sites for the enactment, and thus for the researcher's discovery, of language ideology.

In spite of the many possible points of divergence, the essays gathered here share a fundamental emphasis on the social origins of thought and representation, on their roots in or responsiveness to the experience of a particular social position. Seeking to bring out the social dimensions of cultural conceptualizations of language, most contributors go further, insisting on the tie of cultural conceptions to social power as the crucial feature of the phenomena under study, although power is variously conceived. This recognition of the social derivation of representational practices does not simply debunk them, as long as we recognize that there is no privileged knowledge, including the scientific, that escapes grounding in social life.

There is a danger that in taking the subject matter of, for example, the ethnography of speaking and reconsidering it as ideology, we will simply repeat what anthropology has "always talked about anyway" as culture (Asad 1979:26). A naturalizing move that drains the conceptual of its contingent historical content, making it seem universal or timeless, is often cited as key to ideological process. Ironically, anthropology too often has participated in a kind of naturalization of the cultural, casting culture as a shared and timeless prime motivator. The emphasis of ideological analysis on the social and experiential origins of systems of signification helps counter such naturalization. We intend by the term a reminder that the cultural conceptions we study are partial, interest-laden, contestable, and contested (Hill and Mannheim 1992:382). Cultural frames have social histories, and this demands that we ask how seemingly essential and natural meanings of and about language are socially produced as effective and powerful. As Silverstein and Philips both underline in their essays, this implies a methodological stance, a commitment to consider the relevance of social relations, and particularly of power relations, to the nature of cultural forms.

Such a commitment does not entail an outmoded base-superstructure model, in which material life and relations are seen as primary and real and the ideological as derivative, predictable or illusory (a theme Philips develops further in her commentary). Social relations and materiality are not presymbolic but rather are constituted, not just sustained, through symbolic activity (Thompson 1990:58); ideology and social relations are understood in this volume as mutually constitutive. In their early work in *The German Ideology*, Marx and Engels attacked as ideological (i.e., false in socially significant ways) the notion that ideas are autonomous and efficacious. Contributors to this volume do not cast ideology as autonomous, but they do view it as having effects (though not "efficacious" in the sense of having *desired* effects). Ideology—not as ideas so much as construed practice—is consequential, for both social and linguistic process, although not always consequential in the way its practitioners might envision.

This understanding of ideology as active and effective distinguishes our enterprise from many versions of Mannheim-influenced sociology of knowledge, in which the problem addressed by ideological analysis is the more unidirectional social determination of thought. This isn't the sole concern of the research reviewed in this essay and represented in this volume, which can be as interested in the ideological determination of (linguistic and social) structures as in the structural determination of that ideology (see especially the discussion of the work of Michael Silverstein in the following section). The point is not just to analyze and critique the social roots of linguistic ideologies but to analyze their efficacy, the way they transform the material reality they comment on. The emphasis is on what Eagleton, harking back to Austin's speech act theory, calls the performative aspect of ideology under its constative guise: ideology creates and acts in a social world while it masquerades as a description of that world (1991:19).

In the following sections I turn from the general concept of ideology to the review of studies of language ideology in particular. The work discussed includes a full range of scholars' notions of ideology, as well as much research that has gone on under other rubrics, such as culture, worldview, and metalinguistics. Although I try to touch on the widest possible literature in this sometimes breathless survey, I cannot pretend to be exhaustive (only exhausting). My purpose is to contextualize some of the principal and currently most productive approaches to inquiry and to situate the work in this volume in relation to those trends.

Approaches to Language Ideology

Ideology at the Intersection of Language Use and Structure

A dominant view in American anthropology and linguistics has long cast ideology as a somewhat unfortunate, though perhaps socioculturally interesting, distraction from primary and thus "real" linguistic data. Franz Boas (1911) proposed that language is a cultural system whose primary structure is little influenced by secondary rationalizations and so is an exemplary target of analysis. The American structural linguist Leonard Bloomfield ([1927] 1970, 1944) actually gave considerable attention to speakers' evaluations of speech forms. Although he characterized these as part of the linguist's data, his acerbic remarks make it clear that he saw them as a "detour," of little relevance to the explanation of the structure of "normal" language (1933:22). Modern linguistics in the Bloomfieldian tradition has generally assumed that linguistic ideology and prescriptive norms have little significant—or, paradoxically, only pernicious—effect on speech forms (although they may be recognized as having some less negligible effect on writing).[11]

In contrast to this received wisdom, Michael Silverstein has argued that a grasp of language ideology is essential to understanding the evolution of linguistic structure: "The total linguistic fact, the datum for a science of language, is irreducibly dialectic in nature. It is an unstable mutual interaction of meaningful sign forms contextualized to situations of interested human use mediated by the fact of cultural ideology" (1985:220). According to Silverstein, to the extent that language use is teleological—that is, to the extent that speakers conceptualize language as socially purposive action—we must look at their ideas about the meaning, function, and value of language in order to understand the degree of socially shared systematicity in empirically occurring linguistic forms.

For Silverstein, ideology can quite actively and concretely distort the linguistic structure it represents.[12] In analyses of gender in English, T/V pronoun alternation, and Javanese speech levels, Silverstein (e.g., 1979, 1985) has shown that ideology, understood as rationalization, not only explains but actually affects linguistic structure, "rationalizing" it, often by making it more regular. Ideology thus constitutes an essential moment of the phenomenon of analogical linguistic change. Ideological tenets are derived from some aspect of experience and then generalized beyond that core and secondarily imposed on a broader category of phenomena; this broader category then undergoes restructuring. Structure conditions ideology, which then reinforces and expands the original structure, distorting language in the name of making it more like itself (cf. Bourdieu 1991). In a move that joins the conceptual to the active side of ideology (or the constative to the performative, to echo Eagleton's invocation of Austin), this approach shows that to "understand" one's own linguistic usage is potentially to change it (Silverstein 1979: 233). Rumsey has nicely restated this view:

> Language structure and linguistic ideology are not entirely independent of each other, nor is either determined entirely by the other. Instead the structure provides formal categories of a kind that are particularly conducive to "misrecognition." And partly as a result of that misrecognition, might not the linguistic system gradually change so as to approximate that for which it was misrecognized? (1990:357)

Important linguistic changes can be set off by such ideological interpretation of language structure-in-use. But because they derive only from a larger social dialectic, such changes are likely to take an unintended direction, as exemplified in the historical case of second-person pronoun alternation in English that Silverstein (1985) analyzes and Kulick reviews in his chapter in this volume (see Ehrlich and King 1994). In the seventeenth century, Quakers insisted on use of "thou" forms for all second-person singular address, rationalizing this usage according to the emerging linguistic ideology of the time as more truthful because faithful to numerical realities of the objective world. This practice, soon secondarily ideologized by the larger society as an index of stigmatized Quaker identity, set off a backlash movement away from any productive uses of "thou" by that larger community. A shift to "you" was completed by 1700 (Silverstein 1985:246). In this volume, Kulick presents the loss of the local language of Gapun in Papua New Guinea as a parallel case of unintended shift, triggered by a complex of indexical associations of the vernacular and the language of wider communication.

Errington (1988) observes that although it is standard in sociolinguistic analysis to look for relations between structural change and communicative function, it is more controversial to invoke a notion of native speaker awareness as an explanatory link. As Irvine (1989) has pointed out, Labovian correlational sociolinguistics suggests a direct relation between linguistic variation and social differentiation. This correlation is better viewed as mediated by an ideological interpretation of the meaning of language use, as Irvine demonstrates in her contribution to this volume.

Labov himself, construing ideology as overt political discourse, has explicitly discounted the power of ideology to affect speech forms (1979:329). However, Labovian research attends to measures of "subjective reactions" and of "linguistic insecurity"; in his commentary in this volume, Silverstein characterizes the latter as ideological allegiance to the standard register. Labov differentiates mechanisms of change from below and above the level of speakers' awareness and argues that only changes from below are extensive and systematic, while conscious self-correction—which he labels ideology—leads to only sporadic and haphazard effects on linguistic forms (1979:329).

Errington (1988) argues that Labov's generalization is most applicable to phonological variation, which may be mediated less by speakers' understandings of their conscious communicative projects. In his work on Indonesian speech levels, Errington has developed the notion of pragmatic salience—"native speakers' awareness of the social significance of different leveled linguistic alternants" (1985:294–95). More "pragmatically salient" classes of variables are more susceptible to rationalization and strategic use, being (mis)recognized by speakers as more crucial linguistic mediators of social relations (see also Philips 1991 and discussion in Agha 1994). Because such awareness and use drive linguistic change, says Errington, these variables require a fundamentally different, participant-oriented analysis (see also Hanks 1993, Meeuwis and Brisard 1993, Mertz 1993). Irvine takes up this theme of pragmatically salient phenomena in her essay, examining the relation between ideologies and patterns of honorification not only in Javanese but in several African languages, and briefly considering possible consequences for language change.

Examples from European language communities, and especially American English, reveal a tendency to see reference or propositionality as the essence of language, to confuse or at least to merge the indexical functions of language with the referential function, and to assume that the divisions and structures of language should—and in the best circumstances do—transparently fit the structures of the "real world" (see especially Silverstein 1979, 1981, 1985, 1987). Such views of language are held by expert as well as lay observers, as Irvine comments: "many writers . . . in linguistics and the social sciences . . . have assumed that referential communication is the only function of language" (1989:250; see also Briggs 1986, Reddy 1979).

Silverstein has been understood by some to suggest that this Western objectifying drive for reference and a focus on the surface-segmentable aspects of referentially evaluated language is a nearly universal phenomenon. More accurately, Silverstein's claim is that the referential structure is universally a structuring condition of the consciousness of pragmatic functions. The rationalizing accounts people devise to explain language beyond that vary widely, from reference in our own tradition to fully pragmatic theories for Javanese, which derive the power of language from theories of interaction.[13]

Although not universal, the focus on surface-segmentable aspects and a consequent conception of language as a grammarless collection of words is widely attested (e.g., Blommaert 1994a, Glinert 1991). In his chapter in this volume, Collins considers such a view among the Tolowa, using it as a trigger to reflexively question professional linguistics' privileging of language as structure. (Irvine similarly turns a comparison of Wolof and Javanese ideologies of honorification to a reconsideration of professional linguists' privileging of reference through the construct of linguistic alternants as referentially "the same.") Rumsey (1990) has argued that the focus on lexicon is not characteristic of Australian aboriginal cultures, which do not dichotomize talk and action or words and things. Rosaldo (1982) has asserted that Ilongots think of language in terms of action rather than reference. Among Wasco speakers, the language's disappearance is ideologized differently by two generations, showing how cultural conceptions of language structure are indeed rooted in social position. Younger speakers see language as a collection of words, commodified objects to be brought out and displayed, while for older speakers the language is a matter of myths, not words (Moore 1988, 1993). Hill takes up the question of referential bias in her chapter, identifying an "enactive" Mexicano language ideology that emphasizes not the relationship between reference and reality but rather the proper accomplishment of human relationships through dialogue.

Ethnography of Speaking

The ethnography of speaking was chartered to study "ways of speaking" from the point of view of events, acts, and styles. Hymes (1974:31) insisted early on that a community's own theory of speech must be considered as part of any serious ethnography, and from its inception the ethnography of speaking has given systematic attention to ideologies of language, primarily in the neutral sense of cultural conceptions, particularly those embodied in explicit metalinguistics (e.g., Bauman and Sherzer 1974, Gumperz and Hymes 1972). Ethnographers of speaking have also pursued the grounding of language beliefs in other cultural and social processes (e.g., Feld and Schieffelin 1981, Katriel 1986, Rodman 1991). Language socialization studies, for example, have demonstrated connections among folk theories of language acquisition, linguistic practices, and key cultural ideas about personhood (Ochs and Schieffelin 1984).[14]

Over time, the field has moved toward more concerted attention to the relation between such local linguistic theories and practice. Language ideology has been made increasingly explicit as a force that shapes verbal practices and genres from oratory to disputing. Genres themselves have come to be recognized not as sets of discourse features but rather as "orienting frameworks, interpretive procedures, and sets of expectations" (Hanks 1987:670).[15]

Speech act theory, as developed in the work of the philosophers J. L. Austin (1962) and John Searle (1969), was initially welcomed as compatible with the ethnography of speaking. Later, however, it stimulated critical reflections on linguistic ideology. Silverstein (1979:210) argued that Austin's ideas about language "acts" and "forces" were projections of covert categories typical in the metapragmatic discourse of languages such as English. On the basis of her fieldwork with the Ilongot of the Philippines, Rosaldo (1982) concurred that speech act theory was based in a specifically Western linguistic ideology, what Verschueren (1985:22) characterized as a privatized view of language that emphasizes the psychological state of the speaker while downplaying the social consequences of speech (see also Pratt 1981). Ethnographers, particularly of Pacific societies, have since argued that the centrality of intentionality within speech act theory is rooted in Western conceptions of the self and that it is inappropriate to other societies, where it obscures local methods of producing meaning.[16]

As is true of cultural anthropologists generally, ethnographers of speaking have increasingly incorporated considerations of power in their analyses, again leading to a more explicit focus on linguistic ideology. Bauman's (1983) historical ethnography of language and silence in Quaker ideology was an important development, since it addressed not a neutral variety of ideology but a more formal, conscious, and politically strategic form. Research on language and gender that has responded critically to essentialist readings of gendered behavior and values has helped identify the mediating role of language ideology in the organization of power.[17] Pointing to the "paradoxical power of silence," Gal (1991) in particular reminds us that the social meaning of communicative forms can never be taken as natural and transparent but must always be examined as cultural construction. In this volume, Kulick analyzes the indirect gendering and consequent loss of a bilingual repertoire and the ties of these processes to new forms of social power in Gapun (see also Kulick 1992, Woolard 1995).

The ethnography of language and schooling and of language and the law similarly made early moves to incorporate dimensions of power and ideology into the analysis of communicative practices. Numerous studies in both areas examined how these institutions arrogate truth and value to some linguistic strategies and forms while ruling others out of bounds. Mertz's chapter in this volume brings together work on both institutions, examining the regimentation of linguistic practice in American law schools as a key constituent of the epistemology of the legal profession.[18]

Finally, in considering ideological dimensions of communication, the ethnography of speaking has shifted toward the recognition of variability and contradictions. As Briggs discusses in this volume, early ethnographic critiques of universalist speech act theory, such as Rosaldo's, rested on their own assumptions of cultural uniformity. New directions in the ethnography of speaking move away from the imposition of such homogeneous cultural templates. Claims about "the language ideology of the *x*" are increasingly viewed as problematic. Verschueren (1985) has noted, for example, that English speakers and other Westerners can be seen to hold ideologies rather similar to those of the Ilongots that Rosaldo discusses, depending on the kind of data we look at (see also Rumsey 1990).

Current research recognizes struggles among multiple conceptualizations of talk within a community and even contradictions within individuals (e.g., Briggs 1996a; Gal 1993; Urciuoli 1991, 1996). In her contribution here, Hill locates a Mexicano discourse of nostalgia and respect that is common only in the sense it is known to, but not produced by, all. Rather, women and men possessed of little local capital participate in a counterdiscourse about language. Hill argues, however, that both discourses build on a more fundamentally shared Mexicano linguistic ideology that emphasizes the relation between language use and social order. Advocating a view of linguistic ideology as interactional resource rather than shared cultural background, Briggs also takes up ideology as contentious social process. In his chapter, he shows how Warao strategically deploy varying models for language use as resources for interactional power. Kroskrity, however, argues in his reinterpretation of Arizona Tewa "linguistic conservatism" that there *are* truly dominant language ideologies, in the sense of being widely shared throughout a community as well as being rooted in socially authoritative strata. These may rarely rise to discursive consciousness, but they nonetheless have extensive influence on a group's communicative strategies. Briggs's and Kroskrity's contributions evidence a lively ongoing debate about the relation between ideological dominance and contestation, and the bearing of that relation on our analytic stance.

Language Contact and Conflict

In multilingual communities where there have been self-conscious struggles over language, researchers have long treated language ideologies (in one guise or another) as socially, politically, and even linguistically significant. The traditional topics of sociolinguistic inquiry in these settings have been language maintenance and shift, contact-induced linguistic change, the linkage of language to ethnicity and nationalism, language attitudes, and language planning and development. All of these draw us into Karl Mannheim's question of the "social and activist roots" of conceptions of language(s). Dimensions of language ideology that have been treated in such work include: ideas of what counts as a language and, underlying these, the very notion that there *are* distinctly identifiable languages, objects that can be "had"—isolated, named, counted, and fetishized; values associated with particular language varieties by community members; assumptions that identity and allegiance are indexed by language use.

The extensive body of research on language attitudes in multilingual communities grew up in a social psychological framework (see Baker 1992, Giles et al. 1987). However, we can recast the intrapersonal attitude as a socially derived, intellectualized or behavioral ideology akin to Bourdieu's "habitus" (Attinasi 1983; Bourdieu 1991; Woolard 1985, 1989a).[19] On the other hand, studies of language maintenance and shift initially implicated macrosocial events as direct causes. Later research has insisted that it is only through the interpretive filter of beliefs about language, cognition, and social relations that political and economic events have an effect on language maintenance or shift (Mertz 1989:109). In this volume, Kulick examines the ideological dynamic in one such shift.[20]

The identification of a language with a people and a consequent diagnosis of peoplehood by the criterion of language have been the fundamental tenets of language ideology to which this tradition of research has attended (see Hymes 1984). It is a truism that the equation of language and nation is not a natural fact but rather a historical, ideological construct. This construction is conventionally dated to late-eighteenth-century German Romanticism and Johann Herder's famous characterization of language as the genius of a people, and thus it is often referred to as the Romantic or Herderian concept of language (see Koepke 1990; see also Humboldt

1988). But in fact Herder's formulation can be traced to the French Enlightenment and the French philosopher Condillac (Aarsleff 1982, Olender 1992).

Exported through colonialism, this Herderian or nationalist ideology of language is globally hegemonic today. In this volume, Blommaert and Verschueren trace these assumptions in Western European news reporting, and Spitulnik finds them running throughout Zambian radio decisions. Modern linguistic theory itself has been seen as framed and constrained by the one language / one people assumption (Le Page 1988, Romaine 1989). State policies as well as challenges to the state around the world are structured by this nationalist ideology of language and identity.[21] As Blommaert and Verschueren show in this volume, it underpins ethnic struggles to such an extent that lack of a distinct language can cast doubt on the legitimacy of a group's claim to nationhood.

The belief that distinctly identifiable languages can and should be isolated, named, and counted enters not only into minority and majority nationalisms but into various strategies of social domination. For example, ideas about what is or is not a "real" language have contributed to profound decisions about the civility and even the humanity of others, particularly subjects of colonial domination in the Americas and elsewhere.[22] As Spitulnik's discussion of Zambian mass media, Errington's of Indonesian language development, and Collins's of American Indian language education programs demonstrate, rankings of languages continue to be invoked to regulate the access of speech varieties to prestigious institutional uses and of their speakers to domains of power and privilege.[23]

Written form, lexical elaboration, rules for word formation, and historical derivation all may be seized on in diagnosing "real language" and ranking the candidates (see, e.g., Ferguson and Gumperz 1960, Haugen 1972, Olender 1992). Evaluations of oral language are often implicitly based in literate standards, as Bloomfield noted long ago, although speakers of some minoritized languages hold them in high esteem precisely because they "cannot be written" (King 1994, Taylor 1989). The question of whether a variety has a grammar plays an important part in such debates and diagnostics (Eckert 1983). Academic linguists' extension of the concept of grammar from the explicitly artifactual product of literate scholarly intervention to an underlying natural system only exacerbates the polemics (see controversies reviewed in Morgan 1994).

An equation of change not just with grammarlessness but with decay also pervades judgments about the status of languages. Language mixing, codeswitching, and creolization thus make speech varieties particularly vulnerable to folk and prescriptivist evaluation as grammarless and/or decadent and therefore as less than fully formed (Jourdan 1991, Ludwig 1989, Romaine 1994).

Movements to save minority languages ironically are often structured, willy-nilly, around the same received notions of language that have led to their oppression and/or suppression. Although in some minority language movements the standard terms of evaluation are subverted (Posner 1993, Thiers 1993, Urla 1995), minority language activists often find themselves imposing standards, elevating literate forms and uses, and negatively sanctioning variability in order to demonstrate the reality, validity, and integrity of their languages.[24] Or again, culturally cohesive indigenous groups that enter into struggles for state recognition in the nationalist ideological climate may reconstrue their internal linguistic differences as defining ethnic distinctions (Jackson 1995).

Along with the equation of one language/one people has come an insistence on the authenticity and moral significance of "mother tongue" as the one first and therefore *real* language of a speaker, transparent to the true self (Haugen 1991, Skutnabb-Kangas and Phillipson 1989). Another tenet often clustered with the Herderian ideology in both folk and scientific views demands linguistic purism as essential to the survival of minority languages, a kind of policing of the boundaries that have been drawn to create distinct language forms. Partisans and analysts have criticized all of these assumptions as inappropriate in settings where multilingualism is more typical and where the linguistic repertoire is fluid or complex. But whether waged in Corsica, India, or the American Southwest, the struggle against the nationalist ideological complex has been difficult to win (Anzaldúa 1987, Jaffe 1993, Khubchandani 1983, Pattanayak 1988).

Although the validity of the nationalist ideology of language has often been debated or debunked, less attention has traditionally been given to understanding *how* the view of languages not only as discrete, distinctive entities but as emblematic of self and community comes to take hold in so many different settings (Fishman 1989). In his critical essay on social scientific notions of ideology generally, Geertz ([1964] 1973) long ago called for systematic attention to the social and what I would prefer to call semiotic processes through which ideologies come to signify. The same must be said about ideological conceptions of language.

In analyzing politicized contests over the "true" national language and standard forms, we might ask which linguistic features are seized on, and through what semiotic processes are they interpreted as representing the collectivity? Errington's idea of pragmatic salience, discussed earlier, points out one direction in which the analysis might proceed (see also Thiers 1993). Although linguistic variation may appear to community members and in correlational sociolinguistics as simply a diagram of social differentiation, analysts have begun to examine the ideological production and signifying structure of that diagram in both folk and expert models (Irvine 1989:253). All of the contributors to this volume recognize that simply using language in particular ways is not what forms social groups, identities, or relations (nor does the group relation automatically give rise to linguistic distinction); rather, ideological interpretations of such uses of language always mediate these effects.

The conceptual schema of the semiotician C. S. Peirce (1974) has been used to analyze the processes of semiotic mediation by which chunks of linguistic material gain significance as representations of particular populations, as Gal puts it in her commentary.[25] Working with the Peirician notion of indexicality, Silverstein (1996a, in particular; see his discussion in this volume) has developed a general theory of the "indexical order" that is particularly productive on this question. In the transformation of first-order indexicality into second-order indexicality, instances of speech that are statistically associable with an aggregate of individuals are typified by community members or experts as particular ways of speaking that are schematized as categorically associated with *types* of people.[26]

When a linguistic form-in-use is thus ideologized as distinctive and as implicating a distinctive kind of people, it is often further misrecognized, in Bourdieu's term, or revalorized, as transparently emblematic of social, political, intellectual, or moral character (see Silverstein's discussion in this volume; see also Bourdieu 1991).[27] So, for example, the speaker of the British prestige speech form known as Received Pronunciation is heard not just as a member of a socially privileged sector of English society but also as a person of greater intellectual and personal worth. G. B. Shaw's *Pygmalion* is a poignant if comedic exposition of such reinterpretation. In this volume, Hill, Kulick, Spitulnik, Errington, and Collins all explore the complexes of values taken on by language varieties in contact situations and their interplay with social phenomena such as class, gender and affect.[28]

Iconicity, the interpretation of linguistic form not just as a dependable index of a social group but as a transparent depiction of the distinctive qualities of the group, is one of three semiotic processes that Irvine and Gal (1995) have suggested are widespread in linguistic ideologizations. For example, in a particular community ideology, the 'simple folk' might be characterized iconically by 'plain speech,' in contrast to the 'ornate' speech of another social stratum. Such iconic readings give rise to the other processes Irvine and Gal have identified: recursivity, in which an opposition salient at one level is projected onto other levels of a linguistic and social relationship, and erasure, the rendering invisible of some sociolinguistic activities or actors in a way that bolsters the iconic reading of language differences. So, as 'simplicity' proliferates in the speech of the 'simple folk,' that which might be characterized as complex or ornate is ignored, compartmentalized, or even sometimes stripped from their repertoire through the process of erasure.

The attribution of social, moral, and political meanings to specific language varieties and the erasure of contradictions and variation affect patterns of language acquisition, style-switching, and shift, as Hill, Kulick, and Schieffelin and Doucet show, as well as institutional use, as Spitulnik and Errington discuss in this volume.[29] Moreover, in liberal democratic societies, the misrecognition or revalorization of the indexical character of language may make discrimination on linguistic grounds publicly acceptable where the corresponding ethnic or racial discrimination is not (Gumperz 1992, Lopez 1991, Milroy and Milroy 1985, Sonntag and Pool 1987). For example, although penalizing a student for being African American may be illegal, penalizing a student for speaking African American Vernacular English is not. Where discrimination against Asian Americans in job promotion is illegal, passing over or dismissing an Asian American because of an "accent" that others claim is difficult to comprehend is not (Lippi-Green 1994, Matsuda 1991).

A crude version of Whorfian thinking that treats English as a sine qua non of democratic thought runs through the tradition of American language policy and at times has also enabled attacks on the rights of minority-language citizens (Baron 1990, Leibowitz 1976, Mertz 1982). The identification of discriminatory dynamics in the recent English-only backlash against bilingual policies in the United States has led a number of linguists and social scientists to engage in ideological critique.[30] However, simply asserting that struggles over language are "really about" racism does not constitute analysis. Tearing aside the curtain of mystification in a "Wizard of Oz theory of ideology," as Asad (1979:622) has phrased it, begs the questions of how and why language comes not only to stand for social groups but to do so in a manner that is both dependably readable and nonetheless socially acceptable. This demands attention to both the semiotic and the social process of language ideology, along the lines that Silverstein and Irvine and Gal have developed.

Communities not only evaluate but may appropriate some part of the linguistic resources of groups with whom they are in contact and in tension, refiguring and incorporating linguistic structures in ways that reveal linguistic and social ideologies (Hill 1985; see also Gumperz and Wilson 1971).[31] Linguistic borrowing might appear to indicate speakers' high regard for the donor language. But Hill (1993a, 1995) argues that socially grounded linguistic analysis of Anglo-American borrowings and of humorous misrenderings of Spanish reveals them as racist distancing strategies that reduce complex Latino experience to a subordinated, commodity identity. In a similar example, the appropriation of creole speech, music, and dress by white adolescents in South London, who see only "style" (again, commodified), is in tension with black adolescent views of these codes as part of their distinctive identity (Hewitt 1986). A classic example of the negative loading of language appropriation is Basso's (1979) description of a Western Apache metalinguistic joking genre that uses English to parody "Whiteman" conversational pragmatics, in a scathing representation of and comment on ethnolinguistic differences and inequality. Rampton (1995), however, argues that "language crossing," a limited form of borrowing and mixing used by Asian, Anglo, and Caribbean youths in England, can be a means of ironizing and transgressing recognized ethnic boundaries and of situationally forging an alternative shared identity.

If the linguistic ideology underlying borrowing or mimesis demands scrutiny, so does the ideology underlying differentiation. Irvine (1989) points out that the formal characteristics of the countercultural argots that the linguist M. A. K. Halliday dubbed antilanguages are not arbitrary and that they again suggest the mediation of ideological conceptualizations of linguistic structures. Linguistic inversions such as metathesis, so often characteristic of antilanguages, are an image of the inversion of cultural values. Similarly, subordinate languages in contact situations can acquire not only the functional but also some of the formal properties of antilanguages. Speakers of moribund varieties of Xinca in Guatemala, for example, go "hog-wild" (Campbell and Muntzel 1989:189) with glottalized consonants, which are exotic from the point of view of the dominant Spanish language. This results in the kind of distortion of linguistic structures that Silverstein has described, a distortion that makes a language more like itself. In this case, importantly, it is a linguistic self that is most distinctive from its socially dominant counterpart, Spanish (see Thiers 1993).

Overt Intervention: Policy, Purism, and Standardization

Since Dante, the "questione della lingua"—that is, the selection and elaboration of a linguistic standard—has stood for a complex of issues about language, politics, and power (Steinberg 1987:198). The existence of a language as a discrete entity is always a discursive project, rather than an established fact (Sakai 1991). The formation and particular characteristics of standard languages had indeed been studied earlier by philologists, Prague School functional linguists, and applied linguists (e.g., Cobarrubias and Fishman 1983, Havránek 1964). But new emphasis on the ideological dimension of language practices has given rise to analyses of language standardization as discursive project, treating "standard" more as ideological process than as empirical linguistic fact.[32]

Commentators generally agree that codified, superposed standard languages are tied not just to writing and its hegemonic institutions but to specifically European forms of these. Linguists have typically held standard languages to be artificial or even deliberately antinatural (Emonds 1986, Joseph 1987). However, in the vernacular belief systems of much of Western culture, language standards are no longer recognized as "manmade" constructs but are naturalized by metaphors such as that of the free market (Joseph 1987, Silverstein 1987). Ideological analysis addresses such questions as how doctrines of linguistic correctness and incorrectness are rationalized and how they are related to doctrines of the inherent representational power, beauty, and expressiveness of language as a valued mode of action (Silverstein 1985:223). Moral indignation over nonstandard forms derives from ideological associations of the standard with the qualities valued within the culture, such as clarity or truthfulness (241).[33]

Macrosocial research on language policy has traced culturally distinctive assumptions about the role of language in civic and human life. In modern multilingual language policies, fundamentally different orientations to language exist simultaneously and in tension: visions of language as a resource, problem, or right (Ruiz 1984) or, as Spitulnik discusses in her contribution, ideologies of democratic linguistic pluralism and hierarchical pluralism.[34] Ideologies compete within any given society and historical period, but the struggle among them can give rise to distinctive approaches of states to the public regulation of language, such as those taken by Britain and France. Whereas France has long formalized public control of language development and selection, as in the institutionalization of the French Academy, the English tradition of language treatment is generally privatized and laissez-faire.[35] In their chapter in this volume, Blommaert and Verschueren similarly note contrasts between French and German emphases on language in defining nation and between official Dutch and official Belgian positions. But they also identify an implicit ideological assumption of national uniformity that they dub "homogeneism" and that they find to be widely shared across these European societies.

An ideology of "development" is pervasive in postcolonial language planning, wherein deliberate intervention is deemed necessary to make a linguistic variety suitable for modern functions. Founded on an implicit ranking of languages, development ideology paradoxically condemns languages, like societies, to perennial status as underdeveloped when compared to the metropole (Blommaert 1994a, Gilliam 1984). In his contribution to this volume, Errington gives an extended consideration of the development trope as it affects not only Indonesian, the wonder child of language planning, but traditional Javanese as well. Errington critically evaluates not only Indonesian nationalist rhetoric on language development but also parallel accounts of national language development that derive from functionalist social science.

Purist doctrines of linguistic correctness close off languages to nonnative sources of innovation, but usually selectively, targeting only languages construed as threats on a social or political basis (Weinstein 1989). An examination of purism leads Jernudd (1989) to argue that the effect of ideology on language use is a key problem in contemporary linguistics (see Ferguson 1983). He observes that in spite of the growth of the applied field of language planning, the connection of extralinguistic interests and ideologies to linguistic outcomes through correction acts in discourse has not been theorized (although Silverstein's metapragmatic approach, discussed earlier, offers a promising basis for such a theory).

The linguistic outcome of purism is not predictable, and its social positioning and strategic use are not transparent.[36] In this volume, Kroskrity shows how an apparently purist linguistic conservatism among the Tewa may derive not from resistance to contact phenomena so much as from the strength of theocratic institutions and their ritual linguistic forms as models for other domains of interaction (see also Kroskrity 1992, 1993). In contrast, the sanctity of language in an ultra-orthodox Jewish community leads to the restriction of the Hebrew language to sacred contexts, to prevent its debasement (Glinert and Shilhav 1991).

As Hill discusses in this volume and elsewhere, Mexicano (Nahuatl) vernacular purist ideologies are deployed paradoxically to enhance the authority of those who are least immersed in the vernacular and most enmeshed with the larger Mexican economy (Hill 1985, 1993b; Hill and Hill 1980, 1986). In a related phenomenon, everyday speakers of Galician in northwest Spain may dissociate themselves from revived, linguistically pure Gallego forms, which smack of institutional politics. "Politicians address the 'people' as *pobo*, while the very people . . . view themselves as *pueblo*" (Álvarez 1990, Álvarez-Cáccamo 1993:10). Such complex relations among social position, linguistic practice, and purist ideologies illustrate the importance of problematizing ideology rather than assuming that it can be read from one of the first two elements. Linguistic ideology is not a predictable, automatic reflex of the social experience in which it is rooted.

Literacy and Orthography

Ideologies of literacy are not identical to ideologies of language as they focus on speech. Derrida (1974) famously deconstructs numerous examples of a Western view of speech as natural, authentic, and prior to the mere lifeless inscriptions of alien, arbitrary writing. Following Derrida, Sakai (1991) also identifies a phoneticist ideology in eighteenth-century Japan, one that stresses the primacy and transparency of speech over writing. Mignolo (1992), on the other hand, asserts that the supremacy of the oral as represented in Plato's *Phaedrus*, a key text for Derrida (1981), was inverted in Renaissance Europe. Harris (1980) argues that a European legacy of "scriptism" is smuggled into the apparent oral bias of contemporary linguistic concepts, from the sentence through the word to the phoneme.

The relationship of social groups as well as individual readers—lay and professional—to specific texts depends fundamentally on ideologies of language (e.g., Scollon 1995; see Silverstein and Urban 1996 on the complexities of textuality). For example, Janowitz (1993) shows that conflicting approaches to locating scriptural truth within the Judeo-Christian tradition depend on different ideas about the ways texts are created (see Forstorp 1990). Anthropological studies of literacy—its impact on previously oral societies, its use in schooling—belatedly recognized that literacy is not an autonomous, neutral technology but rather culturally organized, ideologically grounded, and historically contingent. When literacy has been introduced in nonliterate societies, it has been taken up in myriad ways that are mediated by local views of language. Literacy is therefore not a unitary phenomenon but rather a diverse set of practices shaped by political, social, and economic forces in diverse communities.[37]

As with language, ideas about what counts as real literacy have profound political and social consequences. The European tradition that saw civilization as founded in literacy recognized only *alphabetic* literacy, and Mignolo (1992, 1995) argues that this led Spanish conquerors to misconstrue Mesoamerican societies, languages, and cultures. (See Collins 1995 for a summary and a critical discussion of reflexes of this alphabetic bias in modern anthropological theory.) The definition of what is and what is not literacy is never a purely technical but always a political matter. Studies of the emergence and the ongoing imposition of schooled literacy and school English, for example, show that the selective valuation of literate traditions is closely linked to mechanisms of social control.[38]

In countries where identity and nationhood are under negotiation, every aspect of language, including its phonological description and forms of graphic representation, can be contested. Even where nationhood is as classically well established as in France, orthographic battles flare. This means that orthographic systems cannot be conceptualized as simply reducing speech to writing but rather are symbols that themselves carry historical, cultural, and political meanings.[39] In this volume, Schieffelin and Doucet examine such meanings in the case of Haitian kreyòl, showing how debates focus on indexical and iconic readings of both the sound and the look of a language.

Transcription, or the written representation of speech within, for example, academic disciplines and law, is not a neutral mechanical activity, but relies on and reinforces ideological conceptions of language (Du Bois 1991:71; see also Hymes 1981, Ochs 1979, Tedlock 1983). Linguistic anthropologists have recently begun to examine transcripts produced by community consultants for what they reveal not only about local conceptions of language and writing but also about the academic researcher's own assumptions, both in directing the transcribing and in parallel transcription activity.[40] Folklorists, sociolinguists, and conversational analysts who have recorded dialects of English reveal their linguistic biases when they use nonstandard orthography or "eye dialect" to represent the speech of blacks, Appalachians, or southerners more than that of other groups. Given the ideology of the value of the letter, nonstandard speakers thus appear less intelligent (Edwards 1992; Preston 1982, 1985). In the American legal system the verbatim record is an idealist construction, prepared according to the court reporter's model of English, against which incoming speech is filtered, evaluated, and interpreted. It is considered "information" if a witness speaks ungrammatically, but not if lawyers do, and editing is applied accordingly (Walker 1986).

Historical Studies

The "linguistic turn" in historiography in recent decades has given rise to a wave of historical examinations of ideologies of language, influenced by Derrida, by Habermas's (1989) theory of communication and the public sphere, and by Foucault's observation that speech is not merely "a verbalization of conflicts and systems of domination, but . . . the very object of man's conflicts" (1972:216). Western states, and particularly France, England, and the United States, predominate in this literature. Historians, literary theorists, sociologists, anthropologists, and educationists have examined the ideology of language associated with the rise of Western scientific discourse, Protestant religious discourse, mass literacy, and universalistic school curricula. Closely linked are critical histories of linguistics, philosophy of language, and popular linguistics, which join more traditional intellectual histories.[41]

In the late eighteenth through the mid-nineteenth centuries in Western Europe, language became the object of civil concern as new notions of public discourse and forms of participation (and exclusion) were formulated by new entrants in the public sphere.[42] Much of the historical research focuses more on normative ideas about rhetoric than on those concerning grammar, but it demonstrates just how closely linked these topics were. Auroux (1986) and Andresen (1990) find that political conceptualizations of language, rather than meditations on "language itself," dominated French and American debates in the seventeenth through the nineteenth centuries. Hegemonic English ideology drew its political and social effectiveness from a presupposition that language revealed the mind, and 'civilization' was largely a linguistic concept (Baron 1982, Finegan 1980, Smith 1984, Taylor 1987). The nineteenth-century debate over language in the United States was at base a fight over what kind of personality was needed to sustain democracy. Cmiel (1990) argues that the emergence of a compartmentalized democratic personality corresponded to the acceptance of style shifting and a range of linguistic registers.

Where casual generalization has traditionally contrasted, for example, the English and the French attitudes toward language as if they were uniform cultural attributes inhering at the state and individual level, more detailed historical studies recently have shown that an apparently characteristic national stance emerges conjuncturally from struggles among competing ideological positions. States typically waver among orientations or simultaneously act upon more than one in their policymaking.[43]

Colonial Language Ideology

"Language has always been the companion of empire," asserted the early Spanish grammarian Nebrija ([1492] 1946). But which language(s) to use in the administration of empire was not always obvious. Rather than impose their own language, administrators might select an indigenous vernacular, to protect the language of the colonizers from the depredations of nonnative speakers (Siegel 1987). Some of the most provocative recent work on linguistic ideology, clearly tracing the links among linguistic, ideological, and social forms, comes from studies of colonialism.

European missionization and colonization of other continents entailed control not only of speakers but of their vernaculars.[44] Colonial linguistic description, frankly political and conversion oriented in the early colonization of the Americas, came to be conceived by nineteenth-century participants as a neutral scientific endeavor. Yet it was still very much a political one, as analyses of dictionaries, grammars, and language guides show (Irvine 1995, Raison-Jourde 1977). In what Mignolo (1992, 1995) calls the colonization of language, Europeans brought to their tasks ideas about language prevalent in the metropole, and these ideas blinkered them to indigenous language structures, conceptualizations, and sociolinguistic arrangements.[45] As with many other colonial phenomena, linguists constructed rather than discovered distinctive language varieties, a process well documented for Africa (Fabian 1986, Harries 1988, Irvine 1995). According to Cohn, British grammars, dictionaries, and translations of the languages of India created the discourse of Orientalism and converted Indian forms of knowledge into European objects (1985:282–83; see also Musa 1989).

Perceived linguistic structure can always have political meaning in the colonial encounter. Functional or formal inadequacy of indigenous languages, and therefore of indigenous minds or societies, was often alleged as a justification of European "tutelage" (Fabian 1986; see also Raison-Jourde 1977). But on the other hand, a sixteenth-century grammarian read alleged similarities of Quechua to Latin and Castilian as "a prediction that the Spaniards will possess it" (cited in Mignolo 1992:305). Greenblatt (1990, 1991) argues persuasively that nearly simultaneous early European reports of indigenous Americans as on the one hand possessing no language at all and as on the other hand able to communicate freely with the conquerors are two sides of the same ideological coin. Both show that the Europeans were unable to credit the indigenous languages with a reality that Greenblatt calls "opacity" and to appreciate the fact of human cultural diversity.

Because of the availability of documents, historical research on early European colonialism has explored the linguistic ideologies of colonizers more than those of indigenous populations. But some work seeks to capture the encounter and interaction of the two.[46] Rafael (1988), for example, contrasts the structure and focus of a seventeenth-century manual of Castilian written by a Tagalog printer with Spanish missionaries' grammars of Tagalog. The comparison highlights the contrast in political interests that underlay translation for the Spanish and for indigenous Filipinos.

Historiography of Linguistics

The close intertwining of public and scholarly conceptualizations of language in the West and its colonies through the nineteenth century leads directly to more general critical studies of Western philosophy of language and professional linguistics. Foucault's (1970) archaeology of European philological discourses, while disputed (e.g., Aarsleff 1982, Itkonen 1988) has been one trigger to further work on the topic. Contributors to the collection by Joseph and Taylor (1990) examine the intellectual as well as the political prejudices that framed the growth of linguistic theory, from Locke through Saussure to Chomsky, and the role of linguistic ideas in specific social struggles (see Newmeyer 1986). Crowley (1990), for example, finds "discursive violence" not only in ahistorical general linguistics and its mythic delimitation of language but also in the competing school of historical linguistics. Of particular relevance to our topic, Attridge (1988) deconstructs Saussure's linguistics as hostile to and suppressing evidence that the language user and the language community intervene, consciously or unconsciously, to alter the language system. According to Attridge, Saussure saw language as open to external change by humanly uncontrollable forces but rejected the influence of history as intellectual construct.

A number of studies show how philology and emerging linguistics in the nineteenth century contributed to religious, class, and/or nationalist projects. Olender (1992), for example, traces the fundamental links of race and religion to the new sciences of language in eighteenth- and nineteenth-century Indo-European and Semitic philological studies. Crowley (1989, 1991) demonstrates the assumptions of social class on which Standard English was first theorized, while Gal (1995) shows how metropolitan linguistic theories were implicated in the making of Hungarian identity. And, as Irvine (1995) has argued, ideologies of family and gender relations pervade nineteenth-century European descriptions of the grammatical structure and classification of African languages.

Professional, scientific linguistics in the late twentieth century has nearly uniformly, and sometimes rather smugly, rejected prescriptivism. However, a number of authors argue that this rejection hides a smuggled dependence on and a complicity with prescriptive institutions for the very subject matter of the field; "rather than registering a unitary language, linguists helped to form one" (Crowley 1990:48, Haas 1982). The idealism of modern "autonomous" linguistics has come under concerted ideological scrutiny.[47] Sankoff (1988) argues that contemporary positivist linguistic methodologies that invoke a scientific rationale are ideologically imposed by the same interests that propagate normativism and prescriptivism.

More anthropologically oriented linguistics and sociolinguistics have been analyzed ideologically as well (Cameron 1990, Dorian 1991). Schultz (1990) argues that Whorf's writings were constrained by the American folk ideology of free speech, which fosters the sense that speakers control language. Unlike Bakhtin, whose insights Schultz sees as similar, Whorf had first to convince his audience that linguistic censorship exists, and this necessity accounts for contradictory strategies in his writing.

Metaphors of "endangered" and "dying" languages very recently have generated exchanges on the inescapably political, ideologically selective nature of all linguistic and sociolinguistic research (Dorian 1993, 1994a; Hale et al. 1992; Ladefoged 1992; Woodbury 1994). One of the most thoroughgoing ideological analyses of linguistic theory is Rossi-Landi's (1973) treatment of linguistic relativism as bourgeois ideology, in the sense of interest as well as ideation. Rossi-Landi sees the theory as a manifestation of guilt for the destruction of American Indians. The idealism of linguistic relativism transforms linguistic producers into consumers and enables the illusion that the theoretical exhibition of the structures of a language saves the worldview of the extinct linguistic workers (see also Bauman 1995,

Hill and Mannheim 1992). In his contribution in this volume, Collins identifies just such a displacement of "real language" from contemporary speakers in the criticism that academic linguists level at didactic Tolowa materials produced by community members. Such considerations lead him to conclude that the study of language ideology cannot be undertaken as a neutral descriptive project but always demands reflexive interrogation of our own ideological commitments.

Conclusion

A research focus on language ideology makes a promising bridge between linguistic and social theory. In spite of the traditional difficulties posed by the ideology concept, it allows us to relate the microculture of communicative action to political economic considerations of power and social inequality, to confront macrosocial constraints on language behavior, and to connect discourse with lived experiences (Briggs 1993:207, Paul Kroskrity personal communication). As Gal points out in her commentary, populations around the world posit fundamental linkages among such apparently diverse cultural categories as language, spelling, grammar, and nation, gender, simplicity, intentionality, authenticity, knowledge, development, power, tradition. The contributions to this volume attempt to understand when and how those links are forged, whether by lay participants or by their expert analysts, through what semiotic and social processes, and with what consequences for linguistic and social life.

NOTES

Many people, including all of the contributors and anonymous reviewers of this volume, have influenced this version of this essay, and I thank them all. I am particularly grateful to Bambi Schieffelin for allowing me to raid our coauthored review of language ideology (1994) as a basis for portions of this essay (with permission from the *Annual Review of Anthropology*, vol. 23, © 1994, by Annual Reviews, Inc.). Special thanks also to Michael Silverstein, Judy Irvine, and Rob Moore for their careful readings of and excellent suggestions on several sections of this essay. They are not responsible for places where it has proved incorrigible.

1. For distinctions and discussion, see also Mertz and Parmentier 1985, Errington 1988, Parmentier 1986, Lucy 1993b, and Silverstein and Urban 1996. See also Gumperz's 1982a notion of "contextualization cues."

2. There are a great number of useful reviews of the study of ideology. Throughout this essay I draw most heavily on, and I refer the interested reader to, reviews that are particularly well focused for work on language ideology: Eagleton 1991; Friedrich 1989; Geuss 1981; and Thompson 1984, 1990.

3. The assertion of universality is a feature of ideology for those who hold it to be the invention and characteristic of bourgeois society (see, e.g., Gouldner 1976).

4. Note that Thompson does not restrict domination to class domination as the classical Marxist tradition did.

5. For this view of linguistic ideology, see Silverstein 1981 on the "limits of awareness" and Errington 1985, 1988 on "pragmatic salience."

6. Lenin and other Marxists who cast ideology as a positive programmatic tool in a struggle for power are exceptions to the association I posit between power-centered and negative views.

7. But note that not all social scientific uses are actually neutral.

8. Most commentators agree that Mannheim ultimately found himself quite trapped in this reflexive vision of ideology. He attempted to extract himself from relativism by devising a notion of the "relational" in contrast to the "relative," which secondarily enabled him to evaluate the appropriateness (rather than the truth) of an ideology in relation to the social position of its holders (for a discussion, see Goldman 1994).

9. Many of the contributors to this volume participated in a discussion group in which we were struck by the apparent absurdity of nineteenth-century philology's relentless reading of spiritual qualities from linguistic structures. We wondered if the single-minded reading of power into and out of communicative practices that has characterized our own late-twentieth-century sociolinguistics will look as ludicrously obsessive in another century's retrospect and whether we should not attend more to some of these other dimensions of social subjectivity.

10. But see Eagleton 1991 for some amusing stretches of imagination to cases that might not.

11. Note, however, that European "functionalism," as it developed critiques of Saussurean structuralism, long ago attempted to retheorize the nature of the social in language in relation to consciousness of language use. See, for example, the Prague School's theorizing of functional dialectology and particularly of standard language varieties (Havránek and other contributors to Garvin 1964).

12. Kroch and Small 1978 put forward a similar claim about American English speakers' "grammatical ideology."

13. I thank Michael Silverstein for his helpful clarification of this question.

14. On this topic, see also Heath 1983, Schieffelin and Ochs 1986, Kulick 1992, Miller et al. 1990, Ochs 1988, and Schieffelin 1990.

15. For studies of some specific genres, see Brenneis and Myers 1984, Basso 1988, Calame-Griaule 1986, Goldman 1983, Merlan and Rumsey 1991, Briggs 1996b, Lindstrom 1992, Parmentier 1993, Urban 1993, Watson-Gegeo and White 1990. For the reformulation of genre itself, see also Bauman and Briggs 1990, Briggs 1993, Briggs and Bauman 1992, and Hanks 1996.

16. For examples of such challenges to intentionality, see Duranti 1992, 1993; Du Bois 1992; Graham 1993; Hill and Irvine 1992; Morgan 1991; and Stroud 1992.

17. See especially Keenan 1974, Eckert 1989, Ochs 1992, Kulick 1993, and Smith-Hefner 1988. Eckert and McConnell-Ginet 1992, and Gal 1991 offer particularly useful reviews of this substantial literature.

18. On education, see for example, Heath 1983, Cook-Gumperz 1986, and Collins 1991. Collins 1995 reviews much of the voluminous work on school language and literacy. On law, see, for example, Mertz and Weissbourd 1985. Mertz 1994 reviews the also substantial field of language and the law.

19. For socially grounded approaches to linguistic prestige or atttitudes, see Gal 1979, 1987, 1989; Guy 1988; Hidalgo 1986; Hornberger 1988b; Rickford 1985; Hill 1985; Woolard 1989a; and Woolard and Gahng 1990.

20. Schieffelin 1994 and Bell 1990 offer further examples of the specificity of ideologies that can enter into shift or maintenance.

21. For examples, see Blommaert 1994b, Coulmas 1988, Gold 1989, Handler 1988, Maguire 1991, and Trosset 1986.

22. For significant studies of this topic, see Filgueira Alvado 1979; Martinell Gifre

1988; Mannheim 1991; Olender 1992; Mignolo 1992, 1995; Pagden 1993; Greenblatt 1990, 1991; and Irvine 1995.

23. See also, among others, Bourdieu 1991; Gumperz 1982a, 1982b; Haviland 1989; Hurtado and Rodríguez 1989; Labov 1982; and Morgan 1994.

24. Eckert 1983; Jaffe 1993; Urla 1988, 1993a, 1993b; and Schlieben-Lange 1993 provide sensitive discussions of these dilemmas.

25. For a discussion of Peircian notions and "semiotic mediation," see Mertz 1985.

26. If there is any felicity in my formulation of Silverstein's second-order indexicality, it must be credited to Rob Moore. On the workings of first- and second-order indexicality in other kinds of language variation, see Irvine, this volume. See also Urban 1991.

27. See also Gal 1993, Jacquemet 1992, Urban 1991, and Gal and Irvine 1995.

28. Among the myriad studies of the revalorization of languages are: Dorian 1981; Eckert 1980; Errington 1995; Heller 1985, 1988; Limón 1982; Martin-Jones 1989; McDonald 1989; McDonogh 1993; Smitherman-Donaldson 1988; Wolfson and Manes 1985; Urciuoli 1992; Woolard 1985, 1989a; Williams 1988; and Zentella 1997.

29. See also Blom and Gumperz 1972; Gumperz 1982a; Heller 1985, 1988, 1995; Dorian 1989; Eckert 1980; Speicher and McMahon 1992; and Urciuoli 1995 for further examples. Note that although linguistic variation is frequently socially evaluated, it is not always. In more than one situation of ethnolinguistic contact, variability in a minoritized language is less subject to invidious evaluation than is variability in the superimposed variety (see Dorian 1994c, Mannheim 1991).

30. See, among others, Adams and Brink 1990, Crawford 1992a, Fishman 1988, Nunberg 1989, Silverstein 1987, Sonntag and Pool 1987, and Woolard 1989b.

31. On this point, see also Siegal 1986:300, Haarman 1989, and Flaitz 1988.

32. Joseph 1987, Milroy and Milroy 1985, Silverstein 1987, and Crowley 1989 are good examples of such treatments of the status of standard languages.

33. Grillo 1989, Higonnet 1980, Joseph 1987, and Swiggers 1990 pursue this point, particularly in relation to the case of French.

34. For case studies see Hornberger 1988 and Akinnaso 1991; see also Heath 1977, Cobarrubias 1983, Grillo 1985, Coulmas 1991, and Wodak 1989.

35. Heath 1977, 1980; Heath and Mandabach 1983; Grillo 1989; and Haugen 1985 all make this or related points about national stances toward language.

36. On the selectivity, social positioning, and unpredictable/unintended outcomes of purist movements, see Gumperz 1971; Herzfeld 1982, 1996; Thomas 1991; Östman 1996; Dorian 1994b; Frangoudaki 1992; Jernudd and Shapiro 1989; and Gross 1993.

37. These points are developed and illustrated in Besnier 1991; Street 1984, 1993; Boyarin 1993; Ewald 1988; Illich and Sanders 1988; Messick 1993; Schieffelin and Gilmore 1986; Schieffelin 1995; Scollon and Scollon 1981; Kulick and Stroud 1990; Guss 1986; Gewertz and Errington 1991; McKenzie 1987; and Mertz 1996.

38. For studies of schooled literacy, see Foucault 1975; Collins 1991, 1993, 1996; Cook-Gumperz 1986; Gee 1990; Heath 1981; see also Bourdieu 1991; and Michaels and Cazden 1986.

39. For particular orthographic debates, see Neu-Altenheimer, Marimoutou, and Baggioni 1987; Coulmas 1990; Fodor and Hagège 1983–1994; Hornberger 1995; Mühlhäusler 1990; Twine 1991; Brown 1993; Hellinger 1986; and Winer 1990.

40. See, for example, Bauman 1995, Urban 1996, Haviland 1996, and Silverstein 1996b.

41. See Aarsleff 1982, Formigari 1993, Andresen 1990, Busse and Trabant 1986, Gal 1995, and Silverstein 1995.

42. For such considerations of language in the public sphere, see Anderson 1983;

Bailey 1991; de Certeau, Julia and Revel 1975; Fliegelman 1993; Grillo 1989; Gustafson 1992; Balibar 1991; Balibar and Laporte 1984; Gal and Woolard 1995; Kramer 1992; Landes 1988; Lee 1995; Simpson 1988; Warner 1990; and Mugglestone 1995.

43. See Baron 1990; Heath 1972; Heath and Mandabach 1983; Mackey 1991; Reagan 1986; and Crawford 1992a, 1992b.

44. See Bolton and Hutton 1995 for a contemporary version of such colonial control in the banning of antilanguage in Hong Kong.

45. Important examples are also developed in Irvine 1993, Klor de Alva 1989, Samarin 1984, Todorov 1984, and Illich 1981.

46. See Adorno 1986, Boone and Mignolo 1994, Karttunen 1994, Lockhart 1991, Mannheim 1991, Hanks 1987, Philips 1991, and Mignolo 1995.

47. For example, Bourdieu 1991; Harris 1980, 1987; Hymes 1971; Joseph and Taylor 1990; Williams 1977; and Davies 1984.

REFERENCES

Aarsleff, Hans. 1982. *From Locke to Saussure: Essays on the Study of Language and Intellectual History*. Minneapolis: University of Minnesota Press.

Adams, Karen L., and Daniel T. Brink, eds. 1990. *Perspectives on Official English: The Campaign for English as the Official Language in the USA*. Berlin: Mouton de Gruyter.

Adorno, Rolena. 1986 *Guaman Poma: Writing and Resistance in Colonial Peru*. Austin: University of Texas Press.

Agha, Asif. 1994. Honorification. *Annual Review of Anthropology* 23:277–302.

Akinnaso, F. Niyi. 1991. Toward the Development of a Multilingual Language Policy in Nigeria. *Applied Linguistics* 12:29–61.

Althusser, Louis. 1971. *Lenin and Philosophy and Other Essays*. London: New Left Books.

Álvarez, Celso. 1991. The Institutionalization of Galician: Linguistic Practices, Power and Ideology in Public Discourse. Ph.D. diss., University of California, Berkeley.

Álvarez-Cáccamo, Celso. 1993. The Pigeon House, the Octopus and the People: The Ideologization of Linguistic Practices in Galiza. *Plurilinguismes* 6:1–26.

Anderson, Benedict. 1983. *Imagined Communities: Reflections on the Origin and Spread of Nationalism*. London: Verso.

Andresen, Julie Tetel. 1990. *Linguistics in America 1769–1924: A Critical History*. London: Routledge.

Anzaldúa, Gloria. 1987. *Borderlands/La Frontera: The New Mestiza*. San Francisco: Aunt Lute Books.

Asad, Talal. 1979. Anthropology and the Analysis of Ideology. *Man* 14:607–627.

Attinasi, John J. 1983. Language Attitudes and Working Class Ideology in a Puerto Rican Barrio of New York. *Ethnic Groups* 5:55–78.

Attridge, Derek. 1988. *Peculiar Language*. London: Methuen.

Auroux, Sylvain. 1986. Le sujet de la langue: La conception politique de la langue sous l'ancien régime et la révolution. In *Les idéologues: Sémiotique, théories et politiques linguistiques pendant la Révolution française*, ed. W. Busse and J. Trabant, pp. 259–278. Philadelphia: John Benjamins.

Austin, John Langshaw. 1962. *How to Do Things with Words*. Cambridge, Mass.: Harvard University Press.

Bailey, Richard W. 1991. *Images of English: A Cultural History of the Language*. Ann Arbor: University of Michigan Press.

Baker, Colin. 1992. *Attitudes and Language*. Clevedon, England: Multilingual Matters.

Balibar, Renée. 1991. La Révolution française et l'universalisation du français national en France. *History of European Ideas* 13:89–95.

Balibar, Renée, and D. Laporte. 1984. *Le français national.* Paris: Hachette.

Baron, Dennis E. 1982. *Grammar and Good Taste: Reforming the American Language.* New Haven: Yale University Press.

———. 1990. *The English Only Question: An Official Language for Americans?* New Haven: Yale University Press.

Basso, Keith. 1979. *Portraits of "the Whiteman": Linguistic Play and Cultural Symbols among the Western Apache.* Cambridge: Cambridge University Press.

———. 1988. Speaking with Names. *Cultural Anthropology* 3:99–131.

Bauman, Richard. 1983. *Let Your Words Be Few: Symbolism of Speaking and Silence among Seventeenth-century Quakers.* New York: Cambridge University Press.

———. 1995. Representing Native American Oral Narrative: The Textual Practices of Henry Rowe Schoolcraft. *Pragmatics* 5:167–184.

Bauman, Richard, and Charles L. Briggs. 1990. Poetics and Performance as Critical Perspectives on Language and Social Life. *Annual Review of Anthropology* 19:59–88.

Bauman, Richard, and Joel Sherzer, eds. 1974. *Explorations in the Ethnography of Speaking.* Cambridge: Cambridge University Press.

Bell, Allan R. 1990. Separate People: Speaking of Creek Men and Women. *American Anthropologist* 92:332–345.

Besnier, Niko. 1991. Literacy and the Notion of Person on Nukulaelae Atoll. *American Anthropologist* 93:570–587.

Bloch, Maurice. 1985. From Cognition to Ideology. In *Power and Knowledge*, ed. Richard Fardon, pp. 21–48. Edinburgh: Scottish Academic Press.

Blom, Jan-Petter, and John J. Gumperz. 1972. Social Meaning in Linguistic Structures: Code-switching in Norway. In *Directions in Sociolinguistics: The Ethnography of Communication*, ed. John J. Gumperz and Dell Hymes, pp. 407–434. New York: Holt, Rinehart & Winston.

Blommaert, Jan. 1994a. The Metaphors of Development and Modernization in Tanzanian Language Policy and Research. In *African Languages, Development and the State*, ed. Richard Fardon and Graham Furniss, pp. 213–226. London: Routledge.

———. 1994b. Ujamaa and the Creation of the New Swahili. In *Continuity and Autonomy in Swahili Communities*, ed. David Parkin, pp. 65–81. London: School of Oriental and African Studies, University of London.

Bloomfield, Leonard. 1933. *Language.* New York: Holt, Rinehart and Winston.

———. 1944. Secondary and Tertiary Responses to Language. *Language* 20:44–55.

———. [1927] 1970. Literate and Illiterate Speech. In *A Bloomfield Anthology*, ed. Charles Hockett. Bloomington: Indiana University Press.

Boas, Franz. 1911. Introduction to the Handbook of American Indian Languages. *Bulletin of the Bureau of American Ethnology*, pp. 1–83. Washington, D.C.: U.S. Government Printing Office.

Bolton, Kingsley, and Christopher Hutton. 1995. Bad and Banned Language: Triad Secret Societies, the Censorship of the Cantonese Vernacular, and Colonial Language Policy in Hong Kong. *Language in Society* 24:159–186.

Boone, Elizabeth H., and Walter D. Mignolo, eds. 1994. *Writing without Words: Alternative Literacies in Mesoamerica and the Andes.* Durham, N.C.: Duke University Press.

Bourdieu, Pierre. 1977. *Outline of a Theory of Practice.* Cambridge: Cambridge University Press.

———. 1991. *Language and Symbolic Power.* Cambridge, Mass.: Harvard University Press.

Boyarin, Jonathan, ed. 1993. *The Ethnography of Reading.* Berkeley: University of California Press.

Brenneis, Donald L., and Fred R. Myers, eds. 1984. *Dangerous Words: Language and Politics in the Pacific.* New York: New York University Press.

Briggs, Charles L. 1986. *Learning How to Ask: A Sociolinguistic Appraisal of the Role of the Interview in Social Science Research.* Cambridge: Cambridge University Press.

———. 1993. Generic versus Metapragmatic Dimensions of Warao Narratives: Who Regiments Performance? In *Reflexive Language: Reported Speech and Metapragmatics,* ed. J. A. Lucy, pp. 179–212. Cambridge: Cambridge University Press.

———. 1996a. Disorderly Dialogues in Ritual Impositions of Order: The Role of Metapragmatics in Warao Dispute Mediation. In *Disorderly Discourse: Narrative, Conflict, and Inequality,* ed. Charles L. Briggs, pp. 204–242. New York: Oxford University Press.

———, ed. 1996b. *Disorderly Discourse: Narrative, Conflict, and Inequality.* New York: Oxford University Press.

Briggs, Charles L., and Richard Bauman. 1992. Genre, Intertextuality, and Social Power. *Journal of Linguistic Anthropology* 2:131–172.

Brown, Becky. 1993. The Social Consequences of Writing Louisiana French. *Language in Society* 22:67–101.

Busse, Winfried, and Jürgen Trabant, eds. 1986. *Les idéologues: Sémiotique, théories et politiques linguistiques pendant la Révolution française.* Philadelphia: John Benjamins.

Calame-Griaule, Genevieve. 1986. *Words and the Dogon World.* Philadelphia: Institute for the Study of Human Issues.

Cameron, Deborah. 1990. Demythologizing Sociolinguistics: Why Language Does Not Reflect Society. In *Ideologies of Language,* ed. John E. Joseph and Talbot J. Taylor, pp. 79–96. London: Routledge.

Campbell, Lyle, and Martha C. Muntzel. 1989. The Structural Consequences of Language Death. In *Investigating Obsolescence,* ed. Nancy Dorian, pp. 181–196. Cambridge: Cambridge University Press.

Cmiel, Kenneth. 1990. *Democratic Eloquence: The Fight over Popular Speech in Nineteenth-century America.* Berkeley: University of California Press.

Cobarrubias, Juan. 1983. Ethical Issues in Status Planning. *Progress in Language Planning,* ed. Juan Cobarrubias and Joshua A. Fishman, pp. 41–86. Berlin: Mouton.

Cobarrubias, Juan, and Joshua Fishman, eds. 1983. *Progress in Language Planning.* Berlin: Mouton.

Cohn, Bernard. 1985. The Command of Language and the Language of Command. *Subaltern Studies* 4:276–329.

Collins, James. 1991. Hegemonic Practice: Literacy and Standard Language in Public Education. In *Rewriting Literacy: Culture and the Discourse of the Other,* ed. Candace Mitchell and Kathleen Weisler, pp. 229–253. New York: Bergin and Garvey.

———. 1993. The Troubled Text: History and Language in Basic Writing Programs. In *Knowledge, Culture and Power: International Perspectives on Literacy Policies and Practices,* ed. Peter Freebody and Anthony Welch, pp. 162–186. Pittsburgh: University of Pittsburgh Press.

———. 1995. Literacy and Literacies. *Annual Review of Anthropology* 24:75–93.

———. 1996. Socialization to Text: Structure and Contradiction in Schooled Literacy. In *Natural Histories of Discourse,* ed. Michael Silverstein and Greg Urban, pp. 203–228. Chicago: University of Chicago Press.

Comaroff, Jean, and John Comaroff. 1991. *Of Revolution and Revelation: Christianity, Colonialism and Consciousness in South Africa,* Vol. 1. Chicago: University of Chicago Press.

Cook-Gumperz, Jenny. 1986. Schooling and Literacy: An Unchanging Equation? In *The*

Social Construction of Literacy, ed. Jenny Cook-Gumperz, pp. 16–44. Cambridge: Cambridge University Press.

Coulmas, Florian. 1990. Language Adaptation in Meiji Japan. In *Language Policy and Political Development*, ed. Brian Weinstein, pp. 69–86. Norwood, N.J.: Ablex.

———. 1991. European Intergration and the Idea of the National Language. In *A Language Policy for the European Community*, ed. Florian Coulmas, pp. 1–44. Berlin: Mouton de Gruyter.

———, ed. 1988. *With Forked Tongues: What Are National Languages Good For?* Ann Arbor: Karoma Publishers.

Crawford, James. 1992a. *Hold Your Tongue: Bilingualism and the Politics of "English Only."* Reading, Mass.: Addison Wesley.

———, ed. 1992b. *Language Loyalties: A Source Book on the Official English Controversy.* Chicago: University of Chicago Press.

Crowley, Tony. 1989. *Standard English and the Politics of Language*. Urbana: University of Illinois Press.

———. 1990. That Obscure Object of Desire: A Science of Language. In *Ideologies of Language*, ed. John E. Joseph and Talbot J. Taylor, pp. 27–50. London: Routledge.

———. 1991. *Proper English? Readings in Language, History and Cultural Identity*. London: Routledge.

Davies, A. 1984. Idealization in Sociolinguistics: The Choice of the Standard Dialect. In *Georgetown University Round Table on Languages and Linguistics, 1984*, ed. Deborah Schiffrin, pp. 229–239. Washington, D.C.: Georgetown University Press.

de Certeau, Michel, Dominique Julia, and Jacques Revel. 1975. *Une politique de la langue: La Révolution française et les patois*. Paris: Gallimard.

Derrida, Jacques. 1974. *Of Grammatology*. Translated by G.C. Spivak. Baltimore: Johns Hopkins University Press.

———. 1981. *Dissemination*. Translated by Barbara Johnson. London: Athlone Press.

Dorian, Nancy C. 1981. *Language Death: The Life Cycle of a Scottish Gaelic Dialect*. Philadelphia: University of Pennsylvania Press.

———. 1991. Linguacentrism and Language History. In *The Influence of Language on Culture and Thought*, ed. Robert L. Cooper and Bernard Spolsky, pp. 85–100. Berlin: Mouton de Gruyter.

———. 1993. A Response to Ladefoged's Other View of Endangered Languages. *Language* 69:575–579.

———. 1994a. Comment: Choices and Values in Language Shift and Its Study. *International Journal of the Sociology of Language* 110:113–124.

———. 1994b. Purism vs. Compromise in Language Revitalization and Language Revival. *Language in Society* 23:479–494.

———. 1994c. Varieties of Variation in a Very Small Place: Social Homogeneity, Prestige Norms, and Linguistic Variation. *Language* 70:631–696.

———, ed. 1989. *Investigating Obsolescence: Studies in Language Contraction and Death*. Cambridge: Cambridge University Press.

Du Bois, John W. 1991. Transcription Design Principles for Spoken Discourse Research. *Pragmatics* 1:71–106.

———. 1992. Meaning without Intention: Lessons from Divination. In *Responsibility and Evidence in Oral Discourse*, ed. Jane H. Hill and Judith T. Irvine, pp. 48–71. Cambridge: Cambridge University Press.

Duranti, Alessandro. 1992. Intentions, Self and Responsibility. In *Responsibility and Evidence in Oral Discourse*, ed. Jane H. Hill and Judith T. Irvine, pp. 24–47. Cambridge: Cambridge University Press.

———. 1993. Intentionality and Truth: An Ethnographic Critique. *Cultural Anthropology* 8:214–245.
Eagleton, Terry. 1991. *Ideology: An Introduction*. London: Verso.
Eckert, Penny. 1980. Diglossia: Separate and Unequal. *Linguistics* 18:1053–1064.
———. 1983. The Paradox of National Language Movements. *Journal of Multilingual and Multicultural Development* 4:289–300.
———. 1989. The Whole Woman: Sex and Gender Differences in Variation. *Language Variation and Change* 1:245–267.
Eckert, Penny, and Sally McConnell-Ginet. 1992. Think Practically and Look Locally: Language and Gender as Community-based Practice. *Annual Review of Anthropology* 21:461–490.
Edwards, Jane. 1992. Transcription of Discourse. In *International Encyclopedia of Linguistics*, ed. William Bright, pp. 367–371. New York: Oxford University Press.
Ehrlich, Susan, and Ruth King. 1994. Feminist Meanings and the (De)Politicization of the Lexicon. *Language in Society* 23:59–76.
Emonds, Joseph. 1985. Grammatically Deviant Prestige Dialect Constructions. In *A Festschrift for Sol Saporta*, ed. Michael Brame, Heles Contreras, and Frederick Newmeyer, pp. 93–129. Seattle: Noit Amrofer.
Errington, Joseph J. 1985. On the Nature of the Sociolinguistic Sign: Describing the Javanese Speech Levels. In *Semiotic Mediation*, ed. Elizabeth Mertz and Richard J. Parmentier, pp. 287–310. Orlando: Academic Press.
———. 1988. *Structure and Style in Javanese: A Semiotic View of Linguistic Etiquette*. Philadelphia: University of Pennsylvania Press.
———. 1995. State Speech for Peripheral Publics in Java. *Pragmatics* 5:213–224.
Ewald, Janet. 1988. Speaking, Writing and Authority: Explorations in and from the Kingdom of Taqali. *Comparative Studies in Society and History* 39:199–223.
Fabian, Johannes. 1986. *Language and Colonial Power: The Appropriation of Swahili in the Former Belgian Congo 1880–1938*. Cambridge: Cambridge University Press.
Feld, Steven, and Bambi B. Schieffelin. 1981. Hard Words: A Functional Basis for Kaluli Discourse. In *Georgetown University Round Table on Languages and Linguistics 1981*, ed. Deborah Tannen, pp. 350–370. Washington, D.C.: Georgetown University Press.
Ferguson, Charles A. 1983. Language Planning and Language Change. In *Progress in Language Planning*, ed. Juan Cobarrubias and Joshua A. Fishman, pp. 29–40. Berlin: Mouton de Gruyter.
Ferguson, Charles A., and John J. Gumperz. 1960. Introduction. In *Linguistic Diversity in South Asia*, ed. Charles A. Ferguson and John J. Gumperz, pp. 1–18. Bloomington: Indiana University Research Center in Anthropology, Folklore, and Linguistics.
Filgueira Alvado, A. 1979. Capacidad intelectual y actitud del indio ante el castellano. *Revista de Indias* 39:163–185.
Finegan, Edward. 1980. *Attitudes towards Language Usage: A History of the War of Words*. New York: Teacher's College Press.
Fishman, Joshua. 1988. "English Only": Its Ghosts, Myths, and Dangers. *International Journal of the Sociology of Language* 74:125–140.
———. 1989. *Language and Ethnicity in Minority Sociolinguistic Perspective*. Clevedon/Philadelphia: Multilingual Matters.
Flaitz, Jeffra. 1988. *The Ideology of English: French Perceptions of English as a World Language*. Berlin: Mouton de Gruyter.
Fliegelman, Jay. 1993. *Declaring Independence: Jefferson, Natural Language, and the Culture of Performance*. Stanford: Stanford University Press.

Fodor, Istvan, and Claude Hagège, eds. 1983–1994. *Language Reform: History and Future.* 6 volumes. Hamburg: Buske Verlag.

Formigari, Lia. 1993. *Signs, Science and Politics: Studies in the History of the Language Sciences.* Translated by William Dodd. Philadelphia: John Benjamins.

Forstorp, Per-Anders. 1990. Receiving and Responding: Ways of Taking from the Bible. In *Bible Reading in Sweden: Studies Related to the Translation of the New Testament 1981*, ed. Gunnar Hansson, pp. 149–169. Uppsala: Almqvist and Wiksell International.

Foucault, Michel. 1970. *The Order of Things.* New York: Random House.

———. 1972. *The Archaeology of Knowledge and the Discourse on Language.* Translated by A. M. Sheridan Smith. New York: Pantheon.

———. 1975. *Discipline and Punish.* New York: Random House.

———. 1980. *Power/Knowledge: Selected Interviews and Other Writings.* Edited by Colin Gordon. New York: Pantheon.

Frangoudaki, Anna. 1992. Diglossia and the Present Language Situation in Greece. *Language in Society* 21:365–381.

Friedrich, Paul. 1989. Language, Ideology and Political Economy. *American Anthropologist* 91:295–312.

Gal, Susan. 1979. *Language Shift.* New York: Academic Press.

———. 1987. Codeswitching and Consciousness in the European Periphery. *American Ethnologist* 14:637–653.

———. 1989. Language and Political Economy. *Annual Review of Anthropology* 18:345–367.

———. 1991. Between Speech and Silence: The Problematics of Research on Language and Gender. In *Gender at the Crossroads of Knowledge*, ed. Micaela di Leonardo, pp. 175–203. Berkeley: University of California Press.

———. 1993. Diversity and Contestation in Linguistic Ideologies: German Speakers in Hungary. *Language in Society* 22:337–359.

———. 1995. Lost in a Sea of Slavic: Linguistic Theories and Expert Knowledge in 19th-century Hungary. *Pragmatics* 5:155–166.

Gal, Susan, and Judith T. Irvine. 1995. The Boundaries of Languages and Disciplines: How Ideologies Construct Difference. *Social Research* 62:967–1001.

Gal, Susan, and Kathryn Woolard. 1995. Constructing Languages and Publics: Authority and Representation. *Pragmatics* 5:129–138.

Garvin, Paul L., ed. 1994. *A Prague School Reader on Esthetics, Literary Structure, and Style.* Washington, D.C.: Georgetown University Press.

Gee, James Paul. 1990. *Social Linguistics and Literacies: Ideologies in Discourses.* London: Falmer.

Geertz, Clifford. [1964] 1973. Ideology as a Cultural System. In *The Interpretation of Cultures*, pp. 193–233. New York: Basic Books.

Geuss, Raymond. 1981. *The Idea of a Critical Theory: Habermas and the Frankfurt School.* Cambridge: Cambridge University Press.

Gewertz, Deborah, and Frederick Errington. 1991. *Twisted Histories, Altered Contexts.* Cambridge: Cambridge University Press.

Giles, Howard, Miles Hewstone, Ellen Bouchard Ryan, and Patricia Johnson. 1987. Research on Language Attitudes. In *Sociolinguistics: An International Handbook of the Science of Language and Society*, Vol. 1, ed. U. Ammon, N. Dittmar, and K. Mattheier, pp. 585–597. Berlin: de Gruyter.

Gilliam, Angela M. 1984. Language and "Development" in Papua New Guinea. *Dialectical Anthropology* 8:303–318.

Glinert, Lewis. 1991. The "Back-to-the Future" Syndrome in Language Planning: The Case of Modern Hebrew. In *Language Planning: Focusschrift in Honor of Joshua A. Fishman*, ed. David F. Marshall, pp. 215–243. Amsterdam: John Benjamins.
Glinert, Lewis, and Yosseph Shilhav. 1991. Holy Land, Holy Language: A Study of an Ultraorthodox Jewish Ideology. *Language in Society* 20:59–86.
Gold, David L. 1989. A Sketch of the Linguistic Situation in Israel Today. *Language in Society* 18:361–388.
Goldman, Harvey. 1994. From Social Theory to Sociology of Knowledge and Back: Karl Mannheim and the Sociology of Intellectual Knowledge Production. *Sociological Theory* 12:266–278.
Goldman, Laurence. 1983. *Talk Never Dies: The Language of Huli Disputes*. London: Tavistock.
Gouldner, Alvin Ward. 1976. *The Dialectic of Ideology and Technology: The Origins, Grammar, and Future of Ideology*. New York: Seabury Press.
Graham, Laura. 1993. A Public Sphere in Amazonia? The Depersonalized Collaborative Construction of Discourse in Xavante. *American Ethnologist* 20:717–741.
Greenblatt, Stephen. 1990. *Learning to Curse*. New York: Routledge.
———. 1991. *Marvelous Possessions*. Chicago: University of Chicago Press.
Grillo, R. D. 1985. *Ideologies and Institutions in Urban France: The Representation of Immigrants*. Cambridge: Cambridge University Press.
———. 1989. *Dominant Languages: Language and Hierarchy in Britain and France*. New York: Cambridge University Press.
Gross, Joan E. 1993. The Politics of Unofficial Language Use: Walloon in Belgium, Tamazight in Morocco. *Critique of Anthropology* 13:177–208.
Gumperz, John J. 1971. Language, Communication and Control in North India. In *Language in Social Groups*. Stanford: Stanford University Press.
———. 1982a. *Discourse Strategies*. Cambridge: Cambridge University Press.
———, ed. 1982b. *Language and Social Identity*. Cambridge: Cambridge University Press.
———. 1992. Interviewing in Intercultural Situations. In *Talk at Work: Interaction in Institutional Settings*, ed. Paul Drew and John Heritage, pp. 302–327. Cambridge: Cambridge University Press.
Gumperz, John J., and Dell Hymes, eds. 1972. *Directions in Sociolinguistics: The Ethnography of Communication*. New York: Holt, Rinehart and Winston.
Gumperz, John J., and Robert Wilson. 1971. Convergence and Creolization: A Case from the Indo-Aryan/Dravidian Border in India. In *Pidginization and Creolization*, ed. Dell H. Hymes, pp. 151–167. London: Cambridge University Press.
Guss, David. 1986. Keeping It Oral: A Yekuana Ethnology. *American Ethnologist* 13:413–429.
Gustafson, Thomas. 1992. *Representative Words: Politics, Literature and the American Language, 1776–1865*. Cambridge: Cambridge University Press.
Guy, Gregory R. 1988. Language and Social Class. In *Linguistics, The Cambridge Survey*. Vol. 4: *Language: Socio-Cultural Context*, ed. Frederick J. Newmeyer, pp. 37–63. Cambridge: Cambridge University Press.
Haarman, Harald. 1989. *Symbolic Values of Foreign Language Use: From the Japanese Case to a General Sociolinguistic Perspective*. Berlin: Mouton de Gruyter.
Haas, William. 1982. On the Normative Character of Language. In *Standard Languages: Spoken and Written*, ed. W. Haas, pp. 1–36. Manchester: Manchester University Press.
Habermas, Jürgen. 1989. *The Structural Transformation of the Public Sphere*. Translated by Thomas Burger. Cambridge, Mass.: MIT Press.
Hale, Ken, et al. 1992. Endangered Languages. *Language* 68:1–42.

Handler, Richard. 1988. *Nationalism and the Politics of Culture in Quebec.* Madison: University of Wisconsin Press.

Hanks, William F. 1987. Discourse Genres in a Theory of Practice. *American Ethnologist* 14:668–692.

———. 1993. Metalanguage and Pragmatics of Deixis. In *Reflexive Language*, ed. John A. Lucy, pp. 91–126. Cambridge: Cambridge University Press.

———. 1996. Exorcism and the Description of Participant Roles. In *Natural Histories of Discourse*, ed. Michael Silverstein and Greg Urban, pp. 160–193. Chicago: University of Chicago Press.

Harries, Patrick. 1988. The Roots of Ethnicity: Discourse and the Politics of Language Construction in South-East Africa. *African Affairs* 87:25–52.

Harris, Richard. 1980. *The Language Makers.* London: Duckworth.

———. 1987. *The Language Machine.* London: Duckworth.

Haugen, Einar. 1972. Dialect, Language, Nation. In *The Ecology of Language*, pp. 237–254. Stanford: Stanford University Press.

———. 1985. The Language of Imperialism: Unity or Pluralism? In *Language of Inequality*, ed. Nessa Wolfson and Joan Manes, pp. 3–17. Berlin: Mouton.

———. 1991. The "Mother Tongue." In *The Influence of Language on Culture and Thought*, ed. Robert L. Cooper and Bernard Spolsky, pp. 75–84. Berlin: Mouton de Gruyter.

Haviland, John B. 1989. Mixtecs, Migrants, Multilingualism, and Murder. Working Papers and Proceedings of the Center for Psychosocial Studies 25. Chicago: Center for Transcultural Studies.

———. 1996. Text from Talk in Tzotzil. In *Natural Histories of Discourse*, ed. Michael Silverstein and Greg Urban, pp. 45–78. Chicago: University of Chicago Press.

Havránek, Bohuslav. 1964. The Functional Differentiation of the Standard Language. In *A Prague School Reader on Esthetics, Literary Structure, and Style*, ed. Paul L. Garvin, pp. 3–16. Washington, D.C.: Georgetown University Press.

Heath, Shirley B. 1972. *Telling Tongues.* New York: Teachers College Press.

———. 1977. Social History. In *Bilingual Education: Current Perspectives.* Vol. 1: *Social Science*, pp. 53–72. Arlington, Va.: Center for Applied Linguistics.

———. 1980. Standard English: Biography of a Symbol. In *Standards and Dialects in English*, ed. Timothy Shopen and Joseph Williams, pp. 3–31. Cambridge, Mass.: Winthrop.

———. 1981. Toward an Ethnohistory of Writing in American Education. In *Writing: The Nature, Development and Teaching of Written Communication*, Vol. 1, ed. Marcia F. Whiteman, pp. 25–45. Hillsdale, N.J.: Lawrence Erlbaum.

———. 1983. *Ways with Words.* Cambridge: Cambridge University Press.

———. 1989. Language Ideology. In *International Encyclopedia of Communications*, Vol. 2, pp. 393–395. New York: Oxford University Press.

———. 1991. Women in Conversation: Covert Models in American Language Ideology. In *The Influence of Language on Culture and Thought*, ed. Robert Cooper and Bernard Spolsky, pp. 199–218. Berlin: Mouton de Gruyter.

Heath, Shirley B., and Frederick Mandabach. 1983. Language Status Decisions and the Law in the United States. In *Progress in Language Planning: International Perspectives*, ed. Juan Cobarrubias and Joshua A. Fishman, pp. 87–105. New York: Mouton.

Heller, Monica. 1985. Ethnic Relations and Language Use in Montreal. In *Language of Inequality*, ed. Nessa Wolfson and Joan Manes, pp. 75–90. Berlin: Mouton.

———, ed. 1988. *Codeswitching: Anthropological and Sociolinguistic Perspectives.* Berlin: Mouton de Gruyter.

———. 1995. Language Choice, Social Institutions, and Symbolic Domination. *Language in Society* 24:373–406.

Hellinger, Marlis. 1986. On Writing English-related Creoles in the Caribbean. In *Focus on the Caribbean*, ed. Manfred Gorlach and John A. Holm, pp. 53–70. Amsterdam: John Benjamins.

Herzfeld, Michael. 1982. *Ours Once More: Folklore, Ideology, and the Making of Modern Greece*. Austin: University of Texas Press.

———. 1996. National Spirit or the Breath of Nature? The Expropriation of Folk Positivism in the Discourse of Greek Nationalism. In *Natural Histories of Discourse*, ed. Michael Silverstein and Greg Urban, pp. 277–298. Chicago: University of Chicago Press.

Hewitt, Roger. 1986. *White Talk Black Talk*. Cambridge: Cambridge University Press.

Hidalgo, Margarita. 1986. Language Contact, Language Loyalty, and Language Prejudice on the Mexican Border. *Language in Society* 15:193–220.

Higonnet, Patrice L.-R. 1980. The Politics of Linguistic Terrorism and Grammatical Hegemony during the French Revolution. *Social History* 5:41–69.

Hill, Jane H. 1985. The Grammar of Consciousness and the Consciousness of Grammar. *American Ethnologist* 12:725–737.

———. 1993a. Hasta la Vista, Baby: Anglo Spanish in the American Southwest. *Critique of Anthropology* 13:145–176.

———. 1993b. Structure and Practice in Language Shift. In *Progression and Regression in Language*, ed. Kenneth Hyltenstam and Ake Viberg, pp. 68–93. Cambridge: Cambridge University Press.

———. 1995. Junk Spanish, Covert Racism and the (Leaky) Boundary between Public and Private Spheres. *Pragmatics* 5:197–212.

Hill, Jane H., and Kenneth C. Hill. 1980. Mixed Grammar, Purist Grammar, and Language Attitudes in Modern Nahuatl. *Language in Society* 9:321–348.

———. 1986. *Speaking Mexicano: Dynamics of Syncretic Language in Central Mexico*. Tucson: University of Arizona Press.

Hill, Jane H., and Judith T. Irvine. 1992. Introduction to *Responsibility and Evidence in Oral Discourse*, ed. Jane H. Hill and Judith T. Irvine, pp. 1–23. Cambridge: Cambridge University Press.

Hill, Jane H., and Bruce Mannheim. 1992. Language and World View. *Annual Review of Anthropology* 21:381–406.

Hornberger, Nancy. 1988a. Language Planning Orientations and Bilingual Education in Peru. *Language Problems and Language Planning* 12:14–29.

———. 1988b. Language Ideology in Quechua Communities of Puno, Peru. *Anthropological Linguistics* 30:214–235.

———. 1995. Five Vowels or Three? Linguistics and Politics in Quechua Language Planning in Peru. In *Power and Inequality in Language Education*, ed. James W. Tollefson, pp. 187–205. Cambridge: Cambridge University Press.

Humboldt, Wilhelm von. 1988. *On Language*. Translated by P. Heath. Cambridge: Cambridge University Press.

Hurtado, Aída, and Raúl Rodríguez. 1989. Language as a Social Problem: The Repression of Spanish in South Texas. *Journal of Multilingual and Multicultural Development* 10:401–419.

Hymes, Dell. 1971. On Linguistic Theory, Communicative Competence, and the Education of Disadvantaged Children. In *Anthropological Perspectives on Education*, ed. Murray Wax, Stanley A. Diamond, and Fred O. Gearing, pp. 51–66. New York: Basic Books.

———. 1974. *Foundations in Sociolinguistics: An Ethnographic Approach*. Philadelphia: University of Pennsylvania Press.

———. 1981. *In Vain I Tried to Tell You*. Philadelphia: University of Pennsylvania Press.

———. 1984. Linguistic Problems in Defining the Concept of "Tribe." In *Language in Use*, ed. John Baugh and Joel Sherzer, pp. 7–27. Englewood Cliffs, N.J.: Prentice Hall.

Illich, Ivan. 1981. *Shadow Work*. Boston: Marion Boyars.

Illich, Ivan, and B. Sanders. 1988. *ABC: The Alphabetization of the Popular Mind*. San Francisco: North Point Press.

Irvine, Judith T. 1989. When Talk Isn't Cheap: Language and Political Economy. *American Ethnologist* 16:248–267.

———. 1993. Mastering African Languages: The Politics of Linguistics in Nineteenth-century Senegal. *Social Analysis* 34:27–46.

———. 1995. The Family Romance of Colonial Linguistics: Gender and Family in 19th-century Representations of African Languages. *Pragmatics* 5:139–154.

Itkonen, Esa. 1988. A Critique of the "Post-structuralist" Conception of Language. *Semiotica* 71:305–320.

Jackson, Jean E. 1995. Culture, Genuine and Spurious: The Politics of Indianness in the Vaupés, Colombia. *American Ethnologist* 22:3–27.

Jacquemet, Marco. 1992. "If He Speaks Italian, It's Better": Metapragmatics in Court. *Pragmatics* 2 (June):111–126.

Jaffe, Alexandra. 1993. Obligation, Error, and Authenticity: Competing Cultural Principles in the Teaching of Corsican. *Journal of Linguistic Anthropology* 3:99–114.

Janowitz, Naomi. 1993. Re-creating Genesis: The Metapragmatics of Divine Speech. In *Reflexive Language*, ed. John A. Lucy, pp. 393–405. Cambridge: Cambridge University Press.

Jernudd, Björn H. 1989. The Texture of Language Purism: An Introduction. In *The Politics of Language Purism*, ed. Björn H. Jernudd and Michael J. Shapiro, pp. 1–20. Berlin: Mouton de Gruyter.

Jernudd, Björn H., and Michael J. Shapiro, eds. 1989. *The Politics of Language Purism*. Berlin: Mouton de Gruyter.

Joseph, John E. 1987. *Eloquence and Power: The Rise of Language Standards and Standard Languages*. New York: Basil Blackwell.

Joseph, John E., and Talbot J. Taylor, eds. 1990. *Ideologies of Language*. New York: Routledge.

Jourdan, Christine. 1991. Pidgins and Creoles: The Blurring of Categories. *Annual Review of Anthropology* 20:187–209.

Karttunen, Frances. 1994. *Between Worlds: Interpreters, Guides and Survivors*. New Brunswick, N.J.: Rutgers University Press.

Katriel, Tamar 1986. *Talking Straight: Dugri Speech in Israeli Sabra Culture*. New York: Cambridge University Press.

Keenan, Elinor. 1974. Norm-makers, Norm-breakers: Uses of Speech by Men and Women in a Malagasy Community. In *Explorations in the Ethnography of Speaking*, ed. Richard Bauman and Joel Sherzer, pp. 125–143. Cambridge: Cambridge University Press.

Khubchandani, Lachman M. 1983. *Plural Languages, Plural Cultures: Communication, Identity, and Sociopolitical Change in Contemporary India*. Honolulu: University of Hawaii Press.

King, Linda. 1994. *Roots of Identity: Language and Literacy in Mexico*. Stanford: Stanford University Press.

Klor de Alva, J J. 1989.Language, Politics and Translation: Colonial Discourse and Classic Nahuatl in New Spain. In *The Art of Translation: Voices from the Field*, ed. Rosanna Warren, pp. 143–162. Boston: Northeastern University Press.

Koepke, Wulf, ed. 1990. *Johann Gottfried Herder: Language, History and the Enlightenment.* Columbia, S.C.: Camden House.

Kramer, Michael P. 1992. *Imagining Language in America: From the Revolution to the Civil War.* Princeton, N.J.: Princeton University Press.

Kroch, Anthony S., and Cathy Small. 1978. Grammatical Ideology and Its Effect on Speech. In *Linguistic Variation: Models and Methods*, ed. David Sankoff, pp. 45–55. New York: Academic Press.

Kroskrity, Paul V. 1992. Arizona Tewa Public Announcements: Form, Function, Linguistic Ideology. *Anthropological Linguistics* 34:104–116.

———. 1993. *Language, History, and Identity: Ethnolinguistic Studies of the Arizona Tewa.* Tucson: University of Arizona.

Kulick, Don. 1992. *Language Shift and Cultural Reproduction: Socialization, Self and Syncretism in a Papua New Guinean Village.* Cambridge: Cambridge University Press.

———. 1993. Speaking as a Woman: Structure and Gender in Domestic Arguments in a New Guinea Village. *Cultural Anthropology* 8:510–541.

Kulick, Don, and Christopher Stroud. 1990. Christianity, Cargo and Ideas of Self. *Man* (n.s.) 25:70–88.

Labov, William. 1979. Locating the Frontier between Social and Psychological Factors in Linguistic Variation. In *Individual Differences in Language Ability and Language Behavior*, ed. Charles J. Fillmore, Daniel Kempler, and William S-Y. Wang, pp. 327–339. New York: Academic Press.

———. 1982. Objectivity and Commitment in Linguistic Evidence. *Language in Society* 11:165–201.

Ladefoged, Peter. 1992. Another View of Endangered Languages. *Language* 68:809–811.

Landes, Joan B. 1988. *Women and the Public Sphere in the Age of the French Revolution.* Ithaca, N.Y.: Cornell University Press.

Lee, Ben. 1995. Performing the People. *Pragmatics* 5:263–280.

Leibowitz, A. H. 1976. Language and the Law: The Exercise of Political Power through the Official Designation of Language. In *Language and Politics*, ed. William O'Barr and Jean F. O'Barr, pp. 449–466. The Hague: Mouton.

Le Page, Robert B. 1988. Some Premises Concerning the Standardization of Languages, with Special Reference to Caribbean Creole English. *International Journal of the Sociology of Language* 71:25–36.

Limón, José. 1982. El Meeting: History, Folk Spanish and Ethnic Nationalism in a Chicano Student Community. In *Spanish in the United States*, ed. Jon Amastae and Lucía Elías-Olivares, pp. 301–332. New York: Cambridge University Press.

Lindstrom, Lamont. 1992. Context Contests: Debatable Truth Statements on Tanna (Vanuatu). In *Rethinking Context*, ed. Alessandro Duranti and Charles Goodwin, pp. 101–124. Cambridge: Cambridge University Press.

Lippi-Green, Rosina. 1994. Accent, Standard Language Ideology and Discriminatory Pretext in the Courts. *Language in Society* 23:163–198.

Lockhart, James. 1991. *Nahuas and Spaniards: Postconquest Central Mexican History and Philology.* Stanford, Calif.: Stanford University Press.

Lopez, David E. 1991. The Emergence of Language Minorities in the United States. In *Language and Ethnicity: Focusschrift in Honor of Joshua A. Fishman*, ed. James R. Dow, pp. 131–144. Amsterdam: John Benjamins.

Lucy, John. 1993a. Reflexive Language and the Human Disciplines. In *Reflexive Language: Reported Speech and Metapragmatics*, ed. John A. Lucy, pp. 9–32. Cambridge: Cambridge University Press.

———, ed. 1993b. *Reflexive Language: Reported Speech and Metapragmatics*. Cambridge: Cambridge University Press.
Ludwig, Ralph, ed. 1989. *Les créoles français entre l'oral et l'écrit*. Tübingen: Günter Narr Verlag.
Mackey, William F. 1991. Language and the Sovereign State. *History of European Ideas* 13:51–61.
Maguire, Gabrielle. 1991. *Our Own Language: An Irish Initiative*. Philadelphia: Multilingual Matters.
Mannheim, Bruce. 1986. Popular Song and Popular Grammar, Poetry and Metalanguage. *Word* 37:45–75.
———. 1991. *The Language of the Inka since the European Invasion*. Austin: University of Texas Press.
Mannheim, Karl. [1936] 1985. *Ideology and Utopia: An Introduction to the Sociology of Knowledge*. San Diego: Harcourt Brace Jovanovich.
Martinell Gifre, Emma. 1988. *Aspectos lingüísticos del descubrimiento y de la conquista*. Madrid: Consejo Superior de Investigaciones Científicas.
Martin-Jones, Marilyn. 1989. Language, Power and Linguistic Minorities: The Need for an Alternative Approach to Bilingualism, Language Maintenance and Shift. In *Social Anthropology and the Politics of Language*, ed. R. D. Grillo, pp. 106–125. London: Routledge.
Marx, Karl, and Frederick Engels. 1989. *The German Ideology*. Edited by C. J. Arthur. New York: International Publishers.
Matsuda, Mari. 1991. Voices of America: Accent, Antidiscrimination Law, and a Jurisprudence for the Last Reconstruction. *Yale Law Journal* 100:1329–1407.
McCarthy, E. Doyle. 1994. The Uncertain Future of Ideology: Reading Marx. *Sociological Quarterly* 35:415–429.
McDonald, Maryon. 1989. *We Are Not French: Language, Culture, and Identity in Brittany*. London: Routledge.
McDonogh, Gary. 1993. Stop Making Sense: Language, Humor and the Nation-State in Transitional Spain. *Critique of Anthropology* 13:177–208.
McKenzie, Don F. 1987. The Sociology of a Text: Oral Culture, Literacy and Print in Early New Zealand. In *The Social History of Language*, ed. Peter Burke and Roy Porter, pp. 161–197. Cambridge: Cambridge University Press.
Meeuwis, Michael, and Frank Brisard. 1993. *Time and the Diagnosis of Language Change*. Antwerp: University of Antwerp.
Merlan, Francesa, and Alan Rumsey. 1991. *Ku Waru: Language and Segmentary Politics in the Western Nebilyer Valley, Papua New Guinea*. Cambridge: Cambridge University Press.
Mertz, Elizabeth. 1982. Language and Mind: A Whorfian Folk Theory in United States Language Law. Sociolinguistic Working Papers 93. Austin, Tex.: Southwest Educational Development Laboratory.
———. 1985. Beyond Symbolic Anthropology: Introducing Semiotic Mediation. In *Semiotic Mediation*, ed. Elizabeth Mertz and Richard Parmentier, pp. 1–19. Orlando, Fla.: Academic Press.
———. 1989. Sociolinguistic Creativity: Cape Breton Gaelic's Linguistic "Tip." In *Investigating Obsolescence: Studies in Language Contraction and Death*, ed. Nancy Dorian, pp. 103–116. Cambridge: Cambridge University Press.
———. 1993. Learning What to Ask: Metapragmatic Factors and Methodological Reification. In *Reflexive Language: Reported Speech and Metapragmatics*, ed. John A. Lucy, pp. 159–174. Cambridge: Cambridge University Press.

———. 1994. Legal Language: Pragmatics, Poetics and Social Power. *Annual Review of Anthropology* 23:435–455.

———. 1996. Recontextualization as Socialization: Text and Pragmatics in the Law School Classroom. In *Natural Histories of Discourse*, ed. Michael Silverstein and Greg Urban, pp. 229–249. Chicago: University of Chicago Press.

Mertz, Elizabeth, and Richard J. Parmentier, eds. 1985. *Semiotic Mediation: Sociocultural and Psychological Perspectives*. Orlando, Fla.: Academic Press.

Mertz, Elizabeth, and Bernard Weissbourd. 1985. Legal Ideology and Linguistic Theory: Variability and Its Limits. In *Semiotic Mediation*, ed. Elizabeth Mertz and Richard Parmentier, pp. 261–285. Orlando, Fla.: Academic Press.

Messick, Brinkley. 1993. *The Caligraphic State: Textual Domination and History in a Muslim Society*. Berkeley: University of California Press.

Michaels, Sarah, and Courtney Cazden. 1986. Teacher/Child Collaboration as Oral Preparation for Literacy. In *The Acquisition of Literacy: Ethnographic Perspectives*, ed. Bambi B. Schieffelin and Perry Gilmore, pp. 132–154. Norwood, N.J.: Ablex.

Mignolo, Walter D. 1992. On the Colonization of Amerindian Languages and Memories: Renaissance Theories of Writing and the Discontinuity of the Classical Tradition. *Comparative Studies in Society and History* 30:301–330.

———. 1995. *The Darker Side of the Renaissance*. Ann Arbor: University of Michigan.

Miller, Peggy J., Randoph Potts, Heidi Fung, Lisa Hoogstra, and Judy Mintz. 1990. Narrative Practices and the Social Construction of Self in Childhood. *American Ethnologist* 17:292–311.

Milroy, James, and Lesley Milroy. 1985. *Authority in Language: Investigating Language Prescription and Standardisation*. London: Routledge and Kegan Paul.

Moore, Robert E. 1988. Lexicalization versus Loss in Wasco-Wishram Language Obsolescence. *International Journal of American Linguistics* 62:291–320.

———. 1993. Performance Form and the Voices of Characters in Five Versions of the Wasco Coyote Cycle. In *Reflexive Language*, ed. John A. Lucy, pp. 213–240. Cambridge: Cambridge University Press.

Morgan, Marcyliena H. 1991. Indirectness and Interpretation in African American Women's Discourse. *Pragmatics* 1:421–451.

———. 1994. Theories and Politics in African American English. *Annual Review of Anthropology* 23:325–345.

Mugglestone, Lynda. 1995. "*Talking Proper*": *The Rise of Accent as Social Symbol*. Oxford: Clarendon.

Mühlhäusler, Peter. 1990. "Reducing" Pacific Languages to Writing. In *Ideologies of Language*, ed. John E. Joseph and Talbot J. Taylor, pp. 189–205. London: Routledge.

Musa, Monsur. 1989. Purism and Correctness in the Bengali Speech Community. In *The Politics of Language Purism*, ed. Björn H. Jernudd and Michael J. Shapiro, pp. 105–112. Berlin: Mouton de Gruyter.

Nebrija, Elio Antonio de. [1492] 1946. *Gramática castellana*. Madrid: Edición de la Junta del Centenario.

Neu-Altenheimer, Imela, J. Marimoutou, and Daniel Baggioni. 1987. Névrose diglossique et choix graphiques. *Lengas* 22:33–57.

Newmeyer, Fredrick J. 1986. *The Politics of Linguistics*. Chicago: University of Chicago Press.

Nunberg, Geoffrey. 1989. Linguists and the Official Language Movement. *Language* 65:579–587.

Ochs, Elinor. 1979. Transcription as Theory. In *Developmental Pragmatics*, ed. Elinor Ochs and Bambi B. Schieffelin, pp. 43–72. New York: Academic Press.

———. 1988a. *Culture and Language Development.* Cambridge: Cambridge University Press.

———. 1988b. Indexing Gender. In *Rethinking Context,* ed. Alessandro Duranti and Charles Goodwin, pp. 335–358. Cambridge: Cambridge University Press.

Ochs, Elinor, and Bambi B. Schieffelin. 1984. Language Acquisition and Socialization: Three Developmental Stories and Their Implications. In *Culture Theory: Essays on Mind, Self and Emotion,* ed. Richard Shweder and Robert I. Levine, pp. 276–320. Cambridge: Cambridge University Press.

Olender, Maurice. 1992. *The Languages of Paradise: Race, Religion, and Philology in the Nineteenth Century.* Cambridge, Mass.: Harvard University Press.

Östman, Jan-Ola. 1996. Ideology and Contacts. *Pragmatics, Ideology and Contacts Bulletin* 3:3–8.

Pagden, Anthony. 1993. *European Encounters with the New World: From Renaissance to Romanticism.* New Haven, Conn.: Yale University Press.

Parmentier, Richard. 1986. Puffery and Pragmatics, Regulation and Reference. Working Papers and Proceedings of the Center for Psychosocial Studies 4. Chicago: Center for Transcultural Studies.

———. 1993. The Political Function of Reported Speech: A Beluan Example. In *Reflexive Language,* ed. John A. Lucy, pp. 261–286. Cambridge: Cambridge University Press.

Parsons, Talcott. [1959] 1970. An Approach to the Sociology of Knowledge. In *The Sociology of Knowledge: A Reader,* ed. James E. Curtis and John W. Petras, pp. 282–306. New York: Praeger.

Pattanayak, D. P. 1988. Monolingual Myopia and the Petals of the Indian Lotus: Do Many Languages Divide or Unite a Language? In *Minority Education: From Shame to Struggle,* ed. Tove Skutnabb-Kangas and Jim Cummins, pp. 379–389. Clevedon: Multilingual Matters.

Peirce, Charles S. 1974. *Collected Papers,* 2 vols. Edited by C. Hartshorne and P. Weiss. Cambridge, Mass.: Harvard University Press.

Philips, Susan. 1991. Tongan Speech Levels: Practice and Talk about Practice in the Cultural Construction of Social Hierarchy. *Pacific Linguistics,* Series C 117:369–382.

Posner, Rebecca. 1993. Language Conflict in Romance. In *Trends in Romance Linguistics and Philology.* Vol. 5: *Bilingualism and Linguistic Conflict in Romance,* ed. Rebecca Posner and John N. Green, pp. 41–76. Berlin: Mouton de Gruyter.

Pratt, Mary L. 1981. The Ideology of Speech-Act Theory. *Centrum* n.s. 1:5–18.

Preston, Dennis R. 1982. 'Ritin Fowklower Daun 'Rong. *Journal of American Folklore* 95:304–326.

———. 1985. The Li'l Abner Syndrome: Written Representations of Speech. *American Speech* 60:328–336.

Rafael, Vicente. 1988. *Contracting Colonialism: Translation and Christian Conversion in Tagalog Society under Early Spanish Rule.* Ithaca, N.Y.: Cornell University Press.

Raison-Jourde, Françoise. 1977. L'échange inégal de la langue: La pénétration des techniques linguistiques dans une civilisation de l'oral. *Annales* 32:639–669.

Rampton, Ben. 1985. Language Crossing and the Problematisation of Ethnicity and Socialisation. *Pragmatics* 5:485–513.

Reagan, Timothy G. 1986. "Language Ideology" in the Language Planning Process: Two African Case Studies. *South African Journal of African Languages* 6:94–97.

Reddy, Michael J. 1979. The Conduit Metaphor: A Case of Frame Conflict in Our Language about Language. In *Metaphor and Thought,* ed. Andrew Ortony, pp. 284–324. New York: Cambridge University Press.

Rickford, John. 1985. Standard and Non-standard Language Attitudes in a Creole Continuum. In *Language of Inequality*, ed. Nessa Wolfson and Joan Manes, pp. 145–160. Berlin: Mouton.

Rodman, William L. 1991. When Questions Are Answers. *American Anthropologist* 93:421–434.

Romaine, Suzanne. 1989. *Bilingualism*. Oxford: Basil Blackwell.

———. 1994. Hawai'i Creole English as a Literary Language. *Language in Society* 23:527–554.

Rosaldo, Michelle Z. 1982. The Things We Do with Words: Ilongot Speech Acts and Speech Act Theory in Philosophy. *Language in Society* 11:203–237.

Rossi-Landi, Ferruccio. 1973. *Ideologies of Linguistic Relativity*. The Hague: Mouton.

Ruiz, Richard. 1984. Orientations in Language Planning. *National Association for Bilingual Education Journal* 8:15–34.

Rumsey, Alan. 1990. Wording, Meaning and Linguistic Ideology. *American Anthropologist* 92:346–361.

Sakai, Naoki. 1991. *Voices of the Past: The Status of Language in Eighteenth-century Japanese Discourse*. Ithaca, N.Y.: Cornell University Press.

Samarin, William J. 1984. The Linguistic World of Field Colonialism. *Language in Society* 13:435–453.

Sankoff, David. 1988. Sociolinguistics and Syntactic Variation. In *Linguistics: The Cambridge Survey*. Vol. 4: *Language: The Socio-cultural Context*, ed. Frederick J. Newmeyer, pp. 140–161. Cambridge: Cambridge University Press.

Schieffelin, Bambi B. 1990. *The Give and Take of Everyday Life: Language Socialization of Kaluli Children*. New York: Cambridge University Press.

———. 1994. Codeswitching and Language Socialization: Some Probable Relationships. In *Pragmatics: From Theory to Practice*, ed. Judith F. Duchan, Lynne E. Hewitt, and Rae M. Sonnenmeier, pp. 20–42. New York: Prentice Hall.

———. 1995. Creating Evidence: Making Sense of Written Words in Bosavi. *Pragmatics* 5:225–244.

Schieffelin, Bambi B., and Perry Gilmore, eds. 1986. *The Acquisition of Literacy: Ethnographic Perspectives*. Norwood, N.J.: Ablex.

Schieffelin, Bambi B., and Elinor Ochs. 1986. Language Socialization. *Annual Review of Anthropology* 15:163–191.

Schlieben-Lange, Brigitte. 1993. Occitan: French. In *Trends in Romance Linguistics and Philology*. Vol. 5: *Bilingualism and Linguistic Conflict in Romance*, ed. Rebecca Posner and John N. Green, pp. 209–230. Berlin: Mouton de Gruyter.

Schultz, Emily A. 1990. *Dialogue at the Margins: Whorf, Bakhtin, and Linguistic Relativity*. Madison: University of Wisconsin Press.

Scollon, Ron. 1995. Plagiarism and Ideology: Identity in Intercultural Discourse. *Language in Society* 24:1–28.

Scollon, Ron, and Suzanne B. Scollon. 1981. *Narrative, Literacy and Face in Interethnic Communication*. Norwood, N.J.: Ablex.

Searle, John. 1969. *Speech Acts: An Essay in the Philosophy of Language*. Cambridge: Cambridge University Press.

Siegel, James T. 1986. *Solo in the New Order: Language and Hierarchy in an Indonesian City*. Princeton: Princeton University Press.

Siegel, Jeff. 1987. *Language Contact in a Plantation Environment: A Sociolinguistic History of Fiji*. Cambridge: Cambridge University Press.

Silverstein, Michael. 1976. Shifters, Linguistic Categories, and Cultural Description. In

Meaning in Anthropology, ed. Keith H. Basso and Henry A. Selby, pp. 11–55. Albuquerque: University of New Mexico Press.
———. 1979. Language Structure and Linguistic Ideology. In *The Elements: A Parasession on Linguistic Units and Levels*, ed. Paul R. Clyne, William F. Hanks, and Carol L. Hofbauer, pp. 193–247. Chicago: Chicago Linguistic Society.
———. 1981. The Limits of Awareness. Working Papers in Sociolinguistics 84. Austin, Tex.: Southwest Educational Development Laboratory.
———. 1985. Language and the Culture of Gender: At the Intersection of Structure, Usage and Ideology. In *Semiotic Mediation*, ed. Elizabeth Mertz and Richard J. Parmentier, pp. 219–259. Orlando, Fla.: Academic Press.
———. 1987. Monoglot "Standard" in America. Working Papers and Proceedings of the Center for Psychosocial Studies 13. Chicago: Center for Transcultural Studies.
———. 1993. Metapragmatic Discourse and Metapragmatic Function. In *Reflexive Language*, ed. John A. Lucy, pp. 33–58. Cambridge: Cambridge University Press.
———. 1995. From the Meaning of Meaning to the Empires of the Mind: Ogden's Orthological English. *Pragmatics* 5:185–196.
———. 1996a. Indexical Order and the Dialectics of Sociolinguistic Life. *Symposium about Language and Society—Austin* III:266–295.
———. 1996b. The Secret Life of Texts. In *Natural Histories of Discourse*, ed. Michael Silverstein and Greg Urban, pp. 81–105. Chicago: University of Chicago Press.
Silverstein, Michael, and Greg Urban, eds. 1996. *Natural Histories of Discourse*. Chicago: University of Chicago Press.
Simpson, David. 1988. *The Politics of American English, 1776–1850*. New York: Oxford University Press.
Skutnabb-Kangas, Tove, and Robert Phillipson. 1989. Mother Tongue: The Theoretical and Sociopolitical Construction of a Concept. In *Status and Function of Languages and Language Varieties*, ed. Ulrich Ammon, pp. 450–477. Berlin: Walter de Gruyter.
Smith, Olivia. 1984. *The Politics of Language 1791–1819*. New York: Oxford University Press.
Smith-Hefner, Nancy J. 1988. Women and Politeness: The Javanese Example. *Language in Society* 17:535–554.
Smitherman-Donaldson, Geneva. 1988. Discriminatory Discourse on Afro-American Speech. In *Discourse and Discrimination*, ed. Geneva Smitherman-Donaldson and Teun A. van Dijk, pp. 144–175. Detroit: Wayne State University.
Sonntag, Selma K., and Jonathan Pool. 1987. Linguistic Denial and Linguistic Self-denial: American Ideologies of Language. *Language Problems and Language Planning* 11:46–65.
Speicher, Barbara L., and Seane M. McMahon. 1992. Some African-American Perspectives on Black English Vernacular. *Language in Society* 21:383–408.
Steinberg, Jonathan. 1987. The Historian and the *Questione della Lingua*. In *The Social History of Language*, ed. Peter Burke and Roy Porter, pp. 198–209. Cambridge: Cambridge University Press.
Street, Brian V. 1984. *Literacy in Theory and Practice*. New York: Cambridge University Press.
———, ed. 1993. *Cross-Cultural Approaches to Literacy*. Cambridge: Cambridge University Press.
Stroud, Christopher. 1992. The Problem of Intention and Meaning in Code-switching. *Text* 12:127–155.
Swiggers, Pierre. 1990. Ideology and the "Clarity" of French. In *Ideologies of Language*, ed. John E. Joseph and Talbot J. Taylor, pp. 112–130. New York: Routledge.

Taylor, Allan R. 1989. Problems in Obsolescence Research: The Gros Ventres of Montana. In *Investigating Obsolescence: Studies in Language Contraction and Death*, ed. Nancy Dorian, pp. 167–180. Cambridge: Cambridge University Press.

Taylor, Charles. 1987. Language and Human Nature. In *Interpreting Politics*, ed. Michael T. Gibbons, pp. 101–132. New York: New York University Press.

Tedlock, Dennis. 1983. *The Spoken Word and the Work of Interpretation*. Philadelphia: University of Pennsylvania Press.

Therborn, Goran. 1980. *The Ideology of Power and the Power of Ideology*. London: NLB.

Thiers, Ghjacumu. 1993. Language Contact and Corsican Polynomia. In *Trends in Romance Linguistics and Philology*. Vol. 5: *Bilingualism and Linguistic Conflict in Romance*, ed. Rebecca Posner and John N. Green, pp. 253–270. Berlin: Mouton de Gruyter.

Thomas, George. 1991. *Linguistic Purism*. London: Longman.

Thompson, John B. 1984. *Studies in the Theory of Ideology*. Cambridge, England: Polity Press.

———. 1990. *Ideology and Modern Culture*. Stanford: Stanford University Press.

Todorov, Tzvetan. 1984. *The Conquest of America: The Question of the Other*. Translated by Richard Howard. New York: Harper Colophon.

Trosset, Carol S. 1986. The Social Identity of Welsh Learners. *Language in Society* 15:165–192.

Twine, Nanette. 1991. *Language and the Modern State: The Reform of Written Japanese*. New York: Routledge.

Urban, Greg. 1991. The Semiotics of State-Indian Linguistic Relationships: Peru, Paraguay, and Brazil. In *Nation-States and Indians in Latin America*, ed. Greg Urban and Joel Sherzer, pp. 307–330. Austin: University of Texas Press.

———. 1993. The Represented Functions of Speech in Shokleng Myth. In *Reflexive Language*, ed. John A. Lucy, pp. 241–286. Austin: University of Texas Press.

———. 1996. Entextualization, Replication, and Power. In *Natural Histories of Discourse*, ed. Michael Silverstein and Greg Urban, pp. 21–44. Chicago: University of Chicago Press.

Urciuoli, Bonnie. 1991. The Political Topography of Spanish and English: The View from a New York Puerto Rican Neighborhood. *American Ethnologist* 18:295–310.

———. 1992. Time, Talk and Class: New York Puerto Ricans as Temporal and Linguistic Others. In *The Politics of Time*, ed. Henry J. Rutz, pp. 108–126. Washington, D.C.: American Ethnological Society.

———. 1995. Language and Borders. *Annual Review of Anthropology* 24:525–546.

———. 1996. *Exposing Prejudice: Puerto Rican Experiences of Language, Race, and Class*. Boulder Col.: Westview.

Urla, Jacqueline. 1988. Ethnic Protest and Social Planning: A Look at Basque Language Revival. *Cultural Anthropology* 1:379–394.

———. 1993a. Contesting Modernities: Language Standardization and the Production of an Ancient/Modern Basque Culture. *Critique of Anthropology* 13:101–118.

———. 1993b. Cultural Politics in an Age of Statistics: Numbers, Nations and the Making of Basque Identity. *American Ethnologist* 20:818–843.

———. 1995. Outlaw Language: Creating Alternative Public Spheres in Basque Radio. *Pragmatics* 5:245–262.

Verschueren, Jef. 1985. *What People Say They Do with Words: Prolegomena to an Empirical-Conceptual Approach to Linguistic Action*. Norwood, N.J.: Ablex.

Vološinov, V. N. 1973. *Marxism and the Philosophy of Language*. Translated by L. Matejka and I. R. Titunik. Cambridge, Mass.: Harvard University Press.

Walker, Anne. 1986. The Verbatim Record. In *Discourse and Institutional Authority*, ed. Sue Fisher and Alexandra D. Todd, pp. 205–222. Norwood, N.J.: Ablex.

Warner, Michael. 1990. *The Letters of the Republic: Publication and the Public Sphere in Eighteenth-century America.* Cambridge Mass.: Harvard University Press.

Watson-Gegeo, Karen A., and Geoffrey M. White, eds. 1990. *Disentangling: Conflict Discourse in Pacific Societies.* Stanford: Stanford University Press.

Weinstein, Brian. 1989. Francophonie: Purism at the International Level. In *The Politics of Language Purism*, ed. Björn H. Jernudd and Michael Shapiro, pp. 53–80. Berlin: Mouton de Gruyter.

Williams, Glyn. 1988. Discourse on Language and Ethnicity. In *Styles of Discourse*, ed. Nikolas Coupland, pp. 254–293. London: Croom Helm.

Williams, Raymond. 1977. *Marxism and Literature.* Oxford: Oxford University Press.

Winer, Lise. 1990. Orthographic Standardisation for Trinidad and Tobago: Linguistic and Sociopolitical Consideration in an English Creole Community. *Language Problems and Language Planning* 14:237–268.

Wodak, Ruth, ed. 1989. *Language, Power, and Ideology: Studies in Political Discourse.* Philadelphia: John Benjamins.

Wolfson, Nessa, and Joan Manes, eds. 1985. *Language of Inequality.* Berlin: Mouton.

Woodbury, Anthony C. 1994. A Defense of the Proposition "When a Language Dies, a Culture Dies." *Symposium about Language and Society—Austin* I:102–130.

Woolard, Kathryn A. 1985. Language Variation and Cultural Hegemony: Towards an Integration of Sociolinguistic and Social Theory. *American Ethnologist* 12:738–748.

———. 1989a. *Double Talk: Bilingualism and the Politics of Ethnicity in Catalonia.* Stanford: Stanford University Press.

———. 1989b. Sentences in the Language Prison: The Rhetorical Structuring of an American Language Policy Debate. *American Ethnologist* 16:268–278.

———. 1995. Gendered Peer Groups and the Bilingual Repertoire in Catalonia. *Symposium about Language and Society—Austin* II:200–220.

Woolard, Kathryn A., and Tae-Joong Gahng. 1990. Changing Language Policies and Attitudes in Autonomous Catalonia. *Language in Society* 19:311–330.

Woolard, Kathryn A., and Bambi B. Schieffelin. 1994. Language Ideology. *Annual Review of Anthropology* 23:55–82.

Zentella, Ana Celia. 1997. *Growing up Bilingual: Puerto Rican Children in New York.* Oxford: Blackwell.

I

SCOPE AND FORCE OF DOMINANT CONCEPTIONS OF LANGUAGE

2

Ideologies of Honorific Language

JUDITH T. IRVINE

All sociolinguistic systems, presumably, provide some means of expressing respect (or disrespect), but only some systems have those specially conventionalized linguistic forms that linguists have called "honorifics." This chapter compares several languages—Javanese, Wolof, Zulu, and ChiBemba—with regard to their construction of honorific expressions and the social and cultural frameworks relevant to them.[1] The main question to be explored is whether one can identify any cultural concomitants of linguistic systems in which honorifics occur. Asking that question involves attention to language ideologies and their relationships with linguistic form and social life.

Javanese "language levels" are a classic and well-described example of a system for the expression of respect. In the sense in which "honorifics" are usually identified—that is, as involving special lexical and/or morphological alternants (see the next section)—Javanese provides an apt illustration. Wolof, on the other hand, does not. Of course, Javanese is only one of several Asian languages well known for honorific constructions, while Wolof, spoken in Senegal, comes from another part of the globe. But the presence or absence of honorifics is not an area characteristic that opposes Asian languages to African languages. Zulu, for example, has a system of lexical alternants for the expression of respect, as do the related languages Xhosa and SeSwati. Moreover, many other Bantu languages (such as ChiBemba) also have honorifics, although in the morphology rather than in the lexicon.

Focusing on social structure instead of on geographical area, one might hypothesize that honorifics occur where there are royal courts (Wenger 1982; see also Brown and Gilman 1960) and in societies whose traditions emphasize social rank and precedence. In such settings, honorifics would be a linguistic means of expressing conventionalized differences of rank. The languages I compare in this chapter make it evident, however, that such a hypothesis—in which court life and/or entrenched class differences are proposed as necessary and sufficient conditions for the existence of linguistic honorifics—cannot be adequate. While some such link may hold true for Javanese, it does not for the other systems. The Wolof had royal courts until the French conquest a century ago and retain (especially in rural areas) a social system structured on profound inequalities of birth and family origin—inequalities the ethnographic literature on the region usually describes as caste differences. Neither in preconquest times nor today, however, is there any indication of honorific lexical or morphological alternants in the Wolof language, although there were and are other ways to express deference.[2] Zulu society, even at the height of the Zulu state, was somewhat less stratified than Wolof society (to say nothing of Javanese society), and the Bemba polity was less strongly centralized than any of the other cases; yet both Zulu and ChiBemba have honorifics. Courts and social stratification are not irrelevant to deferential language, but they do not predict its linguistic form.

In examining these sociolinguistic systems, I do not believe any simple correlation between forms of "on-the-ground" social structure (such as the existence of a royal court) and forms of talk (such as honorifics) is likely to be found. Instead, as I have argued elsewhere (Irvine 1985, 1989), the relationship between the distributions of social and linguistic forms is more productively sought in cultural ideologies of language—those complex systems of ideas and interests through which people interpret linguistic behaviors. In this chapter, therefore, I pay special attention to the language ideologies that link ideas about language with ideas about social rank, respect, and appropriate conduct—including the native metapragmatic terminology and theories that articulate and rationalize perceptions of language structure and use (see Silverstein 1979, Woolard and Schieffelin 1994). I draw on a concept of ideology, rather than merely a "culture of language," because "ideology," whatever else it may mean, suggests a connection with those power relations and interests that are central in a social order. Some such connection is surely relevant to honorific language.

As Silverstein (1979) points out, language ideology must be clearly distinguished from linguistic structures and from the distribution of uses. It is this distinction that makes the present comparison possible and, further, sheds light on these systems' historical dynamics, as I briefly observe.

Linguistic Structures

Honorifics are deictic forms of speech signaling social deference, through conventionalized understandings of some aspect(s) of the form-meaning relationship in language. It must be emphasized that honorifics are *forms* of speech: that is, the deference payable by person A to person B is understood (by the members of some community of discourse) as an inherently communicated property of particular linguistic expressions, not just the contingent consequence of an expression's deployment in social life. Moreover, the signaling of deference is *conventional* in that it is not merely the literal product of an expression's compositional semantics but requires some further set of shared understandings about the expression's significance and pragmatic potential. One might even say that in a language that has honorifics, the expression of deference is grammaticalized. By this I mean that expressions of deference are incorporated into the language's grammatical rules, rules that include its lexicon.[3]

Thus, a system of honorifics is a system of special linguistic forms that, apart from the expression of deference, supposedly "mean the same thing" as the corresponding nonhonorific forms with which they alternate. To put this another way, the alternants are isosemantic, in that a particular referent may be denoted either by an honorific or by a nonhonorific expression, the difference lying in the expressions' pragmatic values and not in their denotational adequacy (for further discussion, see the last section of this chapter). The pragmatic value, expressing degrees of deference, respect, or social distance, operates as part of sentence-meaning, not utterance-meaning. That is, in honorifics, deference is incorporated in the construction of the sentence per se, rather than depending on how the sentence is deployed in its social or discourse context. (Note that the possibility of regular, sarcastic uses of honorifics depends on this condition; see Levinson 1983:93.)

Potentially, conventions for the expression of deference might involve any level of linguistic organization. For the most part, however, linguists use the term "honorifics" only with regard to special lexicon or morphology. Through co-occurrence patterns and engagement with other linguistic phenomena such as a characteristic phonology or syntax, those honorific forms may give rise to what can be considered "honorific registers" (see Agha 1993, 1994). As we shall see, a register for conveying respectfulness may be constructed on some other basis; yet, in the usage of most linguists, a language that lacks specifically isolable or segmentable honorific forms in its lexicon or morphology is seldom said to "have honorifics."

In Javanese, respectful expression operates through a complex system of lexical alternants. In the sentence in (1), taken from Errington (1988), each word has a set of alternants, whose various orderly combinations define six "levels" of sentence style:[4]

(1) Javanese "language levels" (Errington 1988:90–91):

KRAMA:	1.	*menapa*	*nandalem*	*mundhut*	*sekul*	*semanten*
	2.	*menapa*	*panjenengan*	*mendhet*	*sekul*	*semanten*
MADYA:	3.	*napa*	*sampeyan*	*mendhet*	*sekul*	*semonten*
	4.	*napa*	*sampeyan*	*njupuk*	*sega*	*semonten*
NGOKO:	5.	*apa*	*sliramu*	*mundhut*	*sega*	*semono*
	6.	*apa*	*kowe*	*njupuk*	*sega*	*semono*
Gloss:		Question marker	'you'	'take'	'rice'	'that much'

'Did you take that much rice?'

Though rarely exhibiting the complexity and elaboration of the Javanese language levels, systems of honorific lexical alternants—respect vocabularies—are also found in many other languages. Among such languages are Zulu and its closest relatives, Xhosa and Seswati, in the Nguni branch of the Bantu language family. In Zulu and Xhosa the respect vocabulary is known as *hlonipha*. A few examples are given in (2):

(2) Zulu *hlonipha* vocabulary (Doke and Vilakazi 1958):

	ORDINARY	HLONIPHA
'graze; weave'	*aluka*	*acuka*
'be dejected'	*jaba*	*gxaba*
'affair'	*indaɓa*	*injušo*
'my father'	*uɓaɓa*	*utšatša*
'hippopotamus'	*imvuɓu*	*incuɓu*
'lion'	*imbuɓe*	*injuɓe*
'house'	*indlu*	*incumba*
'chief'	*inkosi*	*inqoɓo, inqotšana* (dim.)
'our'	*-ithu*	*-itšu*
'thy'	*-kho*	*-to*

(*c*, *q*, *x* = clicks; *ɓ* = implosive bilabial stop)

Many Bantu languages found to the northeast of the Nguni group also have respect forms but locate them in the morphology of the noun classification system, rather than in a set of alternant stems. In ChiBemba, a language of Zambia, for example, there are no morphemes or lexical items exclusively reserved for honorific reference; respect is expressed by the conventional use of plural prefixes (or pronouns) for singular human referents, as in (3).[5] Noun classes 1 and 2, the 'singular' and 'plural' classes used for most nouns that denote humans, are the main ones affected. Thus, the class 2 prefix that marks plurality in (3c) marks honorific singular in (3b):

(3) ChiBemba noun prefixes, classes 1/2:

(a) singular (not respectful):

umo	*umukalamba*	*waandi*	*aleelya*	*isabi*
1	1	1	1	9a
one	older-sibling	my	subject-tense-eat	fish

'One of my older siblings is eating fish.'
(*or*, 'My one older sibling is eating fish.')

(b) singular (respectful):

bamo	*abakalamba*	*baandi*	*baleelya*	*isabi*
2	2	2	2	9a
one	older sibling	my	subject-tense-eat	fish

'One of my older siblings is eating fish.'
(*or*, 'My one older sibling is eating fish.')

(c) plural (plain or respectful):

babili	*abakalamba*	*baandi*	*baleelya*	*isabi*
2	2	2	2	9a
two	older sibling	my	subject-tense-eat	fish

'Two of my older siblings are eating fish.'
(*or*, 'My two older siblings are eating fish.')

As is illustrated in these sentences, honorification in ChiBemba applies to the human-denoting regent of a noun phrase (regardless of syntactic position). Because of complex patterns of concord, all modifiers and anaphors of the human-denoting element are marked for honorification also. Thus, in (3b), numerals and adjectives that modify the human-denoting noun stem *-kalamba* ('older sibling') receive class 2 prefixes, as does the subject-marker anaphor on the verb.

In its noun classification system, ChiBemba also provides for various pejorative usages, by shifting the class assignment of a noun with human reference, as in (4):

(4) ChiBemba honorific and pejorative noun prefixes (singular denotatum; based on the stem *-kaši* 'wife'):

		CLASS	VALUE
abakaši	'(respectable) wife'	2	honorific
umukaši	'wife'	1	disrespectful
akakaši	'(insignificant) wife'	12	insult
ičikaši	'(gross) wife'	7	insult
ilikaši	'(egregious [?]) wife'	5	"a little derogatory"

All these languages thus have systems of alternant expressions that can be marshaled to denote the same referent but with a difference in pragmatic value. In all of these cases, the grammatical rules involved apply, fundamentally, to word formation (selection of stem or of prefix); the formation of sentences may be affected in consequence, through concord patterns and co-occurrence constraints. Except in (3c), the pragmatic value is unambiguous and undeniable.

In contrast, Wolof does not have these kinds of rules. Speakers express respect in other ways. Although Wolof does have speech registers that connote speaker's social rank relative to that of the addressee (as I have described elsewhere; Irvine 1990), the registers are constructed quite differently from, for instance, the Javanese language levels. In Javanese, each word selected from an otherwise isosemantic set has its particular pragmatic value. In Wolof, however, individual words or sentences in the two registers are not isosemantic, except insofar as utterances might rely exclusively on prosodic contrasts to create register differences. As outlined in (5), these prosodic patterns, though characteristic and striking, are nonsegmentable and operate more on the level of utterance meaning than on the level of sentence meaning:

(5) Wolof prosodic patterns:

	waxu géér 'NOBLE SPEECH'	*waxu gewel* 'GRIOT SPEECH'
Pitch	low	high
Volume	soft	loud
Tempo	slow	fast
Voice	breathy	clear
Contour	pitch nucleus last	pitch nucleus first
Dynamic range	narrow	wide

Apart from their prosody, the Wolof registers depend on semantic differences and rhetorical elaboration. Pragmatic value is built up over an expanse of discourse, for the registers embody contrasting rhetorical strategies that can rarely be displayed in an individual word or a brief, decontextualized sentence.

Incidentally, in claiming that Wolof does not have an honorific lexicon or morphology of the types described for Javanese, Zulu, and ChiBemba, I exclude from consideration certain kinds of expressions Wolof does have. Some Wolof titles and kinship terms, for example, as in probably every other language in the world, normally connote respectability, but they do so only by virtue of their semantics, not because of a special pragmatic value. More relevant are praise-names and praise-epithets—that is, patriclan names and a set of semantically opaque expressions that may be attached to them to emphasize the clan's praiseworthy place in history. Although these forms do indeed get mobilized in Wolof eulogistic genres, praise-names differ typologically from the lexical honorifics discussed earlier because they have no nonhonorific alternants. There is no way to denote a patriclan non-honorifically, if one is to denote it at all.

In short, Wolof might be said to have eulogistic or honor-paying *registers*, but it does not have honorific *alternants*, particular intrasentential form-shapes that systematically alternate with nonhonorific forms that are supposed to "mean the same" except for the honorific value.

Linguistic Ideologies

Let us turn to the linguistic ideologies pertaining to three of the languages so far mentioned: Javanese, Wolof, and Zulu. How do speakers of these languages perceive these expressions of deference, and how do they theorize about them? How do they connect such expressions with ideas about respect, rank, and appropriate conduct?

For Javanese, I draw on Errington's (1984, 1988) elegant and complex studies of the speech of the *priyayi*, the traditional elite. These speakers evidently recognize the complexity and subtlety of their sociolinguistic system, and they also attribute these characteristics to the system's highest-ranking users. Indeed, ideas about subtlety and refinement, on the one hand, and coarseness and vulgarity, on the other, seem to be crucial to the *priyayi* conception of their language. The "higher" (*basa*, especially *krama*) levels are considered to be governed by an ethic of proper order, peace, and calm. In them one "does not express one's own feelings" (Wolff and Poedjosoedarmo 1982:41). The "lower" levels (*ngoko*) are "the language one loses one's temper in" (Errington 1984:9). Yet, in some ways, the point is really what happens not to one's own temper but to one's addressee's. The language levels are addressee-focused; they are thought of as a means of guarding the addressee's equanimity, of avoiding angering him or her, and of expressing politeness by deferring to the addressee's wishes and effacing one's own (Errington 1988:42–43). Polite conduct toward a respected addressee is conduct that is stylized, depersonalized, and flat-affect, because that is the behavioral environment that such a respected being's "nature" supposedly requires. Still, the use of "high" deferential styles also implies the speaker's own refinement, as shown by the speaker's ability to efface emotion, sensitivity to the equanimity of others, and pragmatic delicacy.

Compare with this the language ideology of rural, "traditional" Wolof. The Wolof ideology includes some quite similar ideas about rank, affectivity, and engagement with the concrete: high rank implies self-control, flat affect, the protection of others, and (especially for the religious elite) disengagement from worldly involvements. Moreover, deferential conduct toward others requires a flow of flattering words. But, unlike the Javanese case, in Wolof a flow of words does not easily display any high rank or refinement on the part of their speaker.

For some insight into this difference, consider the native metapragmatic theories regarding participant roles in speaking. As example (5) has shown, the Wolof metapragmatic terminology firmly identifies the two registers, "noble speech" and "griot speech," with the rank of speakers—nobles and griots being oppositely ranked castes. In the folk-theory that relates ways of speaking to kinds of speakers, the registers take the form they do because persons of these high and low ranks (i.e., nobles and griots) are ideologically accorded certain temperamental characteristics, such as affectivity and excitability. Thus, "noble speech" is flat-affect speech, while "griot speech" is a high-affect, theatrical, hyperbolic style (see Irvine 1990).

Despite the terminology, however, the use of these registers is not limited to the social ranks they are named for. Both registers are used on some occasions by almost everyone. Still, their use always conveys a sense that the participants in a speech situation inhabit contrasting ranks, even if only metaphorically. Normatively, "griot speech" is the way low-ranking griots address high-ranking nobles. Any person may employ this register to flatter an addressee; yet, in so doing, a speaker engages in griot-like, hence low-ranking, conduct.

The Wolof linguistic ideology thus identifies the register system primarily with the speaker (and the speaker's supposed temperament), elevating the addressee only by implication. The Javanese ideology, in contrast, identifies the *ngoko-madya-krama* style system primarily with the addressee (and the addressee's "needs" to receive speech of a particular kind), elevating the speaker only by implication. Table 2.1 compares the Wolof and Javanese metapragmatic systems with regard to the connotations of register choices for participants' rank. Primary connotations, explicitly signaled by the choice of an honorific register, may be distinguished from secondary, implicit connotations.

Although the "implicated" connotations inform participants' strategies, the fact

Table 2.1 Participant role relationships

		Speaker	*Addressee*
Wolof	"griot speech"	Lowering	(Elevating)
Javanese	*basa* (high levels)	Lowering (Elevating)	Elevating

Key: No parentheses = primary, focal effect; Parentheses = secondary, implicational effect.

that the ideological focus lies elsewhere constrains what rhetorical effects are achievable, and how. So, for example, Wolof nobles avoid using the "griot speech" register, and any other suggestion of low-caste conduct, on public, formal occasions. Instead, they hire a lower-ranking intermediary, usually a griot, to speak on their behalf. The noble sponsor of the speech thus manages to get the addressee flattered while nevertheless suggesting his or her own high rank by refraining from engaging in affectively charged speech and by exploiting the fact that griots are known to select high-ranking and wealthy sponsors if they can.

The comparison of Wolof and Javanese is further illuminated by a look at a third case, Zulu, which shares some characteristics of both. Zulu has two types of deferential expression, the native terminology suggests: *hlonipha* 'showing respect', and *ɓonga* 'praise'. These two types of expression are ideologically linked with different social contexts (family and court) and with different users (women and men), respectively.

The Zulu *hlonipha* language has apparently largely fallen out of use today, although it is still reported among rural Xhosa women (see Finlayson 1978, 1982, 1984 for examples of contemporary usage). A few decades ago, however, it was described as being required especially of Zulu married women, who were supposed to use *hlonipha* words in order to avoid uttering the name of the husband's father.[6] Also to be avoided was any other word that contained the root or stem found in the husband's father's name or that sounded similar. If the father-in-law's name just happened to sound like *imvuɓu* 'hippopotamus', the daughter-in-law had to call hippos *incuɓu* instead. (We might think of this pattern as a sort of anti-pun.) Since names were traditionally composed of meaningful expressions, many words could be affected by the need to avoid a particular person's name-sounds.

The norms of *hlonipha* behavior apply to gesture and clothing as well as to words: to *hlonipha* is to avoid eye contact, restrain one's affectivity, and cover one's body in the presence of respected persons. This apparently includes using conventional euphemisms for talk about bodily functions; it certainly used to include covering over, or avoiding, the expression of sound-sequences that would enunciate respected persons' names. The substitute (respectful) term could derive from a descriptive or metaphorical construction, or it could derive from patterned phonological shifts. The phonological shifts sometimes had the effect of neutralizing consonant contrasts, since the tendency was for stem-initial consonants in *hlonipha* words to become [+Coronal] (especially the coronal affricates *tš* and *j [dž]*) or to become clicks. Many *hlonipha* homonyms were created in this way, as illustrated in (6):

(6) Zulu respect homonyms (Doke and Vilakazi 1958):

	ORDINARY	HLONIPHA
'swing'	*lenga*	*cenga*
'annoy'	*nenga*	*cenga*
		(*c* = dental click)

(*Uku-*)*ɓonga* 'to praise', on the other hand, is to 'express gratitude' or 'worship', but in a very different way. In particular, the term identifies an exuberant, poetic style of male public oratory, usually addressed to important political figures (clan leaders, chiefs, kings, visiting dignitaries) at public gatherings. Although anyone can use this style to shout out praises and encouragement, perhaps to a man engaged in a fight or to an important man who appears on the scene, the model performers are the male professional praise-poets (*izimɓongi*, singular *imɓongi*) supported by chiefs or kings. A praise-poet may begin his training by memorizing traditional praises associated with clans and historical personages, and some of this memorized material may be included in his performance. Successful performance does not depend on exact recall of fixed text, however. On the contrary: vivid, detailed imagery and a sense of spontaneous enthusiasm are crucial. Statements by prominent Zulu and Xhosa poets (see Opland 1983) indicate that effective praise-performance ought to be spontaneous, inspired, and visionary. Several poets told Opland (1983:64 ff.) that the impulse to become a praise-performer came to them originally in a dream; that their experiences are like those of a diviner who is summoned by ancestral spirits; and that the words come to them suddenly, unrehearsed and unprepared, the product of inspiration and emotional outpouring.[7]

Zulu praise-utterance has its poeticisms, but it does not seem to rely upon linguistic honorifics (in the sense I have been discussing here—that is, a special set of isosemantic honorific alternants). Thus, the Zulu expressive system includes an utterer-focused, ecstatic, high-affect, engaged style without honorifics, and an addressee- or bystander-focused, flat-affect, disengaged, avoidance style with honorifics.

Notice that the Zulu praise-oratory style resembles, in some ways, the Wolof "griot speech" register: both deliver praise through dramatic, heightened-affect, semantically elaborated discourse. The resemblance is not accidental. Praise-oratory of this type is widespread in Africa; among the Wolof, it is the griots' specialty. But Wolof and Zulu differ in that the Zulu linguistic ideology does not connect praise-performance with low caste, or with particularly low rank of any sort. Speaking in *ɓonga* style does not compromise the speaker's status. Notice, too, a typological parallel between the Zulu *hlonipha* style and the higher levels (termed *basa*) of Javanese. Both involve lowered affect, euphemism, neutralization of certain contrasts, and conspicuous conventionality. The Zulu system, then, incorporates both patterns of deferential talk described earlier for Wolof and Javanese.

Comparing all three languages, Table 2.2 summarizes these relationships between aspects of linguistic structure and aspects of linguistic ideology, as these concern verbal conduct considered appropriate for elevating others.

Table 2.2 Ideology and structure of other-elevating expressions

	Pattern A	Pattern B
Ideology	Lowered affect; conventionality	Heightened affect; spontaneity
Structure	Semantic or sound neutralization; honorific alternants	Semantic or sound elaboration; no honorific alternants
Zulu/Xhosa	*hlonipha* 'respect'	*ɓonga* 'praise'
Wolof		*waxu gewel* 'griot speech'
Javanese		*basa* ('high' levels)

Distribution of Deferential Styles

As Silverstein (1979) observes, though ideology affects speakers' strategies of language use, linguistic ideology is not the same thing as linguistic structure, and native perceptions of use are not the same as the (comparative) distribution of uses as an outside observer might perceive them. Attempts at cross-linguistic comparison, such as the present comparison of deferential styles, are vitiated if ideology and distribution are not clearly distinguished. Were one to suppose, for Javanese, Wolof, and Zulu, that the ideological rationale for the deferential styles was also their description, the three systems might appear not to be comparable at all. For Wolof, "noble speech" and "griot speech" might appear to be social dialects, not registers (see Irvine 1990 for discussion), and the Zulu *hlonipha* vocabulary might appear to be merely a series of idiosyncratic, ephemeral constructions varying from one woman to another, rather than a systematic linguistic resource.

That is to say, the father-in-law name-avoidance rationale for Zulu *hlonipha* would suggest that each set of daughters-in-law would have a different respect vocabulary, depending on the father-in-law's name; that a particular speaker's respect terms might not be very numerous; and that a term would disappear upon the daughter-in-law's death. But *hlonipha* usage is (or was) actually much more widespread, involving male speakers as well as female, court contexts as well as domestic, and various kinds of respected beings. From Krige ([1936] 1950:31) we learn, for example, that *hlonipha* forms were also used by men to avoid using the name of the mother-in-law, though the custom was "not so strict" for men as it was for women. Furthermore, "the whole tribe" must *hlonipha* the name of the king or chief, while those resident at the royal court must *hlonipha* the names of the king's father and grandfather as well (Krige [1936] 1950:31, 233; see also Bryant 1949).[8] In an example that conspicuously does not involve a father-in-law, Bryant (1949: 220) notes, too, that "for a Zulu woman to call a porcupine by its proper name, iNgungumbane, were but to provoke it to increased depredation in her fields; therefore it must be referred to 'politely' as 'the-little-woman', or umFazazana." The Doke and Vilakazi (1958) dictionary, which cites hundreds of *hlonipha* words, includes respect forms for kin terms, chiefly and royal titles, and possessive pronouns. All these forms, apparently long-standing items of Zulu vocabulary, are unlikely to be merely avoidances of a father-in-law's name. The existence of a widely known respect vocabulary seems to be a fact of the distribution of uses, not inherent in its rationale.

The distribution of Zulu speech styles thus does not conform strictly to the linguistic ideology that links them to gender relations and domestic versus public arenas.[9] Nevertheless, the linguistic ideology does suggest that the primary focus and principal set of connotations for the *hlonipha* vocabulary lie in domestic relations and enter the court only by extension. It is likely, in fact, that Zulu *hlonipha* usage antedates the rise of a strongly centralized Zulu state in the late eighteenth century. The existence of *hlonipha* among the Swazi and the less traditionally centralized Xhosa implies its relative antiquity and tends to confirm the idea that the respect vocabulary arose, not in connection with the state, but in the power dynamics of Nguni family and affinal relations.

Comparing the language ideology with the distribution of uses—a distinction essential for cross-linguistic studies—thus affords a glimpse of the historical dynamics of sociolinguistic systems. As Silverstein (1979) argues, the relationships among language ideology, structure, and use form a dialectical process that, in conjunction with local contingencies, induces change. For Zulu honorifics, it is worth noting in this regard that the kinds of sound changes involved in *hlonipha* words resemble some of the sound shifts that differentiate the Nguni language family from its Southeastern Bantu relatives, such as the shifts *ɓ* > *tš*, *mb* > *nj*, and the acquisition of click consonants.[10] Were it possible to delve more deeply into Zulu or Xhosa ideologies of language, one might be able to illuminate this process by investigating notions of sound symbolism, as well as attitudes toward the Khoisan languages (and their speakers) from which the clicks were acquired.

Conceivably, then, the construction of Nguni honorific avoidance forms included the importation of "foreign" words and sounds, some of which may later have lost their specifically honorific value, being replaced by new avoidance forms.[11] If so, this would not be the only case where honorific alternants have behaved like a currency in inflationary conditions. The other cases of honorifics we have examined here, Javanese and ChiBemba, both evidence processes of pragmatic devaluation. (Wolof, lacking honorific alternants of the same type, is not directly comparable.) Thus, Errington comments that some Javanese terms "have undergone pragmatic devaluation as the result of recurring patterns of strategic other-exalting, self-abasing speech style use" (1988:115). For ChiBemba, Richardson (1967) reports a wide extension of honorific usage in urban settings, as a result of which some honorific address forms have lost any specially honorific implication. Differences in honorific usage between my Bemba consultants of rural and urban origin confirm this trend and suggest that urban speakers must resort to additional means if they wish to underscore respectfulness.

To explore further the contemporary dynamics of any of these honorific systems would require recognizing, however, that language ideologies are also subject to change. Increasingly participating in a global political economy of language, these sociolinguistic systems and their ideologies are being reconfigured.

Summary and Reflections

The comparison of these four languages—Javanese, Wolof, Zulu, and ChiBemba—suggests that grammatical honorifics (i.e., honorific lexical or morphological alternants) accompany linguistic ideologies that specify that flattened affect, conventionality, and avoidance of engagement with the concrete or the sensory are appropriate ways to express respect for *others* (rather than ways to express one's *own* rank). Put another way, honorifics are embedded in an ideology in which a low-affect style can be other-elevating. They are connected with the management of affectivity and conventionality, as well as with the ways these relate to rank and power. The kinds of rank and power involved vary from one system to another. Honorifics have no necessary connection with royal courts or with class stratification. Even where courts exist, domestic power relations may be the honorifics' primary arena.

It would not have been possible, I believe, to reach this conclusion without clearly distinguishing the distribution of forms of talk from the linguistic ideology that interprets and rationalizes them. A focus on ideology has been crucial in accounting for similarities and differences among the four cases considered in this chapter, but ideology alone, without consideration of the behaviors and circumstances it interprets, would not be sufficient. Considering all of these—linguistic structures, ideologies, and distributions—facilitates the comparison of cases and helps illuminate the dynamics of historical change.

But perhaps there is also a deeper level of language ideology suggested in the comparison of these cases: a metalinguistic level involving conceptions of language itself and its relation to a world of referents and social interactions.[12] Here one must consider linguists' own cultures and ideologies of language, as well as those of the speakers of the languages in question. Conceptions at this level permit linguists to identify honorifics as such, but implications are sometimes drawn that, like the language ideologies already discussed, are not exactly and solely based on the structure and distribution of linguistic facts.

As we have seen, the systems I have compared all have honorific registers—one system, Zulu, even has honorific registers of two different kinds—but the systems do not all have honorific alternants at the level of intrasentential segmentables. The systems contrast, therefore, in whether honorification is a register characteristic alone—that is, an aspect of situation and comportment in which the conveying of respect is diffuse—or a grammatical characteristic tied to specific (segmentable) linguistic elements and constructions. Apparently, for rural Wolof, honorification attaches primarily to speakers, their motivations, and their characteristic discursive practices. For Javanese, it also, perhaps primarily, attaches to words.

There is nothing about this contrast to suggest that speakers in any of these sociolinguistic systems consider pragmatic value or rhetorical import to be external to the principal functions of language. On the contrary, it would seem that for speakers in these systems, pragmatic values relating to honorification pervade and suffuse all uses of language. But to the extent that this is the case, their conceptions of language differ from those prevalent among many scholars working in European and American traditions of linguistics. For instance, a linguist who identified honorifics strictly as isosemantic alternants differing "only" in pragmatic value—without further exploration of the matter—would imply (or assume) that pragmatic values concerned with the construction of social relations operate independently of semantic values concerned with an objective, external world. That assumption is deep-seated in a linguistics of Saussurean tradition as it is also in the more broadly based Euro-American notions of language as rationalizable toward "pure" denotation of a "real" world external to emotion, intention, and social construction (see Silverstein 1995a, 1995b, and this volume).

If applied to Wolof, such a conception of language would make the pragmatic values involved in respect registers seem to disappear. The language would be described (as indeed it has been in several grammars and dictionaries) in terms of informational functions alone and as if it had no register differences at all. And if applied to Javanese, this conception of language would find it convenient to imagine the language levels as systematically parallel registers, alike in all respects but their sound-shape particulars and their place on a scale of pragmatic value, now conceived as orthogonal to each register.

Though finding some support in Javanese metapragmatic labels for "language levels," this representation of the Javanese system does not entirely succeed in accounting for the distribution of linguistic forms.[13] As Errington (1988) is at pains to show, the "levels" as wholes are not precisely consistent with the degrees of honorification that could be calibrated for each of their ingredients separately.[14] (In (1), for example, the alternants for the verb 'take' do not line up tidily.) There are several reasons the "levels" are not orthogonal. First, Javanese referent-focused and addressee-focused honorifics can operate partly at cross-purposes and affect different semantic domains. Second, the "levels" differ greatly in how many alternants are specific to each. *Madya*, for example, has fewer than fifty special alternants, as compared with many hundreds for *krama*. Third, the idea that honorific alternants have exactly the same semantic contents is not ultimately tenable. *Basa* (high-level) forms are not simply one-to-one replacements for *ngoko* lexemes. Some honorifics are constructed via tropes that remain semantically transparent, and honorific items differ from their nonhonorific alternants in semantic range. Isosemantic only as regards their denotational adequacy, honorifics do not, in fact, operate at the same level of denotational particularity as do the corresponding nonhonorific forms. As Errington (1988:153–154) puts it, the honorific alternants are semantically less determinate than the *ngoko* forms, since it turns out that several *ngoko* words share the same honorific alternant.[15]

In short, the notion that alternants "mean the same" and that honorific registers simply and systematically parallel nonhonorific registers is an ideologized construct that is in some respects misleading. Similar problems arise for other honorific systems (see Irvine 1995). Indeed, these problems do not concern only honorifics but concern register relations in general. A conception of registers as parallel, isosemantic systems deceptively segregates their pragmatics from other aspects of their structure and deflects descriptions of linguistic structure from discussing register relationships at all. The fact that honorific registers are not simply isosemantic parallels, however, suggests that other kinds of registers should not be presumed to stand in that relationship, either.

A broad discussion of register relations and of the relationship between semantics and pragmatics is well beyond the scope of the present chapter. I have not meant to claim that a distinction between semantics and pragmatics can never be appropriate. The point, instead, is that language ideologies, which include theories about language, are not only to be attributed to seemingly exotic people in far-off places.

Some generations ago, linguists sometimes singled out honorific language in Africa and Asia for ridicule or criticism as the signs of what they took to be false pride, decadent overrefinement, or slavish deference to oriental despotism.[16] That they did so says more about those linguists' attitudes toward indigenous social hierarchies than it says about the languages in question or their cultural contexts. Comments of that kind have become rare in scholarly discourse, but if scholars today are less likely to ridicule other people's linguistic structures, it does not follow that they bring no ideological engagements to them. Because honorifics intricately engage linguistic form with social functions concerned with rank and distance, honorific language may be an especially revealing site for exploring language ideologies—both participants' and observers'. Comparing cases and analyses of honorific language shows that language ideologies mediate between the forms of speaking and the conditions of social life in many complex ways.

NOTES

Earlier versions of this chapter were presented at a session on language ideology at the 1991 annual meeting of the American Anthropological Association and in *Pragmatics* 2:251–62 (special issue on language ideologies, edited by Paul Kroskrity, Bambi Schieffelin, and Kathryn Woolard). Thanks are due to Bambi Schieffelin, Paul Kroskrity, Kathryn Woolard, Michael Silverstein, and Debra Spitulnik for their helpful comments.

1. The discussion of Wolof in this chapter draws on my fieldwork in Senegal, mainly during the 1970s. I am grateful for the support of the National Institute of Mental Health, the National Science Foundation, and Brandeis University. ChiBemba citations come from elicitation sessions with ChiBemba speakers at Brandeis University.

2. Titles and praise-epithets, which Wolof does have, are not alternants and therefore differ typologically from honorifics See discussion in the next section.

3. Since the term "grammaticalization" is often used in a different sense, however—mainly, to refer to a process in which lexical items become incorporated into morphology—I do not emphasize it in the present discussion.

4. Errington (1988) does not call the language levels "honorifics" but instead reserves that term for those lexical items that express respect for a referent rather than for an addressee—unlike some other authors who use the term "honorifics" for both. Although a distinction between reference and address forms is important in his analysis and, indeed, clarifies some matters that have been obscured by too exclusive a focus on the language levels, I prefer the broader usage for the comparative purposes of this chapter. Note, however, that the codification of these forms in named "levels" is not forced by the linguistic ingredients but is socially and ideologically constructed.

5. Some other Central Bantu languages do have unambiguous markers of honorific reference. In Yao, for example, where "any noun or pronoun which has human reference must contain a reference to respect" (Nurse 1979:136), complex patterns of prefixation distinguish honorific from ordinary reference for the relevant noun stems, as illustrated in (i):

(i) Yao noun prefixes, class 1/2:

	STEM	ORDINARY		HONORIFIC	
		Singular	Plural	Singular	Plural
'guest'	*-lendo*	*m-*	*va-*	*a-*	*acáá-*
'grandparent'	*-buje*	*m-*	*acáá-*	*am-*	*acáá-*
'woman'	*-mbúmba*	*jwá-*	*acáá-*	*vá-*	*acáá-*
'pot-maker'	*-gúmba ívígá*	*m-*	*a-*	*a-*	*va-*

(Mbaga and Whiteley 1961)

6. See Krige [1936] 1950:30-31; Doke 1961; Bryant 1949. Published sources on Zulu *hlonipha*, though including extensive lists of forms (especially Doke and Vilakazi 1958), describe the patterns of decades ago. It is not clear to me whether the Zulu respect vocabulary is still in use.

7. Although Opland's book concerns Xhosa praise-poetry primarily, he considers Zulu sources as well. Zulu and Xhosa praise-poetry seem virtually alike as genres, as indeed the languages are. Both systems also have *hlonipha* vocabularies, as I have already noted.

8. As Bryant notes, "the men, or indeed the whole clan, may Hlonipa the name of a renowned chief or ancestor, as, for instance, the Zulus, a few generations ago, Hlonipa'd the words, iMpande (root) and iNdlela (path), calling them, respectively, iNgxabo and iNyatuko, owing to certain then great personages being named uMpande and uNdlela" (1949:220).

9. By the same token, Zulu praise-poetry, *iziɓongo,* is not actually limited to male poets. Gunner 1979 discusses the work of some women composers and performers.

10. For a detailed argument about the role of the *hlonipha* respect vocabulary in the Nguni languages' acquisition of click consonants, see Herbert 1990.

11. Although click consonants occur with much higher frequency in the *hlonipha* vocabulary than in ordinary vocabulary—which is one of the reasons for supposing that they entered the Nguni languages via that route—they do occur in ordinary vocabulary also. Presumably, some of those click-bearing "ordinary" words are ex-*hlonipha* words or derivations thereof that have lost their specially honorific value.

12. The reflections that follow are heavily indebted to comments by Michael Silverstein on an earlier version of this paper and others in the group for which he was discussant (see Silverstein 1992) .

13. Thus, *priyayi* and pure-denotationalist ideologies of language overlap insofar as they both identify parallel registers of honorification, but they cannot be assumed to overlap in their conception of the role of rhetoric in language.

14. See also the analysis in Silverstein 1995b of Javanese linguistic structures and their relationship with registers.

15. The relative semantic "indeterminacy" of *basa* as opposed to *krama* alternants in Javanese has a close parallel in many Australian languages, such as Dyirbal (Dixon 1971), where alternants in a "mother-in-law" avoidance register are semantically more abstract than those in the everyday register (for discussion see Irvine 1995). In other respects, the Australian cases' ideology of avoidance, as a concomitant of affinal relationships on the domestic scene, bears some resemblance to the ideology of Zulu *hlonipha.*

16. See, for example, Pumphrey 1937 and Cust 1886:24. These authors, though writing as if from distance and objectivity, actually were themselves engaged in colonial projects aimed at replacing indigenous systems of rank and authority. Pumphrey was a colonial district officer in Sudan; Cust was a retired administrator in British India who became a noted Orientalist and linguistic bibliographer and who also worked for missionary causes, which he saw his linguistic efforts as furthering.

REFERENCES

Agha, Asif. 1993. Grammatical and Indexical Convention in Honorific Discourse. *Journal of Linguistic Anthropology* 3:131–163.

———. 1994. Honorification. *Annual Review of Anthropology* 23:277–302.

Brown, Roger, and A. Gilman. 1960. The Pronouns of Power and Solidarity. In *Style in Language*, ed. Thomas Sebeok, pp. 253–276. Cambridge, Mass.: MIT Press.

Bryant, Alfred T. 1949. *The Zulu People*. Pietermaritzburg: Shuter and Shooter.

Cust, Robert Needham. 1886. *Language as Illustrated by Bible-Translation*. London: Trübner.

Dixon, R. M. W. 1971. A Method of Semantic Description. In *Semantics*, ed. D. Steinberg and L. Jakobovits, pp. 436–471. Cambridge: Cambridge University Press.

Doke, Clement. 1961. *Textbook of Zulu Grammar*, 6th ed. Johannesburg: Longmans.

Doke, Clement, and B. W. Vilakazi. 1958. *Zulu-English Dictionary*, 2nd ed. Johannesburg: Witwatersrand University Press.

Errington, J. Joseph. 1984. *Language and Social Change in Java*. Athens: Ohio University Center for International Studies.

———. 1988. *Structure and Style in Javanese*. Philadelphia: University of Pennsylvania Press.

Finlayson, Rosemary. 1978. A Preliminary Survey of *Hlonipha* among the Xhosa. *Taalfasette* 24:48–63.

———. 1982. *Hlonipha*—the Women's Language of Avoidance among the Xhosa. *South African Journal of African Languages* 1(1) (suppl.):35–60.

———. 1984. The Changing Nature of *Isihlonipho Sabafazi*. *African Studies* 43:137–146.

Gunner, Elizabeth. 1979. Songs of Innocence and Experience: Women as Composers and Performers of *Izibongo*, Zulu Praise Poetry. *Research in African Literatures* 10:239–267.

Herbert, Robert K. 1990. The Sociohistory of Clicks in Southern Bantu. *Anthropological Linguistics* 32:295–315.

Irvine, Judith T. 1985. Status and Style in Language. *Annual Review of Anthropology* 14:557–581.

———. 1989. When Talk Isn't Cheap: Language and Political Economy. *American Ethnologist* 16:248–267.

———. 1990. Registering Affect: Heteroglossia in the Linguistic Expression of Emotion. In *Language and the Politics of Emotion*, ed. C. Lutz and L. Abu-Lughod, pp. 126–161. Cambridge: Cambridge University Press.

———. 1995. Honorifics. In *Handbook of Pragmatics*, ed. J. Blommaert, J. Verschueren, and J. Ostman, pp. 1–22. Amsterdam/Philadelphia: John Benjamins.

Krige, Eileen. [1936] 1950. *The Social System of the Zulus*. Pietermaritzburg: Shuter and Shooter.

Levinson, Stephen C. 1983. *Pragmatics*. Cambridge: Cambridge University Press.

Mbaga, K., and W. Whiteley. 1961. Formality and Informality in Yao Speech. *Africa* 31:135–146.

Nurse, Derek. 1979. Description of Sample Bantu Languages of Tanzania. *African Languages/Langues Africaines* 5(1):1–150.

Opland, Jeff. 1983. *Xhosa Oral Poetry*. Cambridge: Cambridge University Press.

Pumphrey, M. E. C. 1937. Shilluk "Royal" Language Conventions. *Sudan Notes and Records* 20:319–321.

Richardson, Irvine. 1967. Linguistic Evolution and Bantu Noun Class Systems. In *La classification nominale dans les langues négro-africaines*, ed. G. Manessy and M. Houis, pp. 373–388. Paris: CNRS.

Silverstein, Michael. 1979. Language Structure and Linguistic Ideology. In *The Elements: A Parasession on Linguistic Units and Levels*, ed. P. Clyne, W. F. Hanks, and C. L. Hofbauer, pp. 193–247. Chicago: Chicago Linguistic Society.

———. 1992. The Uses and Utility of Ideology: Some Reflections. *Pragmatics* 2:311–324.

———. 1995a. From the Meaning of Meaning to the Empires of the Mind: Ogden's Orthological English. *Pragmatics* 5:185–196.

———. 1995b. Indexical Order and the Dialectics of Sociolinguistic Life. *Symposium about Language and Society—Austin* III:266–295.

Wenger, James R. 1982. Some Universals of Honorific Language with Special Reference to Japanese. Ph.D. diss., University of Arizona.

Wolff, J. U., and S. Poedjosoedarmo. 1982. Communicative Codes in Central Java. Data Paper 116. Ithaca, N.Y.: Cornell University, Department of Asian Studies, Southeast Asia Program.

Woolard, Kathryn A., and Bambi B. Schieffelin. 1994. Language Ideology. *Annual Review of Anthropology* 23:55–82.

3

"Today There Is No Respect"

Nostalgia, "Respect," and Oppositional Discourse in Mexicano (Nahuatl) Language Ideology

JANE H. HILL

"Today there is no respect" (*āxān āmo cah respēto*) is one formula of a discursive system through which speakers of Mexicano (Nahuatl) in the Malinche Volcano region of Central Mexico express "nostalgia" about days gone by, *in achto*. The discourse of nostalgia consists of formulaic pronouncements on a restricted list of themes: *in achto*, language was unmixed; no one knew, or needed to know, *castilla* 'Spanish' but instead spoke *puro mexicano*. In Mexicano, ritual kinsmen greeted each other on the village paths, parents commanded children, and neighbors spoke to each other of the ancient tasks of cultivation. Work was hard, but goods were cheap, measured in traditional quantities and paid for with small coins with ancient names. People ate traditional foods with Mexicano labels, especially *neuctli* 'pulque', fermented from the sap of agaves. The interactional qualities of *in achto* can be summarized as *in achto ōcatca respēto* 'in those days, there was respect'. Today people are educated and know Spanish, but the Spanish is full of errors, and children come out of school *groseros*—that is, rude and disrespectful.

The discourse of nostalgia is "ideological" in both the "ideational" and the "pragmatic" senses (Friedrich 1989). Not only is it made up of a set of propositions about the past, but, through the implicit and explicit positive evaluations of the past that the discourse asserts, people who benefit from practices that they believe are legitimated by tradition put forward their political interests. Central to the discourse of nostalgia is a "linguistic ideology" (Silverstein 1979, Woolard and Schieffelin 1994) that suggests that the Mexicano language, especially in some "pure" form, is a peculiarly appropriate vehicle for the social forms of long ago, *in achto*, and especially for "respect." On the other hand, Spanish, and the mixing of Spanish and Mexicano, are peculiarly associated with the social forms of today, *āxān*, and with the loss of respect.

While the discourse of nostalgia is universally interpretable in the Mexicano towns of the Malinche region, not everyone produces it. Most likely to repeat its formulas are relatively successful men. Women, and men who possess little in the way of the locally relevant forms of capital, seldom engage in the discourse. Instead, they may produce an oppositional discourse, contesting the discourse of nostalgia by exposing its formulas to contradiction and even to parody. This "counterdiscourse" undermines the terms of the linguistic ideology, constituting an "interruption" (Silverman and Torode 1980) of the idea that particular forms of language are inextricably linked to particular forms of social order. Further, this interruption is more radical than are some well-known challenges to language form and use in English. This may be because Mexicano linguistic ideology locates the crucial nexus of representation between dialogic action and social order, not between reference and reality.[1]

Nostalgia as a Discursive System

Before turning to the counterdiscourse, I characterize with greater precision the content and organization of the discourse of nostalgia. Its characteristic formulas develop a small set of major rhetorical themes: (1) "respect": the proper observance of status relationships, especially illustrated by greetings between *compadres* 'ritual kin' and commands from parents to responsive children, contrasted with today's *grosería* 'rudeness'; (2) the sacred nature of the Mexicano community and the ties between its people, contrasted with contractual ties for profit; (3) a favorable economy, in which goods were cheap and life was rigorous but healthy, contrasted with today's high prices and unhealthy ways; (4) cultivation as the prototypical human way of life, contrasted with factory work and schooling, seen as educational preparation for such work; (5) the use of Mexicano long ago, contrasted with the use of Spanish today; and (6) the linguistic purity of *in achto*, contrasted with the language mixing of *āxān*.[2]

These themes and their associated formulas occurred in sociolinguistic interviews conducted with ninety-six speakers of Mexicano in eleven towns in the Malinche Volcano region between 1974 and 1981. No speaker used all of these themes, nor did any speaker connect them in a coherent argument, either in the interview or in everyday conversation (where the discourse occurred quite commonly). Instead, the discourses of nostalgia occurred in fragments, with formulaic elements scattered across the hour or so of conversation in the average interview or used in passing in conversation. Most speakers used only one or two formulas from the discourse of nostalgia. Every theme was mentioned by at least half a dozen speakers (sometimes the use was in the context of the counterdiscourses described later). Most commonly mentioned were "mixing" and the change in greetings.

Three elderly men in three different communities produced the most complete developments of the discourse of nostalgia, using many of its elements during their interviews. Each of these men had achieved high office in the civil-religious hierarchy in his community, and each claimed an identity as a cultivator, a *campesino*. Don Gabriel (S73)[3] mentioned the largest number of themes, using commonly heard formulas about respect, mixing, greetings, the language of traditional agricultural practice, the sacred, how cheap everything used to be, how people used to work hard, and how the schools, while they teach Spanish, seem to make children disrespectful. Don Gachupín (S12) mentioned the *doctrina*, the greeting of *compadres* as an indicator that "there was respect," and the fact that language mixing occurs. Don Abrán (S76) produced routines on the Mexicano language of agriculture, the speeches appropriate to hospitality and the sharing of pulque, greeting *compadres* on the road, and giving orders to children. None of these three men connected all these elements in a single account or argument.

Since the "discourse of nostalgia" does not occur as a single coherent argument, what is the justification for characterizing it as a single discursive system? First, speakers often chain more than one element. Especially common is the contrasting, in a discussion of "respect," of Mexicano greetings and Spanish greetings, which are thought to be not respectful. Or a speaker may mention language "mixing" and immediately turn to a mention of the problem of respect. Exemplifying the chaining of the language theme with the economic theme, Don Gabriel observed in response to an interview question about domains of Mexicano language use that in his youth he spoke Mexicano in shops. He then amplified his reply:

> Everything was cheap then. You could buy chilis for a *centavo*, fish for two *centavos* . . . everything was by the *centavo*, and by the *cuartilla* [a unit of measure no longer used, about 6 pounds], and one requested it in Mexicano. Anyone would wait on us, and there was no problem with short-weighting, like there is today.

One speaker illustrated "mixing" with a comparison of Spanish *dios* and Mexicano *teotl* 'god', linking language use to community sacralization. Another speaker illustrated the Mexicano greetings and extended the quoted conversation (the usual way of illustrating the greetings) to include a discussion of cultivation:

> "Did the *compadre* wake up well?"
> "Well, God be praised, pass on, *Compadre*."
> "And where is the *compadre* going?"
> "Why, to the fields, to scrape the *magueyes*."
> "May the *compadre* pass on."

Some respondents observed that all children now speak Spanish because they go to school; yet the schools make them not polite and obedient but rude and unruly. For instance, Don Gabriel, replying to a question about whether people spoke Mexicano better today or long ago, said,

> It's the same. The same. But today they all want education, but what good does it do? I tell you, it doesn't do any good. They even go to secondary school, but they come out *groseros*. No longer does it make them have more respect. I tell you, today everything is all mixed up.[4]

In addition to the chaining of rhetorical formulas and themes, speakers express connections between the themes through rhetorical parallelism. For instance, Don Abrán produced the following figure, where the *oficio* 'work' was cultivation and the *tlahtōl* 'language' was Mexicano.

> *ye nōn oficio . . . ye nōn totlahtōl.*
> 'That was the work then . . . that was our language then.'

Don Marcos (S83) used parallelism to associate Mexicano with highly desired "respectful" ethical states of "mutual trust" and "gratitude." Remarking that he still spoke Mexicano with some people in his town, he said,

> *titlahtoah mexicano, timonōtzah de confiānza.*
> 'When we speak Mexicano, we speak seriously with mutual trust.'

Don Marcos felt that Mexicano was an "inheritance" from the elders, and said that he urged this position on his children, as follows:

> *mācmo mā ye ingrāto, mācāmo mā quilcāhua in mexicano.*
> May you not be ungrateful, may you not forget Mexicano.'

In addition to syntagmatic chaining and paradigmatic parallelism in speech, a more complex semiotic logic connects the various discourses with the generalized understanding of "long ago." The discourse of nostalgia involves "multiplex signs" (Briggs 1989): elements that not only refer to but call up indexically an entire social order associated with *in achto.* First, to mention the Mexicano language, especially *legítimo mexicano* 'correct, unmixed Mexicano', accomplishes this. Second, the emphasis on the sacred occurs in two highly routinized discourses: the idea that a speaker in the old days who really knew *legítimo mexicano* knew it *hasta la doctrina* 'even to the catechism'. One speaker stated that people spoke so well *in achto* that "even the hymns were sung in Mexicano." People commonly mentioned that greetings in the old days invoked the sacred: people would exchange "*Ave María,*" "*Verás concebida*" [*sic*]. Such formulas place the sacred at the center of Mexicano usage, paralleling the physical placement of churches at the center of communities and paralleling as well many rhetorical claims that constitute the Mexicano community as a sacred space surrounded by a profane periphery (Hill 1990b, 1995). And note that the greeting formula connects this in turn to the order of "respectful" sociality.[5]

Third, the Mexicano greetings between *compadres*, "co-parents" ritually joined in a kinship-like relationship, and the giving of orders to children in Mexicano are especially favored illustrations of the respectful order of *in achto.* These routines require the production of verb forms that index the two most important axes of social differentiation in Mexicano communities, the relationship between ritual kin and the distinction between senior and junior blood relatives. Verbs marked with honorific affixes (or notable for their absence) index the relationship between speaker and addressee (Hill and Hill 1978). This point is developed later in this chapter.

The social order of *in achto* can also be indexed by mentioning cultivation; hence the use of conversations about agriculture to exemplify Mexicano speech. The ideal of agricultural self-sufficiency is constructed by mentioning the cheap prices (and the measures and coins) of bygone days. This is contrasted with the need to find wage labor and the high prices of today. The language of the wage-paying workplace and of purchasing in shops, practices associated with *āxān*, is Spanish; this was confirmed by nearly all speakers. Speakers usually said that children acquire Spanish because they go to school and that such schooling is necessary to prepare for wage labor, but they argued that children come out of school "disrespectful." Thus, universal schooling and literacy, in *letrah*, an important multiplex sign of *āxān*, is linked syntagmatically to the idea of "disrespect."[6]

In summary, "nostalgia" in the Mexicano communities is accomplished through a set of discourses that are intricately interlinked with one another, by syntagmatic chaining, by rhetorical parallelism, and by the fact that the principle formulas of the discursive system are multiplex signs. Accessing as they do the entire order of *in achto*, such signs permit speakers to move from one of its elements to the other without bridging argumentation. The relative coherence of this system makes it possible for us to speak of nostalgia as an "ideology" (cf. Eagleton 1991).

Pragmatic Ideology in the Discourse of Nostalgia

A central theme of the discourse of nostalgia expresses a "linguistic ideology": a "set of beliefs about language articulated by users as a rationalization or justification of perceived language structure and use" (Silverstein 1979:193). Following Whorf, Silverstein argues that the dialectical relationship among ideology, structure, and use is constituted primarily through "referential projection" or "objectification," the projection through which the structure of language—especially "pervasive surface-segmentable linguistic patterns" (1979:202)—is reified as the structure of the world. Through "referential projection," pragmatic categories are interpreted as referential. For instance, tense may be considered to refer to units of time "in the world," not to pragmatic dimensions anchored in discourse. A form of "projection" occurs also with pragmatic ideologies. The discourse of nostalgia claims that Mexicano dialogues are inextricably linked to a desirable social order of the past, and particularly to "respect," and that disrespect, a key problem of today, is linked to the use of Spanish. These claims focus on usage and are thus pragmatic. Such ideologies, Silverstein argues, tend universally to exhibit certain characteristic features. First, pragmatic ideology locates the "power" of language in surface-segmentable items. Second, pragmatic function is held to be "presupposing," rather than "creative" (or "entailing"): the uses of language appear because preexisting social categories require them. Third, pragmatic effects are held to be extended from propositional ones.

Silverstein's first proposal, that the power of language is located in surface-segmentable elements, is borne out in the Mexicano case by the fact that the discourse of nostalgia utterly fails to notice the formal differences between the signaling of deference and distance in Mexicano, which is accomplished by a complex system of verbal suffixes and by honorific suffixes on other parts of speech as well (especially nouns, postpositionals, and discourse particles), and the morphology of deference in Spanish. However, the discourse of nostalgia does not focus on "words," the surface-segmentable element par excellence.[7] Instead, the units chosen by Mexicano speakers to illustrate "respect" are "surface segmentable" only at the discourse level: they are whole dialogues, not single words or phrases. The salience of such dialogic units may link the pragmatic ideology of nostalgia and a more general theme of community and sociality over individuality in Mexicano communities (see Hill 1990a). It may also be linked to a more generally "pragmatic" orientation toward language in Mexicano language ideology (discussed more fully later in this chapter). For instance, in illustrating how respect was conveyed in greetings, many speakers said something like this:

> In the old days, *compadres* would meet, and they would say, "*Míxtōnaltīhtzīnoh*?" "*Mopanōlīhtzīno*" *huān* "*Mopanahuihtzīnoa compadrito.*" ('Did his honor wake up (well)?' 'May his honor pass by,' 'The compadre is passing honorably by.') But today, it is *puro buenos días, puro buenas tardes* ('nothing but "Good day," "Good afternoon"').

Relevant here are the three verbs, appropriate to the first greeting of a *compadre* on the path in the morning. Their structure is as follows:[8]

(1) a. *m-īxtōnal-tīh-tzīn-oh?*
REFLEXIVE-WAKE UP-APPLICATIVE-HONORIFIC-THEME-PAST SING
'Did the day dawn upon his honor?'

b. *mo-panō-l-tīh-tzīn-o*
REFLEXIVE-PASS-APPLICATIVE-APPLICATIVE-HONORIFIC-THEME(IMP)
'Let his honor pass on'

c. *mo-pana-huih-tzīn-oa-h*
REFLEXIVE-PASS-APPLICATIVE-HONORIFIC-THEME-PLURAL
'His honor is passing by'

Here, the level of honorific marking appropriate to interchanges between ritual kin is indicated by verbs in the third person, even though the exchange is in direct address. The verbs are marked also with the honorific suffix *-tzīn*, used for both the elderly and ritual kin. They are also marked as reflexive verbs, with the prefix *mo-* and the applicative suffixes (*-tīh*, *-l*, and *-huih* in the dialogue just presented) that are required to adapt the valence of these intransitive verbs to the presence of the reflexive prefix. These third-person honorific verbs contrast (1) with second-person verbs with reflexive and honorific markings, appropriate for greeting persons who deserve reverence but who have no ritual kinship relationship with the speaker, (2) with verbs that are reflexive but that lack the honorific suffix, which might be used for a well-dressed stranger, (3) with verbs marked with the prefix *on-* 'away', appropriate for senior relatives who are not elderly, and (4) with unmarked verbs, appropriate for greeting children or same-generation, same-sex blood kin.[9]

The Spanish greetings *Buenos días* and *Buenas tardes* contain no verbs, and so can be used without constituting any particular relationship between speakers beyond the phatic. Furthermore, Spanish, even where verb forms and pronouns are present, has only a two-way contrast of distance and deference, compared to the subtle gradations possible in Mexicano.

Nearly all the speakers who illustrated the greetings said explicitly that the Mexicano greetings show respect but that the Spanish greetings lack it. The speakers seemed to be identifying the difference in indexical force between the two types of greetings, yet no speaker ever mentioned the affixes or even observed that the Spanish greetings had any sort of formal difference from the Mexicano ones. Instead, they illustrated by contrasting complete greeting exchanges with one another, as in the earlier example. *Compadrazgo*, ritual kinship, is the single most important social relationship between adults, and "respect" (along with *confianza* 'mutual trust') is the most important element of this relationship, an element that was often articulated by speakers. The invocation of the most characteristic everyday language of *compadrazgo*, the greeting on the road, can stand metonymically for the respectful social order of *in achto* 'long ago'.

Silverstein (1981) extended his theory of linguistic awareness to permit a continuum of salience. The Mexicano case suggests that such salience may be linked, not only to perceptual factors such as surface segmentability, but also to the complexities of local schemas. Commands to children are mentioned only half as often as greetings between *compadres* in order to illustrate "respectful" Mexicano speech. The most likely reason for this difference is that the presence of the affixal system on the verbs in the greetings is in fact the object of awareness, although at a level below that of "discursive consciousness" (Giddens 1976).

The usual discourse for illustrating commands to children goes something like the following:

> In the old days, you could say to a child, "*Xicui in cuahuitl, xiyah xitlapiati*" ['Get the firewood, go take the stock to pasture'], but nowadays, who would understand? They might even say, "Don't talk to me with that old stuff." You have to say, "*Trae la leña, vas a cuidar.*"

Let us examine the structure of the imperative verbs in these expressions:

		MEXICANO	SPANISH
(2)	a.	*xi-c-ui* IMPERATIVE-P3OBJ-BRING	*trae* BRING-P3
	b.	*xi-yah* IMPERATIVE-GO	*va-s* GO-P2
	c.	*xi-tla-pia-tih* IMPERATIVE-INDEF.NONHUMAN.OBJ.-CARE-GO	

In both cases, the verbs are unmarked for deference. In Spanish, with its two-way distinction of distance/deference, *trae* 'bring' and *vas* 'you're going' are contrasted with deferential *traiga* and *vaya*, respectively. In Mexicano, with a more complex system, the imperatives are contrasted minimally with verbs that would be used to an adult stranger: *xicui* versus *xoncui* 'bring', *xiyah* versus *xonyah* 'go', and *xitlapiatih* versus *xontlapiatih* 'Go take the stock to pasture'. Thus, while commands to children illustrate a social relationship where respect is at issue, their linguistic form alone (as opposed to the nature of the children's response), since it is unmarked, does not invoke respect. Nor does it contrast with the Spanish command, which, at this level of the system, is in exactly the same relationship of marking to a more deferential alternative as is the Mexicano imperative.

Silverstein's second property of pragmatic ideology, the tendency to see indexicality as "presupposing," is helpful in understanding characteristic thematic choices of the discourse of nostalgia. The most popular way to illustrate "respect" is with greetings between ritual kin. This is the maximally "presupposed" social category, outside of blood and marriage relationships. Relationships of ritual kinship are created through formal ceremonies, after which the language appropriate to the relationship is used. The use of the correct language with *compadres* certainly reaffirms the relationship, and it is through such usage that the verbal distance and deference considered appropriate to it are constituted. I have also heard speakers attempt to enhance very distant claims of *compadrazgo* by using honorific third-person forms. For instance, Don Abrán used third-person address to the American linguist Jane Rosenthal, who is a *comadre* of his *comadre* Doña Rosalía. Such usages suggest that people feel there might be some transitivity in a chain of the relationships, such that a person who is *compadre* to a *compadre* of a prominent person, for instance, might be *compadre* of the prominent person more directly. However, it is clear that the claims that speakers might have on, or the honors that they might render toward, someone so addressed are very limited compared to their formally constituted ritual kin, and to derive from these facts the social-constructionist interpretation that relationships of *compadrazgo* are constituted through language certainly would not jibe with native theory.

There are honorific usages outside *compadrazgo* that are probably more constitutive or "creative," in contrast to the relatively "presupposing" usage between *compadres*. For instance, no ceremony marks the transition of a person to the level of venerability that prompts high levels of honorific usage to the elderly, and speakers are not clear about exactly when they would do this ("to someone with white hair" or "to someone who walks with a cane" are examples that have been suggested to me). To some degree, then, recognition as an elder is constituted through the way others address that person, with the label *momahuizotzín* 'your reverence' substituted for the pronoun *tehhuātzīn*, and with second-person honorific verbs. A few people illustrate "respect" by saying, "In the old days, when you would meet an old man, or an old woman, you would say . . . ," but this is less common than the illustration of greetings between *compadres*.

The failure of speakers to recognize creative indexicality is evidenced by the fact that no speaker recognizes explicitly a function of Spanish loan words that is very obvious to the outsider: the constitution of the power of important people in public life. Political discourse in the communities is dense with Spanish loans, and both here and in other kinds of talk very high frequencies of Spanish loan material appear in the usage of important senior men. K. Hill (1985) has shown that speakers implicitly recognize this fact by demonstrating that a female narrator used Spanish-loan frequency as one way of representing the relative status of figures in a narrative.

Silverstein's proposal that pragmatic ideologies tend to reduce usage to reference is not clearly illustrated in the discourse of nostalgia. Silverstein's most developed illustration of this tendency is the case of feminist linguistic criticism in English. He argues that feminists correctly perceive the "pragmatic metaphorical relationship between gender identity and status" (Silverstein 1985:240) but erroneously locate this in the system of reference and predication, especially in the use of the gendered pronouns as noun classifiers, rather than in the intricate web of pragmatic patterning. Speakers in the discourse of nostalgia, however, locate respect in formulaic dialogues, not in particular words. This nonoccurrence of the reduction to reference is a manifestation of

a basic linguistic-ideological bent among Mexicano speakers, to think of speech primarily as action. I enlarge on this point later in this chapter.

Counterdiscourses

The discourse of nostalgia is produced primarily by two groups of people: senior men who are relatively wealthy and successful in terms of having achieved high position in the local hierarchy and young and middle-aged men who have full-time work outside the communities.[10] Not a single woman in our sample was "nostalgic." Instead, women strongly contested the idea that the old days were "better," and a number of men, mainly poor elderly cultivators with little land and undistinguished public careers, agreed with them. These speakers argued that the old days had been extremely hard and that many of the changes that occurred between "long ago" and "today" are improvements. In articulating these ideas, they often produced what I call here "counterdiscourses": arguments that take specific formulas of the discourse of nostalgia and expose them to explicit contradiction and, in the most interesting cases, parody.

The next example illustrates contradiction. Speakers who countered the discourse of nostalgia strongly approved of education and literacy and felt that the bilingualism of today was a great improvement over the monolingual "ignorance" of long ago. One elderly woman (S41) explicitly contradicted the discourse that associates schooling with disrespect and decline. She also suggests that bilingualism is a favorable condition:

> Listen, now I hear the kids studying, they learn Spanish, they even learn Latin. I hear the way they talk, even when they're playing. I hear how they quarrel and fight with one another and I say, "Thank God, it's worth something to read, not like the way we grew up, the way we grew up was bad."

A second elderly woman (S54) turned an expression often used in the discourse of nostalgia—*in achto ōcatca rigōr* 'long ago there was rigor (high standards, hard work, and so on)'—back on itself, observing that she had not been allowed to go to school because *āmo ōcatca rigōr* 'there was no rigor'; instead, parents would hide their children from the teachers.

Several speakers countered the nostalgic discourse that offers the giving of orders to children in Mexicano and filial obedience as illustrations of appropriate traditional social order. Instead, they proposed, their own obedience to their parents brought them nothing but poverty and grief. One young woman (S28), who makes and sells tortillas for a living, said,

> When we grew up this was the land of complete stupidity [*tīro tōntotlālpan*]. Our parents didn't send us to school, they brought us up "under the *metate* [stone for grinding maize]." It's not that way today: now, while the stupid ones are doing the grinding, the young girls can escape, they can go to school, they don't have to stay here. But as for us, no, because what our father or our mother said to do was done, because we had to.

An old man (S11) also interrupted the discourse of nostalgia. In the following utterance he addresses it specifically, implying ("Who knows whether . . . ?") that someone is saying that the old people were better. In opposition, he suggests that obeying the commands of parents was not necessarily good:

> We grew up simply in a time of misery. Now the old people are gone, but who knows whether they were better or more intelligent, or whether perhaps they were stupider, eh? Well, who knows what is the right way? Now the kids go to school. In the old days they put us to work. "Work, work!" they said, and off we'd go, but for what? How did we grow up?

Doña Fidencia (S50) used parody in addressing this theme. In the following passage, she reproduces precisely the form of the discourse of nostalgia. But she inverts the discourse of "giving orders to children" by illustrating orders from a child to a mother:

> Well, now the children say, "*Pos mamá, vente; mamá, dame, o mamá, quiero!*" ['Well, mama, come here; mama, give me, or mama, I want something']. And long ago, no, they would say, "*mamá, nicnequi nitlamaceh, nicnequi nitlacuāz, xinechomaca nin, xinechonmaca in necah*" ['Mama, I want to eat, I want to eat, give me this, give me that']. And now, no, here any child will say, "*Dame esto, mamá, deme Usted, mamá*" ['Give me this, Mama, give me, Mama'].

This example is exactly parallel to those of the discourse of nostalgia (*in achto*, parents would say that; *āxān*, they have to say this), but it interrupts it by suggesting that there was no lack of disrespect and whining from children in the supposedly more respectful "olden days" when children spoke Mexicano.

Some speakers challenged the significance of the change in greeting style, obviously replying to the ubiquitous nostalgic voice. An elderly man in Canoa (S13) contrasted greetings in his own community with those in nearby La Resurrección, as follows:

> Well, here it's "*mīxtōnaltīhtzīno, mopanōltīhtzīno comadrita*" [all laugh], O.K., O.K., but listen here, I'm going to tell you, it's something else when you meet a *comadre* from La Resurrección, well, there it's "*Buenos días, comadrita*," but after all she'll still greet you back, whether it's Mexicano or not, well it's still serious talk (*monohnōtzah*) [general laughter].

Parody is available in this domain as well. Thus, Doña Tiburcia (S78) used parody to counter the illustration of the greeting between *compadres*—a particularly scandalous gesture, since relationships of ritual kinship are a very significant part of local identity and most people are quite sanctimonious about them. Exemplifying the greetings between *compadres*, she recited elaborate verb forms like those given in example 1 and the extract above. But the last line of her represented conversation, in answer to whether the *comadre* is well, goes like this (and got a terrific laugh from her audience, proportionate to the scandal):

> *Poz cualli, cualli comadrita, contentos, māzqui jodidos.*
>
> 'Well we are well, we are well *comadrita*, contented, but getting screwed.'

The obvious implication of this remark is that elaborate rituals of respect between ritual kin do not insulate people from life's vicissitudes or guarantee that they will always speak in a solemn and elevated way. Note that this example was as close as anyone came to parodying the sacred discourse between ritual kin, which seems to be somewhat off limits to agnostic critique.

The obverse of the respectful Mexicano greetings is a practice that was remarked on by many of our consultants, especially those in the towns along the industrial corridor on the west flank of the Malinche: making obscene challenges in Mexicano to strangers on the road. Many consultants remarked that an important reason to know Mexicano is to be able to understand and reply to such challenges. Against this background, Doña Fidencia interrupted the discourse of nostalgia with the following parodic witticism:

> Well, perhaps now is better, you won't hear anybody say, "*Xiccahcayāhua in monānah*" ['Fuck your mother'], now they'll say, "*Chinga tu madre.*"

Doña Fidencia is clearly aware of the discourse of nostalgia and reproduces its form ("Then, people said that, but now they say this") almost exactly—but the content has changed. She is suggesting ironically that nostalgia is misplaced: people were as rude to each other in Mexicano in the old days as they are now in Spanish.

The Discourse of Nostalgia as Political Ideology

Producers of the counterdiscourse obviously hear the discourse of nostalgia as glossing over the dark reality of *in achto*, when there was violence, poverty, and patriarchal control over the life chances of women. Why would they care about *in achto*, however, if things have changed? What seems most likely is that producers of the counterdiscourse recognize that the discourse of "nostalgia" is in fact a pragmatic claim on the present, using "pastness" as a "naturalizing" ideological strategy: rhetorically, the claim is that those practices that are most like those of the past are the most valuable. The counterdiscourses, then, constitute a pragmatic claim on the future, when everyone will have an equal chance for education and a decent life.

The successful men who produce the discourse of nostalgia clearly benefit from social relations of the type invoked in the discourse of nostalgia, whether their success is manifested by high position within the community hierarchy or based on resources accumulated through wage labor. Control over family members, whose labor can be summoned on demand, and an extensive network of ritual kin who cannot refuse requests for loans are absolute prerequisites for a career in the civil-religious hierarchy, the only fully approved route to power within the communitarian system. Men who depend heavily on wage labor also have reason to endorse the "traditional system," and especially the secondary position of women within it, to backstop their own forays into an uncertain labor market. Women maintain households, often entirely through their own devices, while men work outside the towns by the week or by the month. Nutini and Murphy (1970) found that wage laborers were even more likely than cultivators to insist that their wives and children live in virilocal extended families, thus increasing control over their wives, usually through the agency of the mother-in-law. Occasions for establishing bonds of ritual kinship are actually proliferating in the communities as wage labor increasingly dominates their economies; ritual kinship, to a large degree, constitutes the savings-and-loan system in the towns. Thus, for these groups, the order of "respect" sustains them. For women, the order of "respect" is less obviously beneficial. Women who have been abandoned by their husbands or who are widows may have great difficulty in finding ritual kin: peasant women, holding their infants and begging prosperous people entering the church to stand up with them to baptize the babies, are not a rare sight in the city of Puebla.

"Enactive" Pragmatic Ideology and Radical Challenge

Eagleton (1991) cites a distinction, made by Raymond Geuss, between "descriptive" and "pejorative" definitions of the term "ideology." "Descriptive" or "anthropological" definitions assimilate ideology to "worldview": an "ideology" is simply a belief system, and no judgment is made of its truth or value. In the "pejorative" definition, an ideology is viewed negatively, because its motivation is to continue an oppressive system, because it involves self-deception, or because it is in fact false, distorting reality.

Silverstein's (1979, 1985) use of the term "ideology" is certainly "pejorative": he sees linguistic ideologies as distorting the actual forms and functions of language, attending to some at the expense of others. Moreover, he implies that such distortions occur universally in human communities, because of relative cognitive limitations on human linguistic awareness. In emphasizing that the distortions of linguistic ideology are universal (with the salutory corollary that linguistic "science" is "ideological"), he predicts that the specific content of ideological discourse, whether it is hegemonic or counterhegemonic, will simply replicate core category errors, such as the confusion of indexicality with reference and predication and of reference with the nature of the world. This "pejorative" atti-

how does he define these?

ok

does explicating these limitations decrease ideology's power?

tude of course extends to the ideology of resistance, as well as to the ideology of domination. Silverstein (1985) implies, in his discussion of feminist discourse and of the Quaker challenge to the seventeenth-century system of distance and deference in England, that these category errors doom counterhegemonic discourse to political impotency over the long run. Is the Mexicano counterdiscourse described earlier similarly vulnerable? I believe that it is not, and that the radical challenge that it makes to the underlying ideology is due not only to the perspicacity and penetration of those who produce it, but to the broader ideological matrix in which it is embedded.

The Mexicano situation exemplifies a subtype of a version of the "enactive" linguistic ideology identified by Rumsey (1990), in which language is seen as embodied in action, with no distinction made between such action and reference. Rumsey contrasts this view with the dominant "referential" linguistic ideology of the West, which insists on the distinction (and which, according to Silverstein, privileges reference). Rumsey argues for a relationship between ideology and formal patterning. Thus, European languages, spoken in communities with the dualistic or referential ideology, distinguish formally between "wording" and "meaning," while the opposite is the case in the Australian language Ungarinyin, whose speakers exhibit the "enactive" ideology. These distinctions are illustrated in the following examples.

Mexicano formal patterning is distinct from that of Ungarinyin in the representation of reported speech. In Ungarinyin there is no distinction between direct and indirect discourse and, therefore, Rumsey argues, between "wording" and "meaning" at this formal locus. This is not the case in Mexicano, where documents from the sixteenth century show clearly devices for representing constructed dialogue as indirect discourse. Thus, indirect discourse is marked by a deictic shift in the person prefixes on verbs, as in the following example:

Yitic quimolhuiāya canah ōztōc calaquīz.
'In his heart he was saying to himself that he would enter some cave.'
Florentine Codex 12:9 (Dibble and Anderson 1975:26)

Contrast the unshifted person marker in direct discourse:

Quimolhuiāya, "Canah ōztōc nicalaquīz."
'He was saying to himself, "I will enter some cave."'

However, Mexicano resembles Ungarinyin in that the "locution" of indirect discourse is not formally distinguished from "intentions." The formal verbal devices for such indirect discourse under a locutionary verb are identical to those used under affective verbs such as "want." Thus, we find the following:

Quinequi calaquīz	'He wants to enter.'
Quihtoa calaquīz	'He says he will enter.'

Contrast this with the well-known formal distinctions in English:

> He says [that] he will enter.
>
> *He$_i$ says to enter (where subject of "enter" is he$_i$)
>
> He wants to enter.
>
> *He$_i$ wants [that] he$_i$ will enter.

In addition to the deictic shift illustrated in the earlier examples, modern speakers have borrowed the Spanish particle *que* to introduce indirect discourse or have extended the semantic range of the dubitative evidential *quil* (which precedes a locution when quoting speakers want to distance themselves from the views of quoted speakers) to calque on the meanings of *que*.

Mexicano resembles Ungarinyin in cross-referencing throughout the discourse without any possibility for "ellipsis," a term proposed by Halliday and Hasan (1976) for situations where wording, as opposed to meaning, is inferred in English. In sentences like "John told all the girls everything, and Bruce did, too," what is elided is wording: "and Bruce did [told all the girls everything], too." The "girls" in question need not, notoriously, be the same girls for Bruce as for John, so "meaning," but not "wording," may be distinct. In contrast, every Mexicano verb must encode the complete argument structure of the sentence through pronominal prefixes. As in Ungarinyin, such pronominal encoding of argument structure permits speakers to neglect full nominal reference for long stretches of speech.

Mexicano linguistic ideology, like that observed in Ungarinyin by Rumsey, is indifferent to the distinction between meaning and action. As I have pointed out previously (Hill and Hill 1986), the Mexicano noun *tlahtōl* means 'word, language, speech' and does not discriminate between structure and use. Mexicano verbs of speaking may distinguish the referential from the rhetorical (for instance, contrast *tlapōhuia* 'to tell a story, to relate, to chat' [literally, 'to count things', like English "recount" or "account"] with *nōtza* 'to summon, to speak with serious intent to someone' or *nahuatiā* 'to give orders'),[11] but such differentiation is not required: all of these are *tlahtōl*.[12] Consistent with this failure to differentiate form and use, Mexicano speakers discussing the nature of language emphasize, not denotation, but performance: the proper accomplishment of human relationships as constituted through stereotyped moments of dialogue.

Like the Ngarinyin, Mexicano speakers are prone to gloss forms in their language by illustrating a usage. However, in the case of Mexicano, this tendency is highly elaborated. The modern discourse of nostalgia continues an ideological pattern apparent in the sixteenth century. The forms of behavior appropriate to various roles were encoded in memorized speeches, the *huēhuetlahtōlli*, 'sayings of the elders'; a substantial body of these orations, as well as related formulas for a wide range of occasions (ranging from the utterances appropriate to the installation of a new emperor to those required of a midwife upon the delivery of a baby and including long sequences of exchanges of courtesies), were recorded by the Franciscan missionary Bernardino de Sahagún in the sixteenth century.

Karttunen and Lockhart (1989) have translated an etiquette book, prepared by a Nahuatl-speaking *maestro* for the use of missionaries in the late sixteenth century, that illustrates the formal exchange of courtesies in many contexts. Mexicano speakers appear to feel that a language consists, not in words with proper reference that matches reality, but in highly ritualized dialogues with proper usage matched to a social order that manifests an ideal of deference.[13]

The counterdiscourse to the Mexicano discourse of nostalgia is produced within a linguistic-ideological matrix that seems to be largely pragmatic or "enactive," inattentive to the "referential" dimension. Thus, the counterdiscourse, and the discourse of nostalgia itself, exhibits a distinctive type of ideological projection. Ideological challengers in English attack by arguing that usage does not appropriately represent reality and so must be changed. But, according to Silverstein, they do not challenge the indexical relationship between reference and reality; this remains covert and inaccessible. Mexicano speakers who use the rhetoric of the counterdiscourse, like English-speaking feminists who challenge claims that women are inferior, interrupt the explicit representations of the nature of the social order produced in the discourse of nostalgia by pointing out that there has always been rudeness and disrespect in society. Ties of *compadrazgo*, Doña Tiburcia suggests, do not prevent anyone from "getting screwed." Obeying the orders of parents did not bring success for old Feliciano, who asks, "And for what?," or for Doña Eugenia, who grew up "under the *metate*." But the counterdiscourse goes further, challenging not only the representation but the link between language and reality. If Mexicano speech permitted rudeness and misery, and Spanish obviously does the same, then the core of the linguistic ideology, that the order of language stands for the order of society, can be directly dismissed. Thus, for Doña Fidencia, language is irrelevant: a person can say "Fuck your mother" in any language.

Doña Fidencia's attack on Mexicano language ideology may be more fundamental than those constituted in similar counterdiscourses in English. This may be so because in "enactive" as opposed to "referential" ideologies there is only one projective link, as shown in Figure 3.1.

Is there a feedback from ideology to structure in the Mexicano communities, as in Silverstein's case of the triumph of the pronoun "you" in English in response to Quaker linguistic ideology? The situation is obscure and paradoxical. While *legítimo*

REFERENTIAL IDEOLOGY (e.g., feminist counterdiscourse):
Change usage to preserve the relationship between reference and reality.

usage ====//====> reference ========> social reality

ENACTIVE IDEOLOGY (e.g., Mexicano counterdiscourse):
There is no link between usage and reality.

usage==============//=================> social reality

Figure 3.1 Loci of Interruption (//) for Counterdiscourses in Reference-based and Action-based Language Ideologies

mexicano (Mexicano without Spanish loan words) is an important metonym of the order of "respect" in the discourse of nostalgia, it is precisely the groups most likely to indulge in the discourse of nostalgia who speak Mexicano in a very hispanicized way. On the other hand, women and low-status men, the groups who argue in favor of bilingualism and who reject the discourse of nostalgia, speak the least hispanicized Mexicano and are most likely to speak poor (or no) Spanish. Silverstein predicts correctly the distorting effect of linguistic ideology; neither producers of the discourse of nostalgia nor producers of the counterdiscourse recognize the most obvious function of Spanish loan words, which is to mark elevated Mexicano registers in which the discourses of power in the communities are conducted. The result of this failure is a nostalgic purism that makes demands on Mexicano speech that cannot be satisfied. Amplifying the dissatisfaction with Mexicano thus induced is the obvious low status within the communities of precisely their "most Mexicano" members—members who cannot, because of their low status, embody "respect." Such contradictions, along with the evident economic advantages of Spanish, yield language shift and the loss of Mexicano in the Malinche towns. It seems possible that enactive language ideology may make such a language shift marginally easier to accomplish than it would be within a reference-based ideological matrix, where the indexical link between reference and "reality" remains even after the projection from usage to reference is under attack.

The example of the linguistic-ideological component of the Mexicano discourse of nostalgia adds to the list of cases where a "linguistic ideology" is obviously part of a "political ideology." The example shows, however, that the dynamics of counter-hegemonic resistance must be understood within their specific cultural matrix and that this includes the nature of the indexical projections constituted within particular linguistic-ideological forms.

NOTES

Work on Mexicano was supported by funding from the National Endowment for the Humanities (NEH RO-20495-74-572), the American Council of Learned Societies, and the Penrose Fund of the American Philosophical Society.

1. The distribution of the discourse of nostalgia and its counterdiscourse across groups in the Mexicano socioscape is not absolute. For instance, Don Gabriel, while praising the *rigor* of olden days, observes that his ancestors were "enslaved," as indeed they were (they were bonded laborers on a hacienda). In contrast, women, while praising the opportunities available today, may speak negatively of the rudeness of children or the danger of crime in the cities.

2. Empirically, we can determine that the general patterns of borrowing from Spanish into Mexicano, which permits loan vocabulary from every grammatical category of Spanish, were well established by the beginning of the eighteenth century (Karttunen and Lockhart 1976). Thus, not even the great-great-grandparents of the oldest generation of contemporary Mexicano speakers lived in a world in which there were no Spanish loans in Mexicano. Nostalgic discourses are recorded from a very early period in Mexicano communities; Karttunen and Lockhart 1987 note a discourse about a "Golden Age" in the Bancroft dialogues, recorded about 1570–1580. Their "Golden Age" discourse reflects

on a time before the Conquest, when children were rigorously trained and sin was swiftly and sternly punished.

A minor point on Mexicano orthography: the symbol "x" stands for [š], as is conventional in orthographies of the indigenous languages of Mexico.

3. S73, speaker 73, and other speaker numbers given here, refers to the list in Hill and Hill 1986:456-459. S73's view of the world is discussed at length in J. Hill 1995.

4. Mallon 1994 reports very similar discourses about the impact of schooling from the Sierra de Puebla (the Nahua-speaking region immediately north of the Malinche) from the nineteenth century. She reports a struggle over schools and their meaning that was at the center of conflict between local and national "liberal" interests. Rockwell 1994 discusses conflicts about schooling in Tlaxcala, including the Malinche region, in the period immediately after the revolution.

5. Becker 1994:251 reports that elderly consultants recalled "deference couched in Catholic terms" from prerevolutionary Michoacán: "peons learned as children that on sighting a landlord (or his bad guy stand-in, the *mayordomo*), they were to doff their caps and murmur, 'Ave María.'" This suggests that such greetings did/do more than place the sacred at the center of ideological space: they incorporate into such space a highly conservative Catholicism, suffused through and through with presuppositions of hierarchy.

6. Women often agree with the evaluation of today's children as rude and disrespectful; however, they never blame this on schooling, which is very common in the discourse of nostalgia.

7. A routinized purist discourse, discussed in Hill and Hill (1986), does focus on a short list of *legítimo mexicano* lexical items.

8. The following abbreviations appear in the examples: IMP = Imperative, INDEF = Indefinite, OBJ = Object, P2 = Second Person, P3 = Third Person, SING = Singular.

9. The system is not perfectly regular: the various marking options of honorific suffix, reflexive-applicative affixation, and prefixation with *on-* are variable at each level; a verb form may have one, two, or all three elements. Sometimes, *compadres* are addressed in the second person. However, third-person direct address occurs only with ritual kin. See Hill and Hill 1978 for more detailed discussion of the honorific system.

10. While these are the two groups of speakers most likely to use Spanish loan words at high frequencies in speaking Mexicano, they are also the two groups most likely to mention "mixing" as an example of decline.

11. In case anyone is tempted, Karttunen 1983 suggests that *nahuatīa* 'to give orders' is not related to *nāhuat(i)* 'to speak clearly, to answer or respond' (the source of *nāhuatlahtōlli* 'the Nahuatl language'). The latter form has a long initial vowel. Only in Ramírez de Alejandro and Dakin's 1979 vocabulary of the Nahuatl of Xalitla, Guerrero is the form for 'to give orders' attested with a long initial vowel. All other sources give the first vowel in *nahuatīa* as short.

12. I do not know whether speakers make the assumption claimed by Sweetser 1987 for English speakers: that if someone says something, he or she believes it to be true, and since beliefs are markedly sincere, what is said is true. It is the case that to quote someone with doubt is the "marked" case: the speaker must use the dubitative evidential *quil*. However, speakers also use the word "lie" to mean any statement that turns out to be wrong, not just a statement uttered with the intent to mislead (comparable to the example of *mentira* 'lie' by Briggs 1989).

13. In fact, Mexicano speakers did not value plain language and literalism. Leon-Portilla 1982 has pointed out that the knowledge of metaphorical couplets such as *in xōchitl cuīcatl* 'the flower, the song' (poetry), *in ātl in tepētl* 'the water, the mountain' (city), and *in*

tlīlli in tlapalli 'the black ink, the coloured ink' (history) constituted a highly valued form of knowledge.

REFERENCES

Becker, Marjorie. 1994. Torching La Purísima, Dancing at the Altar: The Construction of Revolutionary Hegemony in Michoacán, 1934–1940. In *Everyday Forms of State Formation*, ed. Gilbert M. Joseph and Daniel Nugent, pp. 247–264. Durham, N.C.: Duke University Press.

Briggs, Charles. 1989. *Competence in Performance.* Philadelphia: University of Pennsylvania Press.

Eagleton, Terry. 1991. *Ideology.* London: Verso.

Friedrich, Paul. 1989. Language, Ideology, and Political Economy. *American Anthropologist* 91:295–312.

Giddens, Anthony. 1976. *New Rules of Sociological Method.* New York: Basic Books.

Halliday, M. A. K., and Ruqaiya Hasan. 1976. *Cohesion in English.* London: Longman.

Hill, Jane H. 1990a. The Cultural (?) Context of Narrative Involvement. In *Papers from the 25th Annual Regional Meeting of the Chicago Linguistic Society.* Part 2: *Parasession on Language in Context*, ed. Bradley Music, Randolph Graczyk, and Caroline Wiltshire, pp. 138–156. Chicago: Chicago Linguistic Society.

———. 1990b. In Neca gobierno de puebla: Mexicano Penetrations of the Mexican State. In *Indian and State in Latin America*, ed. Joel Sherzer and Greg Urban, pp. 72–94. Austin: University of Texas Press.

———. 1995. The Voices of Don Gabriel. In *The Dialogic Emergence of Culture*, ed. Bruce Mannheim and Dennis Tedlock, pp. 97–147. Urbana: University of Illinois Press.

Hill, Jane H., and Kenneth C. Hill. 1986. *Speaking Mexicano.* Tucson: University of Arizona Press.

Hill, Kenneth C. 1985. Las penurias de doña María: Un análisis sociolingüístico de un relato del náhuatl moderno. *Tlalocan* 10:33–115.

Karttunen, Frances. 1983. *An Analytical Dictionary of Nahuatl.* Austin: University of Texas Press.

Karttunen, Frances, and James Lockhart. 1976. *Nahuatl in the Middle Years: Language Contact Phenomena in Texts of the Colonial Period.* Publications in Linguistics 85. Berkeley: University of California.

———. 1987. *The Art of Nahuatl Speech: The Bancroft Dialogues.* Nahuatl Studies Series No. 2. Los Angeles: UCLA Latin American Studies Center.

Leon-Portilla, Miguel. 1982. Three Forms of Thought in Ancient Mexico. In *Studies in Symbolism and Cultural Communication*, ed. F. Allan Hanson, pp. 9–24. Lawrence: University of Kansas.

Nutini, Hugo, and Timothy Murphy. 1970. Labor Migration and Family Structure in the Tlaxcala-Puebla Area, Mexico. In *The Social Anthropology of Latin America: Essays in Honor of Ralph Leon Beals*, ed. W. Goldschmidt and H. Hoijer, pp. 80–103. Los Angeles: UCLA Latin American Studies Center.

Ramírez de Alejandro, Cleofas, and Karen Dakin. 1979. *Vocabulario náhuatl de Xalitla, Guerrero.* Cuadernos de la Casa Chata 25. Mexico: Centro de Investigaciones Superiores del INAH.

Rockwell, Elsie. 1994. Schools of the Revolution: Enacting and Contesting State Forms in Tlaxcala, 1910–1930. In *Everyday Forms of State Formation*, ed. Gilbert M. Joseph and Daniel Nugent, pp. 170–208. Durham, N.C.: Duke University Press.

Rumsey, Alan. 1990. Wording, Meaning, and Linguistic Ideology. *American Anthropologist* 92:346–361.

Silverman, David, and Brian Torode. 1980. *The Material Word.* London: Routledge and Kegan Paul.

Silverstein, Michael. 1979. Language Structure and Linguistic Ideology. In *The Elements: A Parasession on Linguistic Units and Levels*, ed. Paul R. Clyne, William F. Hanks, and Carol L. Hofbauer, pp.193–247. Chicago: Chicago Linguistic Society.

———. 1981. The Limits of Awareness. Working Papers in Sociolinguistics 84. Austin, Tex.: Southwest Educational Development Laboratory.

———. 1985. Language and the Culture of Gender. In *Semiotic Mediation*, ed. Elizabeth Mertz and Richard Parmentier, pp. 219–259. New York: Academic Press.

Sweetser, Eve. 1987. The Definition of "Lie." In *Cultural Models in Language and Thought*, ed. Dorothy Holland and Naomi Quinn, pp. 43–66. Cambridge: Cambridge University Press.

Woolard, Kathryn A., and Bambi B. Schieffelin. 1994. Language Ideology. *Annual Review of Anthropology* 23:55–82.

4

Anger, Gender, Language Shift, and the Politics of Revelation in a Papua New Guinean Village

DON KULICK

In a number of recent publications, Catherine Lutz (1986, 1990) has explored the network of associations in Western culture that link women with emotion, which in most cases is overtly devalued. A contrasting situation is described by Bambi Schieffelin (1990), E. L. Schieffelin (1976, 1985), and Steven Feld (1990), all of whom argue that among the Kaluli people of Papua New Guinea, it is *males* who are "stereotypically culturally constructed as the emotional gender" (Feld 1990:262) and that this emotionality is encouraged and strongly valued in a wide variety of ritual and mundane contexts. Studies like these, as well as many others by anthropologists (e.g., articles in Lutz and Abu-Lughod 1990, Bloch and Parry 1982, Watson-Gegeo and White 1990, White and Kirkpatrick 1985), have shown that in probably all communities throughout the world, the expression of affect is engendered and that, therefore, in Catherine Lutz's words, "any discourse on emotion is also, at least implicitly, a discourse on gender" (Lutz 1990:69; see also Ochs 1988:177–83, 215–16).

Because both emotion and gender are indexed and expressed in large measure through language, we can augment Lutz's generalization with the observation that discourses on emotion and gender are also bound up with discourses, or ideologies, of language (Ochs 1992:341). We can, furthermore, expect that at certain periods in the history of a language and its speakers, the links that exist among discourses on affect, gender, and language may come to salience and work to compel speakers to engage in linguistic practices that may result in changes in the language itself.

Michael Silverstein has drawn attention to this type of process in his discussion of the Quaker challenge to the seventeenth-century English system of distance and deference (Silverstein 1985). Silverstein argues that two factors were decisive in the shift from a pronominal system signaling deference and intimacy (through the second-person ye/you–thee/thou opposition) to one in which those affects were no longer encoded grammatically. The first factor was an emergent yet widespread idea about the value of "plain English" as a means of both signifying opposition to traditional knowledge and authority and directly apprehending religious and scientific "truth." The second was Quaker applications of this idea in their everyday speech practices and in their rhetoric about language. Quakers defied contemporary sociolinguistic norms by refusing to use the polite deference (ye/you) forms when addressing others, partly because English scriptural prose used the familiar thee/thou forms and partly because they felt that the ye/you forms contradicted their religious doctrine that all people were equal before God. Quaker usage was in this sense "explicitly subversive," as well as being "societally shocking [and] insulting" (1985:249) to non-Quaker interlocutors, who spoke to the Friends with the polite 'you', only to be answered with the familiar 'thou'. A situation thus arose in which:

> Friends [i.e., Quakers] use symmetric T [thee/thou], and hence others had to avoid it, lest they be mistaken for members of the sect; Friends avoid symmetric Y [ye/you], and hence others must use only it. Consequently, a new system emerges, in which societal norms abandon T decisively as usage indexing speaker as Quaker and take up the invariant usage of Y. A STRUCTURAL or FORMAL change in the norms of English has been affected. (1985:251; capitals in original)

Silverstein summarizes and generalizes this process as follows:

> Ideological rationalization [can] engage . . . with language at and through an intersection of structural form and indexical usage, producing tension in the highly charged "metaphoricization" of indexical meanings and forms. The resolution of this tension seems to move the very structural system into new configurations, generally unforseen by the users of the language. (1985:252)

I draw attention to this analysis by Silverstein because in this chapter I focus on a similar, though much more far-reaching, process of ideological and linguistic change that is under way in a small village (population ca. 110) in Papua New Guinea called Gapun.[1] Gapun is located about 10 kilometers from the northern coast of Papua New Guinea, roughly midway between the lower Sepik and the Ramu rivers. It is a relatively isolated village, and the villagers are self-supporting through a combination of swidden agriculture, hunting, and sago processing. Despite their isolation and their consequently low level of participation in cash cropping or other money-generating projects, the villagers of Gapun are very keen to 'develop' (*kamap*), and thinking about how this might happen occupies a great deal of their time. The villagers have been nominally Roman Catholic since the late 1940s, and their hopes for development are pinned in elaborate ways on Christianity and on the imminent second coming of Christ.

In Gapun, a language shift is currently under way from the village vernacular—a Papuan language called Taiap—to Tok Pisin, the creole language that has become Papua New Guinea's most widely spoken national language. Children are no longer learning the vernacular, and when I last visited the village in 1991, no one under fourteen years of age actively commanded it. The reasons behind this shift are complex and many-stranded, but here I focus on what I see as one of the most central reasons behind the shift—namely, links that exist in village discourses among gender, the expression of anger, and particular ideologies of language that see language as indexical of sociability and the ability to handle knowledge.

Two specific speech genres invoke these links very clearly for the villagers. The first is a kind of dramatic public display of anger that occurs virtually daily in the village. The word by which the villagers most commonly call this speech genre is a Tok Pisin word, *kros*, which literally means 'anger' (in the village vernacular, the name is pwapəŋgar nam,[2] literally 'angry talk'). *Kros*es are considered by Gapuners—both men and women—to be stereotypically feminine expressive modes.

The second speech genre I discuss is called 'men's house talk' (ambagaiŋa nam). This talk is oratory, by men, that occurs inside or in the immediate vicinity of one of the men's houses in the village. Unlike *kros*es, which foreground and proclaim anger, men's house talk is not always and explicitly concerned with anger as such. However, a central structuring characteristic of men's oratories is a concern to downplay conflict and reframe disputes so that everyone appears to be content and harmonious. On certain occasions, such as during meetings called to help heal a sick person, anger is made an explicit topic of discussion, and men are urged to "expose" their anger and "reveal" their complaints.[3]

In my discussion of *kros*es and oratories, I concentrate on the ways in which discourses of gender, affect, and language are mutually reinforcing and sustained through specific linguistic practices. Ultimately, my point is that those discourses, and the practices that constitute and inform them, are nowadays invoked by villagers to position women and men in different and opposing relationships to those institutions and values that everyone in the village agrees are important: namely, Christianity, modernity and civilization. This positioning constitutes the kind of "tension" to which Silverstein refers in the preceding quotation. And as he suggests, the resolution of the tension is moving the linguistic situation itself into new, unforeseen configurations, ones that in this case are resulting in the demise of the village vernacular itself.

Language Ideology and Knowledge

A basic tenet of Gapun villagers' language ideology is that speakers do not normally say what they mean. That is, unlike much Western philosphical tradition and unlike the values generally associated with contemporary middle classes, which view language as a "transparent window to truths both formulable and communicable in it" (Silverstein 1985:248; see also Reddy 1979), villagers in Gapun interpret speakers' words neither as a reflection of their inner state nor as an accurate representation of their opinions on a matter. In fact, the general assumption is that language 'hides' (*haitim*/*ambu-*) meanings that the speaker either cannot or will not state openly. Consequently, interpretation in the village is geared toward getting "behind" or "inside" or "underneath" the words actually used in speech.

The realizations and consequences of this linguistic ideology have been discussed in earlier work on Gapun with relation to literacy (Kulick and Stroud 1990), language socialization (Kulick 1992:223–47) and codeswitching (Stroud 1992). In those works, Christopher Stroud and I have examined the villagers' ideas about language by embedding them in local notions of personhood that make it very risky to appear too blunt or demanding. Here, I foreground a complementary consideration that is mentioned but not elaborated in those earlier analyses: in addition to being linked to and reinforced by conceptions of personhood and sociability, village language ideology is also related to particular village ideas about the nature and consequences of knowledge.

In Gapun, a great number of forms of knowledge consistently carry with them associations of danger. All those forms of knowledge that were traditionally valued—such as knowledge of healing chants, knowledge of certain myths, knowledge of the men's *tambaran* cult and of special skills such as yam planting or woodcarving—are bound up with hazard. Knowledge about any facet of the *tambaran* cult, for example, is believed to have the power to cause the deaths of women and noninitiated boys who might somehow acquire such knowledge. Even initiated men must carefully guard their knowledge of the cult secrets, for to reveal them to the noninitiated would cause the cult deities to murder the speaker. Magic chants, even benevolent ones, link their knower to ancestral spirits or men's cult deities that may act entirely on their own to bring harm to anyone who displeases the knower, even if the knower does not wish this. Overhearing certain myths is viewed as having the potential to cause sickness, and uttering secret names may cause environmental disturbances, or even death, for large numbers of people. Even private knowledge is fraught with danger. Unlike some Melanesian societies, such as the Sepik river Avatip, where knowledge appears to be dangerous only to the extent that it is made public (Harrison 1990:102), in Gapun even the private discovery of knowledge is enough to put the knower in danger. On one occasion, for example, a senior man explained to me that he had repeatedly tried and finally managed to re-create, on a fan he was weaving, a specific mythologically important pattern that he recalled seeing as a boy. "Nobody taught me to weave the design," he told me. "I exposed (*kamapim*) it in my thoughts." This exposure, however, apparently angered the ancestral ghost-owners of the design, who retaliated by inflicting the old man with a serious illness.

This kind of understanding of knowledge makes possessing it and imparting it a somewhat risky business. Knowledge is valuable, but it is also—and this, of course, is part of what constitutes its value—potentially lethal. It must be handled, passed on, and made public in very delicate ways. Anthropologists working in Papua New Guinea have noted that this kind of orientation to knowledge seems very widespread throughout the area. They have also noted that practices of knowledge throughout Melanesia tend to pivot around an oscillation between concealment and revelation. At certain times and under certain conditions, knowledge of sensitive matters—say, of cult secrets (Barth 1987) or clan wealth (Strathern 1979:249)—is revealed to initiates or trading partners. But such knowledge, once revealed, is almost immediately hidden away again, and, furthermore, it frequently carries with it an implicit tag (made explicit in subsequent revelations) that the revelation disclosed only part of, or perhaps even a false impression of what there is to know.

Gapun villagers' language ideology, which privileges ambiguity, hidden meanings, and meanings construed by listeners rather than those conveyed by speakers, provides them with ways to traffic in knowledge without putting themselves or their interlocutors in too much danger. By oscillating between "inside" talk and "outside" talk (Stroud 1992:147), by making deliberately ambiguous, self-contradictory statements (Kulick 1992:127–31), by pressing into service specific structural features such as codeswitching (Stroud 1992) and diminutives (Kulick and Stroud 1993), and by deploying discursive features such as repetition and dissociation (Kulick 1992:127–36), speakers in Gapun manage to reveal, discuss, and circulate knowledge even as they conceal it and thereby gingerly sidestep many of the potentially fatal consequences that stark, unmitigated knowledge is known to have.

Anger

Anger enters this discussion as a singularly inflamed object of knowledge. In village discourses on emotion and knowledge, anger in adults is always linked to danger. If anger is not voiced or acted on, it will, villagers explain, remain in the stomach (the seat of emotions) and 'rot' (*sting/pisimb-*). The putrification of anger may mobilize the ancestral spirits associated with the aggrieved person, and these may cause harm to whomever provoked anger in that person. Alternatively, rotting anger may "give bad thoughts" to the aggrieved, driving them to seek out the services of a sorcerer, who will be paid to murder the object of the anger.

If anger is voiced or acted on, there is a risk that its expression will provoke the wrath of the ancestral spirits associated with the person who is abused or attacked. Abusing or attacking another person may also drive that person to a sorcerer. So, no matter how it is ultimately dealt with, anger is dangerous. People in Gapun die from anger. Village deaths (all of which are held be caused by sorcery) are almost inevitably accounted for at least in part by recalling past arguments or fights that the deceased or his or her close family members or matrilineal relatives had with other people.

Anger (*kros/pwap-*) is one of the relatively few affects that villagers regularly speak about and attribute to themselves and others (the other affects that feature in village discourse are shame [*sem/maikar-*], concern and sadness [*wari/punat-*], dissatisfaction [*les/mnda-*], and fear [*pret/rɛw-*]). Of these emotions, anger and dissatisfaction are seen as the earliest and most basic. They are tied to a dimension of personhood that the villagers call *hed* in Tok Pisin and *kɔkɨr* in the vernacular. Both these words mean 'head'. Each individual, the villagers maintain, has *hed*. By this, they mean that each individual has a basic and volatile sense of personal will and autonomy. The concept of *hed* in Gapun signifies egoism, selfishness, and maverick individualism. It denotes emotional bristliness and defiant, antisocial behavior, and it is roundly condemned in village rhetoric.

For the villagers, one of the embodiments of *hed*, of this volatile dimension of personhood, is small children. Babies and toddlers in Gapun are routinely said to be, and treated as if they were, continually dissatisfied and angry. A child cooing softly on its mother's lap may suddenly be shaken lightly and asked "Ai! What are you mad about? Ah?!" (*Ai! Yu belhat long wanem samting? Ah?!*). Likewise, a mother who sees her eight-month-old daughter reaching out toward a dog lying beside her will comment, "Look, she's mad (*kros*) now, she wants to hit the dog," and she will raise the baby's hand onto the dog's fur, telling the child, "That's it, hit it! Hit it!" One of the clearest indications of how villagers view the affective state of children is in the first words they attribute to them. In the village, a child's first word is generally held to be *ɔkɨ*, which is a vernacular word meaning, approximately, "I'm getting out of here." Attributed to infants as young as two months, this word encapsulates the adult belief that babies "do what they want" (*bihainim laik bilong ol yet*) and go where they want to go regardless of the wishes of others. The two words that villagers consider to rapidly follow *ɔkɨ* also underscore the notion of a baby as a gruff, independent individualist with a "strong" *hed*. These are the Taiap words *mnda* (I'm sick of this) and *aiata* (stop it).

In the villagers' view of the socialization process, children should come to understand that *hed* and the display of anger and dissatisfaction that typifies it must be suppressed (*daunim*). The expectation is that, as they mature, children will curtail their expressions of anger, that they will begin to accept and accommodate others, that they will share with others and conduct themselves "quietly" (*isi*/*tɔwɛr*). Anger, in this cultural understanding, in addition to being fraught with danger, is also seen as childish and immature. Although it is explicitly recognized to be a central component of all people, it is one that adults should do their best to suppress and conceal.

Unfortunately, however, people do become angry at the actions of other people: other people who steal betelnut, who neglect to collect firewood for the evening meal, who forget to return a borrowed item, who engage in extramarital affairs, who talk behind people's backs, and so on. Villagers have developed a number of ways of dealing with the anger they see as being provoked in them, including destroying their own possessions and outright fighting (Kulick 1992:50–52). The single most common way in which anger is conveyed, however, is through the village speech genre known as a *kros*.

Proclaiming Anger in a Kros

The best way to give an impression of the general tenor of *kros*es in Gapun is to briefly examine an extract from one that was recorded and transcribed in June 1991. This is a *kros* between two sisters who live next door to each other. It arose because for several weeks the younger sister, a woman in her thirties named Sake, had been complaining loudly about the fact that children who played in the area near her house littered the ground with coffee beans, which they shot at each other and at pigs through bamboo tubes. One afternoon, Sake caught her sister's ten-year-old son red-handed as he stood shooting coffee beans at pigs underneath her house. She chased him and shouted at him and threatened him. At one point during her tirade at the boy, Sake asked him in a loud voice: "Does your mother come and clean up around here?!" (the answer, Sake knew, was no). Hearing this rhetorical question from inside her house, the boy's mother, a woman in her forties named Erapo, began yelling at Sake. Sake strode into her own house and responded with full force. This segment occurs about five minutes into the shouting match:

SAKE No good rotten big black hole!
ERAPO Smelly cunt bloody bastard!
SAKE I was talking to Erapo [sarcastic]. I was talking good about the rubbish [i.e., the coffee beans], Erapo gets up and swears at me. Fucking cunthole bastard you!
ERAPO This hole of yours [(   )
SAKE [Rotten! Your dirty cunt is a big black hole. Bastard. Black guts! What is she, what is Erapo talking to me about, *kros*-ing me about, swearing at me for?! Ah?! Erapo [you have] a rotten black hole!
[one utterance distraction]
SAKE Catfish cunt! Erapo has a black cunthole! A black cunthole Erapo! Erapo has a huge black cunthole! Erapo has an enormous black cunthole! Satan fucks you all the time, Satan is fucking you Erapo! Erapo! Satan is fucking you really good! Your cunt is sagging like loose mud on a riverbank. Catfish cunt!

This is a typical Gapun *kros*. It exhibits many of the conventions that characterize the speech genre, such as the spatial placement of the speakers inside their respective houses, vituperative insults and gross vulgarity, loud voices shouted out over the village, and harsh, explicitly confrontational accusations of wrongdoing. As the *kros* continues, the insults that the women exchange become interwoven with direct threats, and Sake, especially, repeatedly challenges Erapo to come down from her house so that Sake can "beat her till she shits."

*Kros*es in Gapun are gendered speech genres that are associated with and almost inevitably enunciated by women.[4] Whenever Sake or some other woman has a loud *kros*, those village men not directly involved in some way make clucking sounds of recognition, shake their heads disparagingly, and mutter knowingly that "this kind of rubbish talk is the habit of women, it's their way" (*desela kain rabis tok em we bilong ol meri, pasin bilong ol*). Women are collectively held by village men to be more *bikhed* (willful, big-headed) than men. In ways similar to those in most Melanesian societies, women in Gapun are associated with individualism, atomicity, and antisocial behavior. Traditionally, men, through their common residence in the men's house and through their perpetual preparations for and acting out of funerary feasts, initiation rites, and war raids, represented and embodied cooperation and society. The collective actions of men were considered the 'bones' (*bun/niŋg*) of society. The actions of women, even though these were sometimes collective in nature (Kulick 1992:286, n. 7), do not appear to have been accorded the same type of cultural significance as those of men, and women were and continue to be represented as divisive troublemakers whose selfish actions constantly threaten the solid, manly group. Echoing a statement heard all over New Guinea, village men sometimes remind one another that "we fight over women"; that is, we would not fight if there were no women. Women, with their anger, their *kros*es, and their unwillingness to "suppress" their *hed*s, are the root of all conflicts.

Individual women in Gapun do not share this view of themselves as destructive troublemakers. Women who have *kros*es do not interpret their own behavior in reference to the stereotype. When Sake, for example, has a *kros*, she does not consider that she is being divisive; she is legitimately defending herself and her rights from some violation and attack. When another woman has a *kros*, however, Sake is often quick to sniff that the woman is "a woman who always gets angry for no reason" (*meri bilong kros nating nating*).

The existence of a culturally elaborated stereotype of women as quarrelsome means that such a role is available for any woman to act out, however. And as a stereotypically female role, it is unattractive for men. Men in the village like to pretend that they have no conflicts with others, and they dismiss *kros*es as *samting bilong ol meri*/<u>*naŋɔma ɔrak*</u> (what women do). The village stereotype of what represents ideal male behavior puts pressure on the men to be more sociable, generous, dignified, and temperate than their wives, who are expected to fly off the handle and have a *kros* at the slightest excuse. In most cases, in a manner remarkably similar to that described by Elinor Ochs ([1974] 1989:137–38) for Madagascar, a married man is able to uphold this stereotype and simultaneously announce infringements by simply informing his wife about some slight or infraction that he has been subjected to (such as someone's failure to return a borrowed axe or shovel). The wife can usually be counted on to take it from there, and in doing so she reinforces the stereotype of quarrelsome, loud-mouthed women. Even on those occasions when a man publicly *belhat* (gets angry, shouts), the anger is usually directed at his wife or close female relatives. Public arguments thus almost inevitably involve women at some level. Both men and women blame (other) women for making trouble, for not being able to contain their anger, and for "showing *hed*" (see also Goldman 1986:236, Nash 1987:105, Harrison 1990:162).

Concealing Anger in the Men's House

In very marked contrast to women's *kros*es, oratories in the men's house are occasions on which men in Gapun engage in speeches that downplay tension, smooth over disagreement, and stress consensus in the village. Oratories occur whenever meetings are called in the men's house: to announce the need for labor to clear overgrown paths or repair rotten footbridges; to work out the arrangements that have to be made for funerary feasts; to discern the meaning of messages and news items that villagers bring back with them from their travels to other villages or to the Marienberg mission station; to arrange to help a village man and his wife in some task that requires a number of laborers, such as carrying house posts, roofing a house, or clearing the forest to plant a garden; or to discuss any number of other public issues.

Because they are so strongly associated with the men's house, oratories, by definition, are male discourses. Only men in Gapun are considered to orate. There is no rule or explicit consensus in the village that women cannot orate, and there are a few strong-willed women in Gapun who do occasionally speak in public gatherings that concern both men and women. Women's speeches contain many of the same rhetorical features, such as repetition, that are predominant in oratories, but they differ importantly in that they are much briefer than most men's speeches (which usually last about ten to fifteen minutes but which can go on for up to forty-five minutes), and they never contain any of the particular formulaic tags that the men use to mark their speech as oratorical. Furthermore, women, who are not allowed inside the men's house, obviously cannot speak from there, and so their contributions to a discussion have a peripheral character that is underscored by their spatial placement. Because of factors like these, women who make short speeches at public gatherings are not considered to be orating; they are, rather, "complaining."

Usually, anger is not an explicit topic of discussion in contexts dominated by oratorical speechmaking. Quite the opposite. Skillful orators draw on a wide variety of paralinguistic cues (e.g., speakers are called and assembled under the same roof), metalinguistic cues (e.g., speakers address their talk directly to a general public and use politeness markers to assume and relinquish the floor), and linguistic cues (e.g., there is a marked preference for speakers to use diminutives in order to downplay their own status and talk, and oratories are characterized by supportive repetition from listeners). All these semiotic devices are drawn on to pointedly ignore and downplay the tensions that infect daily life in the village and to promote an illusion that everyone is in agreement and that there really is no anger and consequently no conflict at all. In creating this illusion and bringing the villagers together in this way, orators demonstrate for others their own social awareness and skills, even as they work to create a context in which others can demonstrate their sociability by listening and contributing to the buildup of the consensus by repeating and agreeing.

Sometimes, however, village men focus explicitly on anger, and there are contexts in which they spend much time and talk urging one another to 'expose' (*autim/ arɔnɨ gur-*) their anger, to 'break it open' (*brukim/kra-*), to 'reveal' (kamapim/ *mamanj-*) it. This kind of speechmaking occurs whenever somebody in the village is struck down by a serious illness that people conclude is being caused by ancestral spirits. When this happens, men gather together in a men's house and talk about conflicts. When everybody who wants to talk has had a turn, senior men invoke the village ancestors and call on them to stop causing the sickness. Everybody present in the men's house then dips his forefinger in a glass of water, which is subsequently used to wash the sick person. The idea behind this procedure is that the men in this context embody both themselves and their ancestral spirits, and by first "revealing" their anger and then dipping their forefingers in the water, they "cool" the anger that is causing sickness in the afflicted person.

The following text is extracted from a meeting in the men's house, attended by all village men, called to effect a cure for the author of this paper, who in June

1991 became afflicted with disabling pains that the villagers, on hearing the symptoms, immediately identified as "a sickness of the ground" (i.e., a sickness caused by village ancestral spirits). Note how anger is talked about here.

MONE Whoever feels that something isn't right, all right expose it. It's like we're breaking open the talk now. It isn't good if this [anger] remains in our stomachs, because he [i.e., Don] will suffer. We have to expose all the little talk.

KAWRI Yeah.

MONE Like yesterday too I talked about doing work for him [Mone means that yesterday he exhorted the villagers to get to work building a house for me. Work on this house had been progressing extremely slowly, because even though the villagers had volunteered to build it for me, they found themselves unwilling to work together due to various village conflicts]. We were all lazy [and therefore did no work yesterday]. Or maybe we have some worries, or maybe we're tired of doing work, or maybe we're just tired for no reason, or like that.

KRUNI That's it.

MONE All right we're gonna reveal all these little worries: "This man said something to me and so I'm unwilling to work," this kind of thing. All right, when we've finished talking we'll/or we'll talk about the spirits of the village, of the men's house, OK, and we'll put our fingers in the water all right Don will/we'll hold Don's pain, wash it in the water of our talk. Like just try it. It's not this [i.e., a sickness caused by a village spirit], it's a [white man's] sickness he's got, he'll go to the hospital.

KRUNI At the hospital it'll finish. We'll try it our way [first].

MONE There's no talk [i.e., no dissension]. Like we can/maybe we don't have any talk, or maybe we can talk about the spirits of the village, we don't think that something is as it should be/we can talk about work or about something that is amongst us giving illness to him, all right we'll talk straight about that. Talk straight and put fingers in the water.

Later, toward the end of this session, after several men had revealed "little" irritations or conflicts that they were involved in or had heard about, the talk is summarized like this:

KEM We're gonna hold the water and rub his pain. These things, there's not plenty of complaints.

SAIR No.

ANDON There's no complaints.

KEM Our [-little talk, that's it.

KAWI -little crumbs of talk.

KEM We're making it.

The aspect of this talk to which I wish to draw attention is the way in which anger, even though it is explicitly spoken about here, is consistently embedded in speech characterized by hedges ("maybe we don't have any talk"), the presentation of alternative positions ("or maybe we're just tired for no reason," "it's a [white man's] sickness he's got"), and specific denials that the anger the men are supposed to be exposing is in fact anger at all. Choruses like the one here, in which several men hasten to agree with one another that there are no complaints, occur throughout meetings like this, and they become particularly insistent whenever somebody actually does "expose" a happening or occurrence that caused them to feel anger.

At one point during this meeting, for example, a senior man "revealed" that the men present were reluctant to work on my house because they were angry at Allan, my adoptive village "father." The anger, it was pointed out, stemmed from the fact that Allan and his wife had moved into my previous, communally built, house when I completed my original fieldwork and left the village in 1987. The couple made this move in defiance of received village opinion, and the other villagers now accused Allan and his wife of "ruining" that previous house. Every person present at this meeting was acutely aware of the truth of this senior man's "revelation," because in private villagers routinely expressed bitter resentment toward Allan and his wife for having moved into the house. In the men's house, though, the revelation was handled in the following way:

KEM	All right, you all gave up on poor Allan, he's by himself [i.e., working on building my new house by himself]. You all have this thought, I know, you can't cover it up it, we're showing Christian belief here. It's not anger (*kros*), it's like you're talking straight. OK, and you hold the water now and <u>the spirit will go inside it. It's like that</u>.
ANDON	<u>Is it</u> anger? [rhetorical question]
KRUNI	<u>It isn't</u> anger.
MARAME	There's no anger, it's talk.
MONE	<u>Yes</u>.

One of the most significant ways in which men's public talk about anger differs from women's is in this kind of cooperative recontextualizing work, where speakers weave together their words to reframe anger as not-anger, and where they sometimes even go so far as to congratulate themselves on talking about anger as a way of 'showing Christian belief' (*autim Bilip*). I interpret this kind of supportive discursive interaction between men to be a linguistic manifestation of the village orientation to knowledge as something that in many cases is safely revealed only if it is somehow subsequently reconcealed.

And that is the main point. One of the most significant differences between women's *kros*es and men's oratories—and the difference that seems to evoke the greatest degree of discomfort in villagers—is not so much that female speakers publicize anger. In many ways this is, in fact, commendable, since villagers agree that it is much better to express anger than to let it remain unexposed and rotting in one's stomach (indeed, the public exposure of anger is the whole purpose of the kind of gatherings in the men's house just discussed). What is unacceptable and dangerous about *kros*es is that women complete only half the discursive equation. Women reveal anger without subsequently reconcealing it. They expose anger and leave it uncovered, where it is thought to act like a throbbing, hot lightning rod of unleashed dissension, pulling sorcery, sickness, and death into the village.

Women's linguistic practices for dealing with anger are in almost every way inversions of men's practices. In addition to exposing anger without hiding it again, women's *kros*es emanate from inside or nearby private dwelling houses. Men's oratories, on the other hand, occur in or near the communal men's house. *Kros*es are organized as competing monologues. In oratories, the people being orated at are free to contribute sympathetic interjections throughout the speech and follow the orator by producing a speech or a summation in which they "give support" to the orator. *Kros*es are dramatic declarations of self-display in which speakers assert themselves and their personal autonomy by broadcasting throughout the village that these have been violated. Oratories are characterized by self-effacement; speakers repeatedly remind their listeners in polite, muted tones that they only have "little crumbs of talk" or "a little worry" to draw to everyone's attention. *Kros*es are meant to shame a specific, named person or a specific unknown, unnamed culprit. Oratories are intended to generalize and address people as members of a group; even in those cases where the topic of an oratory is some sort of transgression committed by some specific person, blame is inevitably diffused and generalized, and listeners are reminded that others in the village (though not necessarily they themselves) are just as lazy or uncooperative or big-headed as the (always unnamed) individual(s) who committed the transgression. For both men and women, *kros*es are associated with (other) women and divisiveness. Oratories, on the other hand, are seen as concrete evidence that men in Gapun really are more placid, consensus oriented, sociable, and reasonable than their tempestuous, forever bickering wives (Table 4.1).

Language Shift

In the ways I have outlined, we can consider anger as a kind of locus where ideologies of language, gender, and affect all converge, creating in that convergence a discursive space in which gender stereotypes are both imagined and acted out. In

Table 4.1 Summary of contrastive features of *kros*es and oratories

Kroses	*Oratories*
enunciated by women	enunciated by men
emanate from individual houses	emanate from communal men's house
vulgarity	politeness
self-display	self-effacement
competing overlapping monologues	supportive serial monologues
reveal anger	reveal anger only to reconceal it again
address intravillage affairs	link village affairs to outside world
vernacular language (Taiap) predominates	national language (Tok Pisin) predominates

large measure because of their linguistic practices for publicly dealing with anger, men in Gapun are credited by everyone with greater knowledge about how to handle knowledge, as it were. By exposing anger even as they deny it and conceal it, men present themselves, and are understood by others, as providing and embodying a protective buffer against the ravages that naked anger is known to be able to summon forth. Women, by contrast, brazenly expose anger but subsequently do nothing to mitigate the negative consequences that may be generated by this exposure. This particular linguistic practice of handling anger has become representative of "what women do," and it permits the maintenance of a stereotype that demeans women as childish, destructive, and irresponsible.

Although there are differences, this situation in many ways parallels Silverstein's example of the sociolinguistics of seventeenth-century British society, discussed at the beginning of this chapter. In the case of both Quakers in Britain and women in Gapun, a specific group of people comes to be symbolized in meaningful ways through their linguistic practices. Once this symbolic bond becomes marked, it becomes important for people who do not wish to be identified with that group (non-Quakers in Britain and men in Gapun, as well as individual women in the village who do not wish to be negatively labeled by others) to begin avoiding the type of verbal behavior that is seen as indexical of the group. Thus, non-Quakers avoided the familiar second-person address forms, and men in Gapun avoid *kros*es. The question that arises now is the one with which I began this essay: namely, how is the convergence of anger, gender, and the politics of revelation working to produce a tension in Gapun such that the linguistic situation of the village is moving toward new configurations?

The answer to that question lies in the ideology and practice associated with the two languages that villagers use in their day-to-day talk. Basically, the situation is one in which the vernacular language, Taiap, is nowadays associated with tradition, the land, the local concept of *hed*, and women. Tok Pisin, on the other hand, has come to be bound up with modern processes and phenomena. Tok Pisin is tied to Christianity, white people, money, and schooling; significantly, it is also tied to men and those affective stances that are seen to characterize them.

These associative networks are frequently made explicit in men's house talk. At some point during each meeting in the men's house, no matter what the original reason for the meeting happened to be, somebody will inevitably make a speech in Tok Pisin extolling Christian ideals, reaffirming the value of education, devaluing the ways of the ancestors, and urging the villagers, and specifically the village women, to suppress their anger and stop their fighting so that everybody can "come up" (*kamap* 'change, develop'). The men's house has thus become an important arena in which individual men can publicly assert their familiarity with the modern world by reminding others that the Catholic Church, school, "Papua New Guinea," and *bisnis* (cash-generating enterprises) have altered the nature of village relationships and must be accorded a central role in village life. In making those assertions, Gapun men are able to substantiate their claims to knowledge about the modern world by choosing to orate primarily in the language through which that world is understood to be constituted—that is, Tok Pisin (cf. Sankoff 1980:44). Angry women employ what amounts to a similar discursive strategy in their public speeches. They substantiate their dissatisfaction and foreground their claims to having been violated and impinged on by choosing to announce those claims primarily in the language through which affective discourse is constituted—that is, the village vernacular, Taiap.

Those practices and the ideas that inform them are moving the village vernacular toward extinction. Powered by its links with women and the associations bound up with stereotypes of them, it seems likely that the Taiap language itself will increasingly come to be associated with negatively valued aspects of life, such as affective excess, discursive irresponsibility, and dangerous knowledge. This process is already well under way and is evidenced by villagers who sometimes pointedly refuse to speak their vernacular among themselves in order to prove that they are not "hiding" talk (e.g., during periods of millenarian activity or during sensitive meetings with people from other villages) or by village children who understand purposeful parental switches from Tok Pisin into the vernacular as conveying disapproval and anger (Kulick 1992:217).

Like the particular linguistic forms that became connected with seventeenth-century Quakers in Britain, it seems probable that the Taiap language itself will eventually be abandoned. The main relevance of this in the context of a collection of papers on language ideology is that what we see in Gapun is the way in which particular linguistic practices reinforce and are reinforced by particular ideas that exist in a community about language, affect, gender, and the relationships among those phenomena. By speaking in particular ways, women and men in Gapun activate complex webs of associations that link a wide array of discourses. So women in their *kros*es are not only spitting curses, and men in their oratories are not only making dispassionate, measured speeches that smooth over conflicts in the village. By using language in the specific ways they do, speakers embody and re-create salient stereotypes about what women and men are, they engender affect, and they position themselves in socially meaningful ways in relation to Christianity, civilization, and the modern world.

One of the contributions that I believe this example from Gapun can make to our discussions of language ideology is the reminder that language ideologies seem never to be solely about language—they are always about entangled clusters of phenomena, and they encompass and are bound up with aspects of culture like gender, and expression, and being "civilized." Furthermore, this inherently snarled and delicately layered nature of language ideology can provide colonial discourses of Christianity and modernity with numerous sites of entry into local practices and understandings, as well as with ample possibilities to penetrate and, as has happened in Gapun, enmesh themselves with both linguistic practices and local ideas about gender, affect, and language.

NOTES

I am grateful to my colleague Christopher Stroud; to Michael Silverstein, who was my discussant at the invited session "Language Ideologies: Theory and Practice," organized by Paul Kroskrity, Bambi Schieffelin, and Kit Woolard at the Ninetieth Meeting of the

American Anthropological Association, Chicago, November 1991; and to all the participants in that session who commented on an earlier version of this paper.

1. Fieldwork in Gapun was carried out during fifteen months in 1986-87, and for two months in 1991. Fieldwork in 1986-87 was financed by the Swedish Agency for Research Cooperation with Developing Countries (SAREC) and the Swedish Council for Research in the Humanities and Social Sciences (HSFR). Fieldwork in 1991 was conducted as part of a postdoctoral fellowship at the Department of Linguistics, Research School of Pacific Studies, Australian National University, and was financed by that department.

2. Throughout this text, words that are underlined and italicized are vernacular language words. Words that are only italicized are Tok Pisin words. In addition, the following transcription conventions are used in the examples:

( ) unintelligible utterance

[overlapping utterances

/ self-interruption or false start

Notes on situational context and nonverbal action are given in square brackets [ ] in the body of the transcripts.

3. See also my discussion of oratorical harangues in Kulick 1992:139–47.

4. Those men known throughout the village as ones who sometimes have *kros*es are men who are either old widowers or divorced middle-aged men. That is, they are men without access to a woman's voice. Kulick 1993 is a much more detailed anaysis of gender and *kros*es.

REFERENCES

Barth, Fredrik. 1987. *Cosmologies in the Making*. Cambridge: Cambridge University Press.

Bloch, Maurice, and Jonathan Parry, eds. 1982. *Death and the Regeneration of Life*. Cambridge: Cambridge University Press.

Feld, Steven. 1990. *Sound and Sentiment: Birds, Weeping, Poetics and Song in Kaluli Expression*, 2nd ed. Philadelphia: University of Pennsylvania Press.

Goldman, Laurence. 1986. The Presentational Style of Women in Huli Disputes. *Pacific Linguistics* 24:213–289.

Harrison, Simon. 1990. *Stealing People's Names: History and Politics in a Sepik River Cosmology*. Cambridge: Cambridge University Press.

Kulick, Don. 1992. *Language Shift and Cultural Reproduction: Socialization, Self and Syncretism in a Papua New Guinean Village*. New York: Cambridge University Press.

———. 1993. Speaking as a Woman: Structure and Gender in Domestic Arguments in a Papua New Guinean Village. *Cultural Anthropology* 8(4):510–541.

Kulick, Don, and Christopher Stroud. 1990. Christianity, Cargo and Ideas of Self: Patterns of Literacy in a Papua New Guinean Village. *Man* 25:286–303.

———. 1993. Conceptions and Uses of Literacy in a Papua New Guinean Village. In *Cross-Cultural Approaches to Literacy*, ed. Brian Street, pp. 30–61. Cambridge: Cambridge University Press.

Lutz, Catherine. 1986. Emotion, Thought and Estrangement: Emotion as a Cultural Category. *Cultural Anthropology* 1:405–436.

———. 1990. Engendered Emotion: Gender, Power, and the Rhetoric of Emotional Control in American Discourse. In *Language and the Politics of Emotion*, ed. Catherine Lutz and Lila Abu-Lughod, pp. 69–91. Cambridge: Cambridge University Press.

Lutz, Catherine, and Lila Abu-Lughod, eds. 1990. *Language and the Politics of Emotion*. Cambridge: Cambridge University Press.

Nash, Jill. 1987. Gender Attributes and Equality: Men's Strength and Women's Talk Among the Nagovisi. In *Dealing with Inequality: Analysing Gender Relations in Melanesia and Beyond*, ed. Marilyn Strathern, pp. 150–173. Cambridge: Cambridge University Press.

Ochs, Elinor. 1988. *Culture and Language Development: Language Acquisition and Language Socialization in a Samoan Village*. New York: Cambridge University Press.

———. 1992. Indexing Gender. In *Rethinking Context: Language as an Interactive Phenomenon*, ed. Alessandro Duranti and Charles Goodwin, pp. 335–358. New York: Cambridge University Press.

Ochs [Keenan], Elinor. [1974] 1989. Norm-makers, Norm-breakers: Uses of Speech by Men and Women in a Malagasy Community. In *Explorations in the Ethnography of Speaking*, ed. Richard Bauman and Joel Sherzer, pp. 125–143. Cambridge: Cambridge University Press.

Reddy, Michael. 1979. The Conduit Metaphor—A Case of Frame Conflict in Our Language about Language. In *Metaphor and Thought*, ed. A. Ortony, pp. 284–324. Cambridge: Cambridge University Press.

Sankoff, Gillian. [1971] 1980. Language Use in Multilingual Societies: Some Alternate Approaches. In *The Social Life of Language*, pp. 29–46. Philadelphia: University of Pennsylvania Press.

Schieffelin, Bambi. 1990. *The Give and Take of Everyday Life: Language Socialization of Kaluli Children*. New York: Cambridge University Press.

Schieffelin, Edward L. 1976. *The Sorrow of the Lonely and the Burning of the Dancers*. New York: St. Martin's.

———. 1985. The Cultural Analysis of Depressive Affect: An Example from New Guinea. In *Culture and Depression: Studies in the Anthropology and Cross-cultural Psychiatry of Affect and Disorder*, ed. Arthur Kleinman and Byron Good, pp. 103–133. Berkeley: University of California Press.

Silverstein, Michael. 1985. Language and the Culture of Gender: At the Intersection of Structure, Usage, and Ideology. In *Semiotic Meditation: Sociocultural and Psychological Perspectives*, ed. Elizabeth Mertz and Richard J. Parmentier, pp. 219–259. New York: Academic Press.

Strathern, Marilyn. 1979. The Self in Self-Decoration. *Oceania* 49(4):241–257.

Stroud, Christopher. 1992. The Problem of Intention and Meaning in Code-switching. *Text* 12(1):127–155.

Watson-Gegeo, Karen Ann, and Geoffery M. White, eds. 1990. *Disentangling: Conflict Discourse in Pacific Societies*. Stanford, Calif.: Stanford University Press.

White, Geoffery M., and James Kirkpatrick, eds. 1985. *Person, Self, and Experience: Exploring Pacific Ethnopsychologies*. Berkeley: University of California Press.

5

Arizona Tewa Kiva Speech as a Manifestation of a Dominant Language Ideology

PAUL V. KROSKRITY

"What have you learned about the ceremonies?" Back in the summer of 1973, when I first began research on Arizona Tewa, I was often asked this and similar questions by a variety of villagers. I found this strange, even disconcerting, since the questions persisted after I explained my research interest as residing in the language "itself," or in "just the language, not the culture." But my response was very much a managed production. For though my originally formulated object of study was the Arizona Tewa language, even early on in what was to become long-term field research I had become very interested in the tangled relationship of Arizona Tewa language, culture, and society. But despite this interest, I had been coached by my academic advisers and informed by a scholarly tradition of research on Pueblo Indians to recognize the cultural sensitivity of research on religion and the suspicion directed at those who would nevertheless attempt to study it, even in its more esoteric forms. My professional training thus encouraged me to attribute these periodic inquiries to a combination of secrecy and suspicion regarding such culturally sensitive topics as ceremonial language. Yet despite my careful attempts to disclaim any research interest in kiva speech (*te'e hi:li*) and to carefully distinguish between it and the more mundane speech of everyday Arizona Tewa life, I still experienced these occasional interrogations. Did these questions betray a native confusion of the language of the kiva with that of the home and plaza? Was there a connection between these domains of discourse that was apparent to most Tewa villagers, yet hidden from me? In the past few years, after more than two decades of undertaking various studies of Arizona Tewa grammar, sociolinguistic variation, language contact, traditional narratives, codeswitching, and chanted announcements, an underlying pattern of language use has gradually emerged that, via the documentary method of interpretation, has allowed me to attribute a new meaning to these early inquiries.[1] The disparate linguistic and discourse practices of everyday speech, I contend, display a common pattern of influence from *te'e hi:li* 'kiva speech'. The more explicit rules for language use in ritual performance provide local models for the generation and evaluation of more mundane speech forms and verbal practices.

"LINGUISTIC IDEOLOGIES," taken in Michael Silverstein's (1979) sense as "sets of beliefs about language articulated by users as a rationalization or justification of perceived language structure and use," provide a useful frame for understanding the Arizona Tewa pattern. By viewing member's reflectivity, or what Giddens (1984) calls "reflexive monitoring," as an irreducible force in language behavior, the notion of linguistic ideology directs attention to cultural actors' rationalization of their own language activity. "The total linguistic fact, the datum for a science of language, is irreducibly dialectic in nature. It is an unstable mutual interaction of meaningful sign forms contextualized to situations of interested human use mediated by the fact of cultural ideology" (Silverstein 1985:220).

Examining the Arizona Tewa culture of language as a site for the investigation of language ideologies is multiply warranted. As a Pueblo Indian group that removed itself from Spanish influence in 1700 by migrating to the easternmost of the Hopi mesas and, since then, has maintained its indigenous Kiowa-Tanoan language, the Arizona Tewa are "twice blessed" with a cultural self-consciousness about language use. First, as Pueblo Indians, they are paragons of what Joel Sherzer (1976) and others have termed "linguistic conservatism"—that celebrated penchant for resistance to linguistic borrowing. But whatever analytical value this concept may have to students of language contact, it has at best only the most tentative footing in terms of its foundations in Arizona Tewa cultural experience. Examination of Arizona Tewa linguistic ideology, I contend, offers an alternative, socioculturally based interpretation—a deconstruction of "linguistic conservatism" into dimensions that are simultaneously more analytically precise and more rooted in Arizona Tewa local knowledge.

A second source of Arizona Tewa cultural emphasis on language is their own remarkable history of language contact and language maintenance. In the diaspora of the Pueblo Revolts of 1680 and 1696, the Arizona Tewa are the only outmigrating group that has retained its language into the present.[2] Maintenance of the Tewa language has served not only to perpetuate an ethnic boundary and to embody a "contrapuntal" linguistic consciousness (Said 1984:171–72) but also to mask a pattern of dramatic cultural change in adapting to the Hopi, the group to whom the ancestors of the Arizona Tewa migrated almost three hundred years ago. This adaptation was quite necessary for physical survival in the harsh western Pueblo environment. The Arizona Tewa saying *Na:-bí hi:li na:-bí wowa:ci na-mu* 'My language is my life (history)' reveals the intimate relationships among language, history, and identity that this migration has fostered, as well as the cultural salience of the connection. Thus, the culture-specific history of the Arizona Tewa has enhanced a Pan-puebloan attention to language that may account for its magnified local significance.

Local Knowledge and Linguistic Ideology

Though the role of native language maintenance in response to their Hopi hosts is somewhat peculiar to the Arizona Tewa, the cultural prominence of kiva speech—the speech performed in religious chambers when sacred ceremonial altars are erected—is common to all Pueblo societies. As a key symbol of Tewa linguistic values, kiva talk embodies four closely related cultural preferences: regulation by convention, indigenous purism, strict compartmentalization, and linguistic indexing of identity. For each of these I briefly sketch: (1) their basis in kiva talk, (2) their cultural salience as manifested in members' awareness, and (3) the "scope" and "force" with which these preferences are manifested in nonritual speech. By "cultural salience" I mean approximate location on a scale of awareness that ranges from practical consciousness/tacit knowledge, on the one hand, to discursive consciousness/explicit knowledge on the other (Giddens 1984). In using "scope" and "force" I follow Geertz's (1968) study of Islamic belief, in which he used the former to refer to the range of contexts in which some value or belief would be manifested and the later to characterize its intensity.

Regulation by Convention

In the kiva, ritual performers rely on fixed prayer and song texts. Innovation is neither desired nor tolerated. Proper ritual performance should replicate past conventions, and, if such repetition is impossible, the ritual should not be performed at all. Thus, in instances where the ceremonial knowledge has not been effectively transmitted from one priest to his apprentice, the ceremony becomes defunct. This concern with regulation by convention is manifested in everyday speech preferences by adherence to greeting formulae, to the extended use of kinship terms in address forms, to rules of hospitality involving kinsmen and visitors, and to avoidance of direct confrontation in interaction with fellow villagers. Culturally valued native genres, involving either histories or traditional stories, must carefully conform to the traditional formal precedents associated with those genres.

In traditional stories, for example, from the Arizona Tewa genre *pę́:yu'u*, audience members and performers alike honor a tradition that employs stylized, nonverbal accompaniment and uses familiar storytelling conventions. Foremost among these ways of "speaking the past" is the use of evidential *ba* as a genre marker (Kroskrity 1985a). By disclaiming any novelty on the part of the narrator, this particle and its repeated use provide a continuous and obligatory indexing of "the voice" of the traditional narrator. In example 1, the introductory sentence of the story "Coyote and Bullsnake" exemplifies a pattern of multiple occurrence within each sentence uttered in the voice of the narrator (as opposed to story characters' voices or frame-breaking asides in a personal voice).

speaking of the past, authenticity

(1) owę́heyam-ba	long:ago ba	Long ago, so they say
bayɛna-senó ba	Old Man Coyote ba	Old Man Coyote so
na-tha.[3]	he lived.	he lived.

Thus a particle that denotes the secondhand nature and traditional character of what is said—similar to our "so they say"—aptly functions as a discourse marker of a genre of traditional stories.

Even when narrators chose to "speak the present"—to contextualize their stories for specific audiences—such innovations should ideally occur in the voice of the narrator (e.g., through episode editing and elaboration, nonverbal audience specification, or the addition of identifying details that might be tied to specific audience members). Narrators who chose such frame-breaking strategies as code-switching and the introduction of a personal voice (unmarked by *ba*) or who merely forgot to clearly delineate the "voice of the traditional narrator" by excluding *ba* were negatively evaluated for their efforts by audience members, who criticized them for not telling it "right," not telling it the "old way."

If innovation, even in the form of contextualization, is to be culturally sanctioned, it must be cloaked in traditional garb. I encountered an interesting and creative use of traditional linguistic form one summer when I heard what sounded like a traditional Tewa public announcement (*tų́-khę́*). The chanter was clearly using the dramatic rising and falling intonations associated with the "public address" style reserved for crier chiefs to announce upcoming ceremonies or call for volunteers for village projects like cleaning out a spring, replastering the kiva, or for individuals to offer birth announcements or stylized grievance chants (Black 1967). But, while the form was traditional, its content and presenter were not. The chanter was issuing a call for a yard sale and inviting all within earshot to examine items of used clothing and some small appliances that she hoped to sell! An example of this is provided in example 2.

(2) (a) kwiyó:, he:wɛ khe: ʾi-kwʾón wí-tʾolo-kántʾó
women some clothes they-lie I/you-tell-will
Women: I'm telling you there are some clothes lying.

(b) nɛ́ʾɛ́ phíní-bí-kʾege ʾi:-kų-kwín -ɛ́ʾɛ́-mí
here Phini-ʾs-house you:all-buy-look-come-should
You all should come and shop at Phini's house.

(c) kinán dí-tų́-ʾán-dán wí-tʾolo-ʾán
this I/other-say-since I/you-tell-past
This is what I was told to tell you.

Though the "commercial" message was hardly traditional, the chanter won general village approval by conforming to the expected intonational and other prosodic patterns, as well as the verbal formulae associated with the genre. Despite the brevity of this "short notice" announcement, its obedience to such generic norms as initial addressee specification and its explicit acknowledgment of the announcer role, as well as its prosodic fidelity to traditional models, prompted all but the most ultraconservative villagers to overlook the fact that the chanter was a woman (Kroskrity

1992:110–12).[4] Importantly, both the gender of the chanter and the chant's commercial content—both violations in a genre normally performed by men announcing communal activities—were subordinated in public opinion to an approval of its traditional form.

Members' awareness of the value of conventionality is often, as the preceding examples show, quite explicit. While many individuals praise traditionality for its own sake and accept it as a guiding principle, relatively few (with the exception of older members of the ceremonial elite) related this value to the emphasis on replicating past performances or the importance of precedent in calculating ceremonial privilege. One ceremonially well-placed man compared everyday speech to prayers:

> You know when we talk to each other it is like when we pray. We look for a way of saying things that has been handed down to us by our grandfathers and grandmothers. We like something old that has lived into the present. It must be strong and powerful to do that. Only difference between prayers and [everyday] talk is that we don't send our prayers to people.

This analogy suggests that ceremonial practitioners' greater experiential familiarity with the realm of kiva speech may provide them with a greater awareness of the intertextuality of kiva and mundane speech than is accessible to those less experienced.

Indigenous Purism

Indigenous purism and strict compartmentalization are two dimensions of Arizona Tewa linguistic ideology that, though analytically distinguishable, are intimately joined in most linguistic practices. During ritual performance there is an explicit and enforced proscription against the use of foreign words and/or native vocabulary clearly identified with an equally alien social dialect (such as slang, recently manufactured words lacking any association to prestigious individuals or activities [Newman 1955]). As for enforcement, Frank Hamilton Cushing's experience is exemplary. For uttering a Spanish word in a Zuni kiva he was struck forcefully across the arms by a whipper kachina. After being so purified, he was instructed to say the Zuni equivalent of "Thank you." In his discussion of vocabulary levels of the Zuni, Stanley Newman appears to dismiss purism in passages such as the following:

> Likewise obviously borrowed words, such as *melika* "Anglo-American" cannot be used in the kiva. This prohibition against loanwords is obviously not to be equated with traditions of linguistic purism, whereby organizations in many modern national states legislate against foreignisms that threaten to adulterate the native language. It stems rather from the general Zuni injunction against bringing unregulated innovation into ceremonial situations. Using a word like *melika*, as one informant expressed it, would be like bringing a radio into the kiva. (1955:349)

Though Newman has discouraged the interpretation of such kiva practices as strictly analogous to enforced policies of language purism in contemporary nation-states, the kind of purism that Newman is dismissing amounts to an official proscription of linguistic diffusion (e.g., loanwords, grammatical interference) not only in ceremonial speech but in everyday speech as well. But Tewa ceremonial leaders, like those of other pueblos, are not waging a campaign to dictate everyday speech norms. Any purging of foreignisms in everyday speech represents a popular extrapolation, a symbolic "trickle-down" influence of the salient and prestigious model of kiva speech. The primary concern of ceremonial leaders is with maintaining and delimiting a distinctive and appropriate linguistic variety, or vocabulary level, for religious expression, not with minimizing foreign linguistic influence. The strong sanctions against foreign expressions in ceremonial speech, sanctions that involve physical punishment, are motivated not by the linguistic expression of xenophobia or extreme ethnocentrism but by the need for stylistic consistency in a highly conventionalized liturgical speech level. Similarly, the negative evaluation of instances of code-mixing in everyday speech by members of the Arizona Tewa speech community reflects not the prevalence of negative attitudes about these other languages but rather the functioning of ceremonial speech as a local model of linguistic prestige. This role should not be too surprising when we observe that the prestige that accrues to "standard languages" in modern nation-states emanates, in part, from the support of and their use by national governments and in part from their association with formal education. Since Pueblo societies are traditionally theocratic, fusing political power and religious authority, and since ceremonial leaders must acquire appropriate knowledge through rigorous verbal instruction, the functional role and cultural associations of ceremonial speech are actually quite analogous to standard languages that derive their prestige from the institutional support of both government and formal education.

Further supporting this claim that the negative evaluation of codemixing, especially prevalent in older speakers (Kroskrity 1978), is attributable more to local models than to xenophobia are two types of telling observations. First, speakers regulate language mixing from languages that they highly value and use proficiently. Certainly, the Arizona Tewa, as I have argued elsewhere (Kroskrity 1993:46–47, 206–10), have many social identities that are performed in the nonethnic languages of their linguistic repertoire: Hopi and English. Hopi is an essential medium of intervillage communication and the appropriate language for relating to Hopi kinsmen. Command of English has permitted the Arizona Tewa to gain significant economic and political advantages over the Hopi in their role as cultural brokers, mediating between Euro-Americans and the more conservative Hopi. Fluency in these languages is necessary for full participation in Arizona Tewa society. Though fluency in these languages is never criticized by the Tewa, language mixing between these languages is routinely and consistently devalued. Second, there is a well-established tradition of "song renewal" from other linguistic traditions (Humphreys 1982). Entire songs, solely encoded in foreign languages, are often performed in Tewa Village and throughout the Pueblos. It is difficult to explain the popularity of this tradition if one wants to argue for a xenophobic interpretation of ideal speech norms against codeswitching.

Though the Arizona Tewa clearly lack the deliberation and institutional enforcement often associated with "purist" movements, Arizona Tewa indigenous purism may not lack other attributes that language planning theorists associate with linguistic purism. Scholars such as Jernudd (1989:4), for example, view such movements in modern nation states as consisting of a bidirectional process that involves the simultaneous opening of native resources and the closing off of nonnative ones for linguistic change. Manfred Henningsen (1989:31–32) expands on the latter aspect when he says, "the politics of purity . . . originates in a quest for identity and authenticity of a cultural Self that feels threatened by the hegemonic pressure of another culture." Annamalai (1989:225), too, observes that purism is "manifest when there is social change affecting the structure of social control." But while resistance to hegemony and rapid sociocultural change may be the prerequisite of linguistic purism in modern nation-states, these conditions have also prevailed for the Arizona Tewa and their Southern Tewa ancestors since the time of Spanish contact in the sixteenth century. From the repressive colonial program of the Spanish, to postmigration Hopi stigmatization and segregation, to "domestic" colonization by the United States, it is certainly possible to find a consistent pattern of Tewa resistance to hegemonic pressure. But it would be wrong to assume that purism is coincident with such hegemony, that it is largely a component of a "counterlinguistic" response by the Arizona Tewa and their ancestors to a series of oppressions.[5] Data from contact with Apachean languages traceable to the late pre-Spanish contact period shows the same pattern of loanword suppression (Kroskrity 1982, 1985b) and strongly suggests that the practice of indigenous purism was already in place. What has been even more continuous than hegemonic pressure from outside is the prestigious position of the traditional religious leaders—an "internal" hegemonic force—and the speech norms associated with them.

But if Arizona Tewa indigenous purism lacks a social organization dedicated to its systematic enforcement, the Arizona Tewa people themselves are usually quite explicit about its value. In Albert Yava's approximation of a life history known as *Big Falling Snow*, he proudly compares the Arizona Tewa to the Rio Grande Tewa: "We still speak the Tewa language and we speak it in a more pure form than the Rio Grande Tewas do. Over there in New Mexico the Tewa language has been corrupted by other Pueblo languages and Spanish. We also speak Hopi fluently though there are very few Hopis who can converse in Tewa" (1978:1).

Strict Compartmentalization

The third value, strict compartmentalization, is also of great importance to the understanding of Arizona Tewa linguistic ideology. Essential to kiva talk is the maintenance of a distinctive linguistic variety that is dedicated to a well-demarcated arena of use. Kiva talk would lose its integrity if it admitted expressions from other languages or from other linguistic levels. Likewise, if kiva talk were to be spoken outside of ceremonial contexts, it would profane this liturgical variety and constitute a flagrant violation. This strict compartmentalization of language forms and use has often been recognized as a conspicuous aspect of the language attitudes of Pueblo cultures (Dozier 1956, Sherzer 1976:244). What is novel here is the recognition that this value, like regulation by convention and indigenous purism, is traceable to the adoption of kiva talk as the local model of linguistic prestige. Just as ceremonial practitioners can neither mix linguistic codes nor use them outside their circumscribed contexts of use, so—ideally—Tewa people should observe comparable compartmentalization of their various languages and linguistic levels in their everyday speech. The mixing of Tewa with either English or Hopi is explicitly devalued by members of the Tewa speech community, though in unguarded speech some mixing does occur. It is interesting that in the Tewa folk account of speech variation, social categories are ranked in respect to the perceived avoidance of language mixing. Older speakers, for example, are said to approximate this ideal more than younger. Men do so more than women. It should be emphasized that this folk perception can be readily interpreted as a reflection of the different participation of these groups in ceremonial activities, of their differential proximity to the realm of kiva talk.

Examination of both historical linguistic data and more contemporary sociolinguistic studies of the Arizona Tewa confirms the selective influence of indigenous purism and strict compartmentalization. Since I have already extensively reviewed this trend elsewhere (Kroskrity 1993:55–108), it is appropriate to summarize and highlight a pattern of linguistic ideology that shapes the form of linguistic diffusion in three periods of language contact. The pattern features the suppression of linguistic borrowing, especially in the lexicon. In multilingual episodes with Apacheans, the Spanish, and the Hopi lasting 100, 150, and 191 years, respectively, the Arizona Tewa language has admitted two Apachean, seventeen Spanish, and one Hopi loanword (Kroskrity 1982, 1993). Clearly, Arizona Tewa folk linguists have put into practice the indigenous purist and the strict compartmentalization planks of Arizona Tewa linguistic ideology. But there is also clear evidence that folk attention is selective. The approximation of these ideals in actual practice presupposes a folk perception of "alien" linguistic structures, and yet Arizona Tewa linguists, unlike our own, are primarily if not exclusively lexicographers. Abundant evidence suggests that several grammatical structures in Arizona Tewa are the result of linguistic convergence. Thus, as illustrated in example 3, the innovation of a possessive or relational suffix in Tewa appears to be the result of contact with Apachean languages.

(3)	TEWA	NAVAJO
	sen-bí 'é:nu	hastiin bi-ye'
	man-'s son	man 's[6]–song
	(a) man's son	(a) man's song
	'é:nu -bí nų́'ų́	hastiin bi-ch'ą́ą́h
	boy -'s under	man 's-front
	under the boy	in front of the man

These two phrases, in both Arizona Tewa and Navajo, demonstrate both the phonological and the grammatical similarity of the affixes. In both languages, these constituents are used in possessive constructions and with locative postpositions. Significantly, no other Kiowa-Tanoan language has this constituent (Kroskrity 1985b). This strongly suggests grammatical diffusion from Apachean languages as the source for Arizona Tewa *-bí*.

Similarly, Arizona Tewa has innovated a new passive suffix, which now alternates with an inherited one shared by Rio Grande Tewa. Example 4 illustrates the parallel Arizona Tewa and Hopi constructions.

(4)	TEWA		HOPI	
	p'o	na-kulu-tí	taawi	yuk-ilti
	water	it-pour-PASSIVE	song	finish-PASSIVE
	The water was poured.		The song was finished.	

(Kalectaca 1978:132)

Though Arizona Tewa has a passive suffix, *-n,* which it shares with Rio Grande Tewa, the *-tí* suffix represents a grammatical borrowing from analogous Hopi structures. Again, in an instance of ongoing linguistic change emerging from sociolinguistic variation, younger Arizona Tewa speakers now produce only one of the three structural alternatives for realizing phrasal conjunction that are available for the oldest generation of speakers (Kroskrity 1982). Significantly, it is the one that converges with English structures of the type N and N (i.e., N-ádí N), as represented in example 5:

(5) sen-ná-dí kwiyó-wá-dí
sen-ná-dí kwiyó
sen kwiyó-wá-dí
the man and the woman

There is also evidence that some discourse phenomena join grammar in their location outside the awareness of speakers. In comparative studies of Hopi, Arizona Tewa, and Rio Grande Tewa narratives, I found that, though the Arizona Tewa evidential particle *ba,* as discussed in relation to example 1, was clearly related to a homologous one in Rio Grande Tewa, its pattern of usage more clearly resembled that of the Hopi quotative particle *yaw,* as in Arizona Tewa (example 6) and Hopi (example 7):

(6)	'i-wɛ	ba,	di-powa-di ba,	'ó:bé-khwo:li-mak'a-ként'ó-di
	there-at	ba,	they-arrive-SUB[7]	they:INV-fly-teach-SUB

From there so, having arrived so, they were being taught to fly.

(7)	noq	yaw	'ora:yvi	'atka	ki:tava	yaw	piw	'tɨcvo	ki'yta
	and	yaw	Oraibi	below:south	from:village	yaw	also	wren	she-live

And wren also lived below Oraibi, south of the village.

(from Seumptewa, Voegelin, and Voegelin 1980)

In its frequent and multiple occurrence within sentences, as well as its general service as a genre marker, the Arizona Tewa pattern of use appears to have converged with the Hopi and departed from the norms of other Tewa narrative traditions.

As an ideological preference, "strict compartmentalization" is tangible not only in the practical consciousness of Arizona Tewa speech behavior but also in the "discursive consciousness" of some members. One older man who had recently had primary responsibility for the performance of an important village ceremony offered the following agricultural imagery in his explication of the practice of strict compartmentalization and its ceremonial connections.

> This way we keep kiva speech separate from everyday speech reminds me of the way we plant corn. You know those different colors [of corn] just don't happen. If you want blue corn, if you want red corn, you must plant your whole field only in that color. If you plant two together you get only mixed corn. But we need to keep our colors different for the ceremonies. That's why we have so many fields far from one another. Same way our languages. If you mix them they are no longer as good and useful. The corn is a lot like our languages—we work to keep them separate.

This example of native explication demonstrates that strict compartmentalization is not always an unconscious activity but, on occasions and by some individuals, also a discursive strategy that can be both rationalized and naturalized as obedience to ceremonial dictates.

Linguistic Indexing of Identity

The final dimension of Tewa linguistic ideology concerns itself with the Tewa preference for locating the speaking self in a linguistically well-defined, possibly positional, sociocultural identity and the belief that speech behavior in general expresses important information about the speaker's identity. Related to this is a comment once made to me by Albert Yava regarding the way attention to the speech of others is used to locate them in sociocultural space: "I only have to hear someone talk for a short while before I know who they are and where they have been." In addition to this cultural idea that one's speech is a linguistic biography, the model of ritual speech foregrounds the importance of positional, rather than personal, identities and the use of appropriate role-specific speech.

Outside of kiva talk, we find similar emphases in the more mundane genres of traditional stories and public announcements. In stories, as mentioned earlier, the narrator establishes and maintains his status through adoption of the full range of narrative conventions, including the use of evidential *ba*. These practices permit narrators to adopt the voice of the traditional storyteller in order to "speak the past." Similarly, a conventional component of public announcements is the explicit acknowledgment by the chanter of his mediating status as spokesperson. The scope of this penchant for conveying identity through use of an associated code extends to casual conversation. Among trilingual Tewa men conversing in domestic settings it was not unusual to hear codeswitching deployed for just such expressive purposes. Example 8, extracted from a more detailed study of codeswitching (Kroskrity 1993:193–210) is a brief strip of talk in which a codeswitch signals a reformulation of identity for the speaking selves.

(8) F: [HOPI] Tutuqayki-t qa-naanawakna.
'Schools were not wanted.'

G: [TEWA] Wé-dí-t'ókán-k'ege-na'a-di im-bí akhon-i-di.
'They didn`t want a school on their land.'

H: [TEWA] Nɛmbi e:yɛ nɛ̨lɛ̨-mo díbí-t'o-'am-mí ką:yį́'i we-di-mu:di.
'It's better our children go to school right here rather than far away.'

Three senior Tewa men have been discussing then recent news about the selection of an on-reservation site for the building of a high school. This topic follows from prior discussion of other building projects on the reservation. As is customary in discussing extravillage reservation matters, the conversation, to which all three men have contributed, has been conducted in Hopi. Speaker F merely notes the opposition to previous efforts to create an on-reservation high school. But speakers G and H switch to Tewa to reformulate their speaking selves as Tewa—members of a group that historically has opposed Hopi obstruction of building plans. G's use of Tewa further distances him from the Hopi "they" who opposed use of "their" tribal lands as school sites. H states what has historically been the Arizona Tewa argument for a reservation high school. Since, in retrospect, most Hopi and Tewa individuals now recognize the disruptive impact on their children over the past few decades of attending boarding schools, H's remark also evaluates the essential correctness of the position promoted by their ethnic group. In both G's and H's remarks, the selection of the "marked" code given the topic reformulates their relevant interactional identity as Arizona Tewa. Thus, the practice of maintaining maximally distinctive codes through strict compartmentalization provides the Tewa with appropriate linguistic resources in order to invoke a variety of corresponding sociocultural identities in interaction. Awareness (Silverstein 1981) of this aspect of language use on the part of Arizona Tewa speakers is, predictably, selective. Many speakers recognize the resources that their linguistic repertoires provide in permitting them to perform multiple social identities. These speakers often liken their languages and linguistic levels to masks and costumes worn for a specific ceremony.

But it is useful to note that, although the Arizona Tewa openly acknowledge a close association between language and identity, as mentioned earlier, they do not recognize conversational codeswitching as a locus for the expression of identity. This is, no doubt, tied to the fact that most Arizona Tewa trilinguals deny that they codeswitch, even though they routinely engage in this practice. This denial may reflect not only the fact that these behaviors are largely taken for granted but also a popular confusion between culturally devalued "codemixing" and codeswitching. Of much greater cultural salience are members' discourses on language and identity, which either invoke the Tewa practice of multiple names or compare the activity of speaking different languages to wearing different ceremonial masks (Kroskrity 1993:46–47).

Some members view the cultural practice of having many names and acquiring new names as one progresses through the ceremonial system as the most salient connection between language and identity. The discourse involving analogies to impersonation of kachinas is, of course, limited to those men who have "impersonated" kachinas in public ceremonies. The comparisons to such ceremonial performances requires some further commentary, since the dramaturgical imagery of a western view—involving personae, masks, and impersonation—invites a very nonlocal interpretation. For the Arizona Tewa, as for other Pueblo groups, so-called masks are viewed as living "friends" (*k'ema*), and masking is not a means of hiding one's "real" identity or donning a false one but rather an act of transformation in which the performer becomes the being that is iconically represented by his clan's "friend." When such local meanings are taken into account, it is clear that the imagery of ceremonial performance, even if available only to a restricted group, provides a discourse that recognizes the constitutive role of language in iconically signaling a member's relevant identity.

Conclusions

In this chapter I have explored the potentially fruitful application of the notion of language ideology to the Arizona Tewa speech community. In this section, I attempt to highlight some of the uses of a language ideological approach to the Arizona Tewa data by examining its applicability to two general accounts of Pueblo languages and cultures: the "linguistic conservatism" of the Pueblo Southwest and the relationship of Arizona Tewa language ideology to the political economies of Western Pueblo societies. After this, I return to the issue of members' awareness, or consciousness, as a criterial attribute of language ideologies and suggest that successfully "naturalized" and "contending" language ideologies are routinely associated with different levels of member's awareness.

I start by agreeing with Friedrich (1989:309), who distinguishes several especially valuable senses of "ideology." I employ two of these distinctions in my concluding remarks as a means of assessing both what has been accomplished and what remains to be done. Attending to the "notional" sense of ideology as the basic notions or ideas that members have about a well-demarcated area of a culture, an attention to culturally dominant linguistic ideology greatly improves on the limited "etic" understanding provided by the notion of "linguistic conservatism." Though Pueblo Indian communities are often said to exhibit this trait, scholars have also prematurely reified the notion of linguistic conservatism, treating it as if it were both a self-explanatory and an irreducible analytical account (Kroskrity 1993:213–21). Representative of this approach is Joel Sherzer when he attempts to account for why the indigenous Southwest lacks evidence of linguistic sharing despite its relatively high population density and long-term coresidence of neighboring groups:

> The explanation for this situation may be found in a sociolinguistic factor about which we rarely have data—attitude toward language. The Southwest is one area for which many observers have reported attitudes toward one's own language and that of others, perhaps because these attitudes are often very explicit. Southwest Indians are very conservative with respect to language . . . taking pride in their own language and sometimes refusing to learn that of others. (1976:244)

But language ideology, in this notional sense, permits an account that better captures the cultural unity of otherwise disparate linguistic norms and discourse practices and the guided agency of Tewa speakers in exercising their necessarily selective control over their linguistic resources. In the "pragmatic" (Friedrich 1989:297) or "critical" sense (see Woolard, this volume) elaborated here, language ideology provides analytical access to the social processes that construct those practices and attitudes labeled "linguistically conservative" by outside experts. The Arizona Tewa were and continue to be an instructive example of how folk consciousness and rationalization of language structure and use can have a powerful effect on language contact outcomes.

The "pragmatic" sense of ideology—the strategies, practical symbols, and systems of ideas used for promoting, perpetuating, or changing a social or cultural order—directs attention to the role of such local models of language as instruments of power and social control. It is important to remember that Pueblo ceremonial language, like ceremonial behavior in general, is not only the expression of religious belief through the sacred manipulation of cosmic forces but also the implicit justification of rule by a largely hereditary ceremonial elite. Thus, linguistic ideology provides a socially motivated explanation for the sociocultural processes that inform the local beliefs about language and the linguistic products that are labeled merely by the expression "linguistic conservatism." Moreover, linguistic ideology offers an ethnolinguistic account that provides an insightful microcultural complement to recent ethnographic and ethnohistorical efforts to rethink the sociocultural order of "egalitarian" Pueblo societies. Peter Whiteley's (1988) *Deliberate Acts* and Jerrold Levy's *Orayvi Revisited* (1992) have signaled an important turn in a scholarly tradition that had represented the Hopi and other Pueblo groups as if each were an "apolitical, egalitarian society" (Whiteley 1988:64). In Whiteley's analysis of how the Orayvi—the oldest continuously inhabited Hopi village—split as a resolution of factional disputes, he recognizes the importance of local distinctions between *pavansinom* 'ruling people' and *sukavuungsinom* 'common people'. In this ceremonially based system of stratification, ritual privilege—such as ownership and control of group ceremony—symbolizes and rationalizes an indigenous hierarchy that is critical to understanding the accomplishment of order, as well as the occasional disorders that characterize Hopi village societies. Levy's reanalysis of early field research in Orayvi by the anthropologist Mischa Titiev further establishes the stratified nature of Hopi society and also offers an account of why Hopi social inequality was routinely reconfigured in representations by such scholars as Mischa Titiev (1944) and Fred Eggan (1950) as basically egalitarian. Levy reveals a patterned relationship between ceremonial standing and the control of land that indicates that those clans that "owned" the most important ceremonies also had the most and the best land for farming. As Levy (1992:156) observes, "The system of stratification worked to manage scarcity, not abundance." In a subsistence economy in a high desert environment notorious for meager and inconsistent resources, the Hopi religious hierarchy created a stratification, not only of clans but of lineages within clans, that prioritized those most essential to the performance of required village ceremonies. In times of famine, the hierarchy served as a built-in mechanism for instructing low-status clans and lineages to leave the village so as to create the least disruption to the ceremonial order. While Levy's discussion about the management of scarcity is more true of Western Pueblos and their necessary reliance on "dry farming," the notion of an indigenous hierarchy is clearly extendable to Rio Grande Tewa pueblos like San Juan, where Ortiz (1969:16–18) recognizes an opposition between "made people" and "dry food people" that parallels that between "ruling" and "commoner" classes. The Arizona Tewa also recognize a similar opposition between *pa: t'owa* (made people) and *wɛ t'owa* (weed people).[8]

But it is important to emphasize that in Levy's analysis the ceremonial system not only rationalizes a hierarchy but also serves to mask it by offering an alternative ideology of equality and mutual dependence. For village ritual to be successful, it must enjoy the participation not only of sponsoring clans and lineages but also of many others who participate in a variety of ways—from actual ritual performance to the provision of food for performers. In participating in a ritual sponsored by another clan, villagers expected that their efforts would be reciprocated by others when a ceremony sponsored by their own clan was to be performed. The net effect of what Levy calls the "ceremonial ideology" is the erasure of clan ownership and the transformation of a clan-specific ritual into "shared" village ceremony:

> Although an ideology emphasizing the importance of all Hopis and all ceremonial activities was probably an essential counterbalance to the divisiveness of social stratification, it is important to recognize that the integrative structural mechanisms were also an important ingredient. Opportunity for participation in the ceremonial life was sufficient to prevent the alienation of the common people under the normal conditions of life. (1992:78)

Thus, in Levy's analysis, the ceremonial system served to integrate Hopi society by providing crosscutting relationships of responsibility across clans and lineages, making Hopi society more than the sum of its otherwise divisively strong kin groups. Coupled with such structural mechanisms as marriage regulation (the requirement that one marry outside both of one's parents' clans) and the extension of kinship relations along ceremonial lines (e.g., ceremonial "mothers" and "fathers"), the importance of the ceremonial system as a means of both erasing clan and class divisions and fostering village and ethnic identities becomes clear (Kroskrity 1994). Thus, the ceremonial system can be viewed as a source of the "ideal" egalitarian society, as well as the "ideal" person (Geertz 1990), often felt and expressed by members who have, in turn, communicated this vision to anthropologists who have, in turn, represented it as an essential feature of Hopi society.[9] Given the importance and power of ritual performance as a rite of unification, it is no wonder that the kiva serves as the "site" of the Arizona Tewa dominant language ideology (Silverstein 1992, this volume). Associated both with the theocratic "authority" of a ruling elite and the promise of a ceremonially based social mobility to commoners, kiva speech provides a model that crosses the boundaries of class and clan. For as Bourdieu (1991:113) observes, "the language of authority never governs without the collaboration of those it governs, without the help of the social mechanisms capable of producing this complicity."

Although kiva speech is associated with the cultural salience of group ritual, these highly "naturalized" (Bourdieu 1977:164) ritual privileges and events, including kiva speech itself, promote a "taken for grantedness" (Schutz 1967:74) of this language ideological site and a "practical consciousness" (Giddens 1984) of the role of kiva speech as a model for everyday speech. As discussed earlier in this chapter,

members have a partial awareness of this system, which occasionally surfaces in members' "discursive consciousness" of selected aspects of their language structure and use. The consistency of Arizona Tewa beliefs about language, their partial awareness of how these beliefs can affect language practices, their selective success in activating this awareness in actual practice, and the capacity of individuals to alter their consciousness of the system depending on their interests and "zones of relevance" (Heeren 1974) all argue for a treatment as "language ideological," despite the general lack of "discursive consciousness."[10] It is perhaps a further commentary on the internal diversity of the language ideology literature already noted by Woolard in her introduction to this volume that as I argue for the expansion and recentering of "language ideology" to be more inclusive, partly by the inclusion of ideologies of practice and practical consciousness, others have called for its elimination. Charles Briggs (1992:400), for example, argues that "ideology" tends to suggest either a "fixed, abstracted, and circumscribed set of beliefs" divorced from their constitution in action or "erroneous and derivative notions that can only provide insight into the means by which Others celebrate their own mystification."

Noting that "beliefs about language are multiple, competing, contradictory and contested," Briggs proposes a Foucault-inspired conceptual shift to "metadiscursive strategies" (Briggs 1992:398–400). But while such a perspective might better capture the more self-conscious reflections of Warao shamans, or of American feminists in their rejection of generic "he" (Silverstein 1985), it is important to observe that ideological contention and discursive consciousness are in a relationship of mutual dependence. Debates and other displays of contention necessarily problematize formerly taken-for-granted language practices, and this self-consciousness of language is the very condition for rationalizing or challenging conventional practices.

Of course, such an emphasis on strategy and contestation suggests that these are omnipresent in social life and consciousness. But I have already argued that successfully "naturalized" beliefs and practices, such as the role of Arizona Tewa kiva speech as a "prestige model" for everyday verbal conduct, are not publicly challenged and seldom enter members' discursive consciousness. Any rethinking of language ideology that would exclude naturalized, dominant ideologies and thus analytically segregate beliefs about language according to a criterion of consciousness seems to me to be unwise. Since dominant ideologies can become contended ideologies over time and since members vary, both interindividually and intraindividually, in their degree of consciousness, the creation of a categorical boundary between such language beliefs would falsify their dynamic relationship. But while I can hardly second Briggs's proposed shift to "metadiscursive strategies," I do share his concern to avoid associating language ideology with either the pejorative vision of others' "false consciousness" of their linguistic resources or the valorization of the sociolinguist who can truly and exhaustively comprehend the total system.

This may be an appropriate point to respond briefly, as this volume goes to press, to some related remarks that appear in Charles Briggs's chapter in this volume. It is appropriate, in part, because Briggs—despite his many contributions in that work—seems to privilege the analytical perspective associated with the presumably more exhaustive account of the outside expert, rather than the appeal to members' consciousness that is an important aspect of my work here. It is certainly appropriate for Briggs to reassert an important theme in the literature on language ideology—the multiplicity of language ideologies and their association with contestation (Gal 1993, Woolard this volume). I certainly agree with him that even dominant ideologies are contested and that *"contestation is a crucial facet of how particular ideologies and practices come to be dominant"* (emphasis his). But while such contestation may underlie the genesis and reproduction of all ideologies, it is important to observe that members do not seem to regard all language ideologies as debatable or as equally subject to discussion. In other words, my preliminary typology of dominant versus contending was meant to include local knowledge and not just expert knowledge. While it may be epistemologically more sophisticated to axiomatically assume that all ideologies must be contending, as Briggs has done, it is a critical aspect of the very notion of language ideology that we attend to members' awareness and understandings of their language and discursive practices. The very reifications that Briggs cautions students of language ideology to avoid are thus often undeniably conspicuous features of members' local knowledge to which analysts must attend. Though language ideology, in the Silverstein tradition followed here, does begin as a pejorative notion (Hill this volume), it has not been reserved for cultural others (e.g., Collins this volume, Mertz this volume, Woolard 1989). And while linguists and students of language in social life will always be fascinated by the difference between "local" and professional accounts, we should also be prepared to concede that in the multilayered sociocultural worlds in which we live and analyze, our best efforts at understanding, whether we are experts or members, can be only "partial truths" (Clifford 1986).

Given the connections between ceremonial and more mundane speech delineated here, as well as the partial awareness of it reflected in the rejection of my early claims to diplomatic immunity through appeal to an "autonomous" language, it is no wonder that my early Tewa interrogators found their language so valuable and my linguistic research so controversial.

NOTES

1. By "documentary method of interpretation" I mean the ethnomethodological process that provides that retrospective clarity and revised interpretation in the construction of both commonsense and expert knowledge (Garfinkel 1967:77ff.).

2. For a more complete discussion of the Pueblo diaspora, interested readers should consult Sando 1992:63–78, Simmons 1979, and Schroeder 1979. In using the term "diaspora" to describe the impact of the Spanish colonial program and the resulting Pueblo Revolts, I am following the more "descriptive" model suggested by Clifford 1994, rather than the prescriptive model endorsed by Safran 1991 and others. Insofar as the Arizona Tewa are concerned, they certainly qualify as an expatriate minority community, and their history on First Mesa has been characterized by what Said 1984 has described as the "contrapuntal" self-consciousness, the imposed awareness of exile. The Arizona Tewa do not fit models that require that a diasporic group maintain an ongoing memory of the displaced homeland or a desire to return to such an ancestral site. Though this is not the place for an extended discussion on this topic, it is useful to indicate that the Arizona Tewas' lack of nostalgia for their ancestral homeland is importantly connected to their successful

multiethnic integration into First Mesa Hopi society and to the fact that their former villages are not ongoing communities but rather defunct pueblos long since abandoned.

3. For ease of presentation to a diverse audience, I have opted to use an orthography that departs from conventional Americanist practices in at least two respects. I have eliminated superscript indications of secondary articulation (e.g., aspiration, palatalization) and have instead represented these with digraphs.

4. Announcements display varying degrees of elaboration, depending on whether they are seen as "advance" or "short" notice. The latter are often viewed as reminders and do not contain the full details.

5. I am using "counterlinguistic" here as an adjectival form of what Marcyliena Morgan 1993 calls "counterlanguage." In this and other works, she successfully demonstrates how indigenous discourse preferences, especially those involving indirection, inform African American counterlanguage by creating messages that are simultaneously transparent to members yet opaque to outside oppressors. My point here is that purism appears to predate the Spanish colonial program and therefore is not explainable as a response to Spanish hegemony. It is interesting to speculate that kiva speech may have acquired a connotation of counterlanguage during the early colonial program, when native religion was actively suppressed by the Spanish. It is doubtful, however, that such a connotation would have extended to the Hopi mesas, where the Spanish were never a formidable military presence, or last into the period of "cultural adjustment" after the second Pueblo Revolt, when the Spanish terminated the policy of religious persecution (Schroeder 1972:59–67). It is also important to observe that African American "counterlanguage" utilizes African speech values that are embodied in everyday speech practices, whereas kiva speech is a sacred lect conventionally set apart from more mundane speech behavior.

6. Though Apachean *bi-* is the source for Tewa *-bi*, Tewa has overgeneralized it as a general possessive morpheme, whereas in the Apachean languages it is limited to the third person.

7. SUB is an abbreviated gloss for subordinator, a grammatical marker for dependent clauses.

8. Ortiz 1969 also recognizes a third class that mediates this opposition between made people and "dry food people"—the *t'owa 'e*, a level of secular government officials that dates at least to the time of Spanish occupation.

9. Levy 1992 also suggests that once prevailing social science notions such as Redfield's "folk society" contributed to an intellectual climate in which ethnographers like Titiev and Eggan would deemphasize Hopi social stratification.

10. Here I follow a phenomenological approach (Schutz 1966, Heeren 1974) in which "zones of relevance" reflect the degree of relevance to an actor's project of a given interaction. Thus, awareness of interactional or symbolic detail may be heightened or altered, depending on the immediacy of that actor's imposed or intrinsic interests. For example, a young Tewa man might become acutely aware of kinship and the practicalities of the rules of clan exogamy when he begins to "date" women from his own village. Yet this same awareness might have been previously regarded as "relatively irrelevant" before that point.

REFERENCES

Annamalai, E. 1989. The Linguistic and Social Dimensions of Purism. In *The Politics of Language Purism*, ed. Björn H. Jernudd and Michael J. Shapiro, pp. 225–231. Berlin: Mouton de Gruyter.

Black, Robert. 1967. Hopi Grievance Chants: A Mechanism of Social Control. In *Studies in Southwestern Ethnolinguistics*, ed. Dell H. Hymes and William E. Bittle, pp. 54–67. The Hague: Mouton.

Briggs, Charles L. 1992. Linguistic Ideologies and the Naturalization of Power in Warao Discourse. *Pragmatics* 2:387–404.

Bourdieu, Pierre. 1977. *Outline of a Theory of Practice*. Cambridge: Cambridge University Press.

———. 1991. *Language and Symbolic Power*. Cambridge, Mass.: Harvard University Press.

Clifford, James. 1986. Introduction: Partial Truths. In *Writing Culture*, ed. James Clifford and George E. Marcus, pp. 1–26. Berkeley: University of California Press.

———. 1994. Diasporas. *Cultural Anthropology* 9:302–338.

Collins, James. 1992. Our Ideologies and Theirs. *Pragmatics* 2:405–416.

Dozier, Edward P. 1956. Two Examples of Linguistic Acculturation: The Yaqui of Sonora and the Tewa of New Mexico. *Language* 32:146–157.

———. 1966. Factionalism at Santa Clara Pueblo. *Ethnology* 5:172–185.

Eggan, Fred. 1950. *Social Organization of the Western Pueblos*. Chicago: University of Chicago Press.

Friedrich, Paul. 1989. Language, Ideology, and Political Economy. *American Anthropologist* 91:295–312.

Garfinkel, Harold. 1967. *Studies in Ethnomethodology*. Englewood Cliffs, N.J.: Prentice Hall.

Geertz, Clifford. 1968. *Islam Observed: Religious Developments in Morocco and Indonesia*. Chicago: University of Chicago Press.

Giddens, Anthony. 1984. *The Constitution of Society*. Berkeley: University of California Press.

Heeren, John. 1974. Alfred Schutz and the Sociology of Common-sense Knowledge. In *Understanding Everyday Life*, ed. Jack D. Douglas, pp. 45–56. London: Routledge and Kegan Paul.

Henningsen, Manfred. 1989. The Politics of Purity and Exclusion. In *The Politics of Language Purism*, ed. Björn H. Jernudd and Michael J. Shapiro, pp. 31–52. Berlin: Mouton de Gruyter.

Hill, Jane H. 1992. "Today There Is No Respect": Nostalgia, "Respect," and Oppositional Discourse in Mexicano (Nahuatl) Language Ideology. *Pragmatics* 2:263–280.

Humphreys, Paul. 1982. The Tradition of Song Renewal among the Pueblo Indians of North America. *American Indian Culture and Research Journal* 6:9–24.

Jernudd, Björn H. 1989. The Texture of Language Purism. In *The Politics of Language Purism*, ed. Björn H. Jernudd and Michael J. Shapiro, pp. 1–19. Berlin: Mouton de Gruyter.

Kalectaca, Milo. 1978. *Lessons in Hopi*. Tucson: University of Arizona Press.

Kroskrity, Paul V. 1978. Aspects of Syntactic and Semantic Variation in the Arizona Tewa Speech Community. *Anthropological Linguistics* 20:235–258.

———. 1982. Language Contact and Linguistic Diffusion: The Arizona Tewa Speech Community. In *Bilingualism and Language Contact*, ed. Florence Barkin, Elizabeth A. Brandt, and Jacob Ornstein-Galicia, pp. 51–72. New York: Columbia Teachers College Press.

———. 1985a. "Growing with Stories": Line, Verse, and Genre in an Arizona Tewa Text. *Journal of Anthropological Research* 41:183–200.

———. 1985b. Areal Influences on Tewa Possession. *International Journal of American Linguistics* 51:486–489.

———. 1992. Arizona Tewa Public Announcements: Form, Function, and Language Ideology. *Anthropological Linguistics* 34:104–116.

———. 1993. *Language, History, and Identity: Ethnolinguistic Studies of the Arizona Tewa.* Tucson: University of Arizona Press.

———. 1994. Language Ideologies in the Expression and Representation of Arizona Tewa Ethnic Identity. Paper presented at School of American Research Advanced Seminar on Language Ideology. Santa Fe, N.M.

Kroskrity, Paul V., and Dewey Healing. 1978. Coyote and Bullsnake. In *Coyote Stories*, ed. William Bright, pp. 162–170. IJAL Native American Texts Series, Monograph No. 1. Ann Arbor: University Microfilms.

Levy, Jerrold E. 1992. *Orayvi Revisited.* Santa Fe, N.M.: School of American Research.

Mertz, Elizabeth. 1992. Linguistic Ideology and Praxis in U.S. Law School Classrooms. *Pragmatics* 2:325–334.

Morgan, Marcyliena. 1993. The Africanness of Counterlanguage among Afro-Americans. In *Afro-American Language Varieties*, ed. Salikoko Mufwene, pp. 423–435. Athens: University of Georgia Press.

Newman, Stanley. 1955. Vocabulary Levels: Zuni Sacred and Slang Usage. *Southwestern Journal of Anthropology* 11:345–354.

Ortiz, Alfonso. 1969. *The Tewa World.* Chicago: University of Chicago Press.

Safran, William. 1991. Diasporas in Modern Societies: Myth of Homeland and Return. *Diaspora* 1:83–99.

Said, Edward. 1984. Reflections of Exile. *Granta* 13:159–172.

Sando, Joe S. 1992. *Pueblo Nations: Eight Centuries of Pueblo Indian History.* Santa Fe, N.M.: Clear Light.

Schroeder, Albert H. 1972. Rio Grande Ethnohistory. In *New Perspectives on the Pueblos*, ed. Alfonso Ortiz, pp. 41–70. Albuquerque: University of New Mexico Press.

———. 1979. Pueblos Abandoned in Historic Times. In *Southwest.* Vol. 9 of *Handbook of North American Indians*, ed. Alfonso Ortiz, pp. 236–54. Washington, D.C.: Smithsonian.

Schutz, Alfred. 1966. *Collected Papers.* Vol. 3: *Studies in Phenomenological Philosophy.* The Hague: Martinus Nijhoff.

Seumptewa, Evelyn, C. F. Voegelin, and F. M. Voegelin. 1980. Wren and Coyote (Hopi). In *Coyote Stories*, Vol. 2, ed. Martha B. Kendall, pp. 104–110. IJAL Native American Texts Series, Monograph No. 6. Ann Arbor: University Microfilms.

Sherzer, Joel. 1976. *An Areal-Typological Study of American Indian Languages North of Mexico.* Amsterdam: North-Holland.

Silverstein, Michael. 1979. Language Structure and Linguistic Ideology. In *The Elements: A Parasession on Linguistic Units and Levels*, ed. Paul R. Clyne, William F. Hanks, and Carol L. Hofbauer, pp. 193–247. Chicago: Chicago Linguistics Society.

———. 1981. The Limits of Awareness. Working Papers in Sociolinguistics 84. Austin, Tex.: Southwest Educational Development Library.

———. 1985. Language and the Culture of Gender: At the Intersection of Structure, Usage, and Ideology. In *Semiotic Mediation*, ed. Elizabeth Mertz and Richard J. Parmentier, pp. 219–239. Orlando, Fla.: Academic Press.

———. 1992. The Uses and Utility of Ideology: Some Reflections. *Pragmatics* 2:311–324.

Simmons, Marc. 1979. History of Pueblo-Spanish Relations to 1821. In *Southwest.* Vol. 9 of *Handbook of North American Indians*, ed. Alfonso Ortiz, pp. 178–193. Washington, D.C.: Smithsonian.

Titiev, Mischa. 1944. *Old Oraibi: A Study of the Hopi Indians of Third Mesa.* Papers of the

Peabody Museum of American Archaeology and Ethnology, vol. 2, no. 1. Cambridge: Harvard University Press.

Whiteley, Peter M. 1988. *Deliberate Acts: Changing Hopi Culture through the Oraibi Split.* Tucson: University of Arizona Press.

Woolard, Kathryn. 1989. Sentences in the Language Prison: The Rhetorical Structuring of an American Language Policy Debate. *American Ethnologist* 16:268–278.

Woolard, Kathryn, and Bambi B. Schieffelin. 1994. Language Ideology. *Annual Review of Anthropology* 23:55–82.

Yava, Albert. 1978. *Big Falling Snow.* New York: Crown.

6

The Uses and Utility of Ideology

A Commentary

MICHAEL SILVERSTEIN

Quelque grands que soient les avantages des signes, il faut convenir qu'ils ont des inconvéniens; et si nous leur devons presque tous les progrès de notre intelligence, je les crois aussi la cause de presque tous ses écarts.

A. Destutt de Tracy [1801] 1827:267

Without wishing to commit the etymological fallacy in the understanding of a word's meaning, I would like first to comment on the traditions of usage of the term *ideology*, a theme elegantly announced in Woolard's introductory discussion of "issues and approaches."

From **Idéologues** *to Us via Ideologues*

It was Antoine Louis Claude, Comte Destutt de Tracy (1754–1836), who invented the term *idéologie* in that naturalizing move of the French Enlightenment rendition of Locke (or, to be sure, of Condillocke [see Aarsleff 1982:146–224, especially 216–17]) that sought to understand human "nature." Ideology was proposed as that special branch of zoölogy that recognizes the distinctive condition of humans, we animals who have ideas as the content of what we should call our minds. Central here is the fact that any ideas more developed than physiological sensations are dependent on such ideas' being clothed in signs; and the organization of signs by some systematic grammar enables the discursive expression of a logical faculty of mind. Hence, for Destutt de Tracy, there is the general scientific field of ideology proper, the science of ideas; the subfield of grammar studies the signifying externalizations of ideation, as it were, in structured systems of articulated signs, and the subfield of logic studies the modes of rationality oriented to truth and certitude of inferential states of mind (i.e., formation and combinatorics of ideas). Such a science would, for its propounder, also allow us to diagnose and understand "the causes of incertitude and [logical] error," thus presumably leading to an amelioration of the human condition by developing, or perfecting, our natural mental faculties.

It is particularly interesting, therefore, to see the fate of this term. Destutt de Tracy proposed it as a formation parallel to any of the other "-ologies" of a systematic scientific outlook. It has obviously become a word that now denotes a part or aspect of Destutt de Tracy's very object of investigation, not the enterprise of investigating ideas or concepts. And in many appearances the word has the specifically "pejorative" use—to pick up on Jane Hill's (this volume) invocation of Raymond Geuss (1981:12–22)—that presupposes we know certain ideas to be dubious, in error, and therefore suspect or at least suspicious, in the manner of being "mere" ideas as opposed to material, historical, indeed factual "realities."[1]

Some of us have no connotational—i.e., ideological!—problems with considering mental phenomena as historical and factual, if not directly "material," realities. For us the concept of ideology in our current usage does embrace the terminological transition to denoting a concrete object of possible study, while making no judgment—at least in scientific and scholarly usage—about some independent and absolute universe of Truth (with its capital T) and Validity (positivistically, not positively, speaking) in which ideologies are measured for "error" against a presumed "factual" base or are exposed and denounced on the grounds of some politicoeconomic advantage accruing to those holding them. (In this usage, it is no cause for concern that scientific and scholarly discourse, too, is "ideological," not escaping from the universe of human mental activities as these arise in conditions of enculturated sociality.) It is thus with the sociological and anthropological (or more generally "descriptive" [Geuss 1981:4–12] and social scientific) concepts of ideology as one of the immanent and necessary conditions of human action that I should like to see us continue to be concerned as linguistic anthropologists.

Such a clustering of descriptive concepts is, in fact, cross-cutting to Woolard's report on differentiated "strands" of historically attested senses of the term *ideology*, a history that emerges from various writers' desires for theorizing against a backdrop of assumed epistemological and sometimes political absolutes. By contrast, we might consider our descriptive analytic perspective, richly illustrated in accompanying papers in this section, as a species of social-constructionist realism or naturalism about language and its matrix in the sociocultural realm: it recognizes the reflexive entailments for its own praxis, that it will find no absolute Archimedian place to stand—not in absolute "Truth," nor in absolute "Reality," nor even in absolute deterministic or computible mental or social "Functional Process." Analysis of ideological factuality is, perforce, relativistic in the best scientific (not scientistic) sense. It is therefore as much "pejorative" when conscious of itself, in making us realize that there may be limits for (social) scientific knowledge enterprises, as it is "pejorative" as an analytic tool in making claims about limitations-in-principle or -in-praxis of others' semiotic systems when we consider their ideological dimensions. It is important to remember this when thinking about the history of concepts of "ideology" found in the writings of social theorists in the period following Destutt de Tracy.

The Archaeology of Ideology *and of Ideology*

We can discern a history of very different emphases on now one, now another aspect of Woolard's social-theoretic strands in the discourses of *ideology*. There is a kind of palimpsest or geological stratification of connotations serially taken from and then developed out of canonical nineteenth- and twentieth-century authors who read their predecessors and in turn influenced their successors. This has, over time, produced "strands" of conceptualization, constituting in our day the stereotypic components of meaning of the very term *ideology*.

First off, ideology is an intensional characteristic, predicable of a society, or of a group in a social formation abstracted from society; ideology is even predicable as a possession or characteristic of individuals so long as they are understood to be living within some defined population. Ideology can be understood as "mental," therefore, with some of the same problems for us analysts as are shown by approaches to 'culture' or to 'language' when these are taken to be "mental" characteristics. (Recall here the charming, if seemingly oxymoronic, Chomskian concept of—or at least phrase—"mental organ.") If "mental," where do language and culture live with respect to phenomenal individual, group, or social form? And where, indeed, does 'ideology' live?

Thus, note that the sharedness of ideology, like that of culture or language, and the relationship of ideology to (individual) consciousness, are properties—hence, problem areas for investigation—that survive from Destutt de Tracy's usage, which focused on the specifically human condition as "ideational." Certainly, use of the culture concept and the concept of language central to several traditions of anthropology and of linguistics has entailed for their users wrestling, in many different ways, with the nature of such sharedness, and with the modes and degrees of consciousness involved in such cultural and linguistic phenomena.

As every aware practitioner knows, these constitute both ontological and epistemological problems for the validity of our statements in the scientific manner about "the" culture or "the" language we purport to describe. And they will not disappear, as is increasingly being recognized (sometimes more forcefully by external critics than by linguistic practitioners, who then look like threatened "ideological" apologists) by stale, antibehavioristic appeals to the Cartesian certitude of self-examining "intuition" as constitutive of linguistic—or even of sociocultural—fact. For people to have such intuitions about language, and for people to be able consciously to formulate and communicate them (to "share" them in an active, agentive sense), may thus be "ideological" to a degree greater than, and in ways more diverse than, many students of culture and language in one scientistic mode or another find tractable.

For, in this agentive—indeed, communicative-event–bound and thus indexical—perspective, people actively achieve a "sharing" of ideology. This activity may in fact play an essential role in the putatively found condition of language or culture, that they are the "shared" (*sc.*, common) possessions of group or of social formation. Note that this is an assumption of a truly "social constructionist" position on linguistic or sociocultural reality, holding that the dialectic moment of social (or social-historical) process, for example, active, agentive "sharing," is essential to the semblance of sharedness of verbal and other social-actional norms as individuals' mental "grammar" and "culture."

And to what degree essential? Indeed, if all cultural and linguistic phenomena are essentially event linked, even where they appear to be manifestations of people's "intuitions," they are, as it were, ideological "all the way down." And such a state of affairs calls for a reevaluation of how we might creep up on such supposedly "material" or "objective" factuality as scientific students of language and culture have claimed to encounter in "*langue*," in "competence," in "shared norms and values," in "modes of (re)production," in "doxa" and "habitus," and so on—independent of ideological analysis of these putatively "objective" phenomena.

Observe how this leads into the second aspect of the concept-cluster, the social-situatedness of ideology. For, suppose we are dealing with some ideational phenomenon particular to or predicable of societies, groups, and so on that constitutes their uniqueness, like the classic Romantic notion of the worldview of "a people" or "a nation." Then, insofar as ideology is characteristic of any sociocultural phenomenon whatsoever, it must inhere in what gives coherence to social entities of whatever scope. We have only to be able to locate such a social entity, to find the potential for a unique mental or ideological aspect associable with its members or participants; society-in-mind, as it were, indifferently as much as mind-in-society.

But once we yield to distrust of the socially locatable (as opposed to the material and factual realms of early-nineteenth-century pejorative usage) as somehow less factual than "real" facts, we see that the locatedness of ideology takes on a kind of negative connotation. This negative connotation can be contrasted with the neutral to positive connotations of the social locatedness of "culture," in both technical and lay usages. Rather than seeing that there is no such thing as a social fact without its ideological aspect or component, many users of the concept have simply yielded to the negative connotations of a kind of charged political rhetoric when it comes to analyzing the ideational aspect of social formations. But the long-standing textual basis for this bias is not hard to find, revealed as it is even in the historical organization of dictionary attestations in the *Oxford English Dictionary*, as cited in note 1.

Thus, the locatedness of an "ideology" appears to those viewing it as from across a chasm of Bakhtinian voicing when they use the label: opposing the scientistic stance of others who claim to be at or in a falsely objective "Truth," one can see the distortions or mystifications in such an ideology (this is Woolard's third member of the cluster of notions in the word); opposing the discourses of self-legitimation of dominant, powerful, or oppressive groups or institutions, one can declare these to be ideological on behalf of otherwise silent or nondiscerning victims in a move of committed advocacy that demystifies, debunks, and dethrones, as it were. These are the initial intellectual salvos of delegitimation (Woolard's fourth feature of the concept). We can see that strands three and four share the stance of otherness, the one being epistemological, the other rather frankly political.

These two stances can, of course, be combined in creative ways, as in traditions of a politically committed and self-styled scientific analysis of "ideological" formations that some versions of (generally left-wing) political economy declare themselves to be. (And, from such points of view, self-styled scientific and non-politically committed analyses of any social fact can be declared to be "in fact" or "in practice" right-wing politics in disguise, as has emerged in contemporary left-wing intellectuals' positioned engagement in "culture wars," mostly over language, texts, and text-artifacts and their equivalents.)

Observe how the specialized senses Woolard points out are on the order of distinctive Putnamian (1975) stereotypes and indexical presuppositions associable with the denotational capacity of the term *ideology* and its derivatives. Stereotypes are, of course, beliefs about denotata of a word or expression that are not derived from strictly linguistically mapped sense categories but that, notwithstanding, give descriptive backing to uses of the term. Stereotypes are associable with words and expressions as these are used by specific, historically located groups of users in the division of linguistic labor. Processes of semantic change have underlain the emergence of stereotypy (see also n. 1) in the normal, ideologically informed fashion of linguistic history: at a particular point in time, (1) the indexically entailing penumbra of people's denotational usage of linguistic forms-in-context gets revalorized by a group in the realm of (2) ideologically grounded (3) interpretative apprehension of the signs' entailed contextual surround (stereotypes about contexts-of-usage), and this revalorization returns to usage in terms of (1') transformed presupposing indexical value frequently involving (3') new stereotypic components of denotational meaning. A token of the term is extensionalized, and its intensionalization through understanding what has/will have thus been accomplished by its use for some "reality" inevitably *reintensionalizes* its underlying type, but sometimes with widespread and permanent effect, as in linguistic change.

Such a dynamic explains, of course, the charming sociolinguistic fact that Woolard brings up in her introduction, that there are two phonological forms, [ay]*deology* and [ɪ]*deology*, probably indexically locating a speaker in different communities of discourse and probably emphasizing different stereotypic strands of the concept-cluster in actual usage—for example, Cultural Anthropologese [ay] versus Social Anthropologese or even Sociologese / Political Economicist [ɪ], among others. Indeed, to this extent, we are like the New York City woman of the classic Labovian example (1972:251n) who transformed the general indexical value of the class-stratified alternative pronunciations *v*[eys]*es* versus *v*[ahz]*es* into stereotypic denotational content (the first word-type, she claimed, denoting smaller, less valuable objects than the second). Those of us who pronounce and listen to these alternatives probably do behave like native speakers ought to in respect of the term *ideology* and its derivatives, in which the role of certain authorizing, canonical texts read and reread over two centuries of scholarly and political tradition infuses even our phonetic usage with now one, now another dominant conceptual strand, despite ourselves.

Two Themes for "Reading" Ideologies

Turning to the chapters in Part I in my assigned task as respondent, I first emphasize two general themes concerning the ideological aspect of the cases discussed, and then, in my final section, I comment on the utility of the concept of ideology—as opposed to the concepts of culture and language themselves—when dealing with the facts of language. The first theme concerns how ideology mediates what can only be called a dialectic process of indexicality in many orders of contextual abstraction and on many distinct planes of sociality and of social process. The second theme is how ideology is "sited" and to be "sighted" in a number of frameworks relevant to the analysis of language: metaphorically to spatialize matters, Where are we to look for ideology's many manifestations in social life? And what are the implications of the answers to this for social scientific practices of how to go about looking? The essays here have rich material relevant to both of these concerns.

The Immanence of Ideology in the Dialectic of Indexicality

We now recognize that the "realities" of meaningful social practices emerge from people's situated experience of indexical semiotic processes that constitute them. We ought, perhaps, to resign ourselves to enjoying the fact that it's indexicality all the way down, that in any sociocultural phenomenon nothing is manifest beyond this indexicality except semanticoreferential language and its further developments (Barthes 1968:23–34). So, for social actors as well as for us analysts, in a cultural situation in which at least one cultural "text" is generated, meaningfulness is a dialectical property of social semiotics.[2] And the rub is, the only way analytically to enter into understanding such dialectical systems is with the inherently ironic concept of ideology. Ideology, in other words, is defined only within a discourse of interpretation or construal of inherently dialectic indexical processes, as for example the processes of making or achieving text (*entextualization*) by using language and other sign modalities, whether at the *denotational* plane or the more encompassing plane of *interactional textuality* (though of course, for language in particular, both planes of textuality are always in play).[3]

Now any indexical process, wherein signs point to a presupposed context in which they occur (i.e., have occurred) or to an entailed potential context in which they occur (i.e., will have occurred), depends on some metapragmatic function to achieve a measure of determinacy or textual coherence (Silverstein 1993). It turns out that the crucial position of *ideologies* of semiosis is in constituting such a "default" mediating metapragmatics. Such defaults give parties an idea of determinate contextualization for indexicals in the particular phase of interaction at issue. Participants can presuppose that they share a contextualizing interpretation according to interested positions or perspectives that follow on some social fact such as group membership, condition in society, or achieved commonalty of interests.

In short, ideology construes indexicality by constituting its metapragmatics. In so doing, ideology inevitably biases a participant's or analyst's metapragmatic "take" on indexical (contextual) factuality so as to create another order of potentially effective indexicality that bears what we can sometimes appreciate as a truly ironic relation to the first. For any sign, let us term these hypothetical, logically *preideological* and decidedly *postideological* indexicalities respectively the *first-order* and *second-order* planes of indexicality.[4] (Of course, given the unboundedly dialectic nature of the semiotic process, we should understand these relative planar orders to be generalizable to *n*th and *n*+1st; see Silverstein 1996.)

One can approach the analysis of social signs by observing that every system or modality of social signs is infused with indexicality; that, therefore, all such indexicality is possible only in a dialectic process mediated by ideological formations. So there is no possible *absolutely* preideological—that is, *zero-order*, social semiotic—neither a purely 'sense'-driven denotational system for the referential-and-predicational expressions of any language nor a totalizing system of noncontextual and purely "symbolic" values for any culture. Certainly the confluence of deconstructive and Marxist political-economic approaches, insofar as coherent, amounts to an argument to this effect. While I have already characterized one moment of such social-constructionist accounts of sociocultural phenomena, it is not my purpose here to elaborate this theme.

Rather, let us return to this stipulation: that ideologies present invokable schemata in which to explain/interpret the meaningful flow of indexicals. As such, they are necessary to and drive default modes of the gelling of this flow into textlike chunks. Ideologies are, thus, conceptualized as relatively perduring with respect to the indexicals-in-context that they construe. And we recognize such schemata characteristically by the way that they constitute rationalizing, systematizing, and, indeed most importantly, *naturalizing* schemata: schemata that "explain" the indexical value of signs in terms of some order(s) of phenomena stipulatively presupposable by—hence, in context, autonomous of—the indexical phenomena to be understood. In their most elaborated forms, such naturalizing schemata consist of "Just So Stories" about the direct, transparent, indeed sometimes *iconic indexicality* (*emblematicity*) of the phenomena at issue; in this way, they go to the very heart of issues of what, perduringly, human nature is all about, in a universe that has certain absolute characteristics when viewed from the field of indexical semiosis at issue.

We can think of any of the demographic dimensions of identity summoned up indexically in the use of language: for example, men versus women, generation *n* versus generation *m* within a kinship or even age-system order, ethnicities *A*, *B*, or *C*, various differential class-orientations or class-identities within a structure of stratification. Any schema that interprets an indexical value of forms by a presuppositional relationship—"Persons of such-and-such definability use form '. . .', while so-and-sos use '. . .', (because . . .) . . ."—is potentially an ideological one that rationalizes the indexical value in terms of social differentiations and classifications that in such invocations seem themselves to be independent of the usages at issue.

And we should note just how systematic and elaborated such rationalizations can be, constituting explanatory pre- or nonsemiotic frameworks ultimately grounded in a cosmologically or cosmogonically totalizing vision. At their most elaborate, ideological construals/constructions of indexical facts—the ultimate *extensional* ones, note—turn the indexical forms into seemingly "natural" indexical icons, emblems with consubstantial *intensional* content or stuff seeping back from the original contextual surround into the understanding of what constitutes the sign forms themselves. Dialectically produced, such higher-order indexical forms frequently become little detachable design elements for text building that are, in essence, ready-made texts or text-chunks (cf. Homeric and other epic formulae, Shakespearean collocations) deployable for social-interactive effect while preserving their indexically acquired intensional characteristics as a seemingly autonomous "code" of meanings.[5] (We have only to think of the almost literal evaluation of words—such as *v*[ahz]*es*—as $10-items, compared with their $0.10 denotational equivalents in other socioeconomic class registers.)

Thus, also note that in sociolinguistic theorizing, many of our conceptual constructs are inherently suffused with the ideological moment of the semiotic processes in which they figure. For example, consider the concept of *register*, a minimally binary paradigm of ways of "saying the same thing" distinctly indexically appropriate to two (or more) contexts of usage, however defined. Note that the "sameness" of denotational value of two or more distinct word-forms or expressions is built into the register concept; this is an ideologically driven mirage from the structural linguistic point of view on Saussurean 'sense' (*signifié*). For it is a truism that any difference of internal structure or of external distribution of forms that constitute a paradigm of register variation entails Saussurean nonequivalence of the terms. However, from the perspective of users of such enregistered denotational forms, these are indexically pregnant paradigms of "equivalence"—a denotational "equivalence" that founds registers within some sociolinguistic, never merely denotational-structural (and hence Saussurean-Bloomfieldian-Chomskian) order. No examples of analytically equivalent register forms have, to my knowledge, appeared in the literature; yet the construct of register nicely captures the way that native speakers of languages comprehend variation and variability in their linguistic forms by incorporating such ideological understanding of it.

The register concept, moreover, allows us to capture something of what it means to have a *linguistic community* in which we find an ideology of "speaking the same language." In every such linguistic community, indexical processes can be observed and documented that dialectically balance (presupposing) "*dialectal*" and (potentially entailing) "*superposed*" formal variability in usage (the terms are Gumperz's [1968:383–84]). And there is constant reciprocal interconvertibility of the status of formal linguistic variation as now dialectal, now superposed, through different orders of indexicality.[6]

Yet speakers' imagination of indexically functioning variability as organized by registers—their seeing indexicality through the lens of alternatives of denotational usage—presents the social context to them through a particular idiom. It conceptualizes the appropriateness of alternative formulations of one's otherwise identical denotational message so as to make its form "fit" the (preexisting) context. As Don Kulick observes in his essay (chapter 4), "language ideologies seem never to be solely about language—they are always about entangled clusters of phenomena, and they encompass and are bound up with aspects of culture like gender, and expression, and being 'civilized'"—all, we might add, attributes of language's presupposed context of occurrence.

That people have ideologies of language, therefore, is a necessary entailment of the fact that language, like any social semiotic, is indexical in its most essential modality. And that irony is the essential trope lurking always in ideologically informed contemplation of language, whether by "them" or by "us," is a consequence of the actual dialectic manner in which ideology engages with pragmatic fact through metapragmatic function, in a kind of spiral figurement up the planar orders of indexicality (see now Silverstein 1996). All of the chapters in this volume demonstrate this.

Judith Irvine's essay (chapter 2) takes up the distinction between deference-and-demeanor indexicals and honorific registers, perhaps the classic case of first- and second-order indexicality.[7] Honorification, encoding at least a second order of indexicality, always involves a strong ideological component. When explicit, this ideological view is expressed in a metapragmatics of subtle appropriateness of usage of forms that presupposes an *addressee-focused* context. It construes patterns of usage as being at the first order of indexicality, seeing meaning in speaker's compliance with such patterns or rules. The result is that, at a second order of indexicality, the system of honorification ironically operates rather differently, generally as a *speaker-focused* index of distinction.[8]

As Irvine further points out, there is a second way to focus on how ideologies of these indexical forms engage with the forms themselves, based on the nature of the indexical forms at issue. Irvine observes that in some languages these honorific registers organize the lexicon of nounlike grammatical forms insofar as the indexical categories of honorific/neutral/pejorative denotation are expressed systematically through choices, such as of concord prefixes, in the normal paradigms of inflection and agreement.[9] In this sense honorifics are "grammaticalized" in some languages to a very great degree, as in Yao and ChiBemba. In other languages, there are simply paradigms of lexical register-alternants in sometimes one-to-one (Zulu), sometimes many-to-one (Javanese) denotational "equivalence." As linguistic forms, these are all clearly surface-segmentally expressed, systematic morphological and lexical alternations construable within the denotational structure. As such, they are targets of elaborated metalinguistic consciousness (see Silverstein 1981a). This includes not only native-speaker accounts of honorification but also linguistic-theoretically encompassed descriptive responsibility within the Western, semanticoreferentially focused grammatical tradition of describing perceived linguistic "structure."

By contrast, Irvine notes that the Wolof linguistic ideology centers on the binary contrast of articulate *griot*s (bards) and inarticulate nobles (the latter forming a kind of verbal *Lumpenkönigstum*, one can imagine) as *speakers* with immanent social characteristics indexically presented. As Irvine has discussed in an earlier article on greetings (Irvine 1974) and in an essay on the conventional enregisterment of affect versus its situated enactment (Irvine 1990), the ideological alignment of these social identities relative to discursive interaction looks something like the following: *Griot* : Noble :: active, moving : inert, stationary :: low status : high status :: speaker : addressee :: fluent, loud, rapid, clear, intoned speech : dysfluent, soft, slow, breathy, monotone speech :: grammatically and textually rich language : grammatically and textually sparse language :: first pair-part role (active soliciter) : second pair-part role (put-upon responder). Doing something to index a deautomatization of these expected alignments—classic "role-distancing" or "role-heightening" diacritics—is the obvious speaker-centered possibility for effectively troping on, but not trampling upon, these expectations. Thus, a noble's speaking more elegantly in the *griot* manner will not a "nobler" person make, but a somewhat disaffected or unpresentable noble; such facts obviate the possibility of a higher-order indexical effect here that follows from the cultural understanding of usage.

Irvine's article thus nicely problematizes the contrasts between (a) ideologically supported indexical systems of honorification (Javanese) or of avoidance-respect (Zulu *hlonipha*), with their conscious addressee focus, their degrees of enregisterment and even grammaticalization, and (b) the various kinds of text- and event-bound discursive indexicals of speaker-identity, the ideologies engaging which seem to operate distinctly. Highly ideologized, enregistered, grammaticalized (or at least lexicalized) honorific and avoidance-respect indexicals are imperialistic; they underlie an expansive tropic potential in what seems to be a great deal of strategic (hence, agentive) "metaphorical switching" (Blom and Gumperz 1972:425)—*entailing* or *creative* indexicality, that is (Silverstein 1976:34–35). An effectively *second-order* conventionalized indexicality (pointing to speaker characteristics) is always possible in such a situation and, as an historical eventuality (see Silverstein 1985b:244–51), results in a decisive linguistic change.

Not unexpectedly, therefore, in Jane Hill's discussion of the reflective "discourse of nostalgia" among Mexicano (Nahuatl) speakers in the Malinche area (chapter 3), we see the linguistic exhibit of ideological concern in the addressee-focused honorification indexes; these are typically invoked in images of normative interpersonal routines like greetings, where formerly, in this nostalgic construal, real mutual "respect" was demonstrable.

To our analytic view, there are, indeed, at least two paths of dialectical irony to ideologically informed usage of Mexicano: such usage is, first, located by the interpretive scheme of nostalgia with respect to a longed-for past, for the days of mutual "respect"—that is, a time of positionally defined self-certitude in discursive interaction. If not, of course, strictly "egalitarian" in attitude—since it is, after all, a "T/V"-like system sensitive to hierarchy—it certainly is primordialist in its attitude to (presupposed) distinctions; for nostalgia buffs the evidentiary base rests on those quasi-"natural" distinctions of kinship, or "sacred" distinctions of ritual kinship around which honorification centers (Hill and Hill 1978). (This is an irony so palpable to those currently not privileged in the bilingual, Spanish-Nahuatl social order of modern institutions that many commentators, perhaps Doña Fidencia most wittily among them [Hill, chapter 3], catch all of this in their own counternostalgic debunking.)

And yet a second kind of irony pointed up by Hill is doubly like that of Labov's (1972:117–18, 128–33) now famous "lower-middle-class" speakers of New York City English who showed maximal "linguistic insecurity" before—that is, ideological allegiance to, the standard register they seem basically (or at least basilectally) not to use. Around the Malinche, the ideological discourse of nostalgia for the pure, unadulterated Mexicano of ritualized displays of the mutual respect of yesteryear seems to peak among those whose verbal protocols in fact show maximal mixing—that is, interference/codeswitching—between Castellano (Spanish) and Mexicano (Hill and Hill 1980). Here, however, this mixed-language usage seems to have become enregistered as what the Hills call a "power 'code'" in the Bernsteinian sense of the last term [= our 'register'] (Hill 1985:727–28; Hill and Hill 1986:97–141). In this enregisterment, forms are valorized by indexing successful, generally male, entry into the institutional universe of nation-state modernity and its practical discursive regimes. As Hill here notes, "the discourse of 'nostalgia' is in fact a pragmatic claim on the present, using 'pastness' as a 'naturalizing' ideological strategy" that seems to be recommending to others—to those who actually control "pure" Mexicano—a course of self-exclusion from the superordinate "power 'code'" and all it indexes as the first-order system associated with contemporary political and economic success.

Various people in the community obviously see the incoherence if not cynicism in the indexical effects thus legitimated. From their perspective emerges a competing form of "linguistic insecurity," manifested in a discourse of "counter 'nostalgia'." For this discourse has clearly enregistered the "power 'code'" and, relying on its adherents' consciousness of the denotational value of language, whose forms it valorizes on the basis of the reality check about a nation-state framework for identity that such Castellano usage provides.

On the one hand, recall, the discourse of nostalgia is concerned with valorizing "pure" formulaics of speaker-addressee honorification, centered on *compadrazgo* ritual kinship relations (see Hill and Hill 1978:134–35, 1986:144–55); indexically, this constructs/construes a second-order speaker-focused trope of traditionalism and in-groupness—that is, it licenses an indexical gesture of renvoi memorializing a (presumptive) time when everyone knew his or her proper place (and, hence, the other person's too), emblematized by the ritual relation par excellence of coparenthood. On the other hand, by contrast, the antinostalgic counterdiscourse is firmly situated within contemporaneous social stratification and ego-focused mobility, situating the local, traditionally Nahuatl-speaking linguistic community within a nation-state order dominated by Spanish; it "constitute[s] a pragmatic claim on the future," as Hill here tells us, by mocking the very formulaicness of the cited instances of pure Mexicano honorification, in effect, denotationally *translating* them into Castellano—sometimes wittily mock-translating them to add obscenity and other ribaldry—to show that, notwithstanding the indexical loadings for honorification, anything that one can "say" in Mexicano can also be said in this "power 'code'," too.

The counterdiscourses are referentialist in their self-positioning, even though in Nahuatl there is no lexicalized distinction between sense and denotation, nor between reference-and-predication and all other communicative functions.[10] One sees that the very concept of phrasal translation so vividly exemplified in Hill's consultants' formulations align with a modern referentialist sensibility about the value of language: Mexicano and Castellano are different ways of "saying 'the same' thing." And, in these terms, ritual efficaciousness of greeting formulas and other text-fragments cited from the canons of erstwhile *addressee*-oriented good taste among the ancients are, at the second order of indexicality, hardly to the point when what is at issue is authorizing a 'powerful' *speaker* well placed in a dominated system of social stratification.

The ideological matrix of language shift is also the theme of Kulick's paper about the small village of Gapun near the northern coast of Papua New Guinea.

Here, the creole Tok Pisin is the innovative language, the language of desired and desirous modernity and Christianity, while the Papuan language Taiap—in 1991 no longer spoken by anyone younger than fourteen years—is the language indigenous to the local linguistic community. Compendiously summarizing several of the themes he has elsewhere elaborated (see, e.g., Kulick 1992, 1993 and references there), Kulick shows how local beliefs make ideologically driven language shift both culturally plausible and empirically irreversible.

The ideological field Kulick portrays for us brings together several things that starkly demonstrate how profoundly one must probe to see the dialectic of first- and second-order indexicality. First, there are Gapuners' understandings of how knowledge—especially knowledge about people—is dangerous. Hence, in communicative terms, utterers/senders/speakers normatively are expected to reveal little and to do so figuratively, while addressees/receivers/hearers normatively expect to be knowledgeable from communications only by making considerable interpretative effort. We can see that it would be quite rude to force an addressee or overhearer to confront a barrage of straightforward indexical communications "bald on the record," as it were (in the mode of informational content, perhaps something like being spoken to in too *kasar* a manner in Java).

Second, Gapuners' understanding of the matter creates second-order indexes in speech genres that gender female versus male. The female-gendered *kros* is sited domestically, while useful masculine oratory is sited in and near the communal men's house. *Kros*es are invective- and obscenity-filled dialogic outbursts hurled between two houses; they are negatively valued and rationalized as the product of essentially immature personalities, who cannot or do not properly keep their *hed*s from too much communicative revelation, putting thus on display the affective states of their autonomous selves. A person *kros*sed is drenched in unmistakable knowledge about the affect of someone losing her *hed*, whether the addressee wants to be or no. Men's house talk, by contrast, is considered to be well turned and contained, publicly focused monologic thoughts shared at public meetings; they are positively valued and rationalized as the properly allusive communicative products of persons who have achieved *save* 'savvy' and who can display exemplary Christian and civic ideals oriented to the common weal.[11]

At the ironic, second-order of indexicality, behavior modeled on this dichotomy becomes presupposable as a covert or indirect index (Silverstein 1985b:234–40; Ochs 1992:339–45) of being an adult female, "naturally" prone to burning *kros*es, so it is thought, or of being an adult male, "naturally" able to burnish oratory in orderly interaction through serial monologue, as in the ideally low-key ritual politics of the men's house. And yet, exactly parallel to the real irony of male sociopolitical life among the Merina long ago pointed out by Ochs (Ochs[Keenan] 1974), men can strategically orchestrate or authorize a *kros* in which their wives or other female relatives are the talking *hed*s, thus playing a potentially important role in issues of contested interests.

Taiap language occurs in, and is ideologically associated with, femaleness, with displays of affect in *kros* behavior, and with the feared/devalued (and immature) motivation by *hed* (unhygienic communicative matter-out-of-place in public).[12] By contrast, Tok Pisin is ideologically associated with maleness, with suppression of affect, and communicatively therefore with negatively or indirectly tropic displays of *save*, as great public leaders and Christian thinkers are wont to do (see Watson-Gegeo and Gegeo 1991 with respect to Kwara'ae). It is clear from Kulick's transcripts that some Taiap occurs in men's-house talk, just as much Tok Pisin occurs in women's *kros*-talk. The languages have been ideologically emblematized in the opposite way, however. In this elaborate construction of a second-order cultural configuration, these contingently and historically co-occurring languages are located in a framework of the cultural absolutes of "human nature." Being thus rendered intelligible, the contingencies become certainties: Taiap has been disappearing under indexically effectuated devaluation.

Paul Kroskrity's discussion of Arizona Tewa (chapter 5; see also Kroskrity 1993, esp. 36–39) takes up a centering ideology associated with the survival of this linguistic island within a linguistic island, Hopi, within a linguistic island, Navajo, within the vast English-speaking sea of the contemporary United States. What outsiders see as "linguistic conservatism" or "purism" more etically and without further analysis, Kroskrity informs us is really an ideological centering of language use on *te'e hi:li* 'kiva speech', which seems to be conceptualized both as a genre and as a register informing all use of Tewa and other languages. Thus, insofar as a speaker's identity is manifested in-and-by modalities of linguistic usage, all of a person's demographic and attitudinal characteristics are potentially aligned as metaphors one of another by their conceptualized proximity to the kiva, in practice or in entitlement, as usage indexically summons this up.

Functionally similar to the hegemony of standard register in linguistic communities like those of modern nation-states, *te'e hi:li* dominates at the top-and-center of the conceptual array of "enregistered" indexical forms; thus do the linguistic forms of kiva register become potential superposed—or second-order—variables in the repertoire of Tewa speakers as a function of position and contextual speaking strategy. And we see thereby the interesting irony that a woman announcing a yard sale in the manner of the traditional male public crier, using enregistered forms close to, though not at, kiva-"standard," is nevertheless commended for the effort.

Observe with Kroskrity here "that Pueblo ceremonial language . . . is not only the expression of religious belief through the sacred manipulation of cosmic forces but also the implicit justification of rule by a largely hereditary ceremonial elite." This social stratification, recently reemphasized in studies of the political anthropology of the indigenous American Southwest, is, of course, entirely in keeping with the theme of irony in the dialectical workings of ideological formations. Ceremonial here, as Kroskrity notes, emphasizes kin-based tropes of equality and mutual support, rather than stratified asymmetries of clan-based corporate control of resources and wealth. So, too, *te'e hi:li* as the medium known to be that of the kiva gets ascriptively reintensionalized with the qualities of the performed ceremonial context it extends as formulaic denotational language, the celebration of in-group mutuality and thereby uniform access of those in the in-group to cosmically centered riches. Among younger people in the contemporary American context, how long this kiva-centered Arizona Tewa will remain a forceful emblem in a traditional and recognized system of distinctive ethnic wealth is a fascinating issue of values and their generational changes (see Kroskrity 1993:79–108).

Keeping the Sites of Ideology in Sight

I want very briefly to point to the differences in what we might term the *explicitness* of the ideological in regimes of language that mediate social life. We are speaking here not only of discursive explicitness; for a part of explicitness, and thereby transparency to outside analysts like linguistic anthropologists, seems to lie in the special position of certain institutional sites of social practice, as both *object* and *modality* of ideological expression. Again, these chapters in Part I demonstrate something of the commonalty as well as diversity of ideological manifestations.

A first important distinction to note is whether and to what degree ideologies manifest themselves in text—that is, present themselves to us as actualized *discourses about* social practices. Reflexively focusing on using language itself, we would call such discursive practices *metadiscourses*. Ideological representations in the metadiscourse of any one person must, of course, be perspectival, and they are bound up in the genres of metadiscourse that occur on any one occasion of encounter. Thus, ideologies are immanent in only fragmentary, though mutually engaging representations about language and its use on any given interlocutory occasion (see Hill's report on Mexicano, chapter 3). So, as ethnographers we must, in essence, assemble consultants' articulations to yield a group-level representation with respect to which the members of a group can be differentially located, sometimes, we find, as a function of—or at least a correlate of—their positions in a social space.

Further, metadiscourse frequently presents itself as *nomically calibrated metapragmatics*—a metapragmatics that stipulates lawlike regularities, independent of epistemological concern with time, place, or other event-bound contingencies of the pragmatic practice that is its object of discursive focus. (This *nomic* calibration can be contrasted with metapragmatic calibrations of a *reportive* or *reflexive* type [see Silverstein 1993:48–53], which roughly deal with the realms of respectively, "those-there" and "these-(ongoing)-here" pragmatic phenomena.) Myth, liturgy, and similarly generalized historical or etiological explanation of social phenomena tend to be in nomic calibration with their denotational objects-of-exposition, and, hence, such genres are highly susceptible loci to ideologically transparent representation, as Bakhtin and others (see Bloch 1975 and note 14 *infra*) have said, and has long been the implicit heuristic rule-of-thumb of the sociocultural anthropologist, who looks to such genres for their "charter" status with respect to social fact.

Such a metadiscourse frequently takes the explicit form of rationalizing explanation, a model that represents decontextualizable characteristics of people and functional signs as the (presupposable) basis of how indexical relations emerge in experience. Thus, accounts tend to be like the form of the following examples, explaining how characteristics of individuals recruited to certain roles in semiotic events are indexed by certain linguistic forms: women versus men engage in, or are skilled at, distinct genres of discourse—there's the extensional observation or generalization—because, women are such-and-such and men are so-and-so—intensionalization in another, frequently etiological schema giving the "essence" of the social category; such-and-such are the valued versus devalued forms of language because they are in keeping with tradition or the way of the ancestors or not—the Malinowskian "charter myth" about indexically pregnant forms. When people are discovered to have elaborate metalinguistic ideologies of this metadiscursively evidenced sort, this is one place for the social scientist to begin in figuring out the nature of the indexical dialectic constituting pragmatic facts that is the sociocultural object of investigation.

Sometimes, as we have seen, the ideological metadiscourse emerges in descriptive images of linguistic and other semiotic usage particular to certain contexts. These descriptions are genred, event-situated stereotypes of usage that form a kind of imagistic *canon* of realizable or at least conceptualizable ideological values. Hence Kroskrity's kiva style is summoned up as a measure of any contextualized use of language by the degree to which the kiva-talk register can be seen as immanent in it. The contextualized use of kiva talk links this context, through an ideological imaging of it, to any other context in a kind of effectively intertextual—really, *interdiscursive*—ideology. The scenes animated by Mexicano speakers as typical of days gone by also seem to have some of this canonical character as textualized Gestalten: observe that they are not so much constructed ideologically by a discourse of intensional rules or principles as exhibited—"meta"-animated—by a trope of *re-presentation* that functions here to characterize a type, stereotypic instantiation or representation. Note in many of the papers how such textualized, canonical images combine with rationalizing metadiscourses of principle in a complex narrated and expository genre.

Which brings me to point out more explicitly these ritual sites—Arizona Tewa kivas, Gapun meeting houses, Zulu royal courts—and these interactional sites of understood ritualization of usage—prototypic scenes of honorification of a Mexicano *compadre*, for example. How often do these provide the descriptive exemplification in metadiscourses that ground the semiotic value of indexicals in determinate, textualized ways! This is not by chance, of course, since in "interaction ritual" both social scientists and, indeed, any concerned and interested parties can appreciate the co-occurrence of sometimes transparently tractable interactional textuality and ritual's claim to value-setting effectiveness.

Thus, we see also that ritual is a site of tremendous ideological power, in that, as Durkheimian tradition stipulates, it constitutes an autonomous *metatext* for more everyday social practices the indexical semiotic dimensions of which are generally presupposed as the basis of the tropic figurements of ritual. Recall that ritual is semiotically self-grounding in two linked aspects. First, its very enacted (co)textual form, in whatever sign modalities, constitutes its own reflexively calibrated metapragmatics, thus yielding its autonomy. Second, this enacted textual form is at the same time constituted ("literally!") out of tropes—metasigns—that thus presuppose the existence of nontropic—that is, literal and absolute—"reality" substantiated by its very figuration.

This presupposition of the "literal" code[13] by an axially self-grounding entextualization may look non-"real and factual" to the outsider. But such outsider's suspicion is, of course, irrelevant within the semiotic universe of ritual indexicality. We know of no ritual that does not get its effectiveness in this manner, from the most mundane "performative" usage of otherwise denotational language to the most elaborate, scripturally ordained liturgy. Ritual is self-grounding as indexical-icon within its figured universe and, as such, makes a strong, though semiotically implicit case for what can only be called an ideological order within the culture of a social group.

The site of institutionalized ritual and ritualization, then, provides an essential place where societies and social groups in effect articulate the ideological, whether positively, as in the kiva, or negatively, as in the *kros*. Figuring out how a ritual is performatively efficacious, then, in its tropic modalities, is frequently the key to being able to articulate how an ideology gets its seeming effect in social practice. Further, as we see in the accompanying papers, such sites are the foci of metadiscursively evidenced ideological formations about social life more generally, being powerful institutional forms in two senses, both in their ordaining/(re)vitalizing effectiveness with respect to the "denotational" codes they nomically regiment and as genred event-images that are close to ideological consciousness when rationality contemplates itself.[14]

But the cases reported in the accompanying chapters show very clearly the sitedness of ideology in just this sense, with no further comment necessary.

The Utility of the Ideology Concept to Cultural Analysis

Finally, I wish to make an observation on the very fact of existence of this collection of essays, this book—a collection that engages with linguistic "ideologies" in the plural. Each chapter uses an analytic concept of ideology in approaching its cultural data, thus at a certain analytic moment construing some of the data of language use as "ideological" in a particular way. To be sure, this move is not (merely) self-positioning of the analyst.

While these essays might have something of what has been styled a "postmodern" turn in anthropological discourse, that turn is here both intellectually substantive and empirical in its manifestation. For these chapters, it seems to me, are only incidentally similar to the self-styled "postmodern" stance, which, to different degrees, rejects the "modernist" and even "structuralist" differentiations of *culture* and *structure* from *function* or *process/history* and thus from *agency*—though to what end is not always clear. This is not merely a case of such (sub)disciplinary reposturing. I think, rather, that within linguistic anthropology this turn of analytic focus emerges empirically out of the very material these authors address, not out of a more general epistemological, political, or other angst of authorial identity. The analytic moment of understanding the "ideological" grows vividly out of the data of language for these authors, no less than in his own day it did for Destutt de Tracy's attempts to understand the culturalized condition of cognition-and-communication and the cognitive-and-communicational condition of culture.

As linguistic anthropologists dealing with the semiotic complexities of language-use-in-context (thus being expansive in scholarly charge), we are faced first (and ultimately) with indexical facts—indexical facts "all the way down," in fact, as I like to say. They are facts of observed/experienced social practices, of cognizant social humans caught, thus, in interactional events, the systematicity of which relative to their (indexical) surround is our central problem: *Are* they systematic? If so, *how*? *In what* culturally defined *modalities*? And *to/for whom*? With respect to *which* (actionally bounded) institutional forms? (Re)aligning *whose* values in the semiotically seamless dialectic of mind-in-history? We have to engage multiple, obviously partial problems to situate indexical facts in their totality; surely all careful students of indexical facts have learned this, perhaps even the hard way. And surely such careful students have seen the necessity for considering the "ideological" in relation to anyone's ability to engage our analytic consciousness with indexicality in a grounded discourse that goes beyond the phenomenal "happening" itself.

The total cultural fact—and I include here primordially the total linguistic fact—consists of answers to all the indexically centered questions listed here, then, organized in terms of an overall and ultimate claim about how certain local practice/local knowledge is 'cultural'. As Le Maître Saussure himself observed, theoretical concepts are not of real power in the generalizations they allow except as they dictate their own methodology. *Ideology* of linguistic and cultural phenomena is such a concept, I think, epistemologically useful in making the phenomenal "realities" of both participants and observers (these are roles, not individuals, of course!) experience-near and tractable.

The splendid essays on which I have been asked to comment make this abundantly and richly clear.

NOTES

I thank the organizers/editors of the American Anthropological Association Annual Meeting symposium, "Language Ideologies: Practice and Theory," and of its original publication venue, a special issue of the journal *Pragmatics* (vol. 2, no. 3 [September 1992]), for the kind invitation to participate in this next round of revision-and-resubmission for Oxford University Press. Between the original preparation, presentation, and publication of the papers on which this commentary is based, in 1991–1992, and my preparation of this very substantially rewritten commentary, a number of kinds of interaction have been occurring in various combinations among the very same authors. The editors detail in their preface the formal venues. Additionally, there have been numerous viva voce, electronic, and manuscript-centered conversations among the various authors on topics in and around the concepts of linguistic ideology. In particular, I salute and warmly thank the several authors on whose papers I specifically comment for the collegial exchange of ideas that has led to the versions of our papers now before the readership. I offer this entextualized precipitate of ongoing and, to me, lively conversation to draw a wider set of collegial conversationalists into this process.

1. From the perspective of historical linguistics, here is an interesting problem in the shift of meaning from the abstract field-of-scientific-study sense to the concrete sense of (in the singular) one of the objects-of-scientific-study. It seems likely that the actual mechanism involved the early, derived adjectival usage—viz., (French) idéologique, (English) ideological—which construes whatever it applies to as an object characteristically studied by the *field* called "ideology." It is easy to see that a derivational back-formation has occurred in the pair (English) ideology → ideologic(al), reidentifying the derivational base with the *object-of-study* sense, since the (French) -ique, (English) -ic(al) formations of adjectives have moved decisively in the direction of characterizing objects on the basis of their own denoting nouns, especially as these share formally identical stems.

It is clear that, contemporaneous with Destutt de Tracy's introduction of the term idéologie in Paris, there was a stimulated translation coinage of an equivalent in English; attestations from 1796 and 1797 appear (reporting on the French discussion) with the authorially stipulated senses for ideology and ideological (see *Oxford English Dictionary*, s.vv.). Apparently through a kind of delocutionary or "voiced" quotation-translation of (pro-)-Napoleonic French usage ca. 1813-1815, taken over by reactionary political interests afterward, the derivational set ideology, ideologue, ideologist, ideological emerges with a fiercely negative and mocking indexical loading (or "connotation") communicated by the sender about the denotatum, leading to the stereotypic sense of unpractical, speculative, idealist social philosophical thoughts that constitute "ideology" and occur in the thinkers of them, the "ideologues." By the 1830s and 1840s, the opposition is established in English of (negatively valued) ideas versus historical and material facts, especially distinguishing ideas stereotypically associable—according to one 1827 citation of ideology—"with hot-brained boys and crazed enthusiasts"—that is, the negatively valued (mere) social-theoretic ideas of a group clearly indexed as not that of the speaker or writer. Thus, any *ideologist*, or proponent of the intendedly scientific field of *ideology*, has merely *ideological* beliefs, as opposed to ideas that correspond to material, historical, and factual realities.

A probable parallel shift in the noun-adjective derivational structure may be observable in very contemporary times, in English close to home, where we can note the very recent shift away from the erstwhile and older derivational paradigms for the field of study, *linguistics*, and its object, *language*:

(a) [noun] language → [adjective] linguistic [= 'of language'];
(b) [noun] linguistics → [adjective phrase] of linguistics.

This is shown in the form linguistic theory, which uses the morphologically derived adjective, the stem of which resembles the noun of (b) in form more than that of (a). Thus, the emergent complex nominal linguistic theory seems to speakers (linguists themselves!) to mean 'theory (as opposed to descriptive or other practice) *of linguistics*', not '. . . *of language*', as in a productive noun phrase linguistic theory under older derivation (a). This means, in effect, that derivation (b) has been replaced with derivation (b'):

(b') [noun] linguistics → [adjective] linguistic.

This furthermore ousts the adjectival sense of derivation (a) and its kind of noun phrase formation, at least in much technical discourse, for which complex-nominal constructions are used. Hence, linguistic theory winds up being a (pejoratively) "ideological" term—in its newer derivational sense—reflecting a disciplinary social organization of self-styled "'linguistic theor'ists" as against all others, whose work seems to the former not to be "linguistic theory."

2. This does not contradict the understanding that some aspects of denotational language as it occurs in the course of social interaction are justifiably referred to systems of Saussurean-Bloomfieldian-Chomskian sense-generating morphosyntax, to which utterance forms can be said to conform and in terms of which a skeleton of denotational meaningfulness—semanticoreferential usage of language form—can be projected in the usual manner.

3. It is, of course, essential to keep these planes of textuality distinct one from another, since the first answers the question "What has been/will have been *said* in-and-by some use of signs?" and the second "What has been/will have been *done* in-and-by some use of signs?" The answer to the first is a model of denotational (referential and modalized predicational) coherence over some span of event-duration, frequently expressed in terms of propositional or "informational" content; the answer to the second is a model of social-actional coherence,

frequently expressed in terms of social acts in some framework for description. It must be seen, however, that both of these kinds of text are models of gradient, interpersonal, indexically consummated achievements in the processual realtime of using signs. Further, the decontextualizable, genred appearance of text to the user is an important, ideologically informed perspectival reality that makes cumulated indexical presuppositions seem to gel as structure autonomous of realtime contextualization (and thus available, for example, for armchair microsociologizing of linguistic pragmatists and philosophers). And note how such structure becomes vivid when concretized in a *text-artifact* that can perpetually be reanimated—for example, by reading a printed array as a text—in a new entextualizing event. See now Silverstein and Urban, eds. 1996, previewed in Bauman and Briggs 1990:72–78, a volume in which the partials of these processes are examined in elaborate detail through case studies of diverse entextualizing and (re)contextualizing modalities.

4. In my 1979 piece "Language structure and linguistic ideology" I reference Robert K. Merton's differentiation of *manifest* and *latent* functions of social practices (see Silverstein 1979:204), especially as this aligns ideologically informed metapragmatic "takes" (there called function_1) on indexical function (there called function_2) with Merton's manifest dimension, and much of actual indexical effectiveness—especially in the way of entailments of indexical occurrence—with Merton's latent dimension. Given the dialectic of ideological engagement with indexicality, however, the concept of *orders of indexicality* mediated by ideologically informed metapragmatics (see now Silverstein 1996) is a much more useful formulation, since, in certain respects, ideological formations depend on the fact of signs functioning indexically (at whatever order, n), just as, with respect to this functioning, a higher order (call it $n+1$) of indexical function depends on the presupposition of ideological formations informing a metapragmatics for order n.

5. Is this not the essence implied in processes of totemism that has been completely missed by structural-functionalists and structuralists alike? Here note the similarity to phenomena of fetishization, of reification, and of commodification, as they have been termed in their respective literatures informed by Marx, Durkheim, Lukács, among others. I sketch a generalization of these phenomena to the wider semiotic realm, fully in keeping with and developed from scattered insights of the late Roland Barthes (see especially 1968, 1983), as I have detailed in two as yet unpublished papers at American Anthropological Association meetings in 1984 and 1988, "The 'value' of objectual language" and "De-voice of authority." For the more general view of precipitated and transportable "text," see the papers in Silverstein and Urban, eds., 1996.

6. Note that the intuition of "saying the same thing" in the ideologically informed capacity of native speaker contemplating dialectal/superposed indexical variation is a very different one from anything a structural linguist might need for purposes of setting up morphosyntactic and hence 'sense' equivalences in the realm of morphosyntactic *paraphrase* relationships. A paraphrase, in this conceptualization, has nothing to do with an indexical paradigm of equivalence-in-context, of course, contextualization and entextualization being, the theory goes, entirely independent "performance" characteristics distinct from characteristics—like paraphrase relationships—that give evidence for the structure of linguistic (*sc.*, grammatical) "competence." (Small child watching the Emperor parade by: "Or *are* they?")

7. I first drew this distinction at a 1988 National Science Foundation conference on honorifics in Portland, Oregon (John Haviland and Alan Kim, organizers) in my presentation, "Demeanor indexicals and honorific registers," now happily superseded by summaries and rephrasings in Silverstein 1996:274–80; cf. also Agha 1994.

8. Thus, note the case of Javanese deference honorification laid out in Silverstein 1979:216–27 and in greater detail in Errington 1988 (see also Smith-Hefner 1988). The

multiple dimensions of indexicality involved, performed deference by speaker to addressee, by speaker to referent, and—indexing speaker's estimation of such—by Agent-NP denotatum to Dative-NP denotatum, differ from the analysis of the dominant linguistic ideology. Ideologically, by contrast, there seems to be a basic conception of addressee-focused unidimensional degrees of "fineness" of language and of perilinguistic self-display a speaker ought to use as part of the appropriate behavioral envelope for addressee. This constitutes an ego-created, addressee-focused bath of signs in which one should strive to immerse one's interlocutor; the "finer" one's interlocutor (in a metric ultimately cosmologically centered through the king or sultan in traditional social structure), the clearer the demand for a "finer" and, thus, figuratively, for a subdued self-display by the utterer. Ironically, the more "finely" one can speak, the more one shows self—at a second order of indexicality informed by, and depending on, the ideological understanding of the practice—to be deserving of ideologically informed "fineness" of speech and behavior from others!

Janet Morford 1995:245–52 reports on various speakers of French who observe that their families of orientation were so cultured and polite that they would not use reciprocal *T* of familiar intimacy (of the famous Brown and Gilman 1960 set, *T/V*) under any circumstances, even in the domestic group. Note here again the *second-order* indexical value, focused on "culturedness" of *speaker*, in what has obviously emerged in certain social sectors of native users of French as a register of honorification the use of which bespeaks positional identity of speakers, not necessarily of addressees.

9. Interestingly, in ChiBemba it is metaphorical "pluralization" of human-denoting nouns that marks 'honorific singular' speech acts that accompany reference-and-predication, paralleling many similar phenomena where categories of numerosity form the metaphorical base, as in, for example, French and Yokuts (see Silverstein 1976:37–40). By contrast, treating semantically 'human' nouns as though they should have metaphorically "thing"-like concord prefixation is a form of enacted pejoration; consider a scrub nurse in a surgery department in an aloud utterance directed ostensibly to a coworker and referring to the then nearby and shabbily dressed author (July 1963): "*That* goes to Harvard!"

10. In passing, Hill seems to attribute to me a view that *all* ideologies are referentialist in nature. To my knowledge, I have never articulated such a view, indeed contrasting the "Standard Average European" linguistic ideologies from others precisely by the former's centering all linguistic function on denotation—that is, modalized referring and predicating, even attempting to "reduce" all other, as we now see distinctively constituted indexical effects, to "implicatures" (Grice, Sperber, and Wilson, et al.) and/or to implicitly denotational "illocutionary force indicating devices" (Austin, Searle, et al.). What I have claimed is that the *forms* of language on which ideologies tend to concentrate their concerns are, as a consequence of metalinguistic availability, precisely those that would be yielded up by analysis under a referentialist principle (as in our linguists' professional notions of structure), plus forms constructionally compatible with these, regardless of the indexical *function(s)* these forms manifest in pragmatic context and regardless of how the local ethnometapragmatics of ideological rationalization understands their functioning. Cases in Silverstein 1979, 1985a, 1985b, and 1996, as well as the case of the Ngarinjins (who live together with Worora people, with whom I worked) that Rumsey 1990 reported on, show a variety of metapragmatic consciousness, ethnometapragmatics, and ideological rationalizations that include these first two orders of phenomena. One might see the consciousness of the counterdiscourses Hill discusses as maximally "colonized" by referentialist ideologies, in a way—and again, given the social positioning of their formulators, they are maximally ironic with respect to first-order indexicality.

11. It is important to note that from the particular addressee- or receiver-focused understanding of communication in Gapun and more generally in Melanesia (see Kulick,

this volume), very different ideas of agentivity and responsibility-to-communicate (i.e., "send" or "receive") inform whatever are the local concepts akin to our 'monologue' and 'dialogue'. The point is, in a *kros* the sender forces knowledge of affect and so on on receiver(s), while in the men's house there must be lots of what I have termed (1976:47–48) diplomatic nonindexicality going on as a strategy of receivers who can potentially take up a later participatory role in (non)response, making the men's house speech seem potentially more "monologic"—that is, not responded to in every respect, in our Western, sender-focused stereotype.

At some future time we will, as theorists, have to turn our attention to rebuilding the concepts of monologue and dialogue on the basis of number of participants, distribution across role-types over interactional-structural time, and changing understandings of which role is at every moment the fulcrum of agentive authority (or control) and of agentive responsibility (or blame). In the *kros*, the same individual seems to be a fulcrum for both, making it perhaps "monologic" to the Gapuners in their addressee-centric ideology.

12. We might note here, for the American English context, the affective loading of erstwhile immigrant languages of ethnic identity. Words and expressions that become indexes of ethnicity frequently are ascribed an affectivity that seems to their ethnically self-indexing users to be unavailable through the use of their translations in English; in a kind of discourse of ethnic nostalgia, they are said to have a warmth and flavor of in-group coziness. (This can be negatively valued, as well, in technical, legal, or civic institutions, which demand standardized expository "objectivity" and thus evaluate such usage as again matter out-of-place.) When we cross this perception with the understanding that (1) conventionally affective language, as opposed to straightforward expository denotational language, is culturally gendered as female, feminine talk, and (2) there are class-indicating second-order indexicalities associated with the stratification of registers around denotational standard (see Labov 1972 and a generation's follow-up work for studies mostly at the phonological plane), it is not hard to see the enacted tropes being indexed by continuing to speak nonstandard, non-English languages: the very opposite of the ideologically mythic straight-talking, standard-using "real" man of few, denotationally exact, and well-chosen (Standard English) words.

13. Generalizing, Barthes 1968:89–90 calls it the *denotational* code, from Saussurean views of (literal) denotation as *parole* realizable on the basis of only Saussurean signification (relations between signifiers and signifieds in the order of *langue*).

14. There is an immense social anthropological literature on ritual, worrying and developing various Durkheimian, Weberian, and Marxian points (not to mention Freudian ones). For an interesting development of the issue of ritual performativity as tropic figuration, see Tambiah 1985:17–166. Following on Maurice Bloch's views of the relationship between ritual language and ideology (see, for example, 1975, 1989), see the interesting review essay by Kelly and Kaplan 1990. I have elaborated some of the themes about the power of ritual and ritualization in Silverstein 1993: passim and in an as yet unpublished piece, "Metaforces of power in traditional oratory" (1981b). See also now the important piece on "poetics and performance" by Bauman and Briggs 1990, reviewing trends in 1980s literature.

REFERENCES

Aarsleff, Hans. 1982. *From Locke to Saussure: Essays on the Study of Language and Intellectual History*. Minneapolis: University of Minnesota Press.

Agha, Asif. 1994. Honorification. *Annual Review of Anthropology* 23:277–302.

Barthes, Roland. 1968. *Elements of Semiology*. Translated by A. Lavers and C. Smith. New York: Hill and Wang.

———. 1983. *The Fashion System*. Translated by M. Ward and R. Howard. New York: Hill and Wang.

Bauman, Richard, and Charles L. Briggs. 1990. Poetics and Performance as Critical Perspectives on Language and Social Life. *Annual Review of Anthropology* 19:59–88.

Bloch, Maurice. 1975. Inroduction. In *Political Language and Oratory in Traditional Society*, ed. Maurice Bloch, pp. 1–28. London: Academic Press.

———. 1989. *Ritual, History, and Power: Selected Papers in Anthropology*. London: Athlone.

Blom, Jan-Petter, and John J. Gumperz. 1972. Social Meaning in Linguistic Structure: Code-switching in Norway. In *Directions in Sociolinguistics: The Ethnography of Communication*, ed. John J. Gumperz and Dell Hymes, pp. 407–434. New York: Holt, Rinehart and Winston.

Brown, Roger, and Albert Gilman. 1960. The Pronouns of Power and Solidarity. In *Style in Language*, ed. T. A. Sebeok, pp. 253–276. Cambridge, Mass.: MIT Press.

Destutt de Tracy, Antoine, Comte. [1801] 1827. *Elémens d'idéologie*. 1: *Idéologie proprement dite*. Paris: Lévi.

Errington, J. Joseph. 1988. *Structure and Style in Javanese: A Semiotic View of Linguistic Etiquette*. Philadelphia: University of Pennsylvania Press.

Geuss, Raymond. 1981. *The Idea of a Critical Theory: Habermas and the Frankfurt School*. Cambridge: Cambridge University Press.

Gumperz, John J. 1968. Linguistics. 3: The Speech Community. In *International Encyclopedia of the Social Sciences*, vol. 9, ed. D. Sills, pp. 381–386. New York: Macmillan.

Hill, Jane H. 1985. The Grammar of Consciousness and the Consciousness of Grammar. *American Ethnologist* 12:725–737.

Hill, Jane H., and Kenneth C. Hill. 1978. Honorific Usage in Modern Nahuatl: The Expression of Social Distance and Respect in the Nahuatl of the Malinche Volcano Area. *Language* 54:123–155.

———. 1980. Mixed Grammar, Purist Grammar, and Language Attitudes in Modern Nahuatl. *Language in Society* 9:321–348.

———. 1986. *Speaking Mexicano: Dynamics of Syncretic Language in Central Mexico*. Tucson: University of Arizona Press.

Irvine, Judith T. 1974. Strategies of Status Manipulation in the Wolof Greeting. In *Explorations in the Ethnography of Speaking*, ed. Richard Bauman and Joel Sherzer, pp. 167–191, 458–460, 486–487. Cambridge: Cambridge University Press.

———. 1990. Registering Affect: Heteroglossia in the Linguistic Expression of Emotion. In *Language and the Politics of Emotion*, ed. C. A. Lutz and L. Abu-Lughod, pp. 126–161. Cambridge: Cambridge University Press.

Kelly, John D., and Martha Kaplan. 1990. History, Structure, and Ritual. *Annual Review of Anthropology* 19:119–150.

Kroskrity, Paul V. 1993. *Language, History, and Identity: Ethnolinguistic Studies of the Arizona Tewa*. Tucson: University of Arizona Press.

Kulick, Don. 1992. *Language Shift and Cultural Reproduction: Socialization, Self, and Syncretism in a Papua New Guinean Village*. New York: Cambridge University Press.

———. 1993. Speaking as a Woman: Structure and Gender in Domestic Arguments in a Papua New Guinean Village. *Cultural Anthropology* 8:510–541.

Labov, William. 1972. *Sociolinguistic Patterns*. Philadelphia: University of Pennsylvania Press.

Morford, Janet H. 1995. La décontraction: *The Modernization of Middle-class Manners in Contemporary France*. Ph.D. diss., University of Chicago.

Ochs[Keenan], Elinor. 1974. Norm-makers, Norm-breakers: Uses of Speech by Men and Women in a Malagasy Community. In *Explorations in the Ethnography of Speaking*, ed. Richard Bauman and Joel Sherzer, pp. 125–143, 457, 485. Cambridge: Cambridge University Press.

Ochs, Elinor. 1992. Indexing Gender. In *Rethinking Context: Language as an Interactive Phenomenon*, ed. A. Duranti and C. Goodwin, pp. 335–358. Cambridge: Cambridge University Press.

Putnam, Hilary. 1975. The Meaning of "Meaning." In *Philosophical Papers*. Vol. 2: *Mind, Language, and Reality*, pp. 215–271. Cambridge: Cambridge University Press.

Rumsey, Alan. 1990. Wording, Meaning, and Linguistic Ideology. *American Anthropologist* 92:346–361.

Silverstein, Michael. 1976. Shifters, Linguistic Categories, and Cultural Description. In *Meaning in Anthropology*, ed. K. Basso and H. A. Selby Jr., pp. 11–55. Albuquerque: University of New Mexico Press.

———. 1979. Language Structure and Linguistic Ideology. In *The Elements: A Parasession on Linguistic Units and Levels*, ed. P. Clyne et al., pp. 193–247. Chicago: Chicago Linguistic Society.

———. 1981a. The Limits of Awareness. Working Papers in Sociolinguistics 84. Austin, Tex.: Southwest Educational Research Laboratory.

———. 1981b. Metaforces of Power in Traditional Oratory. Lecture to Yale University Department of Anthropology.

———. 1984. The "Value" of Objectual Language. Paper delivered at a symposium of the American Anthropological Association's 83rd annual meeting, Denver, Colorado.

———. 1985a. The Culture of Language in Chinookan Narrative Texts; or, on Saying that . . . in Chinook. In *Grammar Inside and Outside the Clause*, ed. J. Nichols and A. C. Woodbury, pp. 132–71. Cambridge: Cambridge University Press.

———. 1985b. Language and the Culture of Gender: At the Intersection of Structure, Usage, and Ideology. In *Semiotic Mediation: Sociocultural and Psychological Perspectives*, ed. E. Mertz and R. J. Parmentier, pp. 219–259. Orlando, Fla.: Academic Press.

———. 1988. De-voice of Authority. Paper delivered at a symposium of the American Anthropological Association's 87th annual meeting, Phoenix, Arizona.

———. 1993. Metapragmatic Discourse and Metapragmatic Function. In *Reflexive Language: Reported Speech and Metapragmatics*, ed. John A. Lucy, pp. 33–58. Cambridge: Cambridge University Press.

———. 1996. Indexical Order and the Dialectics of Sociolinguistic Life. *Symposium about Language and Society—Austin* III:266–295.

Silverstein, Michael, and Greg Urban, eds. 1996. *Natural Histories of Discourse*. Chicago: University of Chicago Press.

Smith-Hefner, Nancy J. 1988. Women and Politeness: The Javanese Example. *Language in Society* 17:535–554.

Tambiah, Stanley J. 1985. *Culture, Thought, and Social Action: An Anthropological Perspective*. Cambridge, Mass.: Harvard University Press.

Watson-Gegeo, Karen A., and David W. Gegeo. 1991. The Impact of Church Affiliation on Language Use in Kwara'ae (Solomon Islands). *Language in Society* 20:533–555.

II

LANGUAGE IDEOLOGY IN INSTITUTIONS OF POWER

7

Linguistic Ideology and Praxis in U.S. Law School Classrooms

ELIZABETH MERTZ

This article explores the relationship between linguistic ideology and praxis through an examination of the language of U.S. law school classrooms. These classrooms afford an exciting opportunity for examining the socially powerful role of linguistic ideology as it intersects with and regiments linguistic practice. The language of professional socialization is at once a key part of the process whereby social identities are forged and changed and an expression of the epistemologies of professional cultures that have important connections with the power structures of our society.

Legal socialization is particularly intriguing because legal institutions serve a special translating function in Western society. When rendering diverse realms of cultural experience in a common language, legal institutions use language as an important and integral part of a socially transformative process. Thus, the act of translation[1] into legal language is one in which linguistic and social regimentation mesh—and law school classrooms are accordingly heavily focused on the role of language in social process, predictably rich in linguistic ideologies.

Bourdieu and Passeron (1977) have described the educational process as one in which a new relation to language and culture is transmitted, in an apparently autonomous institutional setting that nonetheless constantly contributes to the reproduction and legitimization of the established social order. Similarly, anthropologists and sociolinguists working in classroom settings have frequently found the use of language in the classroom to be a powerful orienting social practice (Anyon 1981, Collins 1986, Gee 1985, Heath 1983, Mehan 1979, Philips 1972). Hidden behind the apparent content of any lesson are deeper messages about how the world operates, about what kind of knowledge is socially valued, and about who may speak and in what manner—a cultural worldview that is quietly conveyed through classroom language. Thus, broader social patterns and struggles are played out and transformed in the smaller-scale dynamics of classroom education (see Wertsch 1985a, 1985b; see also suggestions in Bourdieu 1987 and Halliday 1982 that legal educational institutions play a role in the rationalization of the legal system).

Studying Law School Classrooms

To study the linguistic exchanges that constitute law school classroom interaction, we taped the first semester of a Contracts class in eight different schools across the country. In-class coders kept track of who was speaking, the kinds of turns involved, and various other aspects of the classroom dynamics that weren't adequately captured on tape.[2] The tapes were then transcribed and the exchanges were timed and coded in order to generate an overarching quantitative "map" of the classroom interactions. Each class transcript was also analyzed qualitatively,[3] and we created an "ethnography" for each class and then an overarching qualitative summary for each school in the study. We were also able to interview the professors and small groups of the students in a number of the schools of the study.[4]

The schools were selected from across the status hierarchy range of law schools: there were two of the "elite" or "top-five" law schools, one "prestige" or "top-fifteen" law school, two "regional" and two "local" schools, and, in addition, one night school class.[5] Five of the professors were men; three were women. Two were professors of color; five were "white."[6]

Linguistic Ideology and Language Socialization in the Law School Classroom

In order to frame this material, I build from two theoretical approaches. On the one hand, I draw on work that suggests ways in which linguistic ideology is a crucial part of the social grounding of language use and structure—rather than, for instance, treating ideology as an autonomous "cultural" level of phenomena (see Brenneis 1984; Gal 1987, 1989; Hanks 1989, 1990; Hill 1985; Irvine 1989; Woolard 1985, 1989a, 1989b; Woolard and Schieffelin 1994). In this view, the conceptions that speakers hold about language and how it works—whether at the conscious level or at the less explicit level of presupposed cultural assumptions—affect and are implicated in the daily use of language in social situations that are laden with power dimensions and politics. As Woolard notes in her introduction, the study of linguistic ideology provides a much-needed bridge between linguistic and social theory because it relates the microculture of communicative action to political economic considerations of power and social inequality, confronting macrosocial constrains on language behavior.

On the other hand, my analysis approaches the study of linguistic ideology at the intersection of language use and structure, using a linguistic anthropological framework developed by Silverstein (1993), Bauman and Briggs (1990), Lucy (1993), and others. This framework takes linguistic ideology not as a mere false frame that distorts our vision of "reality," but rather as part and parcel of the linguistic structure and praxis that we study (see Mertz 1989, 1993). Thus, as people interact through language, they draw on and create ideologies about language, thereby developing linguistic worldviews or epistemologies that guide them in deciding how to speak and what to say. For example, if people view speech as a contest, and utterances that are marked in particular (metalinguistic) ways as challenges, this is likely to inform their responses to such utterances. Ideologies of language emerge at the meta-level, where language signals reflexively about its own signaling. A linguistic ideology may be very explicit, as when speakers overtly discuss aspects of language use or when political factions battle over whether monolingualism is necessary for national unity. Alternatively, linguistic ideology may appear more subtly, for example, as when a set of meta-level structural linguistic features indicates what kind of speech is occurring (or ought to occur) (see Silverstein 1979, 1993). In either case, linguistic ideology is a part of the structure and practice of speaking (or writing or signing), emergent in linguistic structure but not completely determinative of or identical with the linguistic praxis in process. Thus, linguistic ideology can simultaneously distort or misrepresent, and shape or reflect, linguistic practice. This approach to linguistic ideology allows us to examine the ways in which social power and change are implicated in language structure—often through this process of ideological reflection and refraction.

Combining these two approaches in order to study the language of law school classrooms, we examine the linguistic exchanges in class, with particular attention to underlying ideologies or meta-level characterizations of language that might be at work in the daily practice and structure of law school teaching. We further ask how these ideologies are involved in power relations both within and beyond the classroom. Is there, for example, an ideology of how language functions that is commonly imparted to students—and, more broadly, is there a shared epistemological structure that powerfully embodies the way legal language "works" in society more generally? Are there points of contest in the law school classroom that evidence struggles over this meta-level? Because the law school process is one in which students are socialized to a new identity and a new way of talking, we can also draw on the language socialization literature for insights into how minute aspects of the linguistic structure and interaction constrain and channel socialization of "new" speakers (see Ochs 1988, Ochs and Schieffelin 1984, Schieffelin and Ochs 1986).

This analysis draws in particular on Silverstein's conception of a dialectic between pragmatics and metapragmatics, one aspect of which is the way "explicit metapragmatic registers instantiated in metapragmatic discourse encapsulate ideologies of language use and play an obvious role in the institutionalization of discursive mechanisms of society" (1993:55). The ongoing pragmatics of discourse achieve coherence only through some kind of metapragmatic structuring, which construes that ongoing discourse as being a certain type of discursive event. There is an affinity between this Silversteinian formulation and Gumperz's conception of "contextualization cues," which are the "constellations of surface features of message form [that] are the means by which speakers signal and listeners interpret what the activity is, how semantic content is to be understood and *how* each sentence relates to what precedes or follows" (1982:131). It is often through very subtle combinations of intonation, meta-level framing devices, and so forth that speakers signal that an utterance is to be interpreted as a particular kind of talk (e.g., a friendly exchange, a request for help, an irritated signal to back off). There is a dialectical process at work here in which ongoing pragmatics—at times even accidently—contribute to a continuing typification process. For example, if one participant inadvertently uses passive constructions to describe an event for which the other participant wants him or her to take responsibility, the pragmatics of the ongoing conversation might contribute to a growing typification on the part of the listener that could be labeled "denial of responsibility." At the same time, the meta-level typification frames and shapes the interpretations speakers make of the ongoing pragmatics. The negotiation of this typification is ongoing in conversation. For instance, an interaction that starts as a fight can become a friendly exchange, all the time marked and created through meta-linguistic signaling. Like Silverstein, Gumperz notes that this process of shifting and reframing through contextualization cues often occurs without conscious recognition—that it is "habitually used and perceived but rarely consciously noted and almost never talked about directly" (1982:131).

Not only is this process of meta-level signaling ongoing throughout linguistic interaction; it is constantly subject to negotiation or even contest. Participants in the same event may, of course, construe it differently, so several meta-level interpretations may be "on the floor" at the same time. Herein lies some of the potential for struggle over the construction of discourse in key institutional arenas.[7] In order to move beyond idiosyncratic interpretations of individual interchanges to a broader social view of this regimenting process, however, it might be productive to focus on moments when this typification process becomes more generally shared and explicit, approaching what Silverstein calls "noncancelability" or "interactional nondeniability." To use a crude example, it may always be possible to retrospectively alter a meta-level formulation ("I didn't mean to insult you"), but it becomes much harder to do so when one has used an explicit metapragmatic marker ("I'm insulting you, you idiot"). An unfamiliar audience listening to an exchange like this might be able to rely less on individualized knowledge of the speakers and more on a socially shared interpretation of "what is happening" (to the degree that explicit markers invoke that more overt and shared level). As struggles over "what is happening" become part of institutional processes, the dialectic between pragmatics and metapragmatics becomes less an issue of the vagaries of individual dynamics among participants and more an articulation of general levels of social definition, redefinition, and contest.

Of course, this use of a register that signals to participants what type of event is being indexed is always enmeshed in linguistic ideology,[8] for only through some sort of ideological formulation about language and how it works do we have a notion of types of discourse or events.[9] At the same time, typologizing discourse also permits it to function socially, even in less institutionalized or socially constrained interactions. This is not to say that at any conceivable moment only one understanding of what is happening in the discourse is possible. Rather, ideological struggle over the social meaning of discourse takes place against the backdrop of explicitly typifying (i.e., socially sedimented) metapragmatic registers. Thus alternative meta-level ideological formulations can provide avenues of resistance to settled practices.[10] And where an exchange takes place within an institutional framework in which one kind of meta-level interpretation fits institutional interests in a particular way, invocation of an alternative metapragmatic filter through and in speech pragmatics may well signal resistance to these very institutional frames and processes.

As noted, this conception of linguistic ideology and its relationship to language pragmatics can fruitfully be brought together with work on the social foundations of language that analyzes language dynamics as deeply implicated in broader social power dynamics and structures (see, e.g., Woolard 1985, 1989a, 1989b; Errington 1988). Combining the two perspectives, we see that there is a point at which the institutionalization of language can be understood at once as constantly at work in the structuring of discourse and as dependent on an ongoing process of ideological sedimentation of metapragmatic types. This understanding is exciting because there are parts of the ideological process that are more accessible to conscious reflection (presumably, the sedimentation of types), and others that are at a level that Bourdieu (1977) refers to as *habitus*, or habitual structure. Applying Bourdieu's notion here, we would say that there is a habitual structure of language pragmatics and metapragmatics that operates without conscious reflection to orient speakers in nonneutral ways. This dual character to linguistic ideology accounts for both the sometimes resistant or nontransparent reactions of language to conscious (ideologically motivated) attempts at change and the central character of ideological reflection in institutionalized language use. As an initial step toward developing an adequate view of this complex process at work in law school classrooms, I now turn to an examination of a number of exchanges that occurred in the classes studied.

Classroom Exchanges

In this section I focus on several classroom exchanges in which students did not conform to the discourse format encouraged by the professor. Note that in these classes the reigning mode of interaction is a highly stylized genre known as the "Socratic method," in which the professor addresses a series of questions to a single student. Each question supposedly builds on the student's previous answer and draws the student closer to the response the professor is seeking (see Philips 1982). Although a frequently expressed ideology in law school teaching is that there are "no right answers" to questions, it is clear that there *are* wrong answers. This is indicated by everything from pitch and intonation of professors' responses to overtly negative assessments of previous answers. The exchange of questions and answers pushes students toward certainty, urging them to take definite positions that they must then defend. (It matters not whether the position taken is "right" or "wrong," for, as one professor told me in an interview, frequently the "wrong" answers are more useful as teaching devices. He noted that these incorrect responses permit a building up of suspense; after the professor gets more and more students to adopt the incorrect position, he can then "spring" the correct answer on them. This is a procedure, I was told, that is designed to burn the correct answer more indelibly into students' brains.) It is therefore a violation of the metapragmatic rules to refuse to take a position—or to refuse to give reasons for a position that lend themselves to this kind of back-and-forth. In particular, references to affect or emotion as a basis for a position just "don't work" within this kind of metapragmatic frame.

In the analysis that follows, I look at Socratic exchanges as both pragmatic structures and instantiated metapragmatic ideology . That is, Socratic dialogue is seen at once as a pragmatic structuring of the ongoing discourse and as a practice that carries with it certain metalinguistic ideological assumptions. These assumptions are deeply linked to the institutional structure to which students are being socialized as they enter the legal profession. I have elsewhere suggested one key aspect of this language-metalanguage link, arguing that in classroom discourse professors rupture the "textualist" ideologies that so many students bring with them from prior educational experiences (Mertz 1996). Instead of being a metapragmatic ideology that approaches texts as fixed and transparent, classroom dialogue imparts an ideology of legal texts as fundamentally always open to—and in a process of—reconstitution and recontextualization. This ideology is conveyed in and through the pragmatic structure of classroom discourse. Susan Philips has also noted that the insistent channeling of discourse through the professor that is a feature of Socratic dialogue prepares students "to function effectively in focused interactions involving many people where a single person controls the talk of others . . . where one key characteristic of the status differentiation is that the person in control, namely the judge, asks repeated questions of the person under control, who must answer those questions in a highly specialized language" (1982:192). This effect is only heightened by the mandatory participation that is often a feature of the Socratic classroom. Thus, the structure of classroom language is focused on breaking down fixed approaches to texts and orienting students to a discourse in which power and authority are seen as manifest in particular ways through language structuring.

Here, I analyze aspects of the pragmatic structure of law school dialogue, focusing on points of conflict and breakdown. At these moments, we can see another fundamental aspect of the pragmatic-metapragmatic dialectic that is occurring in law school language. I begin with an exchange between a male professor and a female student.[11] The student has voiced an objection to the fairness of a case result:[12]

STUDENT The contract, the original contract itself had a provision in it for prices that change due to an advance in case of the rise in the wages which actually happened causing the forward contract to be so much more expensive. So, if we're looking at expectation damages then the point that, I mean, in his contract that he had he would have, his original contract that the coke in that would have been subject to rise as well, would it not?

PROFESSOR I don't know. What's the relevance of that to—

STUDENT —well—

PROFESSOR —how we solve the problem?

(*silence*)

STUDENT (*rising intonation*) It just bothers me. I . . .

(*class laughter*)

PROFESSOR What bothers you?

STUDENT (*silence, smiles, looks down*)

PROFESSOR What bothers you, I take it, is the parties thought about the problem of labor and the increased price in labor. And you're suggesting this was something they recognized. Now, do you want to go from there to say, if they recognized that . . . there was a problem with the cost of the labor . . . if there was going to be a stunningly disturbed market they should have said something about it, is that what you want to say? If that's what you want to say, where does that lead you?

STUDENT (*again, silence, looks down*)

Note that at the end of the exchange, the professor essentially adopts the student's voice, using indirect speech ("you're suggesting this was something they recognized"). The student has refused to budge from her chosen register ("It just bothers me") and has indexed that refusal with silence. And so the professor speaks for her, taking her place in the dialogue, and, in the absence of any cooperation from her, imbues her with the correct voice. His insistent continuation of the dialogue, even without help from his interlocutor, forces on this segment of speech the metapragmatic interpretation he seeks to impose—that this instance of speaking is an event of a particular discourse type (Socratic dialogue with its accompanying metapragmatic rules). One key rule of this type of discourse is that interlocutors keep talking, keep coming up with reasons and justifications for articulated and antagonistically defended positions ("Where does that lead you?"). Her silence indicates a competing interpretation; this chunk of speech is an exchange in which she wishes to express a felt dissatisfaction with a case outcome. The power differential between interlocutors is perhaps evidenced by the fact that the final interpretation goes to the professor; yet her strongly maintained, smiling silence is a resistance that is not ultimately overcome by him. The timing of the class's laughter, incidentally, reinforced the professor's signal that her response was inappropriate.

The technique of taking a student's place in the dialogue when the student does not respond as desired is used in many of the classrooms in the study. More rare, but dramatic illustrations of the general metapragmatic struggle at work here, are times when the professor dictates to the student which words to use, as in one exchange in which the professor, after rephrasing a question several times (and receiving the same, "incorrect" answer—"no") told the student, "Try yes." The student initially responded with silence. The professor repeated, with rising intonation and added stress on each word, "Say yes." "Yes," said the student at last. The professor then proceeded to attempt a continued dialogue by asking, "Why?" Note here that there was a movement from more implicit metapragmatic indicators that the student's answers were unsatisfactory to a breakthrough into very explicit regimentation when all else failed. This more explicit metapragmatic regimentation, directing the student to repeat ("Say yes"), is identical in form to the metalinguistic formulations found across many cultures in child language socialization routines, which typically take "the form of explicit prompting by the caregiver or other member of the group. . . . The prompting routine is itself marked by characteristic linguistic features. For example, the routine is usually but not always initiated by an imperative verb form meaning 'say' or 'do,' followed by the utterance to be repeated" (Ochs 1986: 5).[13] The modeling of correct language use in Socratic routines, then, may be an invocation of one of the more powerful linguistic socialization techniques available in the human repertoire (see also Ochs and Schieffelin 1984).

Here metapragmatic regimentation of the discourse over resistances is the mode of socializing students, molding them into new social identities (lawyers) by literally putting new voices into their mouths and, at the same time, thoughts into their heads. This regimentation occurs through multiple layers of language, from subtler typification of chunks of speech as legal argument to overt appropriation of interlocutors' voices where necessary. At times the connection between putting new voices into students' mouths and reformulating their identities becomes quite explicit, as in the following exchange:

PROFESSOR Tell me. Why are you in law school, Ms. C.? Why are you studying the law? Don't tell me to become a lawyer; I understand that.

STUDENT It interests me.

PROFESSOR Because it interests you. What a quaint way to put it. Why aren't you in business school? where every sensible person probably ought to be now.

STUDENT I'm thinking of changing right now.

PROFESSOR A possibly wise move. But why didn't you go directly to business school?

[I omit several turns in which the student reiterates that law school interests her, and the professor repeats his question about her motivation for choosing law school.]

STUDENT To do something different.

PROFESSOR What is it that's different about the law from business?

STUDENT It's not certain; it's ever-changing.

PROFESSOR Well, it is that. It is ever-changing. Or is it just that you like variety? Come, Ms. C., you're not that shallow a person. Let's be honest. Let's force you to say something maybe you don't

> really mean. Let's psychoanalyze you. You're in law school rather than business school because you find it at bottom more deeply satisfying or at least you thought you could, to study the law than go to business school. You are not some lucre-seeking monster who would go to business school. You may be right, however, to be a lucre-seeking monster at the present time in history, but that's not what you are. There is deep emotional fulfillment that you are supposed to be getting from the law school. That's why you came here.

Here the student is actually put in the position of giving "incorrect" answers about her own inner thoughts and motivations, and the professor in supplying the "correct" answers imports for her not only a way of talking but also an entire persona and set of normative orientations. These orientations oppose the purported purely money-seeking motivations of those who attend business school to the alternative, more lofty goals of those who pursue law.

A more subtle but still powerful and pervasive version of this occurs when professors rephrase students' answers to questions, telling them what they "meant":

> PROFESSOR We can say that the gift was given as an inducement for that behavior, right, because the promise to refrain comes after the gift. That's what you mean when you say that a contract as opposed to the gift has its own [inaudible], right? "I'll give you the money, if you refrain." Not, "I'll give you the money," "Thanks, I'll refrain." All right. That's what you mean when you say it's conditional.

Here, the professor imputed a precise, legally framed meaning to the student's words, telling her what she should have meant when using the term "conditional." As in the previous example, there is an ideological movement from words to thoughts in the professor's reformulation of the student's speech, a powerful metapragmatic reframing that teaches an approach to texts and language as it attempts to reshape identities and ways of thinking.

Professors differed in their rationales for using a Socratic discourse format: it imitates courtroom dialogue, it keeps the students engaged, it is efficient in large classrooms, it imitates the mental process of "thinking like a lawyer" that the class dialogue attempts to inculcate. There was also variation in the degree to which professors followed the most "pure" form of the Socratic method, with some professors using a style that involved fewer lengthy one-on-one exchanges and more free-floating exchanges involving multiple students.[14] What is intriguing are the apparent continuities in metapragmatic structuring beneath these rationales and pragmatic differences, continuities that express a more subtle ideology about language that is part of the larger system to which students are being socialized, of the texts they are being trained to read, of the way of speaking that the professors urge on them.

Language ideology concentrates not so much on why a certain form of classroom speech is useful or desirable, but rather on the transparency of metapragmatic form to social result. This is the case on several levels. The metapragmatic form of at times forced dialogue is ideologically represented as transparent to the social result of a transformed social identity for the students (language form inculcating new forms of talking and, at the same time, professional identity), as we have seen in the examples. However, metapragmatic form is also represented as transparent to the social results of cases that are won by speakers able to hold up their end of similar dialogues, those who are able to take on and speak roles fluidly. At a still deeper level, metapragmatic form mirrors legal epistemology, which derives its legitimacy in part from an act of translation of social events and actors into their legal categories and roles. These categories and roles, like the legal texts re-entextualized in new legal opinions, are always part of an oppositional discourse in which one of two opposing parties—and interpretations—will "win" (see Mertz 1990, 1996).

"Taking a position" as an interlocutor in a dialogue is a necessary part of gaining power for legal actors. This taking of a position is a role-playing, and it doesn't matter which role is played as long as some role is played. Again and again, professors play roles—they take the parts of their students, and of various characters in the case dramas as those dramas unfold in classroom speech. Again and again, professors push students to take these roles themselves and play them with certainty. Indeterminacy, breakthroughs of genuine affect (indexing through tone and gesture a failure to play the role), and silence are gaps in the dialogue or, worse, refusals to acquiesce in the ongoing metapragmatic structuring of discourse.

That structuring is a key ideological message of law school socialization. It prepares students for a legal world that constantly effects a translation of people into their roles (plaintiff, defendant) and actions into their legal categories (tort, breach of contract). This translation occurs within a system in which either of two opposing results is always possible (guilty, not guilty) and in which effectual and "correct" metapragmatic regimentation (in courts, in legal documents, in law office talk) yields powerful social results. A key presupposition of the legitimacy of those results in our society is the untying of the drama as legally translated from its usual social moorings, the putative objectivity of the story once told in the apparently dispassionate language of the law. As the people in the cases become "parties," strategic actors on either side of a legal argument, they are stripped of social position; their gender, race, class, occupational, and other identities become secondary to their ability to argue that they have met one or another aspect of a legal test (for example, the requirement that there be some form of "objectively manifested assent" to an agreement in forming a contract).

Social context enters only through the backdoor, as when the professor warns the students about the way that the "equities"[15] of a situation can skew legal results (for example, if the legal requirements for "assent" are not met, but the judge or jury finds that there is a contract because of sympathetic feelings toward an indigent plaintiff). Even then, these "equities" become one more tool in the strategic toolbox, just one more argument to use in an effort to win. This bracketing of social context is deemed to be a crucial way in which law achieves objectivity and lawyers achieve dispasssionate professional competence (see Mertz forthcoming).

One of students' main tasks in the first year of law school is to gain an understanding of legal categories and how to "use" them.[16] A realistic assessment of the "equities," of the possible effects of social context and emotions, is a small part of this task, necessary to effective strategy. The more central lesson is one of translating people and events into legal categories. To learn this new language, students must learn not to concentrate on the history and politics and emotional import of the situation but to inquire only as to whether the events fit the prescribed legal tests ("Was there an offer and acceptance?" "Did the defendant breach?"). This institutionalized linguistic ideology teaches that professional distance is obtained through translation of people and events into legal categories so that they can be used strategically in a struggle for the dominant interpretation. "Taking a position on either side," "playing either role," is a feature of the metapragmatic regimentation of discourse that takes that institutionalized ideology to the heart of the speaking that constitutes the legal arena.

NOTES

I would like to thank Bambi Schieffelin, Paul Kroskrity, Kathryn Woolard, and a number of anonymous readers for their helpful comments and suggestions. I also wish to acknowledge the assistance of an extremely talented and diligent group of researchers who assisted with the project to date: Nancy Matthews and Susan Gooding (who were project managers), Jacqueline Baum, Janina Fenigsen, Robert Moore, Nahum Chandler, Carolee Larsen, Kay Mohlmann, Leah Feldman, Mindie Lazarus-Black, Shepley Orr, Christine Garza, and Jerry Lombardi. Wamucii Njogu, Steve Neufeld, Carlos de la Rosa, and Tom Murphy assisted with the quantitative analysis. The daunting task of transcription was undertaken with energy and care by Diane Clay and Leah Feldman at the American Bar Foundation, and by Zella Coleman and her group. The project was funded by grants from the Spencer Foundation and from the ABF.

1. James Boyd White 1990 uses essentially this notion of "translation," though there are differences between his approach to language and the anthropological linguistic approach drawn upon here (see Mertz 1992).

2. For example, coders noted nonverbal signals that became part of the interaction—as when a student responded to a professor by nodding or shaking her head or using some other kind of nonverbal signal.

3. Qualitative notes examined aspects of the ongoing discussion, such as how social context or emotion was dealt with; they also traced aspects of the developing classroom "culture," such as the ways in which particular students became regular "characters" on whom the professor drew.

4. I personally interviewed the professors and some of the student groups, and I taped and coded one of the classes; the rest were taped and coded by members of the "team" listed in the acknowledgements. Interviews focused on how professors and students viewed the classroom process. In terms of the transcript coding: at the end of the coding process, each school had been completely coded by a single coder to ensure uniformity (this involved some recoding in a few cases). I performed intercoder checks with the in-class coders; the transcript coders were cross-checked both at the beginning and the end of the lengthy coding process by the project managers.

5. The schools were selected using what could be called a "modified snowball" approach; in many cases it was difficult or impossible to obtain access "cold" or without use of some networks or prior contact (although we were able to obtain access that way in two of the schools in the study). We first located schools of the appropriate status levels in

areas in which it was possible to obtain coders with graduate training in linguistics, anthropology, and/or qualitative sociology. We then sorted out classrooms by gender and race of professors, in an effort to obtain a diverse group of professors. And then we frequently worked through available networks to get access. In several cases, even after using this approach, we were refused. However, over a period of several years we were able to obtain access to classrooms that varied along the dimensions we sought to study. The study, then, can be viewed as a set of case studies that provides an opportunity for comparative analysis not offered by single case studies; it is not a random sample.

6. Because of the small numbers of men and women of color teaching in the first-year curriculum, especially in the limited number of elite schools, I do not give more specific information here to avoid inadvertently identifying study participants.

7. Gumperz's observation that the meta-level process is rarely dealt with at a conscious and direct level may find its limit here, for as speakers come into conflict, it may become more likely that they will consciously reflect on and even argue about meta-level typifications.

8. For example, "Class, please take your seats; we're beginning our lesson now," or, "You jerk, you're going to get an argument from me on that," both of which attempt to impose a meta-level typification of the ongoing speech event (formal classroom speech, argument).

9. When these formulations become part of institutionalized social processes, they are arguably likely to become less fluid—more "set" or "gelled"—less a function of vagaries of individual interpretations and preferences.

10. As, for example, if a pacifist responded to the argumentative comment in note 8 by saying, "I'm not going to fight with you about this," contesting the typification that the first speaker sought to impose.

11. It may seem striking that all of these examples involve female students and male professors. However, there are examples of similar breakdowns that involve male students. Whether there is a gendered distribution to this kind of exchange is beyond the scope of this inquiry.

12. In these transcriptions, use of a dash to end an utterance (—) indicates an interruption with overlap, while use of ellipsis (. . .) indicates that a speaker "trailed off" the ending without using the usual pragmatic markers to communicate that the utterance had ended.

13. A particular apt comparison can be made with the *ɛlɛma* routines used to socialize Kaluli children (see Schieffelin 1990:75–80).

14. Interestingly, it appears that it is the law school from which a professor obtained the original J.D. or L.L.B. degree, in combination with gender and race, that is the best predictor of high degrees of use of "pure" Socratic method in the classrooms of this study. Thus, the three white male professors who were trained in top-five schools stood out as by far the most Socratic teachers (86 percent, 81 percent, and 74 percent of class time spent in one-on-one focused dialogue). The remaining professors ranged from 60 percent to 16 percent of class time and included professors of color (both male and female) who had trained at top-five schools, and white male and female professors who had trained at less elite institutions. (The class with only 16 percent of the turns spent in focused dialogue was something of an outlier; the next lowest class had 34 percent focused dialogue turns.)

15. The concept "equities," deserving of an entire article by itself, is an interesting residual category that includes any social contextual or emotional aspect of the situation not strictly relevant to the legal tests but still likely to sway judges or juries concerned about "fair" results.

16. I assert this on the basis of both how much class time is devoted to teaching this task and comments in professor interviews.

REFERENCES

Anyon, Jean. 1981. Social Class and School Knowledge. *Curriculum Inquiry* 11:3–42.

Bauman, Richard, and Charles Briggs. 1990. Poetics and Performance as Critical Perspectives on Language and Social Life. *Annual Reviews of Anthropology* 19:59–88.

Bourdieu, Pierre. 1977. *Outline of a Theory of Practice*. Cambridge: Cambridge University Press.

———. 1987. The Force of Law: Toward a Sociology of the Juridical Field. *Hastings Law Journal* 38:201–248.

Bourdieu, Pierre, and J. C. Passeron. 1977. *Reproduction in Education, Society and Culture*. London: Sage.

Brenneis, Donald L. 1984. Straight Talk and Sweet Talk: Political Discourse in an Occasionally Egalitarian Community. In *Dangerous Words: Language and Politics in the Pacific*, ed. D. Brenneis and F. Myers, pp. 69–84. New York: New York University Press.

Collins, James. 1986. Differential Treatment in Reading Instruction. In *The Social Construction of Literacy*, ed. J. Cook-Gumperz, pp. 117–137. Cambridge: Cambridge University Press.

Errington, J. Joseph. 1988. *Structure and Style in Javanese: A Semiotic View of Linguistic Etiquette*. Philadelphia: University of Pennsylvania Press.

Gal, Susan. 1987. Codeswitching and Consciousness in the European Periphery. *American Ethnologist* 14:637–653.

———. 1989. Language and Political Economy. *Annual Review of Anthropology* 18: 345–367.

Gee, James. 1985. The Narrativization of Experience in the Oral Style. *Journal of Education* 167:9–35.

Gumperz, John. 1982. *Discourse Strategies*. Cambridge: Cambridge University Press.

Halliday, Terence. 1982. *Legal Education and the Rationalization of Law: A Tale of Two Countries—The United States and Australia*. Chicago: American Bar Foundation.

Hanks, William. 1989. Text and Textuality. *Annual Review of Anthropology* 18:95–127.

———. 1990. *Referential Practice: Language and Lived Space among the Maya*. Chicago: University of Chicago Press.

Heath, Shirley Brice. 1983. *Ways with Words: Language, Life, and Work in Communities and Classrooms*. Cambridge: Cambridge University Press.

Hill, Jane. 1985. The Grammar of Consciousness and the Consciousness of Grammar. *American Ethnologist* 12:725–737.

Irvine, Judith. 1989. When Talk Isn't Cheap: Language and Political Economy. *American Ethnologist* 16:248–267.

Lucy, John, ed. 1993. *Reflexive Language*. Cambridge: Cambridge University Press.

Mehan, Hugh. 1979. *Learning Lessons*. Cambridge, Mass.: Harvard University Press.

Mertz, Elizabeth. 1989. Sociolinguistic Creativity: Cape Breton Gaelic's Linguistic "Tip." In *Investigating Obsolescence: Studies in Language Contraction and Death*, ed. N. Dorian, pp. 355–367. Cambridge: Cambridge University Press.

———. 1990. Consensus and Dissent in U.S. Legal Opinions: Narrative Control and Social Voices. *Anthropological Linguistics* 30:369–394.

———. 1992. Creative Acts of Translation: James Boyd White's Intellectual Integration. *Yale Journal of Law and the Humanities* 4:165–185.

———. 1993. Learning What to Ask: Metapragmatic Factors and Methodological Reification. In *Reflexive Language: Reported Speech and Metapragmatics*, ed. John A. Lucy, pp. 159–174. Cambridge: Cambridge University Press.

———. 1996. Recontextualization as Socialization: Text and Pragmatics in the Law School Classroom. In *Natural Histories of Discourse*, ed. M. Silverstein and G. Urban. Chicago: University of Chicago Press.

———. Forthcoming. Linguistic Constructions of Difference and History in the U.S. Law School Classroom. In *Democracy and Difference*, ed. C. Greenhouse. Albany, N.Y.: SUNY Press.

Ochs, Elinor. 1986. Introduction. In *Language Socialization across Cultures*, ed. Bambi B. Schieffelin and Elinor Ochs, pp. 1–13. Cambridge: Cambridge University Press.

———. 1988. *Culture and Language Development*. Cambridge: Cambridge University Press.

Ochs, Elinor, and Bambi B. Schieffelin. 1984. Language Socialization and Acquisition: Three Developmental Stories and Their Implications. In *Culture Theory: Essays on Mind, Self, and Emotion*, ed. R. Shweder and R. LeVine, pp. 276–320. Cambridge: Cambridge University Press.

Philips, Susan. 1972. Participant Structures and Communicative Competence. In *Functions of Language in the Classroom*, ed. C. Cazden, V. P. John, and D. Hymes. New York: Teacher's College Press.

———. 1982. The Language Socialization of Lawyers: Acquiring the "Cant." In *Doing the Ethnography of Schooling*, ed. G. Spindler, pp. 177–209. New York: Holt, Rinehart, and Winston.

Schieffelin, Bambi B. 1990. *The Give and Take of Everyday Life*. Cambridge: Cambridge University Press.

Schieffelin, Bambi B., and Elinor Ochs, eds. 1986. *Language Socialization across Cultures*. Cambridge: Cambridge University Press.

Silverstein, Michael. 1979. Language Structure and Linguistic Ideology. In *The Elements: A Parasession on Linguistic Units and Levels*, ed. P. Clyne, W. Hanks, and C. Hofbauer, pp. 193–247. Chicago: Chicago Linguistic Society.

———. 1993. Metapragmatic Discourse and Metapragmatic Function. In *Reflexive Language*, ed. John A. Lucy, pp. 33–58. Cambridge: Cambridge University Press.

Wertsch, James. 1985a. *Culture, Communication, and Cognition*. Cambridge: Cambridge University Press.

———. 1985b. *Vygotsky and the Social Foundation of Mind*. Cambridge, Mass.: Harvard University Press.

White, James Boyd. 1990. *Justice as Translation: An Essay in Cultural and Legal Criticism*. Chicago: University of Chicago Press.

Woolard, Kathryn A. 1985. Language Variation and Cultural Hegemony: Toward an Integration of Sociolinguistic and Social Theory. *American Ethnologist* 12:738–748.

———. 1989a. Sentences in the Language Prison. *American Ethnologist* 16:268–278.

———. 1989b. Language Convergence and Language Death as Social Processes. In *Investigating Obsolescence: Studies in Language Contraction and Death*, ed. N. Dorian, pp. 355–367. Cambridge: Cambridge University Press.

Woolard, Kathryn, and Bambi B. Schieffelin. 1994. Language Ideology. *Annual Review of Anthropology* 23:55–82.

8

Mediating Unity and Diversity

The Production of Language Ideologies in Zambian Broadcasting

DEBRA SPITULNIK

> The seven (7) main vernacular languages on the Media represent all seventy three (73) tribes found in Zambia.
>
> Kapeya 1988:3

> The problem is, we have been recognized as a language, so why be mistreated? . . . It remains that the big two or the big four get most of the time. . . . But you can't raise these issues because you may be called a tribalist.
>
> Anonymous

The Production of Language Ideologies in Media Practice

The central concern of this chapter is to investigate the role of powerful institutions in the production and reproduction of language ideologies. While language ideologies are most readily identifiable in explicit metalinguistic discourse (i.e., language about language), I demonstrate here how language ideologies are also embodied in a very fundamental and implicit sense within the everyday practices of institutions.

As several contributors to this volume point out, one of the critical challenges in the analysis of language ideology is to keep the sites of ideology in sight (e.g., Silverstein, Woolard; also see Woolard and Schieffelin 1994:58 and Fairclough 1995:71). Taking the politics of language in Zambian radio as a case study, I argue here that this is not just a matter of locating *where* ideologies are produced but also *how* they are produced. I maintain that the structural grounding of language ideologies in institutional practice is best understood as a process of *language valuation* and *evaluation* which occurs through specific kinds of semiotic processes. These semiotic processes are manifold and complex, but the important thing about them is that in most cases they function to naturalize or neutralize language value; that is, they obscure the historically contingent nature of language values, as well as the relations of power and interest underlying them.

I introduce the concepts of language valuation and evaluation here—borrowing from Saussure's concept of relational value (1959:111ff) and Voloshinov's concept of social evaluation (1986:103ff)—for two reasons. The first advantage is that these terms redirect our attention away from a strictly mentalistic or ideational definition of ideology and toward a concept of ideology as process. Language valuation and evaluation are processes through which different social values and referents come to be associated with languages, forms of speaking, and styles of speaking.

This is not to reject the ideational status of ideology, however. Ideology is at once conceptual and processual, implicit in practice, embodied in lived relations, and explicit in certain kinds of conscious articulations such as metalinguistic discourse.[1] This definition is thus an expansion of Irvine's important formulation of language ideologies as "ideas about social and linguistic relationships, together with their loading of moral and political interests" (1989:255). It replaces the term "ideas" with a wider set of possibilities: language ideologies can be ideas, cultural conceptions, processes of meaning construction, implicit evaluations, and explicit comments "about social and linguistic relationships, together with their loading of moral and political interests" (255).

The second advantage of the concepts of language valuation and evaluation is that they tap into a broader conception of the interpretive and value-laden dimension of all human reality. Every social group has an "evaluative purview," according to Voloshinov, and this social evaluation is the ideological horizon of interests and judgments that mediates structure and action (1986:106). For example, on this view, the use of a language can never be value-free—as we see later in this chapter, even 'neutrality' is socially constructed—because social judgments and orientations are always in play. Linking the concept of ideology to social evaluation in this sense is important because it rescues the concept from the postmodern critique that ideology necessarily presupposes a distinction between appearance and reality. In some cases ideologies do create appearances that mystify or falsify realities. In other cases they are simultaneously appearance *and* reality—that is, a lived truth, "within the true" (Foucault 1972:224; also see Donham 1990:49).

It is crucial to stress that language ideologies and processes of language valuation are never just about language (Kulick, this volume; Woolard and Schieffelin 1994:55–56). Language ideologies are, among many other things, about the construction and legitimation of power, the production of social relations of sameness and difference, and the creation of cultural stereotypes about types of speakers and social groups. Such language ideologies and processes of language valuation are quite comparable to other types of ideological processes, since they are often intricately linked to social relations of power, including "power exercised by the state on behalf of a dominant social class" (Fairclough 1995:17). Moreover, as with other kinds of ideologies, language ideologies tend to be naturalizing and universalizing, disguising the conditions of their own production and their intimate and often strategic ties to power, interest, and the creation of cultural value (see Eagleton 1994).

The place of powerful institutions such as mass media and educational and legal systems in the construction and maintenance of such linguistic hegemonies has been the subject of growing attention over the past decade (Woolard and Schieffelin 1994, Anderson 1983, Bourdieu 1991, Gal 1989, and many of the chapters in this volume). There is also a much longer tradition of sociolinguistic research on language planning and policy that addresses the important ideological functions of these institutions (see Cobarrubias and Fishman 1983). It is only recently, however, that scholars have focused their gaze below the level of the overall ideological function and effect of institutions to look more closely at how *specific practices* within institutions give value to different languages and to different ways of using language.

In the discussion that follows, I propose that the investigation of these practices of language valuation requires attention to the following basic questions: Which particular features of institutions feed into the production of language ideologies? Are different institutions differentially suited for the production of certain kinds of language ideologies? Which aspects of language in particular become important in the institutional construction of language value? Where are the battles fought and in what terms?

Echoing the introductory quotes, we examine how 7 radio languages are made to "represent" 73 ethnic groups, and how some languages are accorded high status, while others are "mistreated." The core argument is that the central task of Radio Zambia is to mediate both national unity and national diversity; in so doing, it regulates sameness and difference across social groups through the differential allocation of airtime to different languages. I demonstrate that the allotment of radio airtime to different languages is structured by two opposing ideologies, one of democratic pluralism and the other of hierarchical pluralism. I explain, further, how the contradiction between these two opposing ideologies creates a situation where contestation can emerge and where hegemony can never be complete.

This case has more general implications for the study of multilingual and multiethnic societies because it illustrates one of the fundamental problems faced by virtually every nation-state in the world today: the challenge of forging a unified national identity while simultaneously giving some recognition to national diversity. The manufacture of national identity also shares many of the same perplexing dilemmas raised in debates about multiculturalism. For example, several of the themes that emerge in the Zambian situation are identical to questions currently being asked in the United States: How can a nation be united without one national language?[2] Is recognizing diversity necessarily divisive? When the state explicitly allocates resources to social groups on the basis of difference, does this "make [the] nation into a racial and ethnic spoils system"[3] (Tilove 1996)? And does this lead to a situation where a seemingly infinite number of social distinctions can be invoked in claims for representation and resources?

Mass media are a particularly volatile domain for such battles over representation, because of their high visibility and because of their inherent publicizing function (Spitulnik forthcoming). As mass media build the communicative space of the nation-state, all of a nation's languages, dialects, and language varieties, and the speech communities associated with them, are *automatically* drawn into relations with one another. For example, some languages and varieties may be dominant, with a greater quantity and quality of media products; some may be represented only minimally, and still others may be completely absent, either silenced or ignored.

In semiotic terms, what this means is that there is an indexical component to the use of a language or a speech variety, which extends beyond the indexing of a social group associated with the code: the code chosen indexes the codes not chosen. These dynamics of relational value are especially salient in the Zambian case, where there are 73 different ethnic groups, more than seventy different language varieties, and roughly fifteen to twenty major language clusters. In selecting which languages and ethnicities to represent in national broadcasting, Radio Zambia maps out a distinct picture of the nation's ethnolinguistic landscape and also publicizes, legitimizes, and empowers certain groups at the expense of others.

As we investigate our central problem of how the grounding of language ideologies in institutional practice occurs through such semiotic processes of language valuation, several other types of semiotic processes become apparent. For example, Radio Zambia's partitioning of the linguistic universe through differential allocation of airtime amounts to an iconic diagramming of social differentiation through a diagram of linguistic differentiation (see Gal this volume and Woolard and Schieffelin 1994:61ff). In addition, as evidenced in the opening quotations, a language can stand, in a complex symbolic and indexical sense, for a group. It is thus possible, according to the second speaker, for a collective group, a "we," to be "recognized as a language." A group can *have* a language and also *be* a language (see Hymes 1984).[4] Another pervasive semiotic process examined here is the indexical transfer of social stereotypes about speakers to the languages themselves. For example, in Zambian broadcasting, some languages are construed as more "intellectually equipped" and others as better suited for "cultural expression," on the basis of certain social evaluations of their speakers as, for example, rural folk, urban consumers, "illiterate," "sophisticated," or "insignificant."[5]

Before turning to the specific investigation of how such ideologies and evaluations are embedded in the practices of media production, the following three sections set the stage for analysis with an overview of Radio Zambia, state ideology, and the political economy of languages in the country.

An Overview of Radio Zambia's Role in the Negotiation of Ethnolinguistic Pluralism

Since its inception in 1941, radio broadcasting has been one of the most visible and contested arenas of language valuation and national language policy implementation in Zambia. Fundamentally, what underlies the political volatility of language use on radio is that Zambian broadcasting is the primary state institution for representing both national unity *and* national diversity.[6]

Radio is by far the most widely consumed medium in the country,[7] and it is the only widespread mass communication form that uses Zambian languages in addition to English, the official language of Zambia. According to the national language policy, mass media are authorized to use eight languages (English, Bemba, Kaonde, Lozi, Lunda, Luvale, Nyanja, and Tonga), from among the roughly fifteen to twenty different languages (or language clusters) that exist in the country.[8] At the same time however, radio is charged with upholding a state philosophy of ethnic egalitarianism (among the nation's "73 tribes") and the obvious aim of political encompassment, as encapsulated in the national motto "One Zambia, One Nation." Collectively, then, the eight radio languages are intended to represent both the nation as a whole and its internal diversity.

In this process, radio operates with two competing visions of the nation's diversity. Radio's use of different languages is structured by both a vision of ethnic egalitarianism in line with state discourse and a hierarchical ranking of the nation's languages which is linked to the political and demographic inequalities among their speech communities. As we see in the following discussion, Radio Zambia balances these different pluralisms in three basic ways: (1) through a differential allocation of radio airtime, which both regulates language equality *and* gives languages different unequal values, (2) through various modes of establishing evaluations of each of the 7 Zambian radio languages vis-à-vis the country's official language, English, and (3) by accommodating the interests of 73 ethnic groups within the programming constraints of these seven languages.

Pluralism in State Politics: The Culturalization of Ethnicity and the Vices of Tribalism

In Zambia's state discourse on pluralism, there are 73 officially recognized ethnic groups that are constructed as *equally different*—that is, different in the same way—in terms of their presumably harmless, apolitical "cultural" differences. Amounting to a virtual *culturalization of ethnicity*,[9] each ethnic group is said to have its own unique traditions, dances, songs, and history, which it is encouraged to preserve and promote for the sake of the youth, tourism, and national identity.[10] State discourse thus attempts to diffuse the political dimensions of ethnicity at the same time that it promotes an image of the state as tolerant of diversity. References to the more volatile differences between ethnic groups, particularly their inequalities in population, political positions, and economic resources, are avoided at all costs.[11]

Instead, politicians constantly invoke the national motto "One Zambia, One Nation" as a symbol of a national unity predicated on being able to hold together and tolerate ethnic difference (Spitulnik 1994, in press). On this note, Zambia is rather exceptional among modern African states, as it has experienced almost no violent ethnic conflict and has prevented any one ethnic group from monopolizing political power. But while claiming to have forged a national unity of "73 tribes united,"[12] the state has always simultaneously attended to the politics of ethnic difference and special interest. Zambia's first and long-ruling President Kenneth Kaunda carefully orchestrated a policy of "tribal balancing" in political appointments, and early on he articulated what became the general consensus in Zambia's political culture regarding the "deadly vice" of tribalism (Kaunda 1967:11). Analogous to racism or sexism, "tribalism" is understood both as discrimination based on ethnic identity and as the more general way in which ethnic affiliation can be interested and partisan. Warnings against "falling victim to tribalism" and denunciations of its divisive, retrogressive, and fundamentally un-Zambian nature pervade political oratory in contemporary Zambia. During one-party rule (1972–1990), arguments against adopting a multiparty system warned about the possibility of political parties dividing along ethnic lines, and the history of multiparty politics since 1990 bears this out to a great degree.

Nevertheless, the state has continued to articulate a rhetoric of encompassing nationalism ("One Zambia, One Nation") *alongside* its philosophy of ethnic pluralism. I argue that these two ideologies of "unity no matter what" and "diversity within the unity" are mutually reinforcing but that they are also in a constant state of tension with the possibility of ideological implosion. The net result is that the state's claim to build unity, fend off tribalism, and *also* encourage unique ethnic cultures amounts to a cautious *pluralism within bounds*, where diversity always verges on divisiveness, and where attention to difference itself borders on subversion. This, in a nutshell, describes Radio Zambia's position concerning language diversity as well.

Democratic versus Hierarchical Pluralism: A Convergence of Language History, Policy, and Demographics

In consonance with its state discourse of apolitical ethnic egalitarianism, Zambia has developed a national language policy that also stresses pluralism but ignores difference. This has been accomplished mainly through sanctioning an extraordinarily high number of "official Zambian languages"—7—which are all subordinated to the ethnically neutral "official language," English.[13] The 7 Zambian languages are Bemba, Kaonde, Lozi, Lunda, Luvale, Nyanja, and Tonga, and they are the only Zambian languages used in broadcasting, schools, and government publications. English, the former colonial language, is the language of government, higher education, and international communication.

The choice of *which* 7 languages, out of more than 70 different language varieties, was fairly well determined before independence by the convergence of several processes: colonial language policy (especially in broadcasting and education), missionary work, and labor migration patterns, which established Bemba and Nyanja as the colony's two urban lingua francas.[14]

Crucially, English, Bemba, and Nyanja were the first languages of Northern Rhodesian broadcasting, which started in 1941 as a World War II information service. After the war, Lozi and Tonga were added as the service expanded with a full range of programs. According to Harry Franklin, the Northern Rhodesian Director of Information, nearly everyone understood these four "main 'root' languages of the country," and thus it was unnecessary to add more languages, despite several requests to do so (1950:16). Significantly, Franklin saw radio as having a key role in helping to standardize languages and promote the dominance of some over others: "Africa's babel of tongues is one of the main causes of its people's backwardness, and we hope eventually to reduce languages broadcast rather than to increase them, and so to play a part in the eventual development of one African tongue . . . and still more remotely, in the universal use of English" (1950:16).

Over time, the selection and dominance of the four languages became mutually reinforcing, and this arrangement was extremely convenient administratively, as their geographic distribution virtually aligned with the four compass points North (Bemba), South (Tonga), East (Nyanja), and West (Lozi), which defined the major provinces of the colony.[15] In 1954, however, the two Northwestern Province languages Lunda and Luvale were added to broadcasting (no single language was prominent in the province), and at independence in 1964 a third Northwestern Province language, Kaonde, was included.

The contemporary linguistic situation is largely a legacy of these trends in colonial administration and the related trends in ethnic politics. The use of numerous Zambian languages in early radio did not help to reduce "the African babel" but helped to permanently establish some of the basic terms in which ethnolinguistic diversity is structured and experienced. For example, the semiotics of the early arrangement—one language : one province—came to define a model of distributional equality that dominates the debates about broadcasting languages. Critically, in this political economy of languages (see Gal 1989), different languages became associated with different prestige values and domains of use, primarily through the "uneven development" of the ethnic groups speaking them[16] and their concurrent unequal valuation in broadcasting. The high status and widespread use of Bemba and Nyanja, "the big two," grew as their value in the urban labor markets became established, and this was accompanied by higher proportions of radio airtime for them. These two, along with Lozi and Tonga, came to be known as "the big four" as their first-language speakers emerged as the major ethnic and regional power blocs in state politics (Molteno 1974). For most of broadcasting history, Lozi and Tonga have had slightly lower proportions of airtime than Bemba and Nyanja but more than the three Northwestern languages, which are associated with much smaller populations and ethnic power bases. The use of these three in contemporary Zambia is fairly limited to their own mother-tongue populations (e.g., 7 percent of all Zambians speak Kaonde, while 3 percent of the country is ethnically Kaonde). By contrast, the Bemba and Nyanja languages far outreach their ethnic populations (19 percent and 16 percent) and are spoken by 56 percent and 42 percent of all Zambians, respectively (Kashoki 1978).

With these factors of language history, ethnic politics, and demographics in mind, what obtains, then, is not a situation of *democratic* linguistic pluralism, as one would predict from the state discourse of ethnic egalitarianism. All languages (or even just the 7 chosen languages) are not equally valued; rather, they are *hierarchically* ranked (Figure 8.1). This language ranking is both a historical product of colonial administration and ethnic politics and a partial diagram of the demographic and status inequalities among speech communities.

The Politics of Language Value in Contemporary Radio

The politics of language value, and especially the grounding of this scheme of hierarchical linguistic pluralism, occur most prominently in three domains in which the Zambian linguistic universe is partitioned through broadcasting practice: the

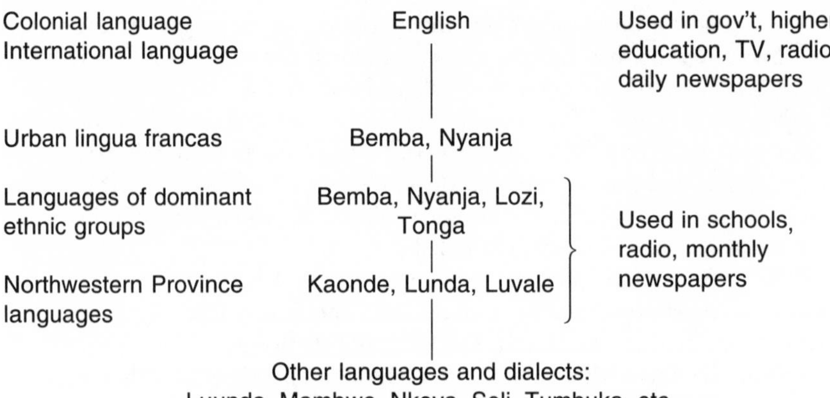

Figure 8.1 Hierarchical linguistic pluralism in Zambia

radio channel, program content, and airtime. The following discussion demonstrates how radio—as a particular medium structured by time, wavelengths, and program types—creates the possibility for an iconic mapping of social divisions through divisions across these three domains. In addition, we examine how the way that radio is temporally and topically carved up establishes basic structural contrasts and relational values that become focal points for the construction and contestation of language value.

Partitioning the Linguistic Universe: The Ongoing Negotiation of Linguistic Pluralism

Since the early days of broadcasting in Zambia, the airwaves have been carefully divided up among different languages, and concurrently distinct administrative units have been assigned responsibility for the output in each of the different languages. Most pronounced has been the segregation of English from Zambian languages, in terms of both airwaves and program types. One of the key issues of attention and contestation has been *which* Zambian languages are treated more (or less) like English, which clearly occupies the privileged position in the language hierarchy. Table 8.1 illustrates the special status of English on radio. Not only are there more than twice as many hours for English as for all Zambian languages combined, but the two English channels also monopolize the more prestigious FM frequencies.[17]

The names "Radio 1" and "Radio 2" were introduced in 1989 with the creation of "Radio 4" and were preceded by five other pairs of labels (Table 8.2).[18] The alterations in both the channels' names and languages are highly significant, as they reveal a constant attention to the politics of language value and illustrate the ongoing practices that are necessary to sustain and justify language valuations.

From the late 1940s until independence in 1964, broadcasting operations for Africans and Europeans were separate. The "African Service" emanated from Lusaka (the Northern Rhodesian capital), and the "English Service" came from

Table 8.1 ZNBC domestic radio operations and time allocations, 1990

	Hours	*Frequencies*	*Languages*	*Total radio time* (%)
Radio 1	04.50–24.05	SW, MW	7 Zambian lgs	31
Radio 2	04.50–24.05	SW, MW, FM	English	31
Radio 4	Continuous 24 hrs	FM stereo	English	38

SW = shortwave, MW = medium wave (same as AM), FM = frequency modulation.

Salisbury (the Southern Rhodesian capital). The African Service carried a few programs in English for Africans, but most English language programs were produced in the Southern Rhodesian studios for the Europeans.

Zambian broadcasting inherited this language segregation at independence, and out of this situation "the Vernacular Service" (with 7 Zambian languages) and "the National Service" (with English only) were created in 1964. Racial overtones were thus eliminated with both the rejection of the label "African" and the revaluing of English as something "National," that is, rightfully belonging to the newly independent nation-state and not to any one race. But even with these new labels, the comparative scopes of the two channels and their implications for language valuations remained fundamentally the same: Zambian languages were still segregated from English, which stood apart as the language of wider, national, and more modern communication.

Oppositions to these distinctions soon erupted, however, as the channels' names were changed three more times in the space of two years. Controversies continued over the allocation of different languages to each channel, as well. In 1965, for example, the National Service was relabeled "the English Service," in an attempt to dispel any implication that the "vernacular" languages of its counterpart were not also 'national'. The implication endured, however, and in 1966 the Vernacular and the English Services were renamed "Home" and "General," thus even further accentuating differences in scope. The Home Service, as something 'not-general', carried connotations of being specific, local, and even narrow. Resonating with Zambian idioms of ethnic origin and rootedness, the word "home" also signaled that the "vernacular" broadcasts were for rural and ethnic-based audiences and tapped into their essential identities: "Zambia National Broadcasting Corporation [ZNBC] realizes the importance of a vernacular language as being the [*sic*] most

Table 8.2 The changing names of Zambian radio services

Date	*Service Name*	*Service Name*
late 1940s	African Service	English Service
Jan. 1964	Vernacular Service	National Service
Feb. 1965	Vernacular Service	English Service
Aug. 1965	Home Service	English Service
Jan. 1966	Home Service	General Service
Feb. 1989	Radio 1	Radio 2

and proper communicator and a true identifier of man's belonging . . ." (Kapeya 1988:2). Even after the Home Service was relabeled "Radio 1" in 1989, broadcasters continued to use themes of home and belonging in promoting the channel, for example in the Bemba slogans *Kumwesu kwaliwama* 'At home (our place), it's nice'. The General Service, on the other hand, as something 'not-home', did not *belong* to anyone in particular. Associated with wider—more general—spheres of communication and seemingly dissociated from locality, ethnicity, and special interest, the General Service used the one language that symbolizes the transcendence of such boundaries—English.

Throughout these various changes, the inherent oppositional nature of this binary system of two channels led to a situation where one channel became automatically associated with what the other one was not. The proportional valuations of the two channels and their associated social evaluations during this period are shown in Figure 8.2.

Shortly after independence, however, the binary scheme was challenged as several controversies erupted over which languages could rightfully share time with English on the General Service. In early 1966 "the big four" (Bemba, Nyanja, Lozi, Tonga) were added, with the rationale that their audiences were larger and that therefore they needed more hours. But a year later, Lozi and Tonga were removed, leaving only "the big two" on the General Service with English. This situation remained stable for nearly twenty years, an index of the more inclusive scope of Bemba and Nyanja as lingua francas and their possible neutrality as not necessarily *belonging* to any one people.

The problem, was however, that while Bemba and Nyanja are widely used by people of all ethnicities, their link to specific ethnic constituencies remains a continually invokable reason for limiting their use at the national level. Bemba and Nyanja are simply not 'general' like English, and in selecting them over others one is open to being "called a tribalist" (as in the opening quotation), as this complaint to the Ministry of Information and Broadcasting implies: "Some languages have more hours than others [and] only two of the seven languages are on the General Service. . . . [This is] unfair as far as the national motto of "One Zambia, One Nation" is concerned" (Letter from Northwestern Province, received 13 August 1981, ZBS/101/1/5). Since the national motto "One Zambia, One Nation" is about *uniting* an ethnically plural society, to this letter writer unity was violated by *separating* out two Zambian languages to share a channel with English. As the pressures increased for the General Service to "include everybody," the other five languages were added in the mid-1980s, but equal time was not granted. The situation was then dramatically reversed in 1988. All Zambian languages were removed from the General Service, and it resumed its much earlier status as English only. Significantly, this "all-or-nothing" decision evoked both praise and criticism, essentially drawing from two competing visions of pluralism.

On the one hand, there was the danger of having too much pluralism—that is, a pluralism verging on divisiveness and confusion ("the African babel")—with the possibility of contamination, especially when it came to mixing on a common channel with English. One listener, for example, lauded the removal of Zambian languages and expressed the "sincere hope that these changes will help bring back

African : European :: Vernacular : National :: Vernacular : English :: Home : General

traditional : modern :: rural : urban :: ethnic : cosmopolitan :: exclusive : inclusive

Figure 8.2 Proportional valuations of the two radio channels and their associated social evaluations

to life the turnished [*sic*] image of the general service" (*Times of Zambia*, October 16, 1988, p. 4). Others felt that the presence of Zambian languages on a channel with English was too disruptive or that only English was necessary for General Service programs such as health, farming, and educational broadcasts. The colonial bifurcation of English and all other languages thus remained, with lingering connotations of English as the sole language of prestige and progress.

On the other hand, there was the view of pluralism as positive and necessary for national communication and the promotion of Zambian culture. Several listeners strongly opposed the removal of all Zambian languages from the General Service, complaining, for example, that "English has the lion's share" while Zambian languages were "deprived of adequate air time" (*Times of Zambia,* October 1988). One commented sarcastically, "I suppose that is the penalty they get for being Zambian languages" (*Times of Zambia,* October 11, 1988, p. 2).

The problem of singling out two languages surfaced again in 1989 when ZNBC introduced Radio 4, a 24-hour FM stereo channel designed to carry a mixture of pop music programming and commercial advertising.[19] At this time, the Home Service was renamed Radio 1 and the General Service became Radio 2, thus replacing the hotly debated descriptive titles with more technical numerical labels (see Spitulnik forthcoming). Initially, some ZNBC staff thought Radio 4 would use all eight languages, but from the outset it was English only. This was justified by claims that advertisers all preferred English and that listeners who spoke only "the home languages" had no buying power and would therefore not be good audiences for a channel that was to be supported by advertising revenue. Other staff noted that since FM radio covered only urban areas, there was no need for the vernaculars, which were "for villagers." But despite all of these seemingly objective appeals to external factors, none of these claims were supported by market research, and in fact they ran contrary to the well-known fact that urban people do listen to Bemba and Nyanja programs.

So why weren't the two lingua francas added to the new urban-based channel? More than two thirds of all Zambians speak at least one of these languages, and nearly half live in urban areas. Certainly the listeners were there. Regarding business interest, one senior executive acknowledged that "Bemba and Nyanja are the only two languages that bring any money [on Radio 1]. That's why they are slotted at lunch time, and they have commercial programs. . . . The sponsors shun some of these other [languages]." ZNBC executives knew that the two lingua francas could have been successful on Radio 4, but the choice was political. In terms of ethnolinguistic impartiality, the issue paralleled that of the embattled General Service languages: either have *all* Zambian languages on the new channel, or *none* at all. Even if Bemba and Nyanja reach wider audiences, their connections to specific ethnic groups lurks in the background of any decision regarding their use.[20] With the additional aim of styling Radio 4 after Western FM pop radio, the exclusive use of English not only dispelled controversies over "tribalism" but was a 'natural' consequence of its status as the modern, international language.

The Linguistic Division of Labor: Program Content and Class Dimensions of Language Value

The "penalty" that Zambian languages "get for being Zambian languages" thus extends beyond the allocation of airtime and channels into an institutionalization of what counts as their appropriate program content. A crucial element at work in this process is not only the familiar phenomenon of languages standing for and indexing social groups but also the pervasive indexical transfer of social stereotypes about speakers to the languages they speak.

In terms of program content, English has long been established as the language of international news, current affairs discussions, and the majority of scientific and formal education programs, while Zambian languages carry mostly cultural and development programs.[21] Ethnolinguistic pluralism is therefore contained not only within one channel but also within topics, and specifically through an equal subordination under English in this linguistic division of labor. Most prominent is the construction of language equality through uniformity in program content. To take one example, the same English script is used to prepare the daily Zambian language newscasts, so the news in each of the seven languages is identical in format and content. The master text—to be translated into 7 languages—is extracted from the script of the English language "Main News," but it is half the length, with the international items usually omitted.[22]

In this equal subordination under English, Zambian languages are often equated with the rural folk, even though nearly half of all Zambians and more than three quarters of all radio listeners live in urban areas. Similar to the Radio 4 case, news staff claim to be just following the norms "out there" when they explain that the "sophistication" of the Radio 1 audience differs from the English language audience and that a five-minute excerpt from the ten-minute English news is adequate for them. As one senior news editor elaborated, "We wouldn't give an item on the SALT talks in Geneva. If they could understand that, they could listen in English." Another said, "You don't pick something in Saigon or China, because you may be reaching illiterates. . . . There are complicated issues which wouldn't even make sense to them." There was no audience research, however, to substantiate these views, and, in a sense, the ability of newscasting to widen people's horizons was short-circuited by the assumption that some listeners' intelligence was unalterably limited. Many Zambians who know little or no English do have an interest in world events and would like more international news in their own languages.

In apparent contrast to the news editors' statements, ZNBC administrators point to the use of seven languages as examples of broadcasting's dedication to the state policy of "taking things to the people." But what is being delivered, and to whom? Most informational programs in Zambian languages are on national politics and development topics such as farming and health. In essence, their audiences are "the imagined Others" for the highly cosmopolitan English-speaking broadcasting elite. The audiences thought of as "illiterates" are basically those who have not reached a certain level of formal education, *in English*, and to some media elite this precludes an ability to comprehend or share the same worldview.

Not only does radio's institutionalization of limited program content for Zambian languages perpetuate this perceived divide, but the use of English master scripts for these informational programs further regulates linguistic uniformity (or egalitarianism) and constructs English's high value as *the* scientific and factual language. By contrast, most independently scripted programs in Zambian languages adhere to the politically acceptable expressions of ethnic diversity, consonant with the culturalization of ethnicity—that is, traditional music, storytelling, and cultural topics. Through these broadcasting practices, then, the 7 vernaculars are valued as equally transparent vehicles for communicating the *same* information to ethnically diverse people, and as equally particularistic codes for gaining access to *different* ethnic cultures.

If Zambian languages are viewed as cultural reservoirs, then English is an economic reservoir, or at least the avenue for tapping into economic resources. This complex facet of the political economy of languages and class dynamics in Zambia is continuously reproduced by radio. As I have shown, English has the exclusive ability to serve as the neutral language of translation and encompassment. In the sense that English is nonethnic (i.e., not the mother tongue of any Zambian ethnic group), it appears politically neutral. It does not *belong* to any one people; it is apparently open to all. But what this really means is that the dominance of English has been naturalized, to the point where it is the unmarked choice. This is far from political neutrality, however, since English language competence does belong to a select group: the elites who hold power. English as 'neutral' thus masks class dimensions and the hegemony of those who command its "standard" usage (Silverstein 1987), including the media elites who play a major role in constructing the seemingly natural neutrality and transcendence of English.

In short, then, radio broadcasting must be seen as both a *source* and a *result* of language evaluations. The semiotics of this process has operated primarily through a scheme of binary oppositions, as shown in Figure 8.3. Over time the privileged position of English in broadcasting was firmly established through its unique allocation to a separate channel, its exclusive use in certain types of programs, and its use as the language of key source material for a whole range of programming. It is the language of scientific explanation, high-level political debate and speechmaking, and the language of international agencies who sponsor programs and write factual information pamphlets—all of which are used as bases for radio programs and scripts. English is thus seen as an avenue to a "wider knowledge," unlike the vernaculars, which are for the commoners and "local knowledge."

The equation of Zambian languages with cultural topics, "illiterates," and stereotypes about "the rural folk" is not just supported by institutional practices at ZNBC; it is also at the core of the class conflicts among broadcasting personnel themselves. While Zambian language broadcasters are highly educated and fluent in English, they are promoted much less. They are often shunned by English lan-

Zambian languages : English language

traditional : modern :: rural : urban :: ethnic : cosmopolitan :: exclusive : inclusive

backwards : sophisticated :: illiterate : literate :: biased : neutral

local news : international news :: cultural programs : scientific programs :: traditional music : Western music

Figure 8.3. Social evaluations of languages and their links to program content

guage broadcasters as inferior and as generally ignorant of modern styles of dress, the right drinking places, and the skills of news gathering. For example, when asked whether the Zambian language broadcasters ever socialize with those who work in English, a senior English language broadcaster responded with a long, critical reflection:

> They don't feel free. They're reserved. OK, we [the English language broadcasters] go around on tours, presidential events . . . so we're exposed. But they aren't, and they feel a bit inferior. And they go to the wrong clubs, like these shebeens . . . and they drink bad beer. They don't go to nice places like the Intercon [Hotel Intercontinental]. Even if they went to these nice places, they wouldn't know their way around, or how to act, and they don't dress nicely. It's this inferiority complex. We get the same salaries. . . . But many General Service programs are sponsored, so we get a bit more from that.

Like the languages they work in, the Zambian language broadcasters are ghettoized within a context of English language domination. Many of them thus view their jobs as critical sites for playing a preservationist role in the maintenance of their language and their culture, and particularly for the preservation of what are viewed as otherwise dying or nearly lost oral traditions. With less than a third of all radio time, their departments receive only a small portion of ZNBC's resources, and they have few chances for national tours, foreign study, commissions from program sponsors, and other perks that enable English-language broadcasters to build up their wardrobes and professional sophistication.

ZNBC's promotional ladder mirrors and maintains these class distinctions and the linguistic hegemony of English. Within ZNBC, the most prestigious broadcasting positions are with, in descending order: Television Zambia (TVZ), Radio 4, Radio 2, and Radio 1. Radio 1 broadcasters are rarely promoted directly to Television Zambia, but many Radio 2 personnel are. Mother-tongue speakers of Northwestern Province languages have, overall, the least representation among the English language broadcasters, while mother-tongue speakers of Bemba and Nyanja are very prevalent on Radio 2, Radio 4, and TVZ. Most strikingly, the ethnolinguistic distribution of broadcasters (but not executives) across media thus parallels the diagram of hierarchical linguistic pluralism (see Figure 8.1).

Time Sharing on Radio 1: Regulating Language Sameness and Difference

As indicated in the previous section, the allocation of radio airtime itself has emerged as one of the key measurements of linguistic equity. Not all languages have the same amounts (and types) of airtime, and thus the promotion of a simple linguistic egalitarianism as one would expect from the state philosophy is far from clear. Instead, Radio Zambia has developed a complex schedule that simultaneously regulates language equality and gives languages different, unequal values. With such a dynamic of language valuation, radio both upholds a vision of balanced pluralism and operates with its seeming contradiction, a scheme of hierarchical linguistic pluralism.

Significantly, the partitioning of radio airtime among 7 Zambian languages and their ability to represent 73 ethnic groups is limited to *one* radio channel. Table 8.3 illustrates how Radio 1's schedule carefully staggers the 7 Zambian radio languages across the different days and times of the week. This establishes a basic icon of one national pie that is getting divided up. As people talk about this radio time sharing, various discourses of ethnolinguistic democracy are invoked that play into and seize on these structural contrasts.

The schedule in Table 8.3 presents a picture of distributional equality, where no particular language seems privileged over others. Each day a different language opens the station, no language dominates any large time blocks, and across the weekly cycle every time slot is shared by two or more languages. A similar construction of distributional equality occurs in the Radio 1 news schedule, where a sequence of back-to-back newscasts in each of the seven languages is broadcast three times daily, starting at 6.00, 12.20, and 17.20. Within each of these three news periods the newscasts are identical in format and content, but the ordering of languages differs at different times of the day; thus, no single language always gets first place at news time.

At the same time, however, there are great disparities in the quantity and quality of airtime allocated to each language, as summarized in Table 8.4. The "big four" all have roughly the same amount of airtime, while the three Northwestern Province languages have much less and do not occur every day, except in newscasts. In terms of measurable hours, then, there are two tiers—Bemba, Nyanja, Tonga, and Lozi on one level, above Luvale, Kaonde, and Lunda. The high valuation and the demographic dominance of Bemba and Nyanja over the other five languages are

Table 8.3 Time allocation of Radio 1 languages, 1990

Time	*Mon*	*Tues*	*Wed*	*Thurs*	*Fri*	*Sat*	*Sun*
04.50–08.00	B	T	Ln/Lv	Lz	K	N	B
08.00–10.00	Lz	K	T	Lv	T	B	B
10.00–12.00	T	Lv	Lz	T	Ln	Lz	T
12.00–14.00	N	B	N	B	N	B	N
14.00–16.00	T	Ln/Lv	Lz	Lz	K	N	Lz
16.00–18.00	Lz	K	T	Ln	Lz	N	N
18.00–20.00	T	Lz	Ln	K	Lv	Lv	T
20.00–24.05	Lz	N	B	N	B	B	B

B = Bemba; K = Kaonde; Ln = Lunda; Lv = Luvale; Lz = Lozi; N = Nyanja; T = Tonga.
Based on Zambia National Broadcasting Corporation Radio One Programme Schedule, First Quarter 1990.

Table 8.4 Time sharing on Radio 1

	Zambians speaking (%)	*Radio 1 Airtime* (%)	*Days*	*Wknd hrs*	*Late nights*	*Lunch slots*
Bemba	56	19	daily	11	WFSu	TuThSa
Nyanja	42	15	daily	7	TuTh	MWFSu
Tonga	23	19	daily	8	Sa	—
Lozi	17	18	daily	4	M	—
Luvale	8	9	Tu–Sa	2	—	—
Kaonde	7	8	TuThF	0	—	—
Lunda	5	8	Tu-Sa	2	—	—

Column 1 is based on Kashoki 1978:39. Other tabulations are based on Table 8.3.

reflected more in the allocation of peak times and through other forms of institutional favoritism. The two lingua francas have the most late-night slots, numerous weekend programs, and the daily lunchtime slots, all of which attract high advertising volume and also correspond with the typical urban laborer's off-work schedule.[23]

The most pervasive theme in both listeners' and broadcasting personnel's discourse about these language valuations is that radio languages represent homogeneous and relatively monolingual speech communities—that is, ethnic groups. Radio's elaborate partitioning of its universe of addressees at the most general level—as separate but equal speech communities based on language—draws from and feeds into this essentialist view. Thus, while management statements say that "the seven (7) main vernacular languages on the Media represent all seventy three (73) tribes found in Zambia" (Kapeya 1988:3), some people simply do not feel represented; they want their piece of the national pie. Many such complaints, as we have already seen, allude to the national motto "One Zambia, One Nation" in making demands for a linguistic democracy. While this motto signifies a vision of equal inclusion, the closely related nationalist slogan "One Man, One Vote" (Spitulnik 1994, in press) has become a major trope for measuring equal representation, as in this letter to Radio Zambia: "If we are all Zambians, then we should all get the same privileges. Kaonde should be on the radio for the same amount of time as the other languages. Equal hours for each tribe" (Mytton 1978:217). Building on the view that one language is "a true identifier" of one people,[24] a series of one-to-one correspondences and distributional tropes have thus emerged as assessments of ethnolinguistic equity: one language, one people, one culture; equal hours for every language, and so on. In this semiotic of proportional distribution, if languages represent people, then equal representation for everyone in radio occurs through equal distribution of radio's resources (e.g., airtime, programs, staff) across these different languages.

In the ongoing debate over the three Northwestern languages, egalitarianism is also measured in terms of another kind of one-to-one correspondence, that of regional distribution. Some broadcasters and listeners say, for example, that the Northwestern Province is unduly favored with *three* radio languages, while the four remaining languages are made to cover the eight other provinces. According to this view, some provinces are actually shortchanged by having no unique radio language of their own or by having their other languages go unrepresented. But Northwesterners see it differently. To them the criterion of impartiality is not one language per province but equal hours per language, as this broadcaster explained in 1989: "The problem is, we have been recognized as a language, so why be mistreated? ... It remains that the big two or the big four get most of the time. ... But you can't raise these issues because you may be called a tribalist."

During 1989, ZNBC's concern over such growing sentiments was considerable. Originally Radio 1, and the Home Service before it, had five departments: Bemba Section, Lozi Section, Nyanja Section, Tonga Section, and Northwestern Section. This bureaucratic division in itself clearly marked the status of "the big four" as against the others. To dispel this implication, ZNBC administratively repartitioned the linguistic universe by dividing the Northwestern Section into three distinct language units: the Kaonde Section, the Lunda Section, and the Luvale Section. An administrative analog of linguistic egalitarianism was thus created: one language, one section. Radio time was not changed, however.

Other voices of contestation come from Zambians whose first languages are not any of the official languages (Mytton 1974, 1978). Indeed, if one fully applies the essentialist notion that a language is a "true identifier" of a people, a very serious problem arises: If languages do emblematize people, then how are 73 different peoples represented by only seven languages?

National statistics suggest that roughly 40 percent of the total population are from ethnic groups other than those associated with the 7 official Zambian languages (Kashoki 1978:19–21). Taking language varieties into consideration, however, a much smaller number (roughly 16 percent) do not speak one of the official languages or a closely related dialect as a first language (38). In addition, multilingualism is extremely high, and there is evidence that nearly 95 percent of all Zambians understand at least one official language (39). Still, periodic demands for recognition are common, as this letter from a Nkoya listener illustrates: "Lozi isn't representative of Nkoya, so we should have our own broadcasts. ... We won't accept a situation of being considered as a sub-group of Lozi!" (received 7/89, ZNBC). The executive handling this said he would check the government policy to determine if Nkoya was "a language or just a dialect," and presumably this would decide whether the Nkoya people could be considered "a subgroup" of the neighboring Lozi people.[25] In the difficult conflation of 73 into 7, ZNBC thus attempts to dispel the essentialist idea that one language represents only one ethnic group.

In a similar vein, some Zambians invoke this argument of 'language' versus 'dialect' to assert that there are no more than six or seven Zambian "languages" and that some radio languages can be removed without sacrificing comprehension. A corollary thus emerges from the first theme "a language equals a people": "a dialect equals a subgroup." While the former are viewed as having real status, the latter are seen as "small" and insignificant. For example, one Zambian explained to me that the Northwestern languages are more like dialects of Bemba: "There are these small languages, what are they, Lunda, Luvale, and Kaonde. No one will argue that they can't use Bemba in the Northwestern Province. Bemba, Nyanja, Tonga, and Lozi would be enough [on radio]."

The apparent superiority of some Zambian languages over others is also rationalized in historical terms. For example, a senior ZNBC executive commented: "I don't have to go into whole history of broadcasting for you . . . . but due to their history the Bemba and Nyanja programs are better equipped in terms of intellectual output." While this executive acknowledged the historically contingent nature of the high valuation of Bemba and Nyanja, he did not acknowledge the contemporary relations of power and interest that continue to perpetuate this. Instead, the superior quality of programs in these languages was taken as a given—unalterable and unattributable to any interests in particular.

For critics of this linguistic status quo, however, the issue is not about historical precedent or comprehensibility; it is about basic representation. Radio language comprehension is extremely high across the Zambian population, with the mean number of radio languages listened to overall at 2.9 (Mytton 1974:26).[26] Indeed, Radio Zambia audiences are not as fragmented along ethnic lines as the schedules would suggest; many listeners listen to programs in several different languages. Comprehension is not the point, however, if languages are viewed as primordial emblems of autonomous ethnic groups: to be excluded from radio is tantamount to being a "subgroup," encompassed by one of the selected seven. To get around this problem of representation, ZNBC has pursued other avenues for allowing linguistic diversity to emerge in its programming. For example, in the Nkoya case, the executive said he would ensure that some Nkoya *songs* were played during the Lozi time slots. Thus, consonant with the linguistic division of labor and the pluralism within bounds discussed earlier, cries for representation are met by the inclusion of cultural material. While the time blocks and named radio languages themselves cannot be tinkered with, small glimmers of linguistic diversity greater than the chosen seven can occur on the airwaves, but they are of the safe cultural kind.

Conclusions

The central trope in all of these debates over radio languages revolves around the question of *which unit of representation* is adequate for quantifying ethnolinguistic equality. Should it be measured by amount of airtime, amount of primetime, inclusion on a specific radio channel, or degree of geographical coverage? In a situation where the actual numbers of speakers are unequal, and where the political and economic valuations associated with different languages are unequal these seemingly external domains with their own 'objective' possibilities for segmentation and quantification become the foci for measuring ethnolinguistic parity.

As we have seen, there is an attempt to regulate language sameness across the weekly schedule, and in newscasting and other translated programs, through a semiotics of distributional equality and through a cultural "codification of diversity" where all diversities are exchangeable (Spyer 1996:26). But this apparent pluralism is not open to all, as evidenced in the Nkoya case. It is a pluralism within bounds. Moreover, it is not an egalitarian pluralism; rather, it is a hierarchical pluralism that mirrors the stratified political economy of languages in the country.

I have argued that language ideologies are both produced and reproduced in such media practices and that this occurs through different processes of language valuation and evaluation which have a powerful semiotic component. For example, this chapter has demonstrated how radio iconically maps social divisions through the divisions of airtime and how relational values between languages (and between speakers) are constructed and indexed through differences in program content. In these processes of valuation and evaluation, different social values are linked with different languages: some are construed as more capable of scientific expression and others as more suited to cultural expression; some are "small," while others are "big"; certain ones have more prestige, and some are considered to stand for people of many ethnicities, while others are not.

Regarding the question of whether different institutions are differentially suited for the production of such language ideologies, the answer here is yes. In the case of radio (and Radio Zambia in particular), I have illustrated that both the structure of the medium and the structure of the institution are critical in establishing some of the terms in which the politics of language gets played out. Radio is a medium shaped by time, wavelengths, and program types, and these three areas are some of the most closely attended to in the construction of language value. A fourth feature of radio, the spoken word, which we have not been able to examine here, is also essential in processes of language valuation, especially in language standardization (Bell 1991) and in setting up models of verbal interaction and linguistic innovation (Spitulnik 1996).

The structural parameters of the particular institution considered here are also highly significant. Battles over language value, and specifically over ethnolinguistic representation, are perhaps nowhere more intense and volatile than in the case of a state-run, centralized radio monopoly. I have claimed that mass media are exceptionally charged arenas for such battles, because of their high prestige, their high visibility, and their inherent publicizing function.[27] With one radio station and only one channel earmarked for Zambian languages, the semiotics of relational value become even more acute, because the playing field is much smaller.

In concluding this chapter, I raise two related issues that bear most directly on questions of where language ideologies are sited and how they work. The first concerns questions of determination and location: To what extent is radio a source of language ideologies, and to what extent it is a result of language ideologies? The second concerns questions of efficacy and consensus: To what extent are these language ideologies hegemonic?

The discussion here demonstrates that media practices are both a source and a result of certain language valuations. As we have seen, radio's role and effectiveness in establishing and reproducing such values is extensive and begins during the colonial period. Without, for example, the identification of four "main 'root' languages" (Franklin 1950:16) or the continued preferential placement of English on a separate channel, a different sociolinguistic landscape might have emerged in Zambia. But radio's determining role in this did not occur in a vacuum. Instead, it has been intricately enmeshed in the country's complex history of ethnic, class, and regional politics. Thus, there are some modes of evaluating languages that, while implicit in broadcasting practice, actually have their sources outside radio—in state discourse, in labor markets, and in more general understandings about the relations between language, culture, and identity. Neither the prestige value of English nor the idea that "a language" emblematizes "a people" actually originates in radio, but they are key language ideologies that are continuously reproduced in radio.

How widespread and how hegemonic are these ideologies? As already suggested, radio gives a fixity and legitimacy to certain language valuations, but they are far from hegemonic. At times they are contested, manipulated, or simply ineffective in producing consensus. For example, in some of the responses considered earlier, listeners protest that "English has the lion's share," and others state that they refuse to be viewed as "a subgroup" of another language. Yet despite these individual objections, radio's powerful impact in the reproduction of social inequalities remains. The differential allocation of resources (such as channels, airtime, office space, and program types) among the eight radio languages is very closely linked to the construction of social inequalities among the speakers of these languages, which broadcasting professionals themselves enact on a daily basis at the workplace. Most prominently, these processes have played a very powerful role in constructing the linguistic hegemony of English and of the nation's English speaking elites. In this sense, language valuations are, following Irvine, "a crucial mediating factor" between linguistic and social differentiation (1989:255). While they are not necessarily causative, they may serve to "rationalize a set of sociolinguistic differences rather than shape them" (255; also see Woolard 1985).

The striking feature of Radio Zambia, however, is that in addition to rationalizing a sociolinguistic hierarchy, it also functions to rationalize its distinct opposite—that is, a state ideology of ethnolinguistic egalitarianism. How effective is Radio Zambia in negotiating these two contradictory versions of linguistic pluralism? Essentially, this is a question not just about radio as an institution but about the people who run it and the interests it represents. Zambian radio—including its top executives, the Minister of Information, and, ultimately, the state and its leader—have been faced with the immensely complex task of reconciling a state ideology of egalitarianism with a fairly rigid linguistic hierarchy grounded in population demographics and the long history of differential language valuation in the country. In comparison to other countries with equally diverse populations and far fewer radio languages (e.g., Kenya, Tanzania, Indonesia), one can say that it is to Radio Zambia's credit that it has supported such a high number of languages within the economic and physical constraints of one broadcasting operation. The only drawback is that in its response to the dominant interpretations of pluralism in state politics—where diversity is seen to verge on divisiveness and acts of recognizing difference are potentially "tribalistic"—broadcasting's extensive promotion of English has weakened its ability to adequately provide for all of its listeners in the seven Zambian languages. In this sense, pluralism is not really negotiated at all; it is muted.

In this complex balancing act of mediating unity and diversity, one perplexing problem remains. We have seen how the national slogan "One Zambia, One Nation," while about unity, very easily becomes an important icon for the measurement of equality and difference, as it translates into other images of one-to-one correspondences—"one tribe, one language," "equal time for each tribe." Within this framework of ethnolinguistic essentialism, it seems almost inevitable that the values of unity and diversity are antithetical. Does this have to be the case? If pluralism is not muted, then what insurance is there that it will not lead to separatism? Indeed, this is why the closely monitored regulation of ethnolinguistic pluralism is so vital for the state's politics of encompassment. What is so striking about these pervasive ideologies of ethnolinguistic essentialism, however, is that they seem to ignore the multilingual, multiethnic reality of many Zambians. Many Zambians today are multiethnic, and most are not monolingual. As Fardon and Furniss have forcefully argued, multilingualism in Africa need not necessarily be seen as a problem to be solved or denied or contained; it is a distinctive richness that is often dramatically undervalued (1994:5). Is there a way, then, to produce language valuations in media practice that does not automatically imply a kind of linguistic essentialism or an oppositional framework in which some languages are "superior" and others are "inferior"? Can powerful institutions represent particular ethnolinguistic *and* multilingual realities without fostering an image of a national spoils system that is to be fought over?

These are wide-open questions. They are ones that are very close to home in our current debates about multiculturalism, public broadcasting, education, and so on. In addition, they have more general consequences for research concerned with the siting of language ideology. They suggest that we need to attend not only to where and how ideologies are produced, but also to the kinds of ideologies that are *not* being produced. Attending to the ideologies that are absent opens up a possibility for discussing alternative kinds of language valuations, ones which may still be instrumental in mediating national communities, but which need not deny the diverse and increasingly multilingual realities that are part of our contemporary world.

NOTES

The material for this chapter is drawn from ethnographic research at the Zambia National Broadcasting Corporation and archival research with Northwestern University's collection of colonial African newspapers. Field research (1988–1990) was supported by Fulbright-Hays and National Science Foundation fellowships and facilitated by the Institute for African Studies at the University of Zambia. I am especially grateful to these institutions; to the numerous ZNBC personnel who generously gave their time and encouragement to this project; and to Donald Donham, Mubanga Kashoki, Salikoko Mufwene, Susan Philips, Bambi Schieffelin, Bradd Shore, Michael Silverstein, and Edwin Wilmsen for their very insightful comments on earlier drafts.

1. This multisitedness of ideology is not a theoretical obstacle if one carefully attends to the methodological question of how ideologies are distilled from empirical data (Silverstein 1992:322, Spitulnik 1992:336, 352).

2. Recently, there have been a number of studies that have examined how claims to nationhood are built on the equation of *a* nation with *a* language (Woolard and Schieffelin 1994:60–61). This equation is particularly problematic for most African nations because of their high degrees of ethnic diversity and the tendency to highly value multilingual repertoires. For an excellent review and critique of the problems associated with the idealized model of the monolingual nation-state in African and the correlated idea that linguistic diversity is dangerous and undesirable, see Fardon and Furniss 1994 and Bamgbose 1994.

3. A comment made by Sally Regiono Vaughn, organizer of the Italian Issues Forum in San Jose, California.

4. Crucially, this equivalence between language and group is explicit in the lexicon of many Zambian languages. For example, in the Bemba language, there are two words for 'language', one of which is synonymous with 'tribe'. The words are *lulimi* 'language, tongue' and *mutundu* 'tribe, race, species, kind; language'.

5. As Silverstein 1987:13ff has argued for English language varieties in the United States, this kind of indexical "totemistic transfer" of stereotypes about social groups to the languages that they speak is part of a wider valorization and commoditization of the "standard," which thus serves to maintain and validate the hegemony of its speakers.

6. Up until 1993, the Zambia National Broadcasting Corporation (ZNBC) had a complete monopoly on broadcasting in the country, operating one television channel and three different radio channels. ZNBC broadcasts are centralized and are transmitted nationally from the capital city; there is no regional broadcasting. Broadcasting was removed from direct state control in 1988 with the creation of the corporation ZNBC, but government influence and censorship is still extensive.

7. A national media survey conducted in 1991 indicates that 57 percent of the national population own a working radio and that 74 percent listen at least once per week (63 percent listen daily or almost daily). By contrast, only 17 percent of Zambians own a television and 30 percent view at least once a week (Claypole and Daka 1993:63–64). (The authors note, however, that audience viewing and listening figures are most likely higher than usual because the study was conducted during an intense election campaign period.) In 1991 the national population was approximately 8.3 million people. For more discussion of radio audiences and the history of broadcasting, see Mytton 1974 and Spitulnik (forthcoming).

8. The most comprehensive studies suggest that there are fifteen to twenty distinct (nonmutually intelligible) language clusters or groupings in Zambia; each cluster contains several closely related language varieties, which are linked to specific ethnic groups (Kashoki 1978, Kashoki and Mann 1978, Lehmann 1978). Nearly all of Zambia's 73 ethnic groups claim to speak their own unique language, and thus one can estimate that there are more than 70 language varieties/dialects in Zambia. This situation is typical of sub-Saharan Africa, where ethnic groups are distinguished by their language varieties. Behind this is the complex, highly political issue of defining "a language" versus "a dialect," which, as we see later, figures prominently in debates over which languages are granted time on the national airwaves.

9. This phrase is my own usage, but one might even more pointedly employ the words of the then Minister of Culture, a "Bantustanization of Zambian culture." This process is fairly widespread across the globe. For example, in Indonesia there is a compartmentalization and "codification of diversity [in which] all diversities become exchangeable" (Spyer 1996:26).

10. While there are several studies on the construction of ethnic identity among specific groups in Zambia (van Binsbergen 1985, 1992, 1994; Papstein 1989; Siegel 1989), there is, to my knowledge, no detailed analysis of the contemporary *state* politics of ethnicity, for example, the state ideology concerning ethnic pluralism and the meanings of ethnic authenticity (or 'culture'). The sources of this ideology, and the historical factors that gave rise to what are identified as the "73 tribes" of Zambia are extremely complex and remain understudied in the literature. Comaroff (1987), Vail (1989), and van Binsbergen (1985, 1994), however, provide some very valuable pointers for examining this "creation of tribalism" as the historical convergence of several factors: (1) the British reliance, in its colonial administration of indirect rule and regulation of industrial labor migration, on the

notion of 'the African tribe' as a fixed population with membership defined by primordial attachment; (2) the roles of anthropologists, missionaries, and African intellectuals in documenting (and canonizing) unique and distinct ethnic cultures, histories, and languages; and (3) the dynamics of regional and national political economies (precolonial, colonial, and contemporary), which give rise to the articulation of ethnic difference and ethnic affiliation. Regarding this latter factor, Molteno 1974 and Ollawa 1979, among others, discuss the political dynamics of ethnic groups and regional power blocks in Zambia's early years, but do little to connect this to either the state discourse on ethnic identity or ethnic consciousness.

11. Issues of ethnic favoritism and conflict have been very important factors throughout the history of Zambian politics. During the period of research, they were distinctly muted by state discourse. It is only recently that national-level politicians (of the opposition parties) have raised in direct discussion what has for quite some time been a frequent topic in everyday conversation.

12. This pervasive rhetoric is exemplified in the following two excerpts: "Dr. Kaunda [then President] was a unifying factor who had tirelessly worked for the unity of all the 73 tribes in Zambia" (*Times of Zambia*, August 30, 1988, p. 7, indirectly quoting the Prime Minister); "At Independence Zambia was rather a divided country in terms of racial, tribal and political cleavages. Therefore, the task of the United National Independence Party was to launch a vigorous attack on these divisive sub-cultures in order to create an atmosphere of national unity, stability and peace . . ." (UNIP 1985:7).

13. The Constitution of Zambia states: "The official language of Zambia shall be English" (Article 1 part 5, as amended by Act No. 18 of 1996).

14. Historical data are drawn from Kashoki 1978, Roberts 1976, and Mytton 1978.

15. The contemporary discourse of regionalism, which flows directly from these relations of power established during the colonial period, is one of the major tropes of ethnic and language politics in Zambia. See, for example, Mitchell's 1956 classic analysis of how regional affiliations (and having closely related languages) shaped ethnic consciousness among urban workers during the colonial period. Significantly, during this early period of intensive multiethnic contact, certain ethnolinguistic labels came into use as the standard cover terms for people of a given region. For example, Northerners were called "Bembas," even if they were ethnically different (e.g. Bisa or Aushi) (Mitchell 1956:28–30); this is still the case today. Also see van Binsbergen 1985:203.

16. See Mitchell 1956 and van Binsbergen 1985, 1994 on how disparities in missionization, rural development, and access to education and labor markets were instrumental in the articulation of ethnic difference and affiliation during the colonial period.

17. Furthermore, until 1991, television broadcast exclusively in English. Presently it carries about one-half hour of Zambian languages per day.

18. Sources: *Handbook to the Federation of Rhodesia and Nyasaland*, 1960 (Salisbury: Government Printer), p. 552; *A Handbook to the Republic of Zambia*, c. 1965 (Lusaka: Government Printer), pp. 105–107; *Nshila*, nos. 183–236 (January 29, 1965–February 10, 1967).

19. Radio Zambia has had commercial advertising since the 1960s, but Radio 4 was created to increase advertising income. As ZNBC is a parastatal body with corporate status, it can generate and invest its own revenues, but it is substantially controlled by the Ministry of Information. Radio 4 is thus not a "commercial" (privately owned) radio channel in the Western sense, and outside commercial interests have had only minimal impact in shaping programming decisions.

20. The dual status of Bemba and Nyanja is somewhat analogous to that of Catalan in Spain, and they present political problems similar to those encountered in attempts at

"de-ethnicizing Catalan identity" (Woolard 1989:58). It seems unlikely that the Bemba and Nyanja languages could ever be fully de-ethnicized.

21. The functional segregation of languages is even more severe in the education system. English is the medium of instruction after Grade 3, and Zambian languages are taught as subjects, with traditional culture as typical content.

22. It should also be noted that the apparent pluralism in having different languages is even further circumscribed by the lack of independent news gathering in Zambian languages. There is thus very little reporting on individual ethnic communities.

23. From their national media survey conducted in 1991, Claypole and Daka 1993 report three major peaks in the daily listening schedule. Of all weekday listeners reporting that they had listened "yesterday" (25 percent of sample), 25 percent listened between 7 and 8 A.M., 25 percent listened at 1 P.M., and 30 to 38 percent listened between 8 and 9 P.M. Listenership at other times ranged from 14 to 23 percent.

24. Kapeya 1988:2.

25. The Nkoya people are roughly 1 percent of the national population, and Nkoya is a distinct language (Kashoki 1978). See van Binsbergen 1985, 1992, 1994 for an examination of the long history of class conflict, uneven development, and "ethnic self-articulation" (1994:142) among the Nkoya in relation to the Lozi.

26. This reflects the fact that there is, to borrow from Laitin 1992, somewhat of a "3 ± 1 language outcome" in practice, if not in policy. Laitin writes that the norm in Africa is that "citizens seeking occupational mobility and middle-class urban opportunities . . . need to have facility in 3 ± 1 languages" (1992:18): the nation's official language (usually an international language), a mother tongue, and possibly one or two regional lingua francas. In Zambia, this multilingual facility is further promoted by the high degree of cross-regional migration and the increasing prevalence of interethnic marriages.

27. The other major arena for such intense battles are educational systems.

REFERENCES

Anderson, Benedict. 1983. *Imagined Communities: Reflections on the Origin and Spread of Nationalism*. London: Verso.

Bamgbose, Ayo. 1994. Pride and Prejudice in Multilingualism and Development. In *African Languages, Development and the State*, ed. Richard Fardon and Graham Furniss, pp. 33–43. London: Routledge.

Bell, Alan. 1991. *The Language of News Media*. Oxford: Basil Blackwell.

Bourdieu, Pierre. 1991. *Language and Symbolic Power*. Cambridge, Mass.: Harvard University Press.

Claypole, Andrew, and Given Daka. 1993. Zambia. In *Global Audiences: Research for Worldwide Broadcasting 1993*, ed. Graham Mytton, pp. 59–70. London: John Libbey.

Cobarrubias, Juan, and Joshua A. Fishman, eds. 1983. *Progress in Language Planning: International Perspectives*. Berlin: Mouton de Gruyter.

Comaroff, John L. 1987. Of Totemism and Ethnicity: Consciousness, Practice, and the Signs of Inequality. *Ethnos* 52:301–323.

Donham, Donald L. 1990. *History, Power, Ideology: Central Issues in Marxism and Anthropology*. Cambridge: Cambridge University Press.

Eagleton, Terry. 1994. Introduction. In *Ideology*, ed. T. Eagleton, pp. 1–20. London and New York: Longman.

Fairclough, Norman. 1995. *Critical Discourse Analysis: The Critical Study of Language*. London: Longman.

Fardon, Richard, and Graham Furniss. 1994. Introduction: Frontiers and Boundaries—

African Languages as Political Environment. In *African Languages, Development and the State*, ed. Richard Fardon and Graham Furniss, pp. 1–29. London: Routledge.

Foucault, Michel. [1971] 1972. The Discourse on Language. Translated by Rupert Sawyer. In *The Archaeology of Knowledge and The Discourse on Language*, pp. 215–237. New York: Harper and Row.

Franklin, Harry. 1950. *Report on "The Saucepan Special": The Poor Man's Radio for Rural Populations*. Lusaka: Government Printer.

Gal, Susan. 1989. Language and Political Economy. *Annual Review of Anthropology* 18:345–367.

Hymes, Dell. 1984. Linguistic Problems in Defining the Concept of 'Tribe'. In *Language in Use*, ed. John Baugh and Joel Sherzer, pp. 7–27. Englewood Cliffs, N.J.: Prentice Hall.

Irvine, Judith. 1989. When Talk Isn't Cheap: Language and Political Economy. *American Ethnologist* 16:248–267.

Kapeya, Mwansa. 1988. The Use of Vernacular Languages in Broadcasting. Paper presented at a broadcasting seminar in Maputo, Mozambique.

Kashoki, Mubanga E. 1978. The Language Situation in Zambia. In *Language in Zambia*, ed. Sirarpi Ohannessian and Mubanga E. Kashoki, pp. 9–46. London: International African Institute.

Kashoki, Mubanga E., and Michael Mann. 1978. A General Sketch of the Bantu Languages of Zambia. In *Language in Zambia*, ed. Sirarpi Ohannessian and Mubanga E. Kashoki, pp. 47–100. London: International African Institute.

Kaunda, Kenneth D. 1967. *Humanism in Zambia and a Guide to Its Implementation*, Part 1. Lusaka: Government Printer.

Laitin, David D. 1992. *Language Repertoires and State Construction in Africa*. Cambridge: Cambridge University Press.

Lehmann, D. A. 1978. Languages of the Kafue Basin: Introductory Notes. In *Language in Zambia*, ed. Sirarpi Ohannessian and Mubanga E. Kashoki, pp. 101–120. London: International African Institute.

Mitchell, J. Clyde. 1956. *The Kalela Dance*. Manchester: Manchester University Press.

Molteno, Robert. 1974. Cleavage and Conflict in Zambian Politics: A Study in Sectionalism. In *Politics in Zambia*, ed. William Tordoff, pp. 62–106. Berkeley: University of California Press.

Mytton, Graham. 1974. *Listening, Looking, and Learning: Report on a National Mass Media Audience Survey in Zambia (1970–73)*. Lusaka: Institute for African Studies.

———. 1978. Language and the Media in Zambia. In *Language in Zambia*, ed. Sirarpi Ohannessian and Mubanga E. Kashoki, pp. 207–227. London: International African Institute.

Ohannessian, Sirarpi, and Mubanga E. Kashoki, eds. 1978. *Language in Zambia*. London: International African Institute.

Ollawa, Patrick. 1979. *Participatory Democracy in Zambia: The Political Economy of National Development*. Devon, U.K.: Stockwell.

Papstein, Robert. 1989. From Ethnic Identity to Tribalism: The Upper Zambezi Region of Zambia, 1830–1981. In *The Creation of Tribalism in Southern Africa*, ed. Leroy Vail, pp. 372–394. London: Currey.

Roberts, Andrew. 1976. *A History of Zambia*. New York: Africana.

Saussure, Ferdinand de. [1916] 1959. *Course in General Linguistics*. New York: McGraw-Hill.

Siegel, Brian. 1989. "Wild" and "Lazy" Lamba: Ethnic Stereotypes on the Central African Copperbelt. In *The Creation of Tribalism in Southern Africa*, ed. Leroy Vail, pp. 350–371. London: Currey.

Silverstein, Michael. 1987. Monoglot "Standard" in America. Working Papers and Proceedings of the Center for Psychosocial Studies 13. Chicago: Center for Psychosocial Studies.

———. 1992. The Uses and Utility of Ideology: Some Reflections. *Pragmatics* 2(3): 311–323.

Spitulnik, Debra. 1992. Radio Time Sharing and the Negotiation of Linguistic Pluralism in Zambia. *Pragmatics* 2(3):335–354.

———. 1994. Radio Cycles and Recyclings in Zambia: Public Words, Popular Critiques, and National Communities. *Passages* 8:10, 12, 14–16.

———. 1996. The Social Circulation of Media Discourse and the Mediation of Communities. *Journal of Linguistic Anthropology* 6(2):161–187.

———. In press. Small Media and the Construction of Communicative Space in Africa. In *Communication and Democracy in Africa*, ed. Goran Hyden and Michael Leslie. Gainesville: University of Florida Press.

———. 1997. Producing National Publics: Audience Constructions and the Electronic Media in Zambia. Unpublished manuscript.

Spyer, Patricia. 1996. Diversity with a Difference: *Adat* and the New Order in Aru (Eastern Indonesia). *Cultural Anthropology* 11(1):25–50.

Tilove, Jonathan. 1996. Whites Seek a Place in Diversity Movement. *Atlanta Journal/ Constitution*, January 28, 1996, B4.

UNIP (United National Independence Party). 1985. *The National Policies for the Decade 1985–1995: Aims and Objectives of the Third Phase of the Party Programme*. Lusaka: Office of the Secretary-General [of UNIP].

Vail, Leroy, ed. 1989. *The Creation of Tribalism in Southern Africa*. London: Currey.

van Binsbergen, Wim M. J. 1985. From Tribe to Ethnicity in Western Zambia: The Unit of Study as an Ideological Problem. In *Old Modes of Production and Capitalist Encroachment*, ed. Wim van Binsbergen and Peter Geschiere, pp. 181–233. London: Kegan Paul.

———. 1992. *Tears of Rain: Ethnicity and History in Central Western Zambia*. London: Kegan Paul.

———. 1994. Minority Language, Ethnicity and the State in Two African Situations: The Nkoya of Zambia and the Kalanga of Botswana. In *African Languages, Development and the State*, ed. Richard Fardon and Graham Furniss, pp. 142–188. London: Routledge.

Voloshinov, Valentin N. [1929] 1986. *Marxism and the Philosophy of Language*. Cambridge, Mass.: Harvard University Press.

Woolard, Kathryn A. 1985. Language Variation and Cultural Hegemony: Toward an Integration of Sociolinguistic and Social Theory. *American Ethnologist* 12:738–748.

———. 1989. *Double Talk: Bilingualism and the Politics of Ethnicity in Catalonia*. Stanford, Calif.: Stanford University Press.

Woolard, Kathryn A., and Bambi B. Schieffelin. 1994. Language Ideology. *Annual Review of Anthropology* 23:55–82.

9

The Role of Language in European Nationalist Ideologies

JAN BLOMMAERT AND JEF VERSCHUEREN

In his book *Nations and Nationalism since 1780*, E. J. Hobsbawm concludes that "the phenomenon [of nationalism] is past its peak" (1990:183). Before he gets to this conclusion (apparently written some time in 1989, before German reunification became a realistic possibility and before the process of fragmentation in some countries of the old communist bloc had gained momentum), he shows quite convincingly, and almost prophetically, that a new "Europe of nations" in the Wilsonian sense (e.g., with independent entities such as Catalonia, Corsica, Slovenia, Estonia) could not produce "a stable or lasting political system" (p. 177). For one, "the first thing most such hypothetical new European states would do is, almost certainly, apply for admission to the European Economic Community, which would once again limit their sovereign rights" (p. 177).

Indeed, nation-states with highly autonomous "national economies" probably belong to the past. However, it is far from clear that such a confrontation with economic reality, which will no doubt change the historical content and direction of nation-building processes, has any direct influence on nationalism from an ideological perspective. After all, as Hobsbawm demonstrates equally convincingly, the essence of nationalism from the nineteenth century on has been the definition of 'imagined communities' along conceptual lines out of touch with 'objective reality' (a theme also developed in Barth 1982 and by Anderson 1983).

An assessment of the ideological processes involved requires access to "the view from below." But, "that view from below, i.e. the nation as seen not by governments and the spokesmen and activists of nationalist (or non-nationalist) movements, but by the ordinary persons who are the objects of their action and propaganda, is exceedingly difficult to discover." This is further complicated by the fact that "national identification and what it is believed to imply, can change and shift in time, even in the course of quite short periods." Hobsbawm adds that "this is the area of national studies in which thinking and research are most urgently needed today." To counterbalance the remark about the "exceeding difficulty" of the research in question, he observes: "Fortunately social historians have learned how to investigate the history of ideas, opinions and feelings at the sub-literary level, so that we are today less likely to confuse, as historians once habitually did, editorials in select newspapers with public opinion" (Hobsbawm 1990:11).

This essay is intended to contribute (1) to the further exploration of the topic identified in these quotations, and (2) to the development of an adequate methodology to approach the complexities of ideology research. Situated in the context of a wider research project, this chapter provides a historical snapshot of mainstream European thinking about nations and national identification, and it reports on a smaller pilot study in which some West European data, mostly dating back to the first weeks of November 1990, were scrutinized in view of the specific role which *language* plays in the overall picture of current nationalist ideologies.[1]

Late 1990 was a period during which Europe was shaken by a wave of what was perceived as ethnic and/or nationalist conflicts, both inside European states (problems of immigration, asylum seekers) and elsewhere (especially in Eastern Europe). It goes without saying that our findings should be interpreted in the light of the regional restrictions on the corpus, a remark that should be kept in mind whenever we use the qualification 'European'. The data sample is very small and in no way representative from a strict methodological point of view.[2] Also, for obvious reasons it cannot allow us to detect diachronical changes in the structure of news reporting. But it may generate a number of hypotheses with regard to the ideologization of language in a nationalist frame, and it may also shed some light on the degree to which specific concepts and views are shared by observers in many European countries.

The nature of the data might raise some worries directly related to Hobsbawm's remark concerning the earlier habits of historians "to confuse editorials in select newspapers with public opinion." There are three ways in which the project avoids this problem. First, the selection criterion for choosing the newspapers to be investigated has been that they should be mainstream publications that together have a maximal readership but each of which has a different target audience. Small-circulation publications have been avoided because they are most likely to represent the opinions of a few people.[3] In practice, extremist texts (in any direction) have, as a result, rarely entered the corpus, though, depending on one's perspective, extremism of some kind may turn out to be the norm under certain circumstances and in some geographical areas.

Second, the investigation pays equal attention to regular news reports and editorials (which are more openly subject to personal interpretation and bias); the character and the genre of the texts are fully taken into account whenever conclusions are drawn from examples.

Third, and most important, more weight is attached to the implicit frame of reference, the supposedly common world of beliefs in which the reports (or the editorial comments) are anchored, than to the explicit statements made by the reporters (or commentators). This approach is crucial for the investigation of widely shared ideologies. And, fortunately, modern linguistics, in particular linguistic pragmatics, provides us with fully adequate tools to undertake exactly this kind of study. Briefly, the basic assumptions are (1) that the authors, just like any other language user in any other communicative context, are unable to express what they want to communicate in a fully explicit way, (2) that therefore their texts leave implicit most of the assumptions they expect their readers to share with them, and (3) that a careful analysis of those implicit assumptions will reveal a common frame of reference or 'ideology'. It follows that isolated examples are never sufficient as evidence: coherence—manifested either as recurrence or as systematic absence—is necessary to warrant conclusions.[4]

Language as a Distinctive Feature

The Significance of a Nonissue

As a surface topic, worthy of an explicit treatment in its own right, language is strikingly absent in our corpus of reports on interethnic conflicts or on issues of "national" identity or nation building. But, far from undermining any attempt to reveal a specific role for language in current nationalist ideologies from the start, this first observation has turned out to touch the very essence of popular linguistic ideology.

Language is raised to the level of an individual issue almost exclusively when reference is made to societies other than the one in which the report in question is itself to be situated. A case in point is a German report entitled "Amerika und Einwanderung: Schmelztiegel oder Salatschüssel?" (America and immigration: Melting pot or salad bowl?), juxtaposed with an article on a dispute over voting rights at the municipal level for minority members in Germany. Though the physical juxtaposition of the two articles is clearly based on a judgment of topical relatedness, the German issue is phrased exclusively in terms of the sharing of political power and the possible infringement of ethnic German rights, whereas language is explicitly focused on as an issue in the United States: "Heute schon spielen sich harte Kämpfe um die Sprache, um die Dominanz des Englischen ab, das vorläufig noch eine verbindende Kraft darstellt" (Already today difficult battles are fought over language, the dominance of English, which—for the time being—still presents a unifying force) (*Die Zeit*, 9 Nov. 1990, p. 7). The Official English movement is indeed a sufficiently interesting phenomenon to deserve special mention in connection with the multiethnicity of the United States.[5] But implicit in this German report is the idea that the coherence of a society strongly benefits from the existence of just one language. It is not accidental that the quoted sentence follows an explicit statement to the effect that "Die ethnisch-rassische Koexistenz scheint zu gelingen solange die Wirtschaft einigermassen floriert" (Ethnic-racial coexistence seems to work as long as the economy is somewhat successful). Linguistic strife is presented as an important force toward social disintegration, triggered by a worsening economy. Because of the need for linguistic coherence, German as the only language of Germany is taken for granted. The issue, which is in reality as acute as in the American case (though there is not one single "threatening" alternative such as Spanish in the United States), does not need to be mentioned. Thus, treating language as a nonissue in relation to German minority problems only reveals how much is really taken for granted.

Language: A Marker of Identity

That language is seen as a unifying force should be clear. Language assumes the character of a clear identity marker. Thus, it appears prominently in an article on Spanish Basque nationalism, entitled "Der Heimat bewusst: Die Basken—gastfreundlich aber nicht servil" (Conscious of the 'Heimat': The Basques: hospitable but not humble):

> Was steckt dahinter? Eine lange Geschichte der allerdings militanten Selbtstbehauptung eines Volkes, dessen Herkunft ebenso wie die Herkunft seiner Sprache, des Euskara, den Ethnologen und Linguisten bis heute Rätsel aufgibt. . . . Diese Ursprache . . . (What's behind it [i.e., behind Basque nationalism]? A long history of clearly militant self-preservation of a people, of which the origin, as well as the origin of its language, Euskara, has until today been a mystery for ethnologists and linguists. . . . This ancient language . . . (*Die Zeit*, 16 Nov. 1990, p. 83)

The language of the Basques, of which not enough may be known to designate it as "Ursprache" (if such a designation has any meaning at all),[6] becomes the romantic focus of the identity of the Basque people in a description that is reminiscent of nineteenth-century scholarship.

Natural Discontinuities

Yet, language is only one identity marker among others. Descent, history, culture, religion, and language are treated as a feature cluster. Their identificational function implies separability, a natural discontinuity in the real world. These discontinuities are "nations" or "peoples"—that is, natural groups, the folk perception of which conceptualizes them in much the same way as species in the animal kingdom. If feathers are predictive of beaks, eggs, and an ability to fly, so is a specific language predictive of a distinct history and culture.[7]

Thus, the absence of the feature "distinct language" tends to cast doubts on the legitimacy of claims to nationhood. Consider the following statements from an article on Ukraine, made in the context of references to the "russification" of the republic:

> The poor old Ukraine has had a bad press. Both the Poles, who dominated the towns of the western part, and the Russians, who dominated those of the east and south, looked down on the Ukrainians as peasants, speaking jargon. The language itself varied greatly from region to region—in the west quite close to Polish, in the east some-

> times indistinguishable from Russian. . . . Politically, the Ukraine was underdeveloped. (*Guardian Weekly*, 4 Nov. 1990, p. 9)

Here the lack of a clearly distinct language is the first item in a list of indicators of cultural erosion or underdevelopment.

In some cases, language is offered as the only distinctive trait of a "group"; others are not really needed, since a distinctive language is predictive of a distinct group identity. This strategy is typically used when little-known ethnic groups are talked about. A case in point is the reporting on the Gagauz people in Moldova:

> . . . the defiant Turkish-speaking Gagauz districts [of Moldova] (*Guardian Weekly*, 4 Nov. 1990, p. 6)

> . . . the Turkish-speaking separatist Gagauz minority (*Guardian Weekly*, 11 Nov. 1990, p. 6)

> . . . the Turkish-speaking Gagauz (*The Guardian*, 1 Nov. 1990, p. 4; *The Guardian*, 12 Nov. 1990, p. 4)

> . . . de Gagaoezen, een Turkstalige minderheid. (. . . the Gagauz, a Turkish-speaking minority)(*NRC Handelsblad*, 2 Nov. 1990, p. 5)

The feature clustering that underlies group identification is such a powerful cognitive mechanism that knowledge about one feature is assumed to be enough, especially when it concerns language. As a result, groups that are distinguished solely on the basis of a distinct language are often treated as "real" ethnic groups. And as such, they can be presented as being involved in inter*ethnic* conflicts, even if their unity along the other parameters of the expected feature cluster does not stand up to scrutiny: "Les violences entre Moldaves et russophones . . ." (The violence between Moldovans and Russian-speakers . . .) (*Le Monde*, 6 Nov. 1990, p. 8). In this report, "Russian-speakers" (referred to alternatingly as "minorité russe" or "minorité russophone") are placed on a par with the Moldovans and the Gagauz. Here we see the dynamics of feature clustering at work. Though "Russians" (the least-preferred denominator in this report) could be reasonably assumed to share some common aspects of ethnicity, "Russian-speakers" can obviously be no more than a residual category, an extremely heterogeneous group of people who may come from all over the Soviet Union, united only by the fact that they speak Russian (though it is certain that not all of them speak it as their mother tongue and though even this feature does not clearly distinguish them from the other groups, as will be shown later in this chapter), and by the fact that they *cannot* be labeled as ethnic Moldovans or Gagauz. But, nevertheless, the "Russian-speakers" are presented, in direct opposition with Moldovans and Gagauz, as an equally solid ethnic unit.

This misrepresentation of the social formations involved in the conflict clearly hampers a fair understanding of what goes on in Moldova: by applying familiar categories, the impression of clear understanding is created, while, in fact, neither the authors nor the readers of the articles have any familiarity with the people talked about. This is further illustrated by another characteristic of our data: after language has been introduced as a categorizing criterion, distinctive features other than language may be dragged in as soon as they are known, irrespective of whether in reality they play an identifying or distinguishing role. This leads to strange descriptions such as the following: . . . "de Gagaoezen—een aan de Turken verwante christelijke minderheid—" (. . . the Gagauz—a Christian minority related to the Turks—) (*NRC Handelsblad*, 5 Nov. 1990, p. 4). Thus, our data show the emergence of religion as a further identifying feature of the Gagauz a few days after the first reports, though Christianity in itself is precisely *not* a minority trait in Moldova.

It may be even more surprising that this language-based identification is maintained even though the distinguishing trait is almost in the same breath denied or downplayed: "They [the Moldovans] claim the Gagauz are strongly Russianised; most speak Russian rather than Turkish and support Russian interests" (*The Guardian*, 1 Nov. 1990, p. 4).

Though this again casts doubt on the legitimacy of a movement (centered around people who have betrayed themselves by adopting another language), we will come back to this example to demonstrate further aspects of the linguistic framing of nationalism.

Before going on, let us briefly point out that the clustering of language, descent, history, culture, and religion, the strength of which we have been trying to demonstrate, is extended even to economic position. Remember the following quote: "Die ethnisch-rassische Koexistenz scheint zu gelingen solange die Wirtschaft einigermassen floriert" (Ethnic-racial coexistence seems to work as long as the economy is somewhat successful) (*Die Zeit*, 9 Nov. 1990, p. 7). The relationship between (multi)ethnicity and economic prosperity is a topic that deserves more than the few lines we can spend here. In general, there seems to be an intuitive, almost automatic, association between the rise of nationalism and economic problems. Thus, a weak economy is a much favored excuse for manifestations of racism. But if economic factors can trigger interethnic conflicts, ethnic groups must be seen as socioeconomically undifferentiated wholes that act and react en masse under economic pressure.[8] The economy, which may soothe slumbering interethnic conflicts in times of general prosperity, is seen as flexible and unstable, whereas ethnicity is seen as a stable and timeless element of social stratification, a stratification that largely coincides with socioeconomic differences.

The Different Faces of Homogeneism

Since the discontinuities—to pursue the lexical semantics metaphor further—are defined in terms of necessary and sufficient conditions that are so strongly clustered that even one of them may be sufficient to characterize a group entity, homogeneity (emphasizing the necessity of the necessary and sufficient conditions) is the norm *within the discontinuities* (i.e., the 'nations' or 'peoples') thus defined. Since such a view is so obviously naive, adherence to it would be most passionately denied by the authors of most of the reports discussed when challenged about this. But here we touch on a deeply engrained dogma that is very coherently—though mostly implicitly—present in discourse about interethnic conflicts. Elsewhere (Blommaert and Verschueren 1991) we have called it the dogma of *homogeneism*:

a view of society in which differences are seen as dangerous and centrifugal and in which the 'best' society is suggested to be one without intergroup differences.

In other words, the ideal model of society is monolingual, monoethnic, monoreligious, monoideological. Nationalism, interpreted as the struggle to keep groups as "pure" and homogeneous as possible, is considered to be a positive attitude within the dogma of homogeneism. Pluriethnic or plurilingual societies are seen as problem-prone, because they require forms of state organization that run counter to the "natural" characteristics of groupings of people. This dogma appears to dominate Belgian (and European) immigrant policies (again, see Blommaert and Verschueren 1991), and—as will be further demonstrated—it is used as an interpretive frame (with the Soviet Union as evidence and example) even for situations outside of Europe in our corpus:

> Wie in die Sowjetunion stellt sich auch in Indien die frage, ob ein Riesenreich, das aus derartig vielen ethnischen, religiösen, sprachlichen und kulturellen Splittern zusammengesetzt ist, zusammengehalten werden kann. (As in the Soviet Union, the question also poses itself for India whether a giant empire consisting of such a plethora of ethnic, religious, linguistic, and cultural fragments can be held together.) (*Die Zeit*, 16 Nov. 1990, p. 11)

The conceptual systematicity with which the norm of homogeneity turns language itself into an interethnic battlefield is discussed in the next section of this chapter.

Though the norm of homogeneity is demonstrably present across Europe, the criteria along which homogeneous nations are defined differ substantially. Let us briefly look at some of the different forms of expression the norm can take. We find it in its purest ethnic form in the German press, where 'das Volk' is systematically contrasted with 'die Bevölkerung': the people versus the population. For instance, the caption accompanying a picture with Turkish immigrants reads: "Soll nur das Volk oder die Bevölkerung auf kommunaler Ebene politisch mitentscheiden dürfen? Türken auf einem SPD-fest in Berlin-Kreuzberg" (Should only the people or the population participate in political decisions at the municipal level? Turks at an SPD-meeting in Berlin-Kreuzberg) (*Die Zeit*, 9 Nov. 1990, p. 7).

Overtly, a clear position of tolerance is advocated: "Deutschland wird, wie in der Geschichte schon oft, die Ausländer, die gekommen sind und bleiben wollen, 'integrieren.'" (Germany will, as often before in history, 'integrate' foreigners who have come and want to stay) (*Frankfurter Allgemeine*, 2 Nov. 1990, p. 1). Yet this claim is embedded in a plea for preserving voting rights at the municipal level for 'Staatsbürger' (citizens) and against giving them to 'Bewohner' or 'Einwohner' (inhabitants). That the plea is intended to protect not so much all those who have acquired German citizenship but mostly ethnic Germans is made abundantly—if unwittingly—clear:

> Mithin ist es konsequent, dass in Deutschland namens des Begriffs der Demokratie . . . Versuche abgewehrt worden sind, die Begriffe Nation und Staat voneinander zu trennen und sie damit aufzulösen. (Therefore it is logical that in Germany, in the name of democracy . . . attempts have been thwarted to tear the notions nation and state apart and hence to annihilate them.) (*Frankfurter Allgemeine*, 2 Nov. 1990, p. 1)

The author continues:

> Bisher is nichts Überzeugendes gesagt worden darüber, das die Verwischung des Begriffs der über die Staatsbürgerschaft verfügenden Angehörigen einer Nation, die in der Handlungseinheit Staat über sichselbst bestimmen, irgendwelche Vorteile habe. . . . Demokratie braucht fesst umrissene Einheiten. (So far, nothing convincing has been said to show that it would have any advantages to eliminate the concept of a "nation" with dependents possessing citizenship and determining their own fate within the action unit "state." Democracy needs clearly defined units.) (*Frankfurter Allgemeine*, 2 Nov. 1990, p. 1)

In the context of this article, the author does not leave any doubt that those 'fesst umrissene Einheiten' are nation-states, the homogeneity of which should not be broken: to the extent that immigrants are tolerable as participants in social and political life, they have to be "integrated."

But it is exactly at this juncture that the paradox—or the deadly logic—of a nationalist ideology becomes clear. The definition of 'das Volk' in terms of a feature cluster makes "integration" impossible, as much as it requires that process. As soon as an 'Einwohner' or member of the 'Bevölkerung' has adapted to one parameter of Germanhood, any other feature may be arbitrarily focused on to preserve the difference. Thus, language is only one feature in the cluster. Just as German Jews (even if indistinguishable in other respects) lacked the proper genetics, any migrant worker fluent in German and respecting all German laws and rules of public life may still be stuck with the wrong descent, historical background, looks, or religion: he or she cannot become a member of 'das Volk'; his or her presence inevitably breaks the "natural groupings" of people, the homogeneity of nations, the strictly separable units needed for democracy. Just consider the categories introduced in the following sentence:

> Nur gebürtige Deutsche und diejenigen, die ihnen kraft "Volkszugehörigkeit" oder durch späteren Erwerb des Staatsangehörigkeit gleichgestellt sind, dürfen wahlen. (Only those born as Germans and those who have been given the same rights on the basis of their "membership in the people" or later naturalization are allowed to vote. (*Die Zeit*, 9 Nov. 1990, p. 7)

Of the two categories who have to be *given* the rights that those born as Germans have "naturally," the first group (including the 'Aussiedler', descendants of earlier German emigrants) are immediately defined as belonging to 'das Volk'. The second group will probably never make it: their children will be second-generation immigrants, not really 'gebürtige Deutsche'.

In contrast to the German emphasis on an ethnic definition of 'das Volk' (in terms of language, descent, culture, and so on), the French version of homogeneism stresses the importance of territoriality. The difference in emphasis has clear historical roots. The German quest for a nation-state was considerably facilitated by the spread of German dialects across a large part of Europe. Though few people actively used a common language of culture, politically the geographical area in question had been so fragmented that language was not only a useful but virtually the only possible focus for unity. Moreover, by the time of German unification in the second half of the nineteenth century, European nationalism was taking a linguistic turn (expressed in the insertion of a language question in national censuses). By contrast, when France needed to identify 'le peuple' after the French revolution, the French language was no more than an administrative means for statewide communication, a language that was shared (even in its dialectal variants) by less than half the population. As a result, the search for self-identification led to a reification of France itself as a natural and indivisible entity, the French "people" consisting of everyone living in its territory. Though from the mid-nineteenth century on France has been "successful" in imposing the French language and reducing the size of all its linguistic minorities, even today "linguistic nationalism" is seen as a distinct type of nationalism with which the French do not ideologically associate themselves. Thus, a sense of bemusement is hardly suppressed in the article "Les forcenés du nationalisme linguistique slovaque" (The fanatics of Slovak linguistic nationalism):

> Grèvistes de la faim, ils campent devant le Conseil national slovaque depuis le vote, jeudi 25 octobre, d'une loi érigeant le slovaque en langue officielle de la Slovaquie. (These hunger strikers have been camping outside the Slovak national Council since the vote, on Thursday October 25, which made Slovak the official language of Slovakia.) (*Le Monde*, 1 Nov. 1990, p. 7)

Thus, having introduced the event ambiguously, leaving open the interpretation that the 'plusieurs dizaines de jeunes' (several dozens of young people) who are conducting a hunger strike are protesting the new law passed by the 'forcenés' (fanatics) of linguistic nationalism, the author then catches the reader by surprise: "Pour eux, cette loi est trop laxiste" (For them, this law is too permissive). The hunger strikers are themselves the fanatics. They do not merely want Slovak to be the official language; they want to take away any linguistic rights that the Hungarian, Gypsy, Polish, Ukrainian, and German minorities within Slovakia might have.

In spite of this expression of astonishment concerning the lack of tolerance for linguistic discontinuity in the Slovak case, the territorially based French version of nationalism has as much trouble accepting discontinuities: within its borders, France is one. This is clearly expressed in the debate over Corsican separatism and, in particular, the official acceptance of the very notion of a "Corsican people." That a debate over the fact that 'Le gouvernement reconnaît l'existence d'un "peuple corse"' (The government recognizes the existence of a 'Corsican people') (*Le Monde*, 2 Nov. 1990, p. 1) is at all necessary, and is treated as front-page news, is already significant. But the phrasing of that recognition is symptomatic of the French version of homogeneism: "M. Mitterrand est intervenu pour que la notion de 'peuple corse' soit retenue en tant que 'composante du peuple français'" [M. Mitterrand has defended the acceptance of the notion of a 'Corsican people' as a 'component of the French people'.) (*Le Monde*, 2 Nov. 1990, p. 1)

In spite of this rhetorical attempt to avert discontinuity, questions are raised about the constitutionality of the government decision, and even about its logical possibility; and it is ridiculed as 'le modèle polynésien' (the Polynesian model), with reference to earlier decisions concerning French Polynesia. The French press avoids any reference to what the German press identifies as an underlying problem for those who are disturbed by the decision:

> Sie sehen voraus, dass wo ein Volk ist, auch ein Staat sein müsse, und sie befürchten, dass nach dem korsischen auch ein "bretonisches," ein "baskisches" oder sogar ein "elsässisches Volk" Ansprüche erheben könnte. (They anticipate that where there is a people, there must also be a state, and they fear that after the Corsicans also a "Bretonic," a "Basque," or even an "Alsatian people" could be making demands.) (*Frankfurter Allgemeine*, 2 Nov. 1990, p. 6)

Corsican nationalists are reportedly satisfied, while the most avid opposition comes from Le Pen's 'Front national':

> Le Front national "souligne les responsabilité [*sic*] que prendraient les parlementaires, les fonctionnaires ou, même, les citoyens qui attenteraient aux liens institutionnels qui placent la Corse dans la République et aux droits historiques et moraux de la patrie française en Corse." (The National Front "emphasizes the responsibilities that would be taken by those representatives, functionaries, or even citizens who would make an attempt on the institutional ties that place Corsica within the Republic and on the historical and moral rights of the French fatherland in Corsica.") (*Le Monde*, 3 Nov. 1990, p. 8)

Here again we find a fundamental paradox of nationalism: though grounded in the observation of "existing" differences, once a separate entity has been defined, nationalism is unable to recognize the legitimacy of any smaller-scale (or larger) group identities.[9]

The data from the British press contain remarkably few references to ethnic or linguistic diversity within Britain. Still, one small article in *The Guardian* (entitled "Welsh militants urge supporters to breed children 'for the cause'") tells a lot. In this article, a meeting of Welsh nationalists is reported. One of their leaders is said to have pleaded for Welshmen to have as many children as possible, so as to perpetuate the Welsh language, in the following terms: "If you cannot speak Welsh, you carry the mark of the Englishman with you every day. That is the unpleasant truth" (*The Guardian*, 12 Nov. 1990, p. 1). Objectively, this is a strong radical statement, revealing a degree of fanaticism mostly associated with radical nationalists. The meeting could, therefore, easily be taken seriously. But the opposite happens. The tone of the entire article is mildly ironical. The proposal to breed children in order to perpetuate the Welsh language is ridiculed. Moreover, the article ends with the suggestion that this proposal is reminiscent of the German Nazi 'Mutterkreuz'—a suggestion that is strongly rejected by the speaker. But even this comparison, grave as it may sound on the surface, is basically ironic. Nationalism (or, even more generally, ethnic diversity), at least within the United Kingdom, is treated as folklore: it is not to be taken seriously as a political movement in Britain. Welsh activists are sketched as picturesque, romantic people, who cherish old customs and values in a harmless way—harmless because of the strength of the centralized, English-speaking state.

In Belgium, homogeneism is most manifest in the domain of immigrant politics. That the Flemish and the Walloons run their own business, quite separately, is taken for granted (to the point where even arms sales can become a regional matter). Real problems of diversity (and the resulting destabilization) are caused only by the presence of immigrants from Maghrebine or of Mediterranean descent. Although the presence of these foreign elements in Belgian society is officially declared to be a form of "cultural enrichment" (invoking a suggestion of tolerance and openness from the Belgian side), a detailed analysis (see Blommaert and Verschueren 1991, 1992, 1993, 1994) reveals that Belgian society wants to be "enriched" only in domains such as exotic cuisine, exotic music, and dance—in sum, folklore. Socially, culturally, and linguistically, if not religiously, immigrants should "integrate" or de-ethnicize themselves, to the point where, as one government party's policy document on immigrants states, "Migrants should become Flemish." An intriguing side effect, but one that cannot be elaborated within the scope of this paper, is the observation that in the discourse about immigrants in Belgium, the age-old division between Flemish and Walloons seems to vanish. The formulation of an attitude toward immigrant minorities has caused the (re)construction of a common Belgian identity, thus allowing two clearly defined (and supposedly homogeneous) groups to form the core structure of a Belgian immigrant policy: "Belgians" as opposed to "Immigrants." Needless to say that neither is, or has ever been, a homogeneous group. The illusion thus created demonstrates the power of homogeneism: it blanks out intrasocietal differences such as age, sex, social status, and power and equates homogeneity with social harmony.

Of Nations and Tribes

Very little disagreement seems to exist with regard to the reality of "nations" in Europe. As we have demonstrated, the "nation" is presented as a natural, objective, and almost biological unit. People are divided on the basis of sex, age, and nation. In spite of the general tendency in our data to accept the existence—in "reality"—of "nations," explicit statements on the subject are rare. Treating this reality as self-evident effectively hides the fact that it rarely stands up to scrutiny. A potentially classical example to disprove the existence of objective criteria of nationhood is a comparison between the Serbs and the Croats, on the one hand, and the Flemish and the Dutch, on the other. In the Serbian-Croat case, existing linguistic differences (underscored by a different orthography) have become highly symbolic for the discontinuity, whereas in the Flemish-Dutch case (where the linguistic differences are of almost exactly the same type and degree) language is the main symbol of cultural unity. On all other counts, the differences are completely analogous as well—history (Ottoman rule for Serbia versus Spanish rule for Flanders, resulting in long periods of political separation from Croatia and Holland, respectively) and religion (Orthodox versus Catholic in the one case, Catholic versus Protestant/Calvinist in the other). In spite of its obviousness, not a single observation of this kind can be found in the corpus.

Interestingly, in the two explicit statements on the reality of nations that we have been able to find (one inside and one outside the restricted corpus that is the starting point for the discussion in this article), a comparison is volunteered between nations or peoples in Europe and "tribes." Consider the following observation from a Belgian newspaper:

> Tijdens zijn jongste bezoek aan Duitsland heeft President Mitterrand met die Franse hooghartigheid die niet zelden wortelt in een gebrekkige dossierkennis, minachtend gewaarschuwd voor een "Europe des tribus." Maar of dat het Franse staatshoofd nu bevalt of niet, het is een feit dat die "volksstammen" bestààn, erkenning, zeggenschap en een eigen plaats eisen in het Europa dat naar vereniging streeft. (During his recent visit to Germany, President Mitterrand, displaying that French sense of superiority which is not rarely based on being ill informed, has warned with disdain against a "Europe of tribes." But whether the French Head of State likes it or not, it is a fact that these "tribes" exist, that they demand recognition, political participation, and a place of their own in the Europe that is trying to reach unity.) (*De Standaard*, 27 Sept. 1991, p. 10)

The term *tribes* has a clear connotation of primitivism and naturalness in this context. And while Mitterrand's use of the term may be seen as ironic, the reaction from the journalist supports the view on nationalism as based on a need for identities analogous to groupings that are supposed to have come about quite naturally and instinctively in the less developed regions of the world. The resurgence of nationalism is therefore normal:

> Overal in Europa zien miljoenen mensen de kans schoon om oude dromen van kultureel zelfbestuur, zelfbeschikking en staatkundige onafhankelijkheid waar te maken. De verdwijning van de loden mantel die de kommunistische regimes over landen en volkeren hadden gelegd, heeft politieke en kulturele krachten vrijgemaakt die de komende decennia de landkaart van het kontinent kunnen hertekenen. . . . Lang vergeten haarden van onrust en gevaar blijken nooit helemaal gedoofd te zijn geweest. (Everywhere in Europe millions of people see the opportunity to realize old dreams of cultural independence, self-determination, and state autonomy. The disappearance of the cloak of lead spread out over countries and peoples by the Communist regimes has released cultural and political forces that are capable of redrawing the map of the continent in the coming decades. . . . Long forgotten centers of unrest and danger seem never to have vanished.) (*De Standaard*, 27 Sept. 1991, p. 10)

The author uses history as the ultimate argument for the reality of the nations of Europe. These nations (e.g., Lithuania, Ukraine, Moldova, Croatia) do not emerge as responses to concrete political or socioeconomic situations—they were always there, but they were suppressed by totalitarian state systems (see the next section). Their reality is historical and, therefore, objectively real.

The same comparison, though in the opposite direction, is made in the opinion columns of the *NRC Handelsblad* (7 Nov. 1990, p. 9). The author, a professor of anthropology, argues against the European view of African "tribes" as homogeneous, traditionalistic groups with rigid group boundaries. An explicit comparison with European nations or "peoples" is not at all central to this well-taken argument. In the text itself it is introduced only indirectly:

> In Europa, zo zeggen Afrikanen, spreekt men van volken; als men het over Afrika heeft gebruikt men het woord stammen. Daarmee is weer bevestigd hoe primitief Afrika is. (In Europe, Africans say, peoples are talked about; but as soon as Africa is the subject, the word tribes is used. This serves to reconfirm how primitive Africa is.) (*NRC Handelsblad*, 7 Nov. 1990, p. 9)

But, maybe as a result of editorial intervention, the comparison is presented as the main focus of attention in the title: "Wat in Afrika stammen heet, wordt in Europa als 'volkeren' getypeerd" (What is called tribes in Africa is characterized as 'peoples' in Europe). Furthermore, by stressing that the view of African tribes that he argues against is a decidedly "European" view, the author implicitly communicates that the properties he rejects for those African tribes are genuine properties of European "peoples" or "nations." Moreover, that similar "nations" exist in Africa is made abundantly clear by stressing the unity of Tutsi and Hutu in Rwanda, in terms of a familiar feature cluster: "Zij leven door elkaar als leden van één samenleving, bezitten één en dezelfde cultuur en spreken één taal" (They live together in one society, possess one and the same culture and speak one language). Thus, again, the objective reality of "nations" is emphasized. Nowhere does it come to mind that groups—wherever they are to be found—have a strongly subjective basis, that "nations" such as Lithuania or the Ukraine are defined territorially more than ethnically, and that they are therefore almost without exception multiethnic in population structure.

Obvious Universality

Such comparisons between Europe and the rest of the world emphasize the universal validity of a nationalist ideology. When criticism of patriotism or nationalism is voiced and reported on, there are clear markers of distance between the opinions described and a more general public opinion. Consider, for example, this review of Peter Glotz's "Der Irrweg des Nationalstaats," in which we read:

> [According to Glotz] Das Geschichtsbild müsse europäisiert und Mehrsprachigkeit zum Bildungsprinzip gemacht werden. Kess spricht er von einer "Hollandisierung Deutschlands"—ein Nationalbewusstsein ohne jeden Bezug zu völkischen, rassischen oder Sprachlichen Elementen.
>
> Schön war's. Das soll kein Spott sein. Es sind solche Argumente, die Glotz in seinem querköpfigen, anregenden, eigensinnigen Essay auch dazu bringen, für Bonn als Regierungssitz zu plädieren. (Our historical perspective should be Europeanized, and multilingualism should be made an educational principle. He speaks boldly of the "Hollandization of Germany"—a national consciousness without reference to people, race, or linguistic elements.
>
> Wouldn't that be nice! And this is not even meant ironically. It is this type of argument that also leads Glotz, in this stubborn and highly personal essay, to a plea for Bonn as capital.) (*Die Zeit*, Nov. 9 1990, p. 16)

Implicit in this is a perception of Holland as a nation untrue to itself because of lack of attention to real national identity and language. Strangely enough, Belgians tend to share this perception with the Germans. Thus, the former Antwerp mayor Cools took every possible opportunity to explain that the Dutch would have been taken over by the French by now if it had not been for the Flemish. And after a recent colloquium, "Dutch in the World," a prominent linguist wrote the following in an opinion article:

> Voor zijn taal *kultuur* zal Vlaanderen zich nu en in de toekomst moeten blijven richten naar het noorden: 15 miljoen geeft meer gewicht dan 5 miljoen. Maar voor de taal *politiek* is het anders. Daar zal Vlaanderen de bescheiden voortrekkersrol . . . zonder meer naar zich toe moeten trekken. In Vlaanderen ziet men de noodzaak in van de . . . instandhouding en verbreiding [van het Nederlands], voor Nederland is dat nog altijd een dubieuze zaak. (For its language *culture*, Flanders has to look to the north now and in the future: 15 million carries more weight than 5 million. But for language *policies* the situation is different. There Flanders will simply have to assume its modest pioneering role. . . . In Flanders one sees the need for the . . . preservation and spread (of Dutch); for Holland this is still a dubious matter.) (*De Standaard*, 22 Oct. 1991, p. 7)

Needless to say that the perception reflected in these German and Belgian texts bears only on Dutch official rhetoric. Our data show that "the view from below" is not so different after all and that the Germans and the Belgians can rest assured that nothing emanating from Holland will disturb their universally valid principles of social and political organization. Unfortunately, this cannot be meant ironically, either.

Language in the Empire

Language as a Battlefield

Our data indicate that language creates identity and discontinuity. It unites and it divides. In the context of conflicts involving nationalist groups in Europe (and elsewhere), these opposite tendencies turn language into the target and the battlefield of interethnic strife. Since language is a distinctive feature of "natural" groups, and since it is an element of divisiveness between such groups, language can also be used as an object of oppression and discrimination in contexts where interethnic differences are not (or no longer) tolerated.

Dominant in the framing of this role of language is the metaphor of the "Empire" in connection with tensions between a central government and "national" linguistic groups. The "Empire" in our corpus mostly refers to the Soviet Union or to state systems based on the Soviet model. In all the examples found in our data, the tensions between the "Empire" and national or ethnic groups are presented as resulting from the systematic denial by the empire of legitimate linguistic, cultural, and political rights. These minority groups claim the right to use their own language (or orthography) or to restore or introduce its official status as "national language." Since language is seen as a natural characteristic of these groups, such rights are held sacred, even if the claims are uncompromising and radical in nature.

Linguistic discrimination by the Soviet government is evoked as an example in statements such as the following:

> Their [the Kazakhs'] culture has been so defiled by the Bolshevikhs that many Kazakhs do not even know how to speak any other language than Russian. (*Guardian Weekly*, 11 Nov. 1990, p. 18)

> . . . a native Russian, Gennadi Kolbin, a party apparatchik who spoke not a word of the Kazakh language and had never been to the republic [of Kazakstan]. (*Guardian Weekly*, 11 Nov. 1990, p. 18)

Soviet oppression is said to have resulted not only in the loss of local language competence among oppressed peoples in peripheral republics. It also resulted in changes in language attitudes and political partisanship:

> The done thing, in the Soviet Ukraine, was to speak Russian if you became educated. (*Guardian Weekly*, 4 Nov. 1990, p. 9)

> They claim that the Gagauz are strongly Russianized; most speak Russian rather than Turkish and support Russian interests. (*The Guardian*, 1 Nov. 1990, p. 4)

The same pattern occurs in Soviet satellites or in regimes that have adopted the Soviet model. Serbia's centralist attitude toward the Albanian population of the Kosovo region is such a case: "The Albanian-language press and radio have been abolished" (*International Herald Tribune*, 12 Nov. 1990, p. 4). When anti-Soviet nationalist groups, once they have gained autonomy or independence, stretch their nationalist fervor to the point of oppressing other minorities within their (supposedly) national territories, this is explained as a direct consequence of the repression and discrimination they have suffered: "Moldawiens Hysterie . . . ist eine Folge des jahrzehntelangen Moskauer Diktats, das der rumänische Sprache sogar ein Kyrillisches Alphabet aufzwang" (The Moldovan hysteria is a consequence of the decennia-long Moscow regulation, which even imposed a Cyrillic alphabet on the Romanian language) (*Die Zeit*, 9 Nov. 1990, p. 1). In other words, the radicalism of newly autonomous or independent nationalist governments is not a product of their own ideology but rather an understandable, yet potentially dangerous, reaction to generations-long oppression by the totalitarian imperial authorities. These hypernationalist reactions, however, threaten the possibilities of future collaboration among newly autonomous regions: "Les violences entre Moldaves et russophones revêtent un aspect potentiellement explosif pour l'ensemble du pays" (The violence between Moldovans and Russian-speakers hides a potentially explosive situation for the country as a whole) (*Le Monde*, 6 Nov. 1990, p. 8).

The new forms of oppression often take the shape of legislation in favor of the majority language, banning other languages:

> In return, the republic's [= Moldova's] government would soften a law that made Moldavian the national language and required people in dozens of occupations to pass tests in Moldavian. The language law has stirred resentment among Russian speakers and the Gagauz. (*International Herald Tribune*, 5 Nov. 1990, p. 5)

> Pour eux [the Slovak hunger strikers protesting against a new language law], cette loi est trop laxiste: elle autorise l'usage des langues minoritaires dans les bureaux et services dans les regions ou les diverses minorités de Slovaquie comptent plus de 20 percent de la population locale. (For them, this law is too permissive: it allows the use of minority languages in offices and services in regions where the various minorities in Slovakia make up more than 20 percent of the local population.) (*Le Monde*, 1 Nov. 1990, p. 7)

These new forms of oppression are supported by standard nationalist arguments that associate national territory with national language. These arguments are, in our data, always presented as direct quotations:

> Lorsque je rentre dans un magasin dans le Sud [de la Slovaquie], on m'aborde en hongrois. Pourtant, je suis sur ma terre natale. (When I enter a shop in the South [of Slovakia], they address me in Hungarian. Yet, I'm on my native land.) (*Le Monde*, 1 Nov. 1990, p. 7)

> Maar waarom zijn er op de Israelische televisie wel programma's in het Arabisch en niet in het Russisch? We zijn nu toch in ons eigen land? (But why are there programs in Arabic on Israeli television and none in Russian? We are in our own country, after all? [said by Russian Jewish immigrants in Israel].) (*NRC Handelsblad*, 7 Nov. 1990, p. 4)

Though the ultimate absurdity of this cycle of oppression is not hidden by the reports, the underlying assumption of the legitimacy of each group's preoccupations is never challenged.

Natural Resistance and Democracy

At an abstract level, these examples invoke the image of an empire, consisting of a wide variety of linguistic, ethnic, religious, and cultural groups, most of which are oppressed by the unitarianism of the central state. Because the empire is oppressive, and because its oppression is directed against features that are absolute, inalienable characteristics of natural groups, the resistance of these groups is seen as necessarily legitimate. The struggle can be conceptualized only in terms of liberation or "freedom" movements.

It is only *natural* that people revolt when they are deprived of their own language and culture. Consequently, the natural, normal, and desired society is one in which these forms of oppression are absent: the nation-state in which people who share one language, culture, religion, and history live together within a sovereign state system. Here again, we find homogeneism as the underlying premise.

The argument in favor of homogeneism remains complex and often obscure. In relation to Eastern Europe, it is blended with the discourse of anticommunism. The natural resistance movements are directed against (the remnants of) Communist Party rule. By a remarkable and largely implicit rhetorical twist that defines communism as being against human nature, East European nationalism thus becomes an equivalent of democratization. The linguistic and cultural liberation of the East European peoples is at the core of the political liberation of the communist world, because nationalist revolt in the communist empire is aimed at liberating the "natural" human group from unnatural communist rule.[10]

In other contexts (such as the "giant empire" India, or minority problems in Belgium), the argument is stripped of its anticommunist connotations and reduced to its supposed naturalness or normality. The backbone of the argument is thus the sole assumption that different people do not like to live together and that successful society building requires as high a degree of similarity as possible among the constituent people.

The conceptual problems involved should be clear. First, homogeneism as a view of society rules out a number of social considerations. Class difference, socioeconomic status, and social mobility do not come up as factors of social coherence or conflict, except as properties of complete groups that correspond to the "natural" criteria for identifying and separating them in the building of a peaceful, harmonious society. This is, to say the least, a partial picture obscured by—admittedly persuasive but necessarily mistaken—monocausalism. Second, the direct association of (homogeneistic) nationalism with democracy and freedom is certainly not warranted by the facts, neither synchronically nor historically. Nationalism has been a notorious cause of conflicts and has led to some of the worst events in history. Also, the "liberated" Moldovans and Kazaks and Slovaks, as well as the liberated East Germans, seem to be building a track record of oppression and racism against minorities. Every minority has its own minorities. And for members of minority groups, be they immigrants in Western Europe or Gagauz people in Moldova, the "national" government may be as bad as the empire, because in both cases very little attention is given to their linguistic, cultural, or whatever rights. Only the structural level of the debate has shifted. Nothing has been achieved to guarantee more democracy in a pluralist sense.

Multilingualism and Tolerance

Still, nationalism is seen as a "natural" development anchored in linguistic and ethnic identities and as a powerful liberation movement, the excesses of which are based on anger and frustration. Our data suggest an intriguing side aspect of the role of language in this process. In three articles, two about the Israeli-Palestinian conflict in Israel and one on Serbian nationalism, reference is made to individual multilingualism as the opposite of fanaticism. The intriguing point is that this reference is made in a negative sense: even tolerant individuals who speak several languages fluently become fanatics. The orthodox bishop of Serbia, Amphilochios, a Serbian extremist, is said to speak fluent German (*Frankfurter Allgemeine*, 6 Nov. 1990, p. 16). So here is an educated polyglot who serves a cause that is mostly associated with lower-class, poorly educated monomaniac masses. The same point is made with reference to some well-educated Palestinian high school students and to a Jewish businessman who has worked with Arab personnel for years. The schoolboys have participated in the violent demonstrations following the Temple Mount shootings; the Jewish shopkeeper does not trust his Arab employees anymore.

> Although such vows are extreme, these boys do not look or sound like "Muslim fanatics.". . . Schooled in an elite institution operated by the Christian Brothers, they are polite and well spoken, able to express themselves in English, French and Arabic. (*International Herald Tribune*, 6 Nov. 1990, p. 7)

> Mr. Samar was born in Tel Aviv to parents who came from Iraq and he speaks fluent Arabic. In the last election he voted for a centrist party. (*International Herald Tribune*, 2 Nov. 1990, p. 5)

The picture that emerges here is the following. The struggle for legitimate national rights is such a central human interest that it eclipses even "intelligent" and practical solutions, such as learning the language of one's counterpart. Individual multilingualism cannot be a remedy for this intrinsically unstable and dangerous societal multiethnicity or multilingualism, for a conflict between people based on nationalist feelings is a fundamental conflict, one that cannot be remedied by slight forms of accommodation between the parties involved. In these references to the failure of individual multilingualism as a solution to interethnic conflicts resides a powerful suggestion about the nature of nationalism. It appears both as an emotional, irrational matter and as a respectable phenomenon. The shortcomings of language learning, or education at large, as a potential solution for interethnic conflicts demonstrate that nationalism is based on the fundamental, natural need for a homogeneous society. Man's political instinct, so to speak, directs him toward homogeneism. *Quod erat demonstrandum.*

It can be noted, in passing, that traditional approaches to language planning in the third world also adopt a homogeneistic frame of reference, in which societal multilingualism is equated with instability and in which a monolingual (or "oligolingual") nation-state is taken as the unquestionable model for progress and development (see Williams 1992). Consequently, language planning efforts in many parts of the world were aimed at reducing the number of official languages (i.e., languages used in administrative and educational practices in institutionalized contexts) to a minimum, the rationale being that nation-building could not proceed successfully in a multilingual situation. Two assumptions seem to have guided these efforts toward the reduction of multilingualism. The first assumption could be called the *integration assumption*—that is, the assumption that multilingualism is an obstacle for societal and national integration into a coherent nation-state. Bamgbose summarizes it as "the assumption . . . that nationhood also involves linguistic unity" (1994:35). The second assumption could be called the *efficiency assumption*—that is, the assumption that efficient government, as well as economic growth and development, are hampered by multilingualism. Both elements were almost dogmatic in language planning discussions about postcolonial African countries. At the same time, however, these assumptions were not used when other parts of the world were discussed. As Fardon and Furniss observe, "Whereas this capacity [for multilingualism] might be lauded elsewhere, it has been a commonplace to stress the negative side of the linguistic complexity of contemporary Africa" (1994:4). Thus, Singaporan political dogma views multiethnicity and multilingualism as one of the essential features of the Singaporan nation, and the European Union propaganda texts consistently stress the linguocultural heterogeneity of Europe as its main claim to uniqueness.

In the case of European states, an intricate web of discourses on multilingualism is created. Individual multilingualism may be encouraged—and it is effectively encouraged in almost every European state—as a key to European citizenship and to socioeconomic prosperity. Intrasocietal institutionalized multilingualism, by contrast, is actively discouraged by the same states (for instance, by means of new and restrictive language legislation), while multilingualism at the level of international (European) institutions is again encouraged and even strongly defended whenever tendencies to reduce the number of "working languages" in these institutions emerge (see, e.g., Deprez and Wynants 1994). This is a paradox, of course, but one that becomes comprehensible in the light of the remarks made earlier in this discussion. Individual multilingualism is a recommendable quality of individuals (who, it is assumed, are monolingual as a norm), and it requires an extra effort from them. On a par with tolerance, dynamism, or a sense of humor, individual multilingualism is relegated to the sphere of personal characteristics and of free individual choice, which cannot be enforced by the state. Societal multilingualism, on the other hand, is problematic and undesirable, because it breaks the "natural," homogeneistic norm of societies. And multilingualism in multinational organizations such as the European Union reflects the fact that the Union is a collection of sovereign nation-states, each having a uniqueness that resides in its language and culture.

Conclusions

Our corpus displays a remarkable consistency with regard to these assumptions. Homogeneism seems to be a widespread ideological premise, underlying much of the opinions reflected in or guided by the European newspaper press (see also Billig 1995, ch. 5). We find a primitive political theory underlying seemingly trivial statements and suggestions about the role of language in nationalism. This theory revolves around the impossibility of heterogeneous communities and the naturalness of homogeneous communities, the 'Volk'. This theory also rationalizes anticommunism, not in terms of an ideological critique, not even in terms of an economic critique, but in terms of the supposedly unnatural character of the communist system. Nationalism thus provides the ultimate evidence for the just cause of the Cold War. The Cold War did not concern political-economic details; it was about fundamental, natural rights, such as the right to use one's mother tongue.

The way in which the role of language in nationalist ideology is presented is largely political. The role of language as an element in feature clusters, corresponding to "natural," objective political units, which makes it a mobilizing force in interethnic conflicts, obliterates the primarily social dimension of language. Language may equally characterize all members of one ethnic group; within that ethnic group its resources may be unevenly distributed along social lines, as so much empirical sociolinguistic work has demonstrated. But the feature cluster of "culture" or "ethnicity" functions as a powerful frame of reference. Less romantic (and maybe less easily accessible) factors virtually disappear from the picture, or their relevance is gravely downplayed.

The way in which language is presented in the overall reporting on nationalist ideologies in Europe reveals (and undoubtedly feeds) a decidedly unsophisticated folk view. Although our analysis in this chapter was based on a relatively small set of data, we believe that we have demonstrated the usefulness of a systematic search for the "view from below" by means of a pragmatic analysis of patterns of wording. If applied with methodological rigor to larger sets of data, we believe that this type of analysis can provide an empirical tool for the investigation of elusive phenomena such as ideologies, public opinion, and ideas.

If nothing else, this brief study may have revealed a significant discrepancy between an aspect of popular language ideology and the way in which language is used in multilingual societies. As demonstrated by Woolard (1989) in connection with bilingualism in Catalonia, language choice is highly symbolic, and language shift is often motivated by the dynamics of social mobility. In popular ideology however, language tends to be a much more fundamental, even natural and inalienable, aspect of ethnicity or group identity in general. The way in which these popular views are sustained, consolidated, and reproduced by various forms of authoritative discourse such as mass media reporting, and the intricate dynamics of hegemony resulting from these processes, await further investigation.

NOTES

This article was written in the context of a research program supported by the Belgian National Fund for Scientific Research (NFWO/FKFO), the Belgian National Lottery, and a Belgian government grant (IUAP-II, contract no. 27). Thanks are due to Gino Eelen, who collected the data we needed, and to Louis Goossens, Johan van der Auwera, Michael Meeuwis, Luisa Martín Rojo, Susan Philips, Bambi Schieffelin, Kit Woolard, Paul Kroskrity, Christina Schäffner, and Anita Wenden for comments on earlier versions. Since its first publication in *Pragmatics* 2(3) (1992), special issue on language ideologies, this article has been reprinted in Christina Schäffner and Anita Wenden, eds., *Language and Peace* (Aldershot: Dartmouth, 1995). The editors' and publisher's permission to integrate it in a new edition of the original collection is hereby gratefully acknowledged.

1. Most of the data used for this specific study date back to the first weeks of November 1990, but they are not strictly confined to that period. The investigated publications are: *Die Zeit*, *Zeit Magazin*, *Der Spiegel*, *Frankfurter Allgemeine*, *Frankfurter Allgemeine Magazin*; *The Guardian*; *The Guardian Weekly*; *NRC Handelsblad*; *Le Monde*; *Le Nouvel Observateur*; *De Standaard*. For the sake of comparison, one non-European source (though clearly "Western" if not specifically American, and widely read in Europe), *The International Herald Tribune*, was studied for the same period. As is clear from the examples, the general tendency turned out to be very similar.

2. The wider research project on news reporting on interethnic problems uses a comprehensive collection of newspapers from twelve European countries, published during the three final months of 1991, as its database. For preliminary reports on this project, see Meeuwis 1993, D'hondt 1994, Langens 1994, Blommaert and Verschueren 1996, and D'hondt, Blommaert, and Verschueren 1995.

3. This statement can be correct only for a free-press tradition in which a wide range of publications is available. By now this is the case in most of Europe, though in the countries of the old communist bloc the situation is less stable than in the rest of Europe, and

hence future repetitions of the same research design may reveal more rapid historical change there.

4. Further justification for this approach is to be found in Blommaert and Verschueren 1991, 1993, and aspects of a full-length theoretical and methodological explanation are provided in Verschueren 1995a, 1995b.

5. For further discussions of this particular movement, which strongly relates national identity to language, see Adams and Brink 1990.

6. The translation of *Ursprache* as 'ancient language' does not do justice to the German term, which is strongly associated with romantic ideas of a people's age, purity, and authenticity.

7. Exactly the same ideological phenomenon is observed by Uli Windisch 1990 in his study of Swiss nationalism and xenophobia. He calls it "essentialism" and describes it as follows: "Every system of political and social representation is organised around essences, natures or noumena which are regarded as, by nature, transcendent, unalterable and historical" (p. 40). What we call feature clustering is identified by Windisch as follows: "This very common mechanism results in the creation of systems of objects, properties and values which can be defined as 'crystallised', as each element in the system is linked to another by ideological association" (p. 47).

8. The main exception to this rule seems to be the attempt, in official European rhetoric, to explain away racism and to preserve the European self-image of tolerance by demonstrating that expressions of racism are restricted to the lower socioeconomic classes and that low socioeconomic status is itself the *cause* (see Blommaert and Verschueren 1991). But this is just one manifestation of another rule: that it is easier to perceive significant distinctions in one's own group than in other groups. The phenomenon indicated here also explains the occurrence, in our restricted corpus, of a long article ("Wider die falschen Apostel," *Die Zeit*, 9 Nov. 1990, pp. 54–56) in which an attempt is made to define "normal nationalism," and in which economic problems are presented as a risk factor that may transform normal nationalism into xenophobia.

9. Uli Windisch 1990 reports that Swiss nationalism has the same profile as French nationalism, being based necessarily—because of the diversity of the people living in the country—on territoriality. Thus, Swiss nationalists cannot understand Jura separatism because "The only sociological division they recognise is that based on national frontiers: '[within Switzerland] there aren't any frontiers, we're all Swiss'" (p. 57).

10. Some recent scholarship about the Soviet Union shares the same assumptions. Thus, Diuk and Karatnycky 1990 say: "Yet all these current tensions [in the Soviet Union] arise from a common source—the imperial nature of the Soviet Union" (p. 16). Their book is a perfect example of unshakable belief in the fundamental reality of the Soviet Union's separable and authentic 'hidden nations.' These nations' holy rights to self-determination are strongly advocated, and "the idea that the non-Russian national movements are anti-democratic and xenophobic" (p. 39) is discarded as a new Western myth-in-the-making. How could they be?

REFERENCES

Adams, Karen L., and Daniel T. Brink, eds. 1990. *Perspectives on Official English: The Campaign for English as the Official Language of the U.S.A.* Berlin: Mouton de Gruyter.

Anderson, Benedict. 1983. *Imagined Communities: Reflections on the Origin and Spread of Nationalism*. London: Verso.

Bamgbose, Ayo. 1994. Pride and Prejudice in Multilingualism and Development. In *African Languages, Development and the State*, ed. Richard Fardon and Graham Furniss, pp. 33–43. London: Routledge.

Barth, Fredrik, ed. 1982. *Ethnic Groups and Boundaries: The Social Organization of Culture Differences*. Oslo: Universitetsforlaget.

Billig, Michael. 1995. *Banal Nationalism*. London: Sage.

Blommaert, Jan, and Jef Verschueren. 1991. The Pragmatics of Minority Politics in Belgium. *Language in Society* 20:503–531.

———. 1992. *Het Belgische migrantendebat: De pragmatiek van de abnormalisering* (The Belgian migrant debate: The pragmatics of abnormalization). Antwerp: International Pragmatics Association.

———. 1993. The Rhetoric of Tolerance, or, What Police Officers Are Taught about Migrants. *Journal of Intercultural Studies* 14:49–63.

———. 1994. The Belgian Migrant Debate. *New Community* 20:227–251.

———. 1996. European Concepts of Nation-Building. In *The Politics of Difference: Ethnic Premises in a World of Power*, ed. Patrick McAllister and Edwin Wilmsen, pp. 104–123. Chicago: University of Chicago Press.

Deprez, Kas, and Armel Wynants. 1994. La Flandre nationaliste face à l'Europe. *Language Problems and Language Planning* 18:113–127.

D'hondt, Sigurd. 1994. *Nationalistische ideologie in de berichtgeving over interetnische conflicten in twee Nederlandse kranten* (Nationalist ideology in new reporting on interethnic conflicts in two Dutch newspapers). Antwerp: UIA-GER.

D'hondt, Sigurd, Jan Blommaert, and Jef Verschueren. 1995. Constructing Ethnicity in Discourse: The View from Below. In *Migration, Citizenship, and Ethno-National Identities in the European Union*, ed. Marco Martiniello, pp. 105–119. Aldershot: Avebury.

Diuk, Nadia, and Adrian Karatnycky. 1990. *The Hidden Nations: The People Challenge the Soviet Union*. New York: William Morrow.

Fardon, Richard, and Graham Furniss. 1994. Introduction: Frontiers and Boundaries—African Languages as Political Environment. In *African Languages, Development and the State*, ed. Richard Fardon and Graham Furniss, pp. 1–29. London: Routledge.

Hobsbawm, E. J. 1990. *Nations and Nationalism since 1780: Programme, Myth, Reality*. Cambridge: Cambridge University Press.

Langens, Isabel. 1994. *Nationalistische ideologie in de berichtgeving over interetnische conflicten in "The Independent" en "The Daily Telegraph"* (Nationalist ideology in news reporting on interethnic conflicts in "The Independent" and "The Daily Telegraph"). Antwerp: UIA-GER.

Meeuwis, Michael. 1993. Nationalist Ideology in News Reporting on the Yugoslav Crisis: A Pragmatic Analysis. *Journal of Pragmatics* 20:217–237.

Verschueren, Jef. 1995a. The Pragmatic Return to Meaning: Notes on the Dynamics of Communication, Conceptual Accessibility and Communicative Transparency. *Journal of Linguistic Anthropology* 5(2):127–156.

———. 1995b. Aspects of Contrastive Ideology Research: A Pragmatic Methodology. *Toegepaste Taalkunde in Artikelen* 52:55–70.

Williams, Glyn. 1992. *Sociolinguistics: A Sociological Critique*. London: Routledge.

Windisch, Uli. 1990. *Speech and Reasoning in Everyday Life*. Cambridge: Cambridge University Press.

Woolard, Kathryn A. 1989. *Double Talk: Bilingualism and the Politics of Ethnicity in Catalonia*. Stanford, Calif.: Stanford University Press.

10

Language Ideologies in Institutions of Power

A Commentary

SUSAN U. PHILIPS

Chapters 7, 8, and 9 in Part II are distinguished from those in the rest of this book by their focus on language ideology in specific institutional settings. Jan Blommaert and Jef Verschueren (chapter 9) deal with language ideology promulgated by Western European newspapers. Debra Spitulnik (chapter 8) addresses language ideology in Zambian radio broadcasting. And Elizabeth Mertz (chapter 7) focuses her attention on language ideology in classrooms in law schools, which are both legal and educational institutions. Like Errington, and Schieffelin and Doucet in chapters 13 and 14, Part III of this book, these authors are concerned with language ideologies that play a role in the constitution of nation-states as political and social units, but the chapters I am concerned with here provide analyses that are more connected to a specific institutional context.

Until recently, analyses of language use in state-connected institutional settings by linguistic anthropologists and sociolinguists have conceptualized those institutional settings as bureaucracies, with particular attention to school classrooms, medical encounters between doctors and patients, and courtrooms (e.g., Erickson and Schultz 1982, Philips 1983). This work, which emerged in the 1970s and 1980s, was considerably influenced by conversation analysis, though it was often distinguished by some of those analysts from their own work because of its context dependence and context specificity. Studies of language use in bureaucratic settings described rules for the organization of talk and linguistic forms that differentiated bureaucrats' and clients' contributions to talk. Often sources of miscommunication between bureaucrats and clients of differing ethnic backgrounds were also a focus of attention. Bureaucrats' control of talk was clearly identified as a form of power that was associated with their control over the definition of reality in the bureaucratic setting and with their imposition of a bureaucracy-specific interpretive perspective. With some exceptions, there was little concern in this work with the content of what was said or with the relation between content and form of utterance. The emphasis on rules and linguistic form reflected the influence of not only conversation analysis but also formal linguistic theory. But this work stands out as the single most coherent body of sociolinguistic work focused on the role of language in the exercise of power done during these decades.

The three chapters I consider here, however, reflect significant analytical shifts that have taken place over the past decade in the study of language in bureaucratic settings. The most important shift has been a reconceptualization of language use in institutional settings as constituting and reproducing the ideological hegemony of the state. This reconceptualization can be thought of as one important sociolinguistic manifestation of the growing attention in the social sciences and humanities to the nation as a sociocultural phenomenon. The dissolution and reformulation of nations in Eastern Europe and in the former Soviet Union and the emergence of a European Union in Western Europe are the real-world events that have stimulated this academic interest in nations and caused nationness to be problematized. In anthropology, theoretical attention to the emergence of a global political economy, to the history of European colonization of the rest of the world, to decolonization and the emergence of nationalisms and new nation states, and to transnational cultural processes has stimulated anthropologists to consider how the local communities and institutional settings they examine articulate with these broader processes, including the cultural constituting of nation states.

With this shift to awareness of the nation as a cultural phenomenon, and of the role of some familiar bureaucracies such as schools and courts in its constitution, has also come a growing interest in powerful institutions that were not analyzed as bureaucracies, most notably public media organizations like the newspapers and radio stations analyzed in two of the essays I consider here. Particularly in Western Europe, a revival of interest in the Frankfurt School's (e.g., Bronner and Kellner 1989) attention to the role of public discourses in the constitution of national political culture has made a focus on language and communication in the media an obvious target of ideological critique. Benedict Anderson's (1991) emphasis on the importance of print media in the emergence of national consciousnesses in the New World has similarly stimulated interest in the connection among media institutions, the cultural constitution of nations, and the cultural experience of being part of a nation.

Another important and related shift in approach to language in bureaucracies that these chapters represent is a shift from a focus on the *form* of language in use to a focus on the *content* of language in use. In the essays here, it is the content of the language ideologies in the various institutional settings that is explicated.

Finally, attention to language ideologies as such is also a new focus for those studying language in public and state institutional settings. This new focus reveals how language is implicated ideologically in political rule in a very different way than through the organization of turns at talk—that is, through the content of the interpretive perspectives promulgated by the bureaucrats. These analyses also happily connect language ideologies in powerful institutions to language ideologies in activities conceptualized very differently in other parts of this book. Through a shared focus on language ideologies, the study of discourse in bureaucracies is here brought into a common frame of reference with the study of other kinds of discourse, mitigating, one hopes, the sometime intellectual isolation of the analysis of language use in institutional settings from other kinds of analysis in linguistic anthropology.

I argue here that the most significant shift in our understanding of language in powerful institutions as reflected in the chapters in this section stems from the awareness of the language ideologies these institutions promulgate as hegemonic in a Gramscian sense—that is, as contributing to the constitution and maintenance of nation-states as political entities.

In the introduction to this collection, Kit Woolard reveals the great range of approaches to ideology that inform the essays in this volume, including those in Part II. My own approach to ideology here is somewhat different, for in the discussion to follow I focus attention specifically on Marxist conceptualizations of ideology and on the way these traditions inform the chapters under discussion. I do this in order to keep an awareness of the *exercise of power* involved in the constitution of language ideologies in the forefront. Linguistic anthropologists' use of "ideology" rather than "culture" to refer to the interpretive perspectives of the people whose ideas we document is a relatively new practice. The shift in terminology should signify a shift in theoretical orientation. It should not just be a substitution of the term *ideology* for the term *culture*, where "culture" in the sense of shared knowledge or worldview is still what is actually being talked about. From my point of view, this shift in terminology within linguistic anthropology signals new awareness of and attention to the way in which the salience and prevalence of particular ideas are themselves forms of power. Ideology carries with it connotations of the exercise of power primarily because Marxist writings about ideology and reactions to them in the nineteenth century have given the term those connotations. It is also my intent through this focus on Marxist approaches to ideology to make clear how they have influenced and can influence present anthropological treatments of linguistic ideologies, whether or not these influences have been made explicit, because I think the influence is important, exciting, and productive.

In the discussion to follow I first talk about the place of ideology in present-day understandings of Marx, giving particular attention to Antonio Gramsci's (1971) ideas about the importance of the ideological role of "the state," which he felt had been neglected by Marx, because of the relevance of these ideas for an understanding of the ideological role of powerful institutions considered in the essays in this section. Then I focus attention on Gramsci's concept of "hegemony" and how this concept has been transformed by Raymond Williams's influential interpretation of Gramsci and by related work by Bourdieu and Foucault.[1] Then I discuss chapters 7, 8, and 9 in turn, giving consideration to how each represents a particular institution's language ideology as a hegemonic imagining of the nation-state.

Ideology in Marxist Traditions

In Marx's vision of European industrialized societies, the ruling class that dominated the working class did so by virtue of its control of the means of production and also through the production of ideology that justified the relations between dominant and subordinate classes. Such ideology concealed from the working class the fact that its interests were not best served by capitalist domination. Marx saw that the critique of dominant ideology, which revealed the vested interests of the ruling class, could lead to working-class resistance to the dominant order. The base-superstructure distinction was a crucial feature of Marx's vision: the material relations of production (base) were primary and gave rise to particular ideological formations (superstructure).

One great appeal of a Marx-inspired approach to ideology is that, through anticipation of the rise of a working-class consciousness that resists the dominant ideology of the ruling class, class-specific and class-generated ideological diversity *within* a society is posited. From this has come the more general idea that a person's structural position within society determines her or his interpretive perspective. Through such generalization, and by analogy, feminists of the late 1960s and 1970s were able to assert a need for women in a classlike structural position of subordination to men to carry out ideological critique of patriarchy. Transformations of this sort have led Giddens (1979) to propose that we speak not of class when considering ideology generated by structural position, but rather of "sectional interests."

Antonio Gramsci arrived at a rather different conceptualization of group-based interest and ideological production through his intellectual efforts to apply Marxist thinking to political struggle in Italy. He criticized Marx for his failure to integrate a conceptualization of the state into his theory of class struggle. Gramsci argued that, although some combination of interests might succeed in taking control of a state by force, that control could not be sustained over time without consent of the governed through ideological persuasion—that is, through hegemony. His vision was one of, among other things, state institutions that articulated with civil society in such a way that the boundaries between government and not-government are not clear. Political party ideologies and interests, economic interests, religious interests, and regional interests could be mutually constituted and could unite or fragment in efforts to control the state or particular institutions.[2]

Gramsci's conceptualization of ideological diversity and contestation has so many sources that it is difficult to see how a single coherent perspective could come to dominate a state. But that is part of the point. For Gramsci, hegemony is never complete; the struggle of the state to maintain the consent of the governed is constant. On the other hand, Gramsci saw evidence in the history of Italy that historic blocs, coconstructed sectional interests that were able to unify around a common ideological core, could and did dominate the state for long periods of time.

One appeal of Gramsci's way of conceptualizing struggle for state hegemony is that although he himself characterized the nation-internal process he was trying to represent as specifically that of late-capitalist Western European nations with economies shaped by imperialist histories, his sectional interests and the way they articulate with the state are sufficiently diverse that we are encouraged to be open-ended in our search for analogues to the processes he identifies in other kinds of nation-states (e.g., Chatterjee 1986).[3]

Hegemony

Although Gramsci is the source of the term "hegemony" as many anthropologists use it today (Woolard 1985, Comaroff and Comaroff 1991), the word has come to have rather different associations from those that Gramsci gave it. He really did associate it with a state's ability to govern through ideology as well as through force. There is no evidence in his writing that he saw hegemony overall as somehow more implicit than explicit, though he certainly meant to uncover what he saw as unrecognized organizational and ideational processes in the constitution of state hegemony. Nor was there a special place for language or language ideologies in the core dimensions of his concept of hegemony.

Three particularly influential European scholars have played a major role in shifting the meaning of hegemony to that of an interpretive perspective that is implicit and taken for granted, in locating ideology in discourse practices, and in loosening, decoupling, or disconnecting the idea of ideological domination from *state* hegemony located in state and state-serving civil institutions: Raymond Williams, Michel Foucault, and Pierre Bourdieu. I give greatest attention here to Williams for two reasons: first, it is Williams who most clearly derives his vision of hegemony from Marxist thinking and from Gramsci's writings in particular, and, second, Williams's ideas and their influence on anthropological thinking about ideology in discourse practices are the least acknowledged and recognized in anthropology.

In *Marxism and Literature* (1977), Williams articulates a critique of the base-superstructure distinction that moves us theoretically to a vision of all activity as imbued with ideological significance. Echoing other critics of Marx, he objects to Marx's privileging of the factory worker's work as the only true form of labor. Like the feminists who see production in reproduction, he finds work that should be valued in the full range of human activities that positively sustain humans, though for Williams it is particularly important to represent the writing of literature as such an activity. If the concept of material production is expanded in this way, then it follows that the activities formerly distinguished from *material* production as *ideological* production, derivative of and dependent on the material, can no longer be so distinguished. The material and the ideological become merged as one; all human action is at once material and ideological.

It is in this context of having loosened ideology from any privileged institutional moorings that Williams takes up the concept of hegemony. For Williams, the meaning of hegemony in Gramsci's writings was that of lived reality and practical consciousness, the unarticulated experiences of domination and subordination of different classes. This meant, of course, that hegemony was experienced differently by people in different structural positions. Taking Gramsci's point that state hegemony is never complete but constantly contested, Williams coined the term "counterhegemony" to refer to resistance to ideological hegemony that is nevertheless profoundly shaped by the hegemony being resisted. He coined the term "alternative hegemony" to refer to alternatives to hegemonic ideology that are not shaped by dominant ideology. Like Gramsci, he was particularly interested in identifying conditions that could give rise to an alternative hegemony. And like Gramsci, Williams located those conditions in activities that were marginal to the functioning and control of formally articulated institutions centrally involved in the reproduction of hegemonic ideology. For Williams, the key marginal activities were the creative practices of artists, while for Gramsci they were the activities of working-class subaltern intellectuals. And Williams envisioned the initial emergence of alternative hegemonies in the form of unarticulated "structures of feeling," his key concept for representing the ideologically implicit in social practices.

I doubt I need to elaborate the point that both Bourdieu and Foucault also developed visions of ideology implicit in practice. From Bourdieu's writings, the most relevant concept that captures this idea of implicitness is the concept of habitus, an embodied and unconscious set of dispositions enacted in specific contexts (Bourdieu 1977). In Foucault's writings (e.g., 1972, 1980), he is clear that the dominant interpretive perspective of an epoch is experienced as a lived reality, a "will to truth," a discourse that spreads across institutional contexts over time through and in actual specific discourse practices. Of these three scholars, Foucault is easily clearest that the power exercised through and by the regimentation of a dominant discourse has no specific locale, in spite of the fact that throughout his work he focuses analytically on precisely the kinds of institutions that Gramsci saw as central to state hegemony.

All three of these scholars are clear that ideological hegemony entails a pervasive implicitness, although Williams allows for degrees of explicitness, and that this implicitness is the source of the power of hegemonic ideas. They also have in common that in their broadest theoretical statements, they reject the locating of ideological hegemony in specific institutional contexts, although, as I have tried to suggest, each actually privileges certain kinds of activities or institutional contexts over others in conceptualizing the kind of ideological work done through discourse practices. But none of them develops a concept of *state* hegemony in the way that Gramsci did.

I suggest here that the three essays on language ideology that I am covering here show the influence of the range of approaches to hegemony just discussed. They are Gramscian in their recognition of the power that state-affiliated institutions exercise through the promulgation of particular kinds of language ideologies. They are more Foucauldian in stressing the implicit taken-for-granted qualities of the language ideologies they document and the power that derives from the naturalization of particular kinds of ideas. However, I must add that they are probably also still rooted in earlier traditions of the analysis of the discourse of one seemingly bounded bureaucratic setting in that they do not convey much of a sense that language ideologies can and do cross fluid or ephemeral institutional boundaries, a sense definitely conveyed in the writings of Gramsci, Williams, and Foucault.

Discussion of Essays

Chapters 7, 8, and 9, the three essays in Part II, have a good deal in common. They all deal with language ideologies in institutional settings that contribute to the constitution of nation-states. The authors are primarily concerned with the *content* of these ideologies, although each highlights dimensions of the language ideology in question to which semiotic concepts of indexicality and iconicity can be applied. In their content, the language ideologies explicated in these essays all contribute to a sense of nationness, although this may not be as obvious in Mertz's discussion of law school classroom discourse regimentation as it is in the discourses examined in the other two chapters. The authors of all three chapters are clear that ideologies that they view as at least partially implicit, as naturalizing relations between language and social order, are being made explicit through *their* analyses. And the authors critique these naturalized representations by offering alternatives to them.

These authors also suggest or imply that there are hegemonic dimensions to the language ideologies they describe. They give evidence of ideological diversity, and Spitulnik and Mertz are clear that there is contestation associated with this diversity. But there is still a real sense of domination associated with at least some aspects of the language ideologies explicated. Actual practical domination and imposition of a reality is particularly clear in Mertz's documentation of law school professors' regimentation of the speech of law school students.

Even so, to leave a characterization of the chapters at this would be to obscure important differences among them. There is particularly a contrast between Spitulnik and Blommaert and Verschueren, on the one hand, and Mertz, on the other, in the kind of language ideology documented and in the way the ideology is promulgated. Gramsci was clear in his distinction between the positive role of education and the negative role of law in the constitution of state hegemony, a lead pursued by Althusser (1971) in his comparative analysis of "ideological state apparatuses." Spitulnik also asks how the features of institutions shape the production of language ideologies. I follow up on her query by discussing factors that may have contributed to the obvious differences between language ideologies in different powerful institutions documented in the three essays considered here.

Using newspapers from several Western European nations, Blommaert and Verschueren document a language ideology shared across these nations that assumes that speakers of a common language constitute a culturally homogeneous ethnic group, which in turn is the potentially or actually most stable and enduring basis for nationhood. In this language ideology, they argue, common language is one of a cluster of features, including descent, history, culture, and religion, that together form the basis for "natural groups." One feature is treated implicitly as if it entailed the others. Mention of speakers of a given language, then, indexes all of the other features in the cluster and indexes the speakers' natural belonging to a social group. Within this framework, multilingualism has little or no significant place, although it is valued in the individual, disvalued for a nation, and valued for the transnational European Union.

Blommaert and Verschueren are quite clear that the broadest assumptions in this language ideology are implicit and taken for granted and that this implicitness is an important source of its power. As they acknowledge near the end of the chapter, while they view the ideology they document as authoritative, they do not see themselves as addressing "the intricate dynamics of hegemony." And, indeed, the institutional production of newspaper discourses is not within the purview of their research project. In examining written rather than spoken discourse that is out of and apart from its contexts of production, they differ from the authors of the other two chapters being discussed.

There is some irony in the fact that, while Blommaert and Verschueren document a language ideology that assumes each natural nation has one culture and one language, the ideology itself is transnational, shared by newspapers in different nations. And these newspapers function in a Western European political climate that is overtly committed to denationalization through the European Union, a denationalization to which these authors contribute through their deconstruction of nationalist language ideology. At the same time, they *do* find diversity within this broader common ideology among the newspaper articles, depending on the nation out of which it came and the nation being talked about—a diversity that they use to further denaturalize, undermine, and critique the common-language ideology.

The interplay between the national and the transnational in this essay highlights the limits of a strictly Gramscian approach to hegemony, which focuses on nation-internal processes. Blommaert and Verschueren show us that newspapers produce nation-imagining language ideologies, and they contribute to the cultural hegemony of the nation-state by virtue of such nation-imagining. But the capacity of newspapers for transnational cultural transmission and replication also plays a role in the production of a world order of nations: newspapers themselves and the language ideologies they carry can literally be moved across national borders. And the newspaper is a kind of institution that can be set up in any nation to speak about that nation. In other words, the transnationalism and the nationalism of institutions that produce nation-imagining language ideologies are mutually interdependent and reinforcing.

Spitulnik's superb essay makes very clear the nation-imagining work that Radio Zambia does through the language ideology expressed in its allocation of radio airtime to different African languages and to English. Only some of the African languages spoken in Zambia are represented through radio time, and those that are represented are allocated different amounts of time. These allocations have been shaped by colonial relations with various ethnic groups in the past, as well as by present-day differences in the number of speakers of each language.

Like Blommaert and Verschueren, Spitulnik shows how the social order is represented in a one-language-equals-one-ethnic-group framework in Radio Zambia practices, as if Zambian ethnic groups were both discontinuous and homogeneous, even though Spitulnik assures us they are neither. Spitulnik also discusses actual patterns of multilingualism, about which there is silence in Radio Zambia rationales for radio time allocations, in a way that makes clear the ideologized nature of language-ethnic group associations.

A comparison of the time and program content allocated to English with the time and program content allocated to Zambian African languages provides a second dimension to Spitulnik's analysis. There is far more broadcasting in English, and the content of the programming is international and Western, rather than local and traditional. There is a rhetoric that English is available to all, the *national* language for the whole nation, but in fact English is accessible to only a small national elite.

Spitulnik is more explicit in her semiotic analysis of these allocations than Blommaert and Verschueren are. She too suggests that language indexes features of ethnic groups, but she also points to an all-encompassing coherent semiotic representation of the nation in its airtime policies in that Radio Zambia's partitioning of the linguistic universe amounts to an iconic diagramming of social differentiation through a diagram of linguistic differentiation.

Spitulnik finds the dominance of English to be far more taken for granted and less contested than the hierarchical allocation of the African languages and, in this sense, more truly hegemonic.

Certainly this essay suggests the relevance of transnational processes in the use of language ideologies to imagine a nation, which I discussed for the Blommaert and Verschueren paper. Radio, like newspapers, is a mass medium. Zambian radio can provide a simultaneous national experience of the kind Benedict Anderson suggested print media provided in emerging nations in the New World. But what it provides through English broadcasting is at least a putative national experiencing of transnational cultural transmission. Radio stations, like newspapers, are replicable institutions. They can be set up anywhere in the world, and the setting up of them, in this case by the government itself, as is common around the world, is a way of signaling to the world the ongoing constituting of a modern nation-state.

Even more obviously, it is difficult to escape the inference that the idea in Zambia that speakers of a language index a homogeneous ethnic group is itself a transnational cultural idea that came in with the colonization of the region by Europeans. The Zambian view that one nation can happily be welded out of diverse languages and ethnic groups can itself be seen as counterhegemonic to the European view, articulated by Blommaert and Verschueren, that such a nation is not natural and will be plagued by conflict, particularly between economically differentiated ethnic groups. In suggesting that ethnicity is an imported European concept, I have been influenced by the argument that in Africa ethnic groups and/or tribes have been a creation of European colonizers, a view promulgated with a great deal of passion recently by anthropologists as well as by politically engaged African nationalists (Vail 1991, Wilmsen 1995). But I do recognize that this view, too, is an ideological construct. My point here is simply that the Zambian language ideology documented in Spitulnik's essay is clearly transnational in character.

Of the three chapters in this group Spitulnik's provides the clearest vision of a state institution promulgating a nation-imagining language ideology with hegemonic dimensions, and in this sense her vision is the most Gramscian of the three. She is also the only author who explicitly states that the language ideology she documents does not originate in the institution whose promulgation of it she documents. This raises some interesting questions. Where *does* she think it comes from? And can we not see that the same is true for the language ideologies documented in the other chapters—that they are being put forward not just in the institutional settings with which they are associated but in other institutions as well (and here I mean within the nation, rather than transnationally)? To answer this question, it would be useful to think in Gramscian terms about the way groups (religious, party, ethnic, class) and institutions are coconstructed and about how historic blocs that come together around a particular view are formed. In so doing, we would develop a richer and more sophisticated understanding of the way power is exercised through language ideologies.

Mertz's chapter on language ideology in the law school classrooms of the United States seems very different from the other two essays, inviting questions about why it is different. In contrast to the other authors, Mertz constrains her analysis to account for transcripts of tape-recorded speech. In this respect, her work is more in the tradition of analyses of language in bureaucratic settings that I characterized at the beginning of this commentary than are the other two essays.

Mertz is like the other authors in conveying to us that she is making the implicit explicit. But, in contrast to the other authors, she theorizes this aspect of what she is doing. She draws on some of Silverstein's (1993) efforts to address different kinds and degrees of explicitness in speakers' encoding of their ideas about language, locating the promulgation of legal language ideology in metalinguistic signaling and metapragmatic regimentation. This chapter brings to life the idea of regimentation, with its vivid examples of the way law school professors humiliate their students to coerce them into talking in a certain way about the appellate decisions that are the typical substantive focus of the law school classroom. Her discussion shows clearly the problems with Gramsci's binary distinction between physical coercion and the consent of hegemony, as speech is revealed for the coercive force it often is.

Mertz's chapter, unlike the other two, is not overtly about the way language ideologies play a role in the imagining of nations, and it is also not overtly about the language-group-nation representations the other two deal with. It is also not about the way a shared language ideology is presupposed in discourse practices, as the other two chapters are, but, rather, about imposing a *new* interpretive framework on reality, a specifically legal framework.

Some key aspects of Mertz's analysis, however, show very clearly the way legal language ideology contributes to nation-imagining. Mertz points out that a central and pervasive feature of law school classroom talk about people and events in the law cases is that the people are stripped of their social identities as these are made sense of in everyday talk in relation to events. The cases are generally not about poor consumers and rich capitalists, or about women and men, or about blacks and whites, but about "parties" and what might give them legal standing in a case, in morally neutral terms. I argue that this dimension of the way law students learn to think and talk about people is a key aspect of the legal interpretive framework that enables it to be the national discourse that it is. What makes people part of a nation is that they are citizens of it, and nothing else.

When we consider in Gramscian terms that legal institutions are more centrally part of the state and constitutive of it and of nations than either newspapers or radio stations, a striking feature of what law school discourses convey regarding the role of language in nation-imagining or even about the role of law in nation-constituting is that they have *nothing* to say about it. When Spitulnik makes the point that the widespread multilingualism in Zambia is not acknowledged in Radio Zambia language ideology, she also points out that the silences in language ideologies are as important as what is expressed. Surely law school silence on the nation-making character of law and the language of law is such an important silence. It suggests that this aspect of legal language is among the most deeply naturalized and implicit dimensions of legal language ideology.

These three essays, then, show us the role of language and language ideologies in the imagining of nations. This makes sense for institutions strongly connected to the state and seen as having a state-hegemonizing role. The essays show that different state-connected institutions constitute rather different kinds of language ideologies and do so in quite different ways.

In the media organizations discussed in Spitulnik and in Blommaert and Verschueren, the language ideologies are statements about national social orders and the nature and role of language in those social orderings. Discrete codes signal discrete social groups, and both codes and groups are treated as homogeneous. It could be argued that media express such language ideologies because their purpose is conceived of as to speak to whole nations about the nation. It is not actually true that most media have an audience of an entire nation, but they do have large audiences, and the size of their audiences is undoubtedly a factor in the broad accessibility of media messages. And they certainly have a central role in conveying information about the nation to local audiences.

In the law school classroom, the language ideology being transmitted is not about codes or about how groups and codes index one another but about reality transformation, how through language use everyday realities are transformed into legal realities. In this setting, linguistic code is taken for granted. Here the social ordering of everyday reality is overtly rejected, denied, and covered up, though never really gone, in favor of a more universalistic discourse that is suited to the national practice of law and the legal constituting of a nation. The messages of legal institutions are not, like those of the media, meant for broad audiences. Most legal messages are for other legal specialists trained in the same interpretive tradition, or they involve legal specialists translating that tradition to nonspecialists in contexts where the state is essentially processing the concerns of the nonspecialists in a bureaucratic setting. Law is like other forms of specialized knowledge relevant to particular institutional settings, particularly medicine, but also, arguably, religion, in which the ideologization of language similarly serves the constitution of specialized interpretive perspectives or social realities.

The diversity in the nature of language ideologies we see in these three essays, then, is due in part to the very different ways their institutions incorporate individual citizens into the nation-state. But I think this diversity is also due to the somewhat different analytical traditions that have been drawn on to study the constitution of ideology through language in different institutions. As I suggested at the beginning of this commentary, media analyses by sociolinguists have been done under different influences than have analyses of law and education. Media analyses have focused on how ideology is constituted in the language and discourse structure of the product of the media (Fowler 1979), in the tradition of what is these days called critical discourse analysis, as we see in the chapter by Blommaert and Verschueren. Spitulnik's analysis is more grounded in an actual media institution than theirs is, but the language ideology she describes still floats relatively free from specific discourses in specific contexts, a point that may be clearer if we think of how relatively grounded Mertz's analysis is in specific discourse in a specific setting.

Analyses of ideology in legal and educational discourse since the late 1960s, in contrast, have typically focused on the actual taped speech of legal and educational specialists engaged in interaction with nonspecialists. Mertz shows us what could be done with the nonscripted interaction of media practitioners (one thinks of Goffman's [1981] analysis of radio talk here) in their actual work settings. On the other hand, the media analyses here and elsewhere establish important links between ideologies in media discourse and broader national economic and political processes that are often not attended to in analyses of language use in legal and educational settings.

Minimally, then, the differences in the analyses we see in these three essays are due not only to differences in the hegemonizing roles of the institutions promulgating the language ideologies but also to the analytical traditions that have most influenced the kind of work done in different institutional settings.

These chapters do, however, still have in common that all clearly ground their analysis of language ideologies in specific institutions. I want to emphasize the virtues and strengths of such grounding. It is easiest to do this by talking about what cannot happen when there is no such grounding. Without such grounding, it is not possible to take the next interesting step of talking about how language ideologies are socially ordered across institutions and groups within a nation and transnationally. Without such grounding, we cannot understand where there are and are not commonalities across institutions in the language ideologies they promulgate. Without such grounding, it is very difficult to talk about fluidity, about the flow or transmission of language ideologies from one institution or group to another, or about how language ideologies are transformed as they move from one setting to another. But there is a need for those of us who *are* institutionally grounded to take these next interesting steps.

On Making the Implicit Explicit

As I have already noted more than once, it is striking that all three of the chapters discussed here adopt the position that the language ideologies they are documenting are implicit in at least some respects and to varying degrees, and all show clearly the implicit being made explicit. Scholars who have worked on language ideologies can be expected to have differing reactions to this strategy. Some would say that an interpretive perspective cannot be considered "ideology" unless it is to some extent implicit, for without that implicitness, without a taken-for-granted quality, an ideology cannot do its work, cannot take hold of people to the extent that it does not occur to them to think otherwise. This view is strongly associated with Marxist treatments of ideology, as is the goal of the deconstruction of the ideology, which entails making it explicit so as to loosen its hold on people, opening the way for other possible perspectives on the same issues. Certainly Spitulnik and Blommaert and Verschueren deploy strategies specifically intended to show that the language ideologies they document are not the truth, or not the only truth.

But, as Woolard notes in her introduction to this volume, some would argue that linguistic ideology must be treated as distinct from and not implicit in language use. Certainly, Silverstein has encouraged a separating out of the metalinguistic from the linguistic, the metapragmatic from the pragmatic. And as I noted earlier, he has recently refined these distinctions by addressing degrees and kinds of explicitness in the ways people's ideas about language are encoded in their speech.

It makes sense to think carefully about kinds and degrees of explicitness, and about their locations and relations, in characterizing language ideologies. Accordingly, it was surprising to me to find that none of these essays posit or address relations between the metapragmatic and the pragmatic, and none direct attention to the varying degrees of explicitness in the data of their own that they display for us. In taking the position that they are making the implicit explicit, they set aside the pragmatic-metapragmatic distinction others have found useful. Or, perhaps it would be more accurate to say that they appropriate the metapragmatic function to themselves, a strategy particularly compatible with ideological critique but one that anthropologists have been faulted for because of the way it allocates true vision to the anthropologist alone.

I speculate here about some of the reasons these authors might have had for pursuing this strategy (without, of course, implying that these reasons were conscious or explicit!), apart from the possibility of a principled commitment to pursuing a particular concept of "ideology," because such possible reasons can help us understand why studies of linguistic ideologies might be going in one direction or another, now and in the future.

One possibility is that these authors are simply more interested in the content of their language ideologies than in the process of *ideologizing* in language use. They may be more interested in revealing the political importance and power-laden nature of language ideologies and the political nature of language than in certain semiotic dimensions of language ideologies. Another possibility is that they may find it difficult to distinguish and to sustain distinctions having to do with kinds and degrees of explicitness in language ideologies. We may need more examples of empirical studies that do this successfully before we can decide which kinds of distinctions are most productive. A third possibility is that the maintenance of some distinctions, such as that between talk and talk about talk, can be sustained only with certain kinds of data or when data have been collected in a particular combination of ways, and these authors may not have been thinking about such distinctions when they gathered their data. I find I can sustain this distinction only with certain kinds of data myself. A fourth possibility is that it may be difficult to integrate the political and semiotic dimensions of linguistic anthropological conceptualizations of language ideologies, particularly in a balanced way. Mertz articulates her desire to achieve such an integration, and her essay suggests that the conscious pursuit of this goal can yield productive results.

Conclusion

Taken as a group, these essays make a strong case for the power of language and language ideologies in the imagining of nations in institutions centrally involved in the production of state hegemony. They show how different state-affiliated institutional complexes deploy rather different kinds of language ideologies, depending on the way the institution articulates its publics with the nation-state. They also invite us to think more about the extent to which nation-imagining language ideologies specific to particular institutions are also shared across institutions and nations.

NOTES

1. Williams 1977, Bourdieu 1977, and Foucault 1972, 1980.

2. Such processes are more visible and well known in some areas of American political life than in others, but I can apply and illustrate Gramsci's thinking with an example from the judicial branch of the government. Appointments of judges to state courts of general jurisdiction in the United States are in some states more under the control of political parties and in others more under the control of state bar associations. But bar associations themselves can be dominated by one political party or another, and both parties and bar associations can be dominated by particular ethnic and religious groups, depending on their locale, and each of these types of sectional interests has an ideological disposition that influences the kinds of lawyers it will try to get appointed to the bench. I have argued elsewhere that bar associations have been engaged in ideological struggle with political parties in a way that has influenced the political ideologies of lawyers appointed as judges in Arizona over time (Philips 1998).

3. For example, Gramsci's way of thinking about the articulation between state and civil society helps me recognize that in Tonga, a country that has no political parties, where I do research, the Free Wesleyan Church (the King's church) is *the* linchpin "civil" institution in the historic bloc that presently sustains the monarchy, because of the way it ideologically embraces and mediates between the "chiefly" royal family and the "commoner" democratic movement in its "religious" discourse.

REFERENCES

Althusser, Louis. 1971. Ideology and Ideological State Apparatuses. In *Lenin and Philosophy and Other Essays*, pp. 127–186. New York: Monthly Review Press.

Anderson, Benedict. 1991. *Imagined Communities*. New York: Verso.

Bourdieu, Pierre. 1977. *Outline of a Theory of Practice*. Cambridge: Cambridge University Press.

Bronner, Stephen E., and Douglas MacKay Kellner. 1989. Introduction to *Critical Theory and Society*, ed. Stephen E. Bronner and Douglas M. Kellner, pp. 1–21. London: Routledge.

Chatterjee, Partha. 1986. *Nationalist Thought and the Colonial World: A Derivative Discourse?* Minneapolis: University of Minnesota Press.

Comaroff, Jean, and John Comaroff. 1991. *Of Revelation and Revolution*. Chicago: University of Chicago Press.

Erickson, Frederick, and Jeffrey Schultz. 1982. *The Counselor as Gatekeeper*. New York: Academic Press.

Foucault, Michel. 1972. The Discourse on Language. Appendix to *The Archaeology of Knowledge*, pp. 215–237. New York: Pantheon.

———. 1980. *The History of Sexuality*. Vol 1: *An Introduction*. New York: Vintage Books.

Fowler, Roger. 1979. *Language and Control*. Boston: Routledge and Kegan Paul.

Giddens, Anthony. 1979. Ideology and Consciousness. In *Central Problems in Social Theory*, pp. 165–197. Berkeley: University of California Press.

Goffman, Erving. 1981. Radio Talk. In *Forms of Talk*, pp. 197–327. Philadelphia: University of Pennsylvania Press.

Gramsci, Antonio. 1971. *Selections from the Prison Notebooks*. New York: International.

Philips, Susan U. 1983. *The Invisible Culture: Communication in Classroom and Community on the Warm Springs Indian Reservation*. New York: Longman.

———. 1998. *Ideology in the Language of Judges: How Judges Practice Law, Politics, and Courtroom Control*. New York: Oxford University Press.

Silverstein, Michael. 1993. Metapragmatic Discourse and Metapragmatic Function. In *Reflexive Language: Reported Speech and Metapragmatics*, ed. John A. Lucy, pp. 33–58. New York: Cambridge University Press.

Vail, Leroy, ed. 1991. *The Creation of Tribalism in Southern Africa*. Berkeley: University of California Press.

Williams, Raymond. 1977. *Marxism and Literature*. Oxford: Oxford University Press.

Wilmsen, Edwin N. 1995. Who Were the Bushmen? Historical Process in the Creation of an Ethnic Construct. In *Articulating Hidden Histories: Exploring the Influence of Eric R. Wolf*, ed. Jane Schneider and Rayna Rapp, pp. 308–321. Berkeley: University of California Press.

Woolard, Kathryn. 1985. Language Variation and Cultural Hegemony. *American Ethnologist* 12:738–748.

III

MULTIPLICITY AND CONTENTION AMONG IDEOLOGIES

11

"You're a Liar—You're Just Like a Woman!"

Constructing Dominant Ideologies of Language in Warao Men's Gossip

CHARLES L. BRIGGS

I would like to take up an issue that is succinctly raised by Pierre Bourdieu in his *Outline of a Theory of Practice.* The notion that social groups produce arbitrary modes of thinking and acting, social structures, and the like is common anthropological fare. Interested in the Marxist problematics of power and ideology, Bourdieu (1977:164) goes on to suggest that "every established order tends to produce (to very different degrees with very different means) the naturalization of its own arbitrariness." A similar concern guides Michel Foucault's work on the emergence in the seventeenth and eighteenth centuries of "a new technology of the exercise of power" that gained its productive capacity through its ability "to gain access to the bodies of individuals, to their acts, attitudes, and modes of everyday behavior" (1980:124, 125). Antonio Gramsci (1971, 1995) was interested in the way that hegemony, resistance, and revolution both create and challenge dominant structures; literary critics, such as Frederic Jameson (1981) and Raymond Williams (1977), and anthropologists, such as Jean and John Comaroff (1991) and James Scott (1985), have drawn on Gramsci's insights in exploring the politics of culture. Michael Taussig has demonstrated the power of commodity fetishism (1980) and of terror and shamanism (1987, 1991) for naturalizing social and racial inequality in postcolonial South America.

My goal in this chapter is to link this question to a subject of growing interest in linguistic anthropology—the study of ideologies of language. As Dell Hymes

(1974) pointed out years ago, perspectives on language structure and use vary as widely between speech communities as do linguistic structures and speech norms. While linguistics has generally considered speakers' reflections on linguistic structure and use to be uninformative and unreliable, a number of writers have opened up fruitful perspectives on these issues. While the contribution of Roman Jakobson's writings on the metalingual function (1960), shifters (1957), and metalanguage (1976) is widely recognized, his earliest published paper also focused attention on the role of literature in moving linguistic structures into and out of conscious awareness ([1921] 1973). Research on the ethnography of speaking has produced a great deal of data not only on the many ways that people think about language but on the relative importance of language use and linguistic reflexivity (contrast Bauman 1983 with Sherzer 1983). Michael Silverstein (1979) has explored the role of linguistic ideologies in shaping scholarly characterizations of language and in attempting to regulate or transform linguistic structures and practices (1985, 1987). Much recent research has focused on the relationship between linguistic ideologies and nationalist agendas (Anderson [1983]1991; Gal 1979, 1991a, 1993; Woolard 1985, 1989a, 1989b).

In this essay, I suggest that bringing together research on the naturalization of social relations with studies of linguistic ideologies can be extremely productive. The success of this enterprise rests, however, on an adequate conceptualization of the nature of linguistic ideologies, their social distribution, and their location within the processes by which power is produced, naturalized, and challenged. I argue against viewing ideologies of language simply as part of the linguistic background shared by the members of a speech community. I maintain that such a perspective is not only empirically unsound and unenlightening but also figures among the means by which scholars naturalize their own interpretive authority. My data are drawn from research conducted with speakers of Warao, an indigenous language of eastern Venezuela, between 1986 and the present. I begin by discussing the importance of age, gender, and social status in shaping the way that social relations constrain access to linguistic ideologies.

The main focus of the chapter is on a particular example that illustrates the deployment of ideologies of language in discursive interaction—an exchange of gossip between two male curers. I use it to explore some of the ways that ideologies of language are contested within the social formations and sites in which people produce and receive discourse. At first glance, the exchange of gossip between two senior and powerful men would seem to constitute an odd focus for a discussion of contestation, in that the dialogue draws in large measure on one ideology of language in assessing the 'truth' of a wide range of narratives. Suggesting that it stands as the proverbial exception that proves the rule, I argue that the ideological framework that the two men advance is not simply *a* or *the* (dominant) Warao ideology of language, a manifestation of some sort of shared cultural or cognitive foundation. Nor would it be accurate to say that it reflects the linguistic ideology of a particular social group—older male curers. I rather characterize it as a collaborative construction of an ideological stance on language and an attempt to delegitimate competing ideologies. I argue that such cases, in which one ideology appears to dominate, provides fascinating vantage points from which to examine how ideologies of language, to paraphrase Clifford Geertz (1966), become both constructions of and for social inequality, provided that scholars become critically aware of (rather than seduced by) the ways that dominance over competing ideologies and practices is naturalized.

Approaches to the Comparative Study of Linguistic Ideologies

If one accepts the value of studying linguistic ideologies, a number of potential theoretical and methodological pitfalls are close at hand. How are we to locate linguistic ideologies? How can they be extracted for scholarly examination? What strategies can we adopt as means of forestalling the emergence of postcolonial dichotomies between "ourselves" and "Others" or between "the West" and "the rest"? I find an article published 15 years ago by the late Michelle Rosaldo (1982) to be quite useful in focusing these issues. Rosaldo draws on extensive fieldwork with the Ilongot of the Philippines in critiquing Searle's (1969) presentation of speech act theory. She draws on Ilongot ideologies of language in showing how Searle "falls victim to folk views that locate social meaning first in private persons—and slight the sense of situational constraint" (Rosaldo 1982:212). She argues that Western ideologies of language are so deeply embedded in Searle's analysis of performative verbs that his work should be read less as presenting universal laws of speech acts than as "an ethnography—however partial—of contemporary views of human personhood and action as these are linked to culturally particular modes of speaking" (228).

One of the most interesting implications of Rosaldo's comparison of Western and non-Western linguistic ideologies is its potential for discrediting what I call the myth of the linguist as hero. This myth has two facets: first, even such a cultural relativist as Boas (1911) believed that linguistic categories "always remain unconscious" for native speakers; anything that the uninitiated may say about their own language constitutes a patently false "secondary elaboration." The linguist is purportedly the only individual who can discern patterns of language structure and use without falling victim to the distorting influence of her or his own "native language." Rosaldo's analysis suggests that linguistic ideologies are much too pervasive and subtle to enable students of language the luxury of transcending their own linguistic ethnocentricity. Her work also points to the fruitfulness of treating scholarly studies of language as objects of analysis in the study of linguistic ideologies rather than simply as (ideally) transparent tools for analyzing speech (see also Silverstein 1979 and his contribution to this volume).

While I find the goals of Rosaldo's project to be clearly laudable, I have a number of reservations regarding the way she sets up the comparison. First, like a number of students of linguistic ideology, she presents Ilongot thinking about language in essentialist terms, positing a single linguistic ideology that would seem to be distributed homogeneously throughout the community. Interestingly, although Rosaldo argues that Ilongot speech acts must be studied in terms of the way they emerge in social relationships and interactive settings, she treats linguistic ideologies as unconscious residues that provide unproblematic bases for speech and action. Nevertheless, data from her own writings and those of Renato Rosaldo point to important points of social/cultural differentiation among Ilongot. Michelle

Rosaldo (1980) details important contrasts between the social experience of women and younger men on the one hand and that of senior males on the other. Renato Rosaldo (1980) has shown that these Ilongot cultural patterns have been shaped by colonial and postcolonial contexts of missionization, World War II, guerrilla insurrections and counterinsurgency campaigns, and encounters with anthropologists. It seems likely that ideologies of language deployed in Ilongot communities are no less complex, contested, differentially distributed, and historically produced than other dimensions of social life.

While the opposing, Western view is identified mainly with a particular brand of philosophical discourse, Michelle Rosaldo concludes that "certain of *our* culturally shaped ideas about how human beings act have limited *our* grasp of speech behavior, leading *us* to celebrate the individual who acts without attending to contextual constrains on meaning" (1982:228; emphasis mine). Exactly how the first-person plural is constituted in this assertion is not entirely clear. Reading directly from particular statements regarding language structure and use to some sort of cognitive common denominator that is evenly and passively inserted into "the brain of each member of a community" (in Saussure's [1916] 1959:19 famous words) seems highly unsound.

While I believe that the cultural roots of linguistic ideologies are profound, I suggest that they can be best characterized not as a homogeneous cultural substratum but as dimensions of practices that are deployed in constructing and naturalizing discursive authority. In this chapter I point to the advantages of the latter approach through an examination of how influential men in indigenous communities in eastern Venezuela attempt to assert the dominance of ideologies of language that are closely associated with their positions of authority.

The Social Distribution of Warao Ideologies of Language

Where the Orinoco River, which traverses Venezuela, flows into the Caribbean, it explodes into a broad fan of tributaries that create a swampy delta region. Some 24,000 persons who are designated and refer to themselves as "the Warao," as members of an *étnia* 'indigenous ethnic group', live in marshlands of the delta and surrounding areas.[1] I have worked primarily in two areas, the Mariusa region in the central delta and the Murako-K^{w}amuhu region to the southeast. Formerly, the Warao lived by harvesting forest products, fishing, and hunting in the moriche palm groves near the coast. The Mariusa group continues to live primarily in this fashion, while horticulture is now of more importance than gathering in Murako and K^{w}amuhu.

In turning initially to the ways that men talk about language, one is struck by the amount of time that men spend talking about talk, discussing the nature of discourse and its role in social action.[2] I have discussed elsewhere the salience of competing models of language use in *monikata nome anaka*, dispute mediation events, and their crucial role in rendering these procedures effective (Briggs 1996a). Linguistic ideologies are similarly foregrounded in *ahokona serebuyaha*, predawn exhortations and demonstrations of ritual knowledge delivered by curers and political leaders.

In this section I contrast two types of Warao discursive practices—women's performances of ritual wailing and men's performances of curing songs. I discuss the fundamentally contrastive character of the ideologies of language that are associated with these two types of discursive practices.

Ritual Wailing

When a relative dies, women sit next to the corpse and wail from the time of the death until the mourners return from the burial site. The texted songs composed by each woman consist of *refrains*, which consist of a kinship term and a formula expressing grief, and *textual phrases*, longer stretches of discourse that tell of the deceased, his or her life, the victim's relationship to the wailer and other members of the community, and the circumstances that led to the death. Women take turns (on the basis of kinship) sitting next to the body, and the person occupying that location generates a much higher percentage of textual phrases. While other wailers continue to compose their own textual phrases, their content is derived in part from the verses sung by the principal wailer.

Two facets of ritual wailing are particularly striking. First, the complex poetic structure of lament texts includes extensive use of reported speech. Stretches of discourse are extracted from discourse events in which women are rarely able to participate actively, such as political rhetoric, as well as from gossip and everyday conversation. Reported speech is used in creating a critical portrait of what is said and done in the community, one that takes male political leaders and curers to task (see Briggs 1992b). Second, ritual wailing is highly polyphonic and intertextual; while all performers embody their own perspective in a distinct text, both verbal and musical parameters are coordinated in producing a collective performance (see Briggs 1993b).

In talking about ritual wailing, women emphasize the importance of the collective nature of the performance, noting that *emo onakumoni—aweresike onaya* 'we couldn't cry apart from one another—we cry very close to one another'. The referent in these expressions is not simply spatial; the women are referring to social relations as indexed by pitch, timbre, and rhythmic coordination. Note that these acoustic features convey powerful affect.[3] Both men and women assert that only by expressing the sorrow and rage engendered by the death in ritual wailing can the performers and their audiences put the disruptive effects of mourning behind them. Several of my interlocutors attributed the success of this process to a special form of intersubjectivity: *onayakore, aobohona ekó tia* 'when they cry, their thoughts are emptied out'. *Obohona* can be translated as 'thoughts', 'consciousness', and 'intentionality'. The locus of personal identity, the *obohona* contains the cognitive and affective elements that are unique to a given individual. When one's *obohona* is 'emptied out', intentionality and personal agency disappear. The voice that emerges is quintessentially collective, being jointly constructed by a number of performers in concert, and it creates shared understandings of recent events. This voice is accordingly unimpeachable: *nome sike onaya; obohonamo onakumoni* 'they only cry the truth; they couldn't cry lies'. Even individuals who are being denounced in bold and salacious terms as having caused the death find it difficult to deny the validity of the claims made in laments.

Curing Songs

I now contrast ritual wailing with *hoa*, songs used by *hoarotu* curers in curing and killing (see Olsen 1996, Wilbert 1972). Initiates learn to use songs, ritual cigars, the breath, and massage in controlling malevolent spirits. Practitioners emphasize two aspects of curers' discourse. First, curers stress the power of the 'names' of *hoa* spirits that emerge in songs. *Hoa* songs draw on a specialized lexicon that is unintelligible to noninitiates. This lexicon, when lodged in the poetic, acoustic, and musical patterning of the song, enables the curer to access the transformative energy that lies behind invisible dimensions of the natural world. Proper use of these 'names' forces the spirits to attend to the curer's discourse; they also demonstrate the practitioner's knowledge of and power over the distinctive attributes of the spirit in question and its *obohona*.[4] A second feature, the linear structure of the song, is referred to as *anaru* 'its path'; moving correctly along the 'path' is crucial if the song is to achieve performative efficacy. The overall rhetorical structure of the song and the parallelistic patterning evident in clusters of lines and verses enable the practitioner to draw the *hoa* along a 'path' that leads either from the patient back to the spirit's home or from the *hoa*'s dwelling through the curer and into a victim's body.

Comparison of Ideologies Connected with Ritual Wailing and Curing Songs

The ideologies associated with ritual wailing and curing songs are similar in one important way—both are regarded as powerfully performative uses of speech. While *hoa* songs can either kill or cure, ritual wailing creates collective structures of feeling that enable communities to overcome the disruptive effects occasioned by death and that significantly affect future events. Beyond this shared feature, however, the two ideologies are highly contrastive. A first difference is gender—while ritual wailing is cited as a quintessential embodiment of women's social power, curers' discourse is the ultimate manifestation of men's social power.[5] The ideological contrasts are also tied to a vast difference in the roles of performer and audience. Ritual wailing not only is by definition collective discourse but also exhibits a high degree of recipient-design, in Sacks's (1992) terms. Performers often declare openly who should be listening, how they should interpret what is being sung, and what action should be taken. In *hoa*, on the other hand, no human audience need be present. Curers sing alone, often out in the forest, when using *hoa* to cause illness. Even though the patient and her or his relatives may be listening when the goal is to cure, the discourse is not directed at them. This exclusion from the overt role of audience is marked by the use of curers' lexicon.[6]

A key difference in the way that men and women contrast the uses of language associated with the two types of discourse lies in the realm of *intentionality*.

Research conducted by Du Bois (1992), Duranti (1988), Rosaldo (1982), and others has pointed to contrasts between speech communities with respect to the role accorded to intentionality. The contrast evident in the way that intentionality is constructed in ritual wailing as opposed to *hoa* songs is as sharp as the gulf that Rosaldo perceived between Western (scholarly) and Ilongot discourse. *Hoa* songs can be characterized as *hyperintentional* speech, as means of imposing the curer's *obohona* on the *obohona* of both spirits and victims through the use of "names" and "paths." The social power of wailing is seen as emerging through the *displacement of intentionality* by "emptying out" the *obohona* (rather than using it purposively to control the *obohona* of others) and by sharing authorship via the process of collective composition.

The Deployment of Linguistic Ideologies in Gossip

I would like to forestall two possible readings of the comparison I have just made. First, I do not wish to imply that competing ideologies of language are evident only in speech settings that revolve around highly marked formal patterns and social contexts; to the contrary, I argue in this section that the deployment of linguistic ideologies also plays a crucial role in everyday discourse. Second, I argued earlier that access to ideologies of language is socially distributed. I suggest, however, that the relationship between contrastive ideologies and social differentiation is vastly more complex than a mere one-to-one correlation would suggest. It is not simply the case that men conceive of language in *X* terms and women in *Y* or that curers assert *A* and noninitiates *B* about language. In order to tease out some of these complexities, I now examine the way that two men give voice to competing ideologies of language in an exchange of gossip.

The sorts of narrative exchanges generally termed "gossip" provide an ideal ground on which to examine how power is created and legitimated in the circulation of discourse. Scholars have long documented the crucial role that gossip plays in creating and contesting intimacy, knowledge, and reputation (see Abrahams 1983, Gluckman 1963, Haviland 1977, Szwed 1966, White 1994). Research has focused more recently on the reflexive or metadiscursive (Bauman and Briggs 1990, Briggs 1993b, Silverstein and Urban 1996) power of gossip; tellers and audiences seek to regulate the circulation of discourse not only within and between gossip sessions but also in other sorts of discursive settings (Besnier 1989, Brenneis 1996, Goodwin 1990, Hannerz 1967, Shuman 1986). Building on Gluckman's (1963) classic interpretation of gossip as an instrument of informal social control, Merry (1984) suggests that the representations formulated in gossip are often incorporated into more "formal" agencies of control. White (1994) argues that gossip about others provides people with a particularly poignant way of revealing things about themselves. The case I examine here is particularly interesting in that the two principal participants attempt to counter and reconfigure widely dispersed representations of themselves under the guise of gossiping about how others are gossiping about them. As such, their exchange provides a fascinating window on the power and the limitations of gossip and its purveyors to control multiple and often conflicting representations, discourse genres, and ideologies of language.

In Warao, gossip is generally termed *dehe wara-* 'to tell stories or gossip'. As is true of a wide number of languages and social groups, the term *gossip* is used in two contrastive senses. It can be used to refer to the pleasurable exchange of everyday narratives about people: *Dehe waraki!* 'Let's tell gossip!' Particularly when the suffix *-witu* (which denotes intensity and/or exclusivity) is attached, *dehe* can also denigrate particular narratives as vicious and vacuous—*tamaha dehewitu!* 'that's nothing but a bunch of lies!' Exchanges of gossip can take place nearly anywhere and in the midst of nearly any activity—except the sorts of performances (such as dispute mediation, ritual wailing, and ritual events) that open up discourse to broad audiences and increase accountability for what is said.[7] As in many types of communities and settings, a wide range of speech forms emerge in exchanges of gossip; since gossip includes a great deal of reported speech, things that were spoken previously in dispute mediations and public proclamations are just as likely to get recontextualized as intimate whisperings. Gossip is much like ritual wailing in this regard. Finally, while everyone has the right to tell and to listen to gossip, people are careful about *what* they say to *whom;* gossip is thus most commonly exchanged between relatives and friends. Gender, age, sexuality, and, as we shall see, social status affect how particular people tell gossip and with whom they choose to exchange it.

The example on which I focus is an exchange of gossip between two senior men, Manuel Torres and Santiago Rivera,[8] which took place shortly after I took up residence in the Mariusa region in May 1987. These men, both of whom were about sixty years of age at the time, were two of the three most powerful leaders in the region. Mr. Rivera was the *kobenahoro* 'governor', the paramount indigenous authority in the area, and he was also one of the most widely feared *hoarotu* practitioners in the delta. He died in 1992, one of the first victims of a cholera epidemic that killed hundreds of Warao (see Briggs and Mantini Briggs 1997). Mr. Torres is deemed by many to be *the* most powerful *hoarotu.* Both men were skilled in other types of curing practice as well. They each had three wives, a clear indication of their social stature. Apprenticeships that provide expertise in curing also enable one to use the same body of knowledge, coupled with a slightly different set of techniques, in sorcery. Thus, while gaining a reputation as being quite skilled in using at least one form of curing/sorcery confers a great deal of authority and social status, this sort of recognition also invites sorcery accusations, which can have very serious consequences. Curers use exchanges of gossip to learn what others are saying about them and to circulate counterassertions designed to undermine the credibility and legitimacy of charges that have been lodged against them.

After the morning meal, Mr. Rivera, his wives, several of their children, and I visited Mr. Torres at his house, which was located at the juncture of the Mariusa River and the Caribbean. Once they had exchanged greetings, the two men sat on the floor of the house, face-to-face, less than two feet apart. Lowering their voices and maintaining eye contact with each other, they excluded others from primary roles in the conversation. Their wives and several of their older children and sons-in-law, who were sitting in an adjacent section of the house or lying in nearby hammocks, broke into the conversation from time to time. These interventions are indeed significant, and I will analyze these contributions from the sidelines in a future paper; here I concentrate on Mr. Rivera's and Mr. Torres's roles in the exchange. Since I had turned off a larger tape recorder that was attached to two semi-shotgun microphones shortly before the dialogue began, they forgot that my small cassette tape recorder was still in operation.[9]

The two men are concerned mainly with questions of health, sickness, and death, not only in their community but throughout the delta as a whole. Statistics provided by Miguel Layrisse, George Salas, and H. Dieter Heinen (1980:66) for five areas of the delta suggest that approximately 50 percent of the children die before reaching puberty. Unfortunately, health conditions appear to have significantly worsened since the years from 1950 through the 1970s, when these data were collected; various diarrheal diseases and malnutrition continue to kill children, and mortality related to tuberculosis appears to have risen dramatically. It thus seems far from surprising that daily talk in Mariusa, as in much of the delta, centers on questions of health, illness, and curing. The role of Warao medical practitioners in both curing patients and causing illness is a particularly common topic of conversation by people in general. Given Mr. Rivera's and Mr. Torres's status as prominent curers, many of the charges they discuss had been leveled against them. I focus on the way that the two men use linguistic ideologies in representing these accusations and—as you might imagine—denying their validity.

Early in the conversation, both Mr. Torres and Mr. Rivera admit that they have retaliated through the use of *hoa* against practitioners who live in other regions in response to what they deemed to be acts of sorcery. These self-incriminating statements would never have been made in a setting in which they could be held accountable, that is, if an audience were present, rather than overhearers, and if anyone who might be listening were not a close relative or ally. Such an indiscretion might leak this information to the two men's enemies.

Mr. Rivera then contrasts the persona that he has just constructed for himself—as a powerful and vengeful sorcerer—with the way he conducts himself at present in his capacity as 'governor':

(1) *Conversation between Santiago Rivera* (SR) *and Manuel Torres* (MT); *Mariusa, 1987*[10]

a. SR *Atuesike debu asidaha debuya.*
'Long ago I really did use bad speech'.

b. SR *Ama ine debu moaya,*
'Now I counsel people',

c. SR *maribu nokokitane;*
'and they must listen to my words';

d. SR *tatuka uriabane debu moaya.*
'I counsel them slowly and carefully'.

Here Mr. Rivera juxtaposes two basic modes of discourse production. The first, *debu asidaha* 'bad speech', is generally used in reference to utterances that reflect anger (*yari*), jealousy (*miahi*), or the like. Such discourse does not emerge from careful consideration of one's *obohona*, the locus of personal identity, cognition, affect, and intentionality. Such uncontrolled speech also fails to respect the *obohona* of one's interlocutors, and it is likely to generate conflict (see Briggs 1996a). When used in the context of talk about curing, particularly when the suffix *-ha* is present, *debu asidaha* is often used to refer to the expression of anger through sorcery. These practices are, as I have noted, deemed to be the epitome of hyperintentionality and individual, asocial agency. Mr. Rivera seems to be using the term 'bad speech' both in reference to unreflective speech and to sorcery.

In (1) Mr. Rivera contrasts his former use of 'bad speech' with his current reliance on *debu moa-* 'counseling'. This discourse mode embodies an idealized model of discourse production. *Aidamo* 'leaders' must 'counsel' the members of their community regarding how one should talk and act. A great deal of 'counseling speech' consists of model utterances that are designed for recontextualization in the mouths of their addressees. 'Leaders' assert that if people speak in this way, social conflict can be avoided. 'Counseling speech' is deemed by leaders to be the quintessential embodiment of order. Since *aidamo* 'leaders' counsel *nebu* 'followers' or 'workers', parents counsel children, and husbands 'counsel' wives—but not vice versa—'counseling speech' constitutes a central discursive means for constructing social inequality (see Briggs 1996a).[11]

The conversation between Mr. Torres and Mr. Rivera then turns to recounting the accusations against them. Not surprisingly, the two attempt to refute the charges by labeling them as 'bad speech'. These narratives are characterized as *dehe* 'gossip'. How could the two men establish the falsity of these widely circulated narratives? Stories are deemed to be 'gossip' when they do not reflect authoritative knowledge of the events they claim to represent. Determining the 'truth' or 'falsity' of such narratives involves uncovering the many layers of intertextuality that have been built into the narratives, or, as Bauman and I (1990) have referred to it, the process of decontextualization and recontextualization. Mr. Torres and Mr. Rivera thus carefully trace the chain of transmission backward, as it were, assessing how each narrator purportedly told the narrative, how she or he extracted it from previous accounts, and why. The crucial point in the discussion of each narrative is the determination of *ahotana* 'its beginning'; the story can be assessed as 'the truth' or 'just a lie' once it has been traced to the purported first telling and the narrators' knowledge of the events in question has been assessed; motives for narrativizing the events are also examined. Mr. Torres and Mr. Rivera use this process of reconstructing the successive recontextualizations of these narratives as a means of asserting that the stories are based on a lack of authoritative knowledge as to what took place.

The concepts of 'bad speech' and 'counseling speech' provide an ideological basis for a great deal of talk—and talk about talk—in Warao communities. *Ahotana* 'its beginning' similarly holds the key to linguistic ideologies presented by Warao men in a wide variety of speech genres. Crucially, this concept motivates a generative system for transforming *dehe nobo* 'ancestral narratives', what we would call myths, into curing songs. Known to curers alone, these songs invoke and harness supernatural power by revealing the *ahotana* of each element of the social and natural world, as I discussed in the case of *hoa* songs. *Ahotana* also provides a key to grasping the complex system of epistemic evaluatives in Warao—suffixes and particles that grammatically encode assertions as to the nature and reliability of the evidence on which one's utterance rests. It would similarly be possible to connect these facets of linguistic ideologies with Warao ideologies of emotion, the person, the body, and so forth (see Briggs 1992b, 1996a). Indeed, I believe that the concepts that I have outlined are quite telling with respect to the way Warao construct language, agency, action, subjectivity, truth, and knowledge.

I submit, however, that it would be misleading to simply assert that the concepts of 'counseling', 'bad speech', and 'the beginning' form key elements of the linguistic ideologies that underlie Warao men's speech. Let us return to the conversation between Mr. Rivera and Mr. Torres. Recall their status as two of the most respected—and feared—curers in the delta. Directly confronting such individuals would be viewed as suicidal. As the gossip they report bears witness, however, people spend a great deal of time criticizing what are seen as their abuses of power—once they are safely out of earshot. While the two men often adopt a mocking, parodic tone when recounting this gossip and an air of bravado in reporting their own responses, hushed, serious, and genuinely fearful reactions to particularly poignant charges also emerge. Indeed, such gossip provides a powerful—if precarious—means of constraining their actions. A host of subversive recontextualizations of these narratives could spark such an extensive expansion and legitimation of lines of rivalry and resistance against the two men that they might lose power, be expelled from the area, be denounced to government authorities (as "evil *hoa* sorcerers"), and/or become the objects of serious retaliation. If these sorcery accusations were tied to a death in the community, the gossip narratives would certainly gain even more weight once they were broadcast to the community in a number of voices through ritual wailing.

The two men have a great deal of fun attempting to discredit a series of charges leveled against them by a man named Francisco Gómez, who is not a curer, Basilio López, a specialist of much lesser stature who practices a different sort of curing, and a number of unnamed female narrators. Mr. Rivera and Mr. Torres trace the gossip back to contentions by Mr. Gómez and Mr. López that the latter "saw" the two curers in their dreams. The two *hoa* practitioners deem Mr. Gómez's accusations to be particularly laughable—since he possesses no supernatural capital himself, he could not possibly have "seen" a *hoarotu* in his dreams.[12] While Mr. López is a curer, he is a *bahanarotu*, not a *hoarotu*, and it is accordingly deemed impossible for him to have 'seen' a *hoarotu* in his dreams. The manner in which Mr. Rivera claims to have refuted Mr. López's charges in a confrontation with his accuser is particularly telling:

(2) *Continuation of conversation;* SR = *Santiago Rivera,* MT = *Manuel Torres*

a. MT *Warao are era.*
'People tell a lot of gossip'.

b. SR *Warao arebu.*
'People's gossip'.

c. MT *Warao, warao arebu.*
'People's, people's gossip'.

d. SR *"Ama ihi obohonamo, obohonamo, obohonamo, obohonamo—tida monuka!"*
"'So you're a liar, a liar, a liar, a liar—you're just like a woman!'"
[

e. MT *"obohonamo, obohonamo"*
"'a liar, a liar'"

f. SR *"¿Qué pasa, pues?"*
"'So what's the matter with you?'"
g. *"Ihi noboto?"*
"'Are you a child?'"
h. *"Ihi idamo diana, ihi kate kayamo idamo diana!"*
"'You're an old man already, and you aren't even as old as we are!'"
[
i. MT *"ihi kate idamo mi diana!"*
"'look, you're old too!'"
j. SR *Tanaha mi diana ine.*
'That's what I said to him'.

People very seldom witness curers' attempts to inflict *hoa* or other purported acts of supernatural violence. Instead, the most reliable evidence is provided by the dreams that come to curers after treating patients. Access to the *ahotana* 'beginning' of these sorcery accusations is thus predicated on forms of symbolic capital, to use Bourdieu's (1991) term, that only curers possess. Lacking the symbolic capital that accrues to a powerful *hoa* practitioner, Mr. López is reduced to the status of those individuals who are most impotent, in the terms advanced by Mr. Rivera and Mr. Torres—women and children. The way that Mr. Rivera focuses on his accusers' age is important. A generation younger, Mr. Gómez and Mr. López enjoy much more limited access to the discursive regime associated with curing and sorcery. It is, on the other hand, precisely the members of their generation who are posing significant challenges to the positions of leadership enjoyed by Mr. Rivera, Mr. Torres, and other senior men. I return to this point later.

Mr. Rivera and Mr. Torres dismiss the narratives told by women (as repeated by the two men's wives and daughters). They claim that *naminanaharone, are dehe waraya, dehe waraya, dehe waraya*—'even though they don't know what they're talking about, they're always telling gossip and telling gossip and telling gossip'. What basis do they have for asserting that their female accusers are ignorant of the events in question? Except in the case of those few women who become skilled curers, the concept of *ahotana* marginalizes women's narratives—and thus their attempts to call the authority of men like Mr. Rivera and Mr. Torres into question—by fiat.

The implications of the situated use of these linguistic ideologies is not confined to this conversation or these particular events. I claim that deploying linguistic ideologies plays an important role in contesting social inequality and social power in Warao communities. Performances of such discourse forms as ritual wailing and gossip narratives, along with curing songs, ancestral narratives, and political rhetoric, constitute powerful forms of social action. I noted earlier that women's ritual wailing provides a crucial means of appropriating and criticizing types of authoritative male discourse to which women are seldom granted access as performers. Gossip plays an important role in Warao social life not simply by virtue of its potential uses in generating collective criticism of 'leaders' but also in that it is accessible, *mutatis mutandis*, to everyone. It thus enables women and men who are not political leaders or curers to contest issues of power and violence. When leaders stand accused of having flagrantly abused their power, gossip provides a means of attempting to create the consensus needed to force public disclosure of their actions in a dispute mediation.[13] Mr. Rivera and Mr. Torres were not only two of the most powerful 'leaders' in the region, but they entered into social conflict frequently, purportedly using sorcery to achieve their ends. At the time of the gossip session, they were jointly countering efforts by other men to usurp their authority and negotiating (sometimes fractious) relations with members of nearby communities. Their alliance ended some two years later, and the complex discursive constructions of hostility and competition that each leveled against the other became an important focus of social life in Mariusa.

Recounting this gossip and attempting to discover its *ahotana* thus constituted crucial means of both constructing and deploying their alliance (while it lasted). If either man should be forced to defend himself in a dispute mediation session, it would be extremely useful to have worked out a good defense in advance in a setting in which accountability was lower and the possibilities for recontextualization were greatly constrained. This tactic was particularly valuable in that the other ally, being a 'leader' (*aidamo*), would likely serve in the role of either key witness or officiating 'leader' in a dispute mediation, thereby creating an excellent opportunity to recontextualize the lines of defense that had been devised in this gossip session. Note that the two men devote much of the conversation to asserting what they *would* say in response to the charges advanced through gossip, should an open confrontation take place. The social power of what they are saying lies not just in its utterance in the present interaction itself but in its potential recontextualization; the two men thus exploit the way that conflict talk circulates between a variety of agencies of social control, as Merry (1984) reminds us.

The entextualization process, the shaping the discourse into textual segments that can be lifted out of the conversation for future use (see Bauman and Briggs 1990), is not oriented simply toward dispute mediation events. During the conversation, the two men were clearly aware that their families were listening and, at times, collaborating in revealing the gossip that was being told about them. As they traced the *ahotana* of the 'gossip', Mr. Rivera and Mr. Torres issued a number of warnings that were designed to be relayed to the individuals who were spreading the 'gossip'. They asserted that they would use their power as 'leaders' in assessing a cash fine against the women for concocting 'mere gossip'. The warnings for the two men who claim to have seen Mr. Rivera and Mr. Torres in their dreams were more pointed. They threatened to send *hoa* against them: if Mr. Gómez and Mr. López were *truly* practitioners of *hoa*—as their claims to having "seen" *hoarotu* curers in their dreams would suggest—they could simply deflect the invading spirits; if not, they would die.

In mustering linguistic ideologies in the service of discrediting the gossip directed against them, Mr. Rivera and Mr. Torres claimed to reveal the "truth," asserting that their detractors were only telling "lies." As Michel Foucault argues, presenting truth claims goes much deeper than simply validating a particular body of facts:

> Each society has its régime of truth, its 'general politics' of truth: that is, the types of discourse which it accepts and makes function as true; the mechanisms and instances

> which enable one to distinguish true and false statements, the means by which each is sanctioned; the techniques and procedures accorded value in the acquisition of truth; the status of those who are charged with saying what counts as true. (1980:131)

Foucault's statement provides an important impetus to push the analysis toward understanding how power relates not just to discourses but to the mechanisms through which discourses are produced, circulated, and legitimated. In contrast, the way that he posits one-to-one correlations between societies and regimes of truth casts the relationship in much too static, homogeneous, and unitary a fashion. As Gal (1993) suggests, linguistic ideologies are contested by powerful social actors within European nation-states. The assumptions that are embedded in Foucault's notion of a "régime of truth" similarly lessen its usefulness as a framework for analyzing the production of truth in the Delta Amacuro of Venezuela. Mr. Rivera and Mr. Torres used linguistic ideologies in attempting to exercise tighter control over the economy of truth and, consequently, to deny their adversaries access to the socially significant discourses that are regulated by this economy. These ideologies naturalize a hierarchy of discursive forms; since women and nonspecialist men lack direct access to the *ahotana*, their discourse can be characterized as "mere gossip" that lacks the power associated with curing speech, accounts of dreams, ancestral narratives, and political discourse. Such uses of linguistic ideologies can play a crucial role in efforts by elder men to naturalize the construction of their substantial political and supernatural capital. Only individuals who enjoy access to the "beginning" of recent events and of curing power—which also emanates from the dreams of initiated practitioners—can speak authoritatively and expect their words to become the basis for collective action. Linguistic ideologies thus provide crucial means of attempting to naturalize the social structural status quo.

White (1997) argues that gossip reveals how penetrable even the most prominent reputations may be, disclosing not only areas of greatest vulnerability but also the boundaries of attack. By entering into the stream of gossip about themselves, individuals can attempt to shore up weak lines of defense, reposition the boundaries that limit offensive and defensive actions, and raise or lower the stakes. By placing such rearguard actions in a venue that is open to many and not tightly controlled by any, however, the objects of gossip risk heightening the visibility and social consequences of attacks on their reputation. It is small wonder that individuals who enjoy privileged access to other discursive institutions often loudly signal their refusal to respond to such charges—that is, assert that they are unwilling to participate in the circulation of gossip about them.

Nor would it be accurate to suggest that the regimes of truth in which Warao communities operate are entirely shaped by the economy of spirit dreams and its resistance by women and younger men. Indeed, if this were the case, I doubt that Mr. Rivera and Mr. Torres would have been so concerned with the accusations that had been made against them. The ideologies of language that they use operate within the sphere of influence of four powerful sets of institutions: the Capuchin (Catholic) Mission, which was established in the delta in 1925; national political parties, especially the Acción Democrática, Partido Cristiano Social, and Movimiento al Socialismo; national and regional governmental bureaucracies; and business enterprises and corporations operating in the delta, which range in scale from one-family fishing operations to factories that export palm hearts to Europe and the United States to British Petroleum. None of these institutions has ever opened an office in the Mariusa region, and the positions of authority occupied by Mr. Rivera and Mr. Torres were not conferred on them by agents of the nation-state, political parties, corporations, or missions. Nevertheless, Mr. Rivera's considerable power as *kobenahoro* was based in part on his ability to obtain at least some goods and bureaucratic support from priests, politicians, capitalists, and bureaucrats and to provide some measure of resistance against the exploitation of Mariusans by these parties. While his ability to present himself as the "traditional" leader of the region—and thus to counsel and cure his followers—was crucial, knowledge of Spanish, literacy, and familiarity with bureaucratic procedures were also extremely useful skills.

While Mr. Rivera was much better versed in this area than his peers, his rudimentary competence was greatly inferior to that of a number of younger men who had been employed for years by commercial fishermen who operate in the Mariusa area. These younger individuals were increasingly threatening his authority; they talked of seizing the position of *kobenahoro,* and several tried to gain the post of *comisario* 'commissioner', which is granted directly by the government. Literacy is required for such appointments, and neither the Capuchins nor the government has ever attempted to establish a school in the Mariusa area; to date, therefore, illiteracy has precluded the possibility that the *kobenahoro* might have to confront the authority of a government-appointed official in Mariusa. Nevertheless, in 1987, the authority of senior men was being contested by individuals who could draw on new possibilities for building alliances with institutions of the nation-state; the regime of truth that Mr. Rivera and Mr. Torres used in exerting power over women and younger men was thus being confronted with new forms of contestation. In sum, it was becoming quite clear by 1987 that Mr. Rivera and Mr. Torres could not fend off attempts to usurp their power for terribly long.

Again I wish to make it clear that I am not asserting that one social group (senior males) and one ideology of language are facing off with competing sectors (women, younger men, and older men who lack the status of curers) and a competing ideology; the construction of difference and inequality is much more complex in political-economic and historical terms than this simple opposition would suggest. As I noted earlier, the alliance between Mr. Rivera and Mr. Torres exploded and was supplanted by highly acrimonious rivalry some two years after this conversation was recorded. Unable to muster support for displacing Mr. Rivera as *kobenahoro,* Mr. Torres endeavored for several years to draw on the power of the nation-state, seeking to become a government-endorsed (and -remunerated) local official. Monolingual and unable to sign his name, he failed to obtain an appointment as a *comisario.* He eventually moved with some one hundred other Mariusans to a town on the mainland where he could gain government recognition as a *cacique,* a term used by Spanish speakers to designate persons whom they consider to be traditional leaders of Native American communities. Thus, Mr. Rivera and Mr. Torres were also willing to participate in competing regimes of truth in advancing their claims to power.[14] When Mr. Rivera was killed by the cholera epidemic in 1992 (his death was initially blamed on Mr. Torres), his son was named *kobenahoro.* Lacking training as a curer, the younger Mr. Rivera was chosen precisely because he could speak Spanish relatively well and was able to deal more effectively with bureaucrats. My point here is not that spirit dreams no longer play a crucial role in constructing authority, for this is not the case. Rather, the growing penetration of ideologies of language and discourse practices associated with the nation-state and other institutional nexuses underlines the importance of Mr. Rivera's and Mr. Torres's interventions within this contested discursive economy.

Ideologies, Contestation, and Practices

I have suggested that this gossip session revolved around the imposition of a single dominant ideology and discursive regime. How does it relate to the questions regarding the *contestation* of ideologies of language that I raised in the introduction to this chapter? If contesting language ideologies is at stake here, why don't Mr. Rivera and Mr. Torres take on these competing ideologies more directly?

Let us reexamine the three major ways that ideologies of language emerged in this portion of the gossip exchange in addressing these questions. In the opening segment of the transcript, Mr. Rivera contrasted his former use of sorcery in aggressive and highly successful acts of vengeance with his current concern with "counseling" members of his community. As I have detailed elsewhere (1996a), the use of discourse in creating conflict as opposed to imposing order and interpersonal harmony is associated respectively with representations of discourse as "bad words," tools for aggressive and sometimes violent self-assertion, versus "counseling speech," discourse that quintessentially embodies social order and authority. These ideologies of language are presented as a part of representations of particular, situated discursive practices—that is, as an important dimension of the ways that social relations are created and sustained within and between communities.

The question of the accusations that had been leveled against Mr. Rivera and Mr. Torres by women is complex, and I included more in-depth discussion in another essay (see Briggs 1993a). The two men's representation of this gossip is confined largely to signaling the content of the accusations themselves; rather than criticizing the sorts of evidence that the women marshal to legitimate their accounts, Mr. Rivera and Mr. Torres simply dismiss the narratives as lacking a factual basis: "even though they don't know what they're talking about, they're always telling gossip and telling gossip and telling gossip." The two men may not know all that much about the evidential underpinnings of the women's narratives. Women often base the authority of their gossip narratives on detailed knowledge of everyday activities, such as gathering, preparing, and distributing food and caring for the sick, about which they have particularly detailed information. Since women generally exchange gossip with other women, Mr. Rivera and Mr. Torres learned about these accusations through their wives and daughters. When such narratives are recontextualized for the benefit of male relatives, very little of the detailed description that provides their evidential basis is retained.

A very complex form of contestation is thus going on here. On the one hand, the two men's attempt to impose the ideology of language associated with the curers' discursive regime on gossip affects the relative legitimacy—and thus the social force—of narratives associated with these contrastive ideologies; accepting *ahotana* as the only basis for legitimating such narratives would deprive women's gossip of a great deal of its social and political force. On the other hand, women's selective use of silence, the withholding of detailed information regarding the ways they represent language and experience in gossip, helps shield the discursive regimes over which they exert more control from attempts by senior males to belittle women and their narratives. Here ideologies of languages are closely tied to highly gendered practices—curing and sorcery, on the one hand, and such activities as securing, preparing, and distributing food and caring for the sick, on the other hand. The opposition that Mr. Rivera and Mr. Torres invoke between men's and women's gossip is thus closely tied into the social construction of gender and the overall economy of relations between women and men. The relationship here between women's and men's gossip points to the complexity of the issue of women's silence, as poignantly delineated by Susan Gal (1991b). To analyze this issue adequately, we must attend to men's denigration of women's gossip, women's attempts to limit male access to their gossip, and the way that women pass along gossip to their male relatives (Briggs 1993a).

The attack on the stories told by Mr. Gómez and Mr. López seems at first glance to revolve a great deal less around contesting contrastive ideologies of language than around restricting access to the ideologies of language that Mr. Rivera and Mr. Torres are constructing as dominant, and to some extent this is the case. By succeeding in according hegemony to a particular ideology, one can enjoy a position of authority by virtue of having demonstrated control over the *process* of shaping how discourse can legitimately be produced, circulated, and rendered authority—that is, in Foucault's terms, over regimes of truth and knowledge. If access can be restricted to the use of discursive practices that are deemed to embody these dominant ideologies, then the champions of these ideologies can provide themselves with an even more effective means of creating social power. By tying the production and legitimation of "knowledge" and "truth" to the discursive practices that provide access to *ahotana,* Mr. Rivera and Mr. Torres can largely restrict rights to practitioners like themselves with respect to what they are constructing as the most authoritative discursive realm. Since they are recognized as being more knowledgeable than nearly all of the remaining curers, they can potentially exercise a great deal of control over the social construction of discourse and power. Crucially, the practices to which they attach discursive authority also greatly shape, through curing and sorcery, the overall economy of life and death.

Nevertheless, I believe that this interpretation stays rather too close to Mr. Rivera's and Mr. Torres's representation of the nature of these accusations. As I noted earlier, Mr. Gómez and Mr. López, a generation younger than Mr. Rivera and Mr. Torres, were at the time beginning to compete for leadership roles with the senior generation. In launching their challenge, Mr. Gómez and Mr. López were attempting to draw on the experiences they gained as employees of the commercial fishermen who exploit Mariusan natural resources and labor. Since Mr.

Rivera and Mr. Torres lacked this experience, Mr. Gómez and Mr. López enjoyed more fluency in Spanish and more in-depth knowledge of petty capitalist production. Moreover, the owners of these small-scale fishing enterprises lent material and sociopolitical support to members of the junior generation due to the closer social ties they enjoy and the owners' ability to exert greater control over them; senior men, particularly Mr. Rivera, seek to maintain much more autonomy from individuals, such as the commercial fishermen, who have their own sources of social and economic power. Bureaucrats, politicians, and missionaries have also frequently shifted their alliances from older and established leaders to younger aspirants. Ventriloquizing the words of the owners and of government officials thus played a crucial role in the way that Mr. Gómez, Mr. López, and others articulated their challenges.

What Mr. Rivera and Mr. Torres failed to mention in characterizing the charges that Mr. Gómez and Mr. López leveled against them is that the accusations included a threat to denounce the two men to magistrates and police in Tucupita—as malevolent sorcerers who were creating conflict in their own communities. Mr. Rivera and Mr. Torres were aware that if these younger men brought their conflicts with senior men to the attention of government officials (particularly magistrates and police officers in town), revealing spirit dreams that lay the blame on other practitioners' shoulders would evoke only ridicule from officials. They were well aware that being accused by women and younger men of generating conflict and abusing power could undermine their credibility in the eyes of government officials entirely—if not land them in jail. Note the interesting contradiction in Mr. Gómez's and Mr. López's position. On the one hand, they declared that sorcery must stop and that the power of the nation-state must supplant it as a means of creating social order. They were similarly, as I noted, quite interested in gaining remunerated positions as representatives of that order. On the other hand, they claimed to be able to prove that Mr. Rivera and Mr. Torres are sorcerers by telling about their *own* spirit dreams. Mr. Gómez and Mr. López thus combined two largely patriarchal modes of establishing social dominance—as associated with curing/sorcery and the nation-state—in such a way as to erode the authority of the former and greatly enhance that of the latter.

This is not to say that Mr. Rivera and Mr. Torres did not also attempt to draw on discourses associated with the nation-state; as I noted, Mr. Torres attempted several years later to be designated as a *comisario* in order to effectively challenge Mr. Rivera's position as *kobenahoro.* Nevertheless, in their gossip they sought to incorporate ideologies and practices associated with the state while at the same time maintaining the preeminent discursive authority of the curing/sorcery régime over which they enjoyed a virtual monopoly. In sum, the process of contesting ideologies and practices is very much at stake in the discussion of the accusations by Mr. Gómez and Mr. López.

That Mr. Rivera and Mr. Torres undertook this process in an exchange of gossip adds, I think, an interesting twist to our understanding of gossip as a social and discursive institution. Gossip sessions are heteroglossic events par excellence in which interlocutors enjoy a great deal of freedom to juxtapose a diverse range of genres, topics, styles, and perspectives. Mr. Rivera and Mr. Torres exploit the discursive openness and heterogeneity of gossip in quoting the words of women, younger men, and other types of curers, and they draw on a range of discursive forms and contexts. As competing perspectives are introduced, however, the range of discursive goals and modes of building authority associated with them are reduced to truth claims about supernatural knowledge. Rather than presenting these claims as emanating from alternative formations—equally systematic bodies of ideologies and discursive practices that are tied to other individuals, identities, and sites—the two men simply reduce them to the status of defective versions of the one sphere of ideology and practice that they are promoting. As successive narrative performances are recounted in reverse, competing discursive propositions are demolished until only one ideological framework and one mode of imposing it emerge as dominant. If they can construct the discursive regime that they closely control as being the only valid path to 'knowledge' and 'truth', its deployment will continue to provide a dominant means of regulating the production, circulation, and legitimization of discourse. Brenneis (1996) has argued that Fijian Indians celebrate heteroglossia and polyphony when they gossip. The present case points to the way gossip can ironically draw on these properties in attempting to suppress them.

This exchange illustrates the metadiscursive power—and the pitfalls—of gossip. The intertextual reach of gossip positions it as an excellent means of exploring the tensions between multiple and often competing forms and sites of discourse and social control and of attempting to change their relationship to each other and one's own position within them. Paradoxically, the least regulated and least authoritative discourse form is used in an attempt to regulate the production, circulation, and reception of much more authoritative and tightly related discursive institutions. But the move is just as risky as it is powerful—circulating representations in gossip can drag participants into these other arenas, such as dispute mediations and demeaning and possibly dangerous encounters with police and judicial officials. Gossip sessions provide excellent venues for constructing and pre-testing rhetorics that could be collectively deployed in such encounters. But if these representations are transformed into public accusations of sorcery in one of these contexts, the new mix of players, interests, and alliances may well depart drastically from prefabricated dialogues.

Gluckman (1963) pointed out long ago that gossip is a powerful tool of social control. I am arguing here that this capacity is tied not only to the much touted value of gossip for representing persons, events, and social relations but to its status as talk at the limits of metadiscursive regulation that can be used to regulate other discourses. In doing so, I want to distance myself from the teleological functionalism that underlies both Gluckman's and many other formulations. Gossip does not simply seek to bring behavior and discourse in line with preexisting shared and stable norms and social constructions. Generally deemed to be a violation of social and discursive rules itself, the relationship between gossip, other discursive institutions, and social control is as contradictory, contested, unstable, and uncontrollable as it is productive.

I devote the remainder of this essay to proposing two responses to the following question: What sort of analytic approach would best prepare us to study how dominant ideologies of language are created, sustained, and legitimated?

A useful point of departure for addressing the first aspect is provided by an issue raised by Paul Kroskrity in his contribution to this volume; it is relevant to the present discussion not only in that Kroskrity focuses on how ideologies of language become dominant but in that his formulation is framed, in part, as a critical response to my own work (Briggs 1992a). Generalizing on the basis of his assessment of a religious structure and institution—the ceremonial kiva—as "the 'site' of the Arizona Tewa dominant language ideology" and as providing "'a prestige model' for everyday verbal conduct," Kroskrity argues that "successfully 'naturalized' beliefs and practices . . . are not publicly challenged and seldom enter members' discursive consciousness" (chapter 5, this volume). Distinguishing "dominant ideologies" of language from "contended ideologies," he argues that dominant ideologies can be characterized by such a high degree of "taken for grantedness" (see Schutz 1966:74) that their discursive authority rests on a cultural consensus that effectively shields them from contestation.

I have never attempted to suggest that the naturalization of language ideologies does not constitute a valuable topic of research—to the contrary, I believe that it is of tremendous scholarly and political importance. Kroskrity's extensive documentation of the complex place that dominant language ideologies and practices occupy in the Arizona Tewa community is thus particularly valuable (see Kroskrity 1993). I do differ from Kroskrity, however, in my analysis of how domination and naturalization are created and sustained. The Arizona Tewa are no less enmeshed in postcolonial relations that involve the penetration of discourse practices associated with the nation-state, capitalism, missionaries, and the media than are Warao communities in Venezuela. Given both this historical and political-economic positioning and the presence of marked social inequality, it would be difficult to imagine that no other ideologies and practices potentially impinge upon the dominance of "the Arizona Tewa dominant language ideology." As Raymond Williams has noted, *"no mode of production and therefore no dominant social order and therefore no dominant culture ever in reality includes or exhausts all human practices, human energy, and human intention"* (1977:125; emphasis in original). To be sure, the two examples differ in that linguistic purism and cultural compartmentalism are highly salient among Arizona Tewa, while cultural and linguistic hybridity is celebrated in most dimensions of social life in Warao communities. Nevertheless, even if notions of pure and traditional Arizona Tewa culture are constructed as standing in opposition to and in isolation from modern, non-Pueblo forms, they must be continually redefined and relegitimated in the context of changing historical circumstances. As Gal (1993) has argued, heterogeneity and contestation are evident in the language ideologies that are championed by administrative (and, one might add, capitalist) elites of nation-states; insofar as "the Arizona Tewa dominant language ideology" resists the complex and contested array of ideologies imposed on Arizona Tewa by missionaries, schoolteachers, bureaucrats, politicians, employers, merchants, and the media, such resistance must be, at least to some extent, complex, dynamic, heterogeneous, and dialogic.

Accordingly, if other language ideologies and discursive practices do not overtly compete with the forms associated with kiva ceremonialism, then the question remains as to how we can account for this situation analytically. As I have argued for Warao gossip, asserting the legitimacy of dominant forms not only affects the value of other possible ways of organizing discursive relations but can serve as a means of attempting to suppress explicit discussion of their bases in contrastive epistemologies, practices, and social identities. I thus suggest that contestation is not simply a feature of *some* ideologies (Kroskrity's "contested ideologies") or a process that emerges in special circumstances that lead people to begin questioning taken-for-granted ideologies; to the contrary, *contestation is a crucial facet of how particular ideologies and practices come to be dominant.* The apparent absence of competing ideologies and practices should give us clues as to the nature of the processes through which alternative forms have been erased or suppressed—that is, to the particular means by which dominance has been established for particular forms. My fear is that when scholars suggest that forms derive their dominance from a cultural consensus that leaves no space for alternative forms and processes of contestations, they run the risk of further reifying the processes through which dominance is created, sustained, and legitimated.

These issues lead me to a second way of taking up the question of analytic approaches to studying dominant ideologies of language. I suggest that gaining a deeper understanding of how ideologies of language become dominant and how others are suppressed and discerning the broad range of ways that contestation takes place involves developing more and more sophisticated ways of studying the complex relations that obtain between language ideologies and discursive practices. Clearly, ideologies of language are not to be equated with discursive practices, as Silverstein (1979) has argued, and they are important social facts in their own right. Nevertheless, I have tried to show that relationships between ideologies and practices are not inherent or fixed but form a central facet of the process of situated social construction that Mr. Rivera and Mr. Torres undertook in their conversation. Recent research suggests that this active process of linking ideologies of language and discursive practices has played an important role in creating, legitimating, and challenging social inequality in the course of the creation and transformation of nation-states (see, for example, Bauman and Briggs 1994, Fraser 1992, Gal 1991a, Gal and Woolard 1995, Habermas [1962]1989, Joseph and Taylor 1990, Landes 1988, Woolard 1985).

I believe that the essays included in this volume are quite helpful in advancing our understanding of the way that language ideologies are constructed as models of and models for discursive practices. While I am clearly paraphrasing Clifford Geertz (1966) here, I am shifting the image in such a way as to grant agency less to "symbols" and "meanings" (for Geertz) or to language ideologies than to the producers and receivers of discourse. The way that ideologies of language and discursive practices are linked is not somehow fixed by or inherent in cultural and/or linguistic patterns but is created, legitimated, and challenged as discourse is produced and circulated. The cultural and political effectiveness of ideologies of language derives from the iconic, synecdochic, and highly reductive ways that they are linked to discursive practices. This relationship simultaneously involves powerful processes of mimesis, construction, and regimentation. Work on metapragmatics and reflexive speech (see Silverstein 1976, 1979; Lucy 1993), performance approaches (see Bauman 1977, Hymes 1975), ethnopoetics (see Hymes 1981), and the social significance of formal patterning (see Jakobson 1960; Feld 1990[1982]; Graham 1995; Haviland 1996; Urban 1986, 1988) suggests that a wide range of representational processes can be packed into particular discourses. At the same time that ideologies of language highlight and thus transform certain aspects of discursive practices, they erase or minimize others. Forms of writing and electronic mediation are also powerful tools for metadiscursive selection and reification, and they are similarly dependent on the objects that they purport to represent at the same time that they constitute powerful means of constructing their objects.

It is, in my estimation, particularly crucial for students of language ideologies to attend closely in both empirical and analytic terms to the way that particular ideologies are discursively linked to competing ideologies and modes of representation. The problem is that scholars, like other producers and consumers of discourse, have their own vested interests in particular sorts of reifications. Thus, while attending to the representational practices that are framed as language ideologies can help open up broad questions of reification, this line of investigation can lead in the opposite direction when ideologies of language are characterized as standing in one-to-one, uncontested relationships with social or linguistic groups. When scholars reify dominant ideologies in this way, they can play a conspicuous role in naturalizing attempts to erase questions of difference, inequality, and contestation.

NOTES

My primary debt in this paper is to the residents of the Mariusa region, particularly Santiago Rivera and Manuel Torres, and of the communities of K^{w}amuhu and Murako. Rosalino Fernández, Librado Moraleda, and Santiago Rivera kindly helped me transcribe and translate the recordings. Portions of this paper were presented at the Annual Meeting of the American Anthropological Association in Chicago in a session on language ideology, organized by Bambi B. Schieffelin, Paul Kroskrity, and Kathryn Woolard (1991) and in a colloquium in the Department of Anthropology, New York University (1992). The support of the Linguistics Program of the National Science Foundation, the Wenner-Gren Foundation for Anthropological Research, and Vassar College are deeply appreciated, as are critical readings by Bambi Schieffelin and Kit Woolard.

1. The *Censo Indígena de Venezuela, 1992* (OCEI [1993]) places the Warao population in the Delta Amacuro State at 20,942, while 2,716 are listed as living in the neighboring state of Monagas and 266 in Sucre. Warao also live in adjoining areas of Guyana.

2. Note that Sherzer 1983 reports that metalinguistics similarly pervades the discourse of Kuna political leaders.

3. For comparative data on this point, see Urban 1988.

4. See Sherzer 1982 for a strikingly similar ideology of ritual language that is evident in Kuna society.

5. I do not mean to suggest here that only women wail or that only men sing *hoa* songs. While I have never seen a man wail, I have heard that some individuals do perform alongside women in certain areas of the delta. Similarly, although most *hoa* practitioners are men, women are occasionally able to become skilled in these practices; I had the good fortune of being able to work with one of them.

6. An important exception in this regard pertains to certain sections of curing songs used by *wisidatu* curers; here a relative of the patient engages in a dialogue with the ma-

levolent spirits—as embodied in the voice of the practitioner (see Briggs 1996b). I have not encountered any examples of such dialogic interaction in attempts to cure victims of *hoa* spirits.

7. This is not to say, however, that exchanges of gossip do not take place away from the social and spatial centers of these events. For example, when the residents of various Mariusan communities gather for the *nahanamu* ritual cycle, exchanges of gossip seem to take place everywhere and at all times—except on the dance platform and in the "spirit house."

8. In view of the complex restrictions regarding the use of Warao names, particularly curers' names, I use pseudonyms in this article.

9. I was not seeking to lead the two men into thinking that I was not recording the conversation. I had been using a larger tape recorder with two large microphones earlier in order to document the exchange of greetings between the two families and other aspects of the conversation. The small tape recorder, which was clearly visible and had been in operation the entire time, provided a backup, ambient recording of the entire encounter between the families. When we later listened to this recording, the two families gave me permission to use it.

10. The narrative is broken into lines in accordance with prosodic and grammatical features and in keeping with turn taking. Brackets between lines indicate overlaps in adjacent turns.

11. For a fascinating parallel situation, see Haviland's 1996 study of the role of parallel couplets in Tzotzil-language Zinacantecan dispute mediation.

12. Francisco Gómez is skilled in treating lacerations, venomous stings, and the like; this type of curative practice does not, however, involve contact with powerful malevolent spirits, such as *hoa*.

13. See Abrahams 1983; Besnier 1989; Brenneis 1984; Goodwin 1980, 1990; Haviland 1977; and Shuman 1986 for comparative data on the interpersonal dynamics and sociopolitical effects of information disclosure and withholding in gossip.

14. In another article (1996b), I document a curing ceremony in which a different type of practitioner (a *wisidatu*) ventriloquized the voices of *hebu* spirits in legitimating Mr. Torres's position in the course of the struggle with Mr. Rivera. Treating Mr. Torres's grandson for an acute respiratory infection thus evoked the "regime of truth" associated with curing in attempting to validate Mr. Torres's (and an ally's) attempt to harness the power of the nation-state for their own ends. This event took place in June 1990, just over three years after I recorded the gossip session.

REFERENCES

Abrahams, Roger D. 1983. *The Man-of-words in the West Indies: Performance and the Emergence of Creole Culture*. Baltimore: Johns Hopkins University Press.

Anderson, Benedict. [1983] 1991. *Imagined Communities: Reflections on the Origin and Spread of Nationalism*. London: Verso.

Bauman, Richard. 1977. *Verbal Art as Performance*. Prospect Heights, Ill.: Waveland Press.

———. 1983. *Let Your Words Be Few: Symbolism of Speaking and Silence among Seventeenth-century Quakers*. Cambridge: Cambridge University Press.

Bauman, Richard, and Charles L. Briggs. 1990. Poetics and Performance as Critical Perspectives on Language and Social Life. *Annual Review of Anthropology* 19:59–88.

———. 1994. Language Philosophy as Language Ideology: John Locke and Johann Gottfried Herder. Paper presented at the Seminar on Language Ideology, School of American Research, Santa Fe, N.M.

Besnier, Niko. 1989. Information Withholding as a Manipulative and Collusive Strategy in Nukulaelae Gossip. *Language in Society* 18:315–341.

Boas, Franz. 1911. Introduction to *Handbook of American Indian Languages*, pp. 5–83. Washington, D.C.: Government Printing Office.

Bourdieu, Pierre. 1977. *Outline of a Theory of Practice*. Translated by Richard Nice. Cambridge: Cambridge University Press.

———. 1991. *Language and Symbolic Power*. Translated by Gino Raymond and Matthew Adamson. Cambridge, Mass.: Harvard University Press.

Brenneis, Donald L. 1984. Straight Talk and Sweet Talk: Political Discourse in an Occasionally Egalitarian Community. In *Dangerous Words: Language and Politics in the Pacific*, ed. Donald Lawrence Brenneis and Fred R. Myers, pp. 69–84. New York: New York University Press.

———. 1990. Dramatic Gestures: The Fiji Indian *Pancayat* as Therapeutic Event. In *Disentangling: Conflict Discourse in Pacific Societies*, ed. Karen Ann Watson-Gegeo and Geoffrey M. White, pp. 214–38. Stanford, Calif.: Stanford University Press.

———. 1996. Telling Troubles: Narrative, Conflict and Experience. In *Disorderly Discourse: Narrative, Conflict and Inequality*, ed. Charles L. Briggs, pp. 41–52. New York: Oxford University Press.

Briggs, Charles L. 1992a. Linguistic Ideologies and the Naturalization of Power in Warao Discourse. *Pragmatics* 2(3):387–404.

———. 1992b. "Since I Am a Woman I Will Chastise My Relatives": Gender, Reported Speech, and the Reproduction of Social Relations in Warao Ritual Wailing. *American Ethnologist* 19:337–361.

———. 1993a. Men's Evidence, Women's Words: Evidence, Deixis, and Power in Warao Women's Gossip Narratives of Shamanic Illness. Paper presented at the Annual Meeting of the American Anthropological Association, Washington, D.C.

———. 1993b. Metadiscursive Practices and Scholarly Authority in Folkloristics. *Journal of American Folklore* 106(422):387–434.

———. 1993c. Personal Sentiments and Polyphonic Voices in Warao Women's Ritual Wailing: Music and Poetics in a Critical and Collective Discourse. *American Anthropologist* 95:929–957.

———. 1996a. Conflict, Language Ideologies, and Privileged Arenas of Discursive Authority in Warao Dispute Mediation. In *Disorderly Discourse: Narrative, Conflict and Inequality*, ed. Charles L. Briggs, pp. 204–242. New York: Oxford University Press.

———. 1996b. The Meaning of Nonsense, the Poetics of Embodiment, and the Production of Power in Warao Shamanistic Healing. In *The Performance of Healing*, ed. Carol Laderman and Marina Roseman, pp. 185–232. New York: Routledge.

Briggs, Charles L., and Richard Bauman. 1992. Genre, Intertextuality, and Social Power. *Journal of Linguistic Anthropology* 2:131–172.

Briggs, Charles L., and Clara Mantini Briggs. 1997. "The Indians Accept Death as a Normal, Natural Event": Institutional Authority, Cultural Reasoning, and Discourses of Genocide in a Venezuelan Cholera Epidemic. *Social Identities* 3:439–469.

Comaroff, Jean, and John Comaroff. 1991. *Of Revelation and Revolution: Christianity, Colonialism, and Consciousness in South Africa*. Chicago: University of Chicago Press.

Du Bois, John W. 1992. Meaning without Intention: Lessons from Divination. In *Responsibility and Evidence in Oral Discourse*, ed. Jane H. Hill and Judith T. Irvine, pp. 48–71. Cambridge: Cambridge University Press.

Duranti, Alesandro. 1988. Intentions, Language, and Social Action in a Samoan Context. *Journal of Pragmatics* 12:13–33.

Feld, Steven. [1982] 1990. *Sound and Sentiment: Birds, Weeping, Poetics, and Song in Kaluli Expression*, 2nd ed. Philadelphia: University of Pennsylvania Press.

Foucault, Michel. 1980. *Power/Knowledge: Selected Interviews and Other Writings, 1972–1977*. Translated by Colin Gordon et al. New York: Pantheon.

———. [1976] 1978. *The History of Sexuality*. Vol. 1: *An Introduction*. Translated by Robert Hurley. New York: Vintage.

Fraser, Nancy. 1992. Rethinking the Public Sphere: A Contribution to the Critique of Actually Existing Democracy. In *Habermas and the Public Sphere*, ed. Craig Calhoun, pp. 109–142. Cambridge, Mass.: MIT Press.

Gal, Susan. 1979. *Language Shift: Social Determinants of Linguistic Change in Bilingual Austria*. New York: Academic Press.

———. 1991a. Bartók's Funeral: Representations of Europe in Hungarian Political Rhetoric. *American Ethnologist* 18(3):440–458.

———. 1991b. Between Speech and Silence: The Problematics of Research on Language and Gender. In *Gender at the Crossroads of Knowledge: Feminist Anthropology in the Postmodern Era*, ed. Michaela di Leonardo, pp. 175–203. Berkeley: University of California Press.

———. 1993. Diversity and Contestation in Linguistic Ideologies: German Speakers in Hungary. *Language in Society* 22(3):337–359.

Gal, Susan, and Kathryn A. Woolard, eds. 1995. Constructing Languages and Publics. *Pragmatics* 5(2):129–282.

Geertz, Clifford. 1966. Religion as a Cultural System. In *Anthropological Approaches to the Study of Religion*, ed. Michael P. Banton, pp. 1–46. London: Tavistock.

Gluckman, Max. 1963. Gossip and Scandal. *Current Anthropology* 4:307–316.

Goodwin, Marjorie Harness. 1980. He-Said-She-Said: Formal Cultural Procedures for the Construction of a Gossip Dispute. *American Ethnologist* 7:674–695.

———. 1990. *He-Said-She-Said: Talk as Social Organization among Black Children*. Bloomington: Indiana University Press.

Graham, Laura. 1995. *Performing Dreams: The Discourse of Immortality among the Xavante of Central Brazil.* Austin: University of Texas Press.

Gramsci, Antonio. 1971. *Selections from the Prison Notebooks of Antonio Gramsci*. Translated by Quintin Hoare and Geoffrey Nowell Smith. New York: International Publishers.

———. 1995. *Further Selections from the Prison Notebooks*. Translated by Derek Boothman. Minneapolis: University of Minnesota Press.

Habermas, Jürgen. [1962] 1989. *The Structural Transformation of the Public Sphere: An Inquiry into a Category of Bourgeois Society*. Translated by Thomas Burger. Cambridge, Mass.: MIT Press.

Hannerz, Ulf. 1967. Gossip, Networks and Culture in a Black American Ghetto. *Ethnos* 32:35–60.

Haviland, John Beard. 1977. *Gossip, Reputation, and Knowledge in Zinacantan*. Chicago: University of Chicago Press.

———. 1996. "We Want to Borrow Your Mouth": Tzotzil Marital Squabbles. In *Disorderly Discourse: Narrative, Conflict and Inequality*, ed. Charles L. Briggs, pp. 158–203. New York: Oxford University Press.

Hymes, Dell. 1974. *Foundations of Sociolinguistics: An Ethnographic Approach*. Philadelphia: University of Pennsylvania Press.

———. 1975. Breakthrough into Performance. In *Folklore: Performance and Communication*, ed. Dan Ben-Amos and Kenneth S. Goldstein, pp. 11–74. The Hague: Mouton.

———. 1981. *"In Vain I Tried to Tell You": Studies in Native American Ethnopoetics*. Philadelphia: University of Pennsylvania Press.

Jakobson, Roman. 1957. *Shifters, Verbal Categories, and the Russian Verb*. Cambridge, Mass.: Harvard University Russian Language Project.

———. 1960. Closing Statement: Linguistics and Poetics. In *Style in Language*, ed. Thomas A. Sebeok, pp. 350–377. Cambridge, Mass.: MIT Press.

———. [1921] 1973. Modern Russian Poetry: Velimir Khlebnikov. In *Major Soviet Writers*, ed. Edward Brown, pp. 58–82. London: Oxford University Press.

———. 1976. Metalanguage as a Linguistic Problem. In *Roman Jakobson: Selected Writings*. Vol. 7: *Contributions to Comparative Mythology: Studies in Linguistics and Philology, 1972–1982*, ed. Stephen Rudy, pp. 113–121. Berlin: Mouton de Gruyter.

Jameson, Frederic. 1981. *The Political Unconscious: Narrative as a Socially Symbolic Act*. Ithaca, N.Y.: Cornell University Press.

Joseph, John E., and Talbot J. Taylor, eds. 1990. *Ideologies of Language*. London: Routledge.

Kroskrity, Paul V. 1993. *Language, History, and Identity: Ethnolinguistic Studies of the Arizona Tewa*. Tucson: University of Arizona Press.

Landes, Joan. 1988. *Women and the Public Sphere in the Age of the French Revolution*. Ithaca, N.Y.: Cornell University Press.

Layrisse, Miguel, George Salas, and H. Dieter Heinen. 1980. Vital Statistics of Five Warao Subtribes. In *Demographic and Biological Studies of the Warao Indians*, ed. Johannes Wilbert and Miguel Layrisse, pp. 60–69. Los Angeles: UCLA Latin American Center Publications.

Lucy, John A., ed. 1993. *Reflexive Language: Reported Speech and Metapragmatics*. Cambridge: Cambridge University Press.

Merry, Sally Engle. 1984. Rethinking Gossip and Scandal. In *Toward a General Theory of Social Control*. Vol. 1: *The Fundamentals*, ed. Donald Black, pp. 277–301. New York: Academic Press.

OCEI (Oficina Central de Estadística e Informática). 1993. *Censo indígena de Venezuela, 1992*. 2 vols. Caracas: Oficina Central de Estadística e Informática.

Olsen, Dale. 1996. *Music of the Warao of Venezuela: Song People of the Rain Forest*. Gainesville: University of Florida Press.

Rosaldo, Michelle Z. 1980. *Knowledge and Passion: Ilongot Notions of Self and Social Life*. Cambridge: Cambridge University Press.

———. 1982. The Things We Do with Words: Ilongot Speech Acts and Speech Act Theory in Philosophy. *Language in Society* 11:203–235.

Rosaldo, Renato. 1980. *Ilongot Headhunting, 1883–1974: A Study in Society and History*. Stanford, Calif.: Stanford University Press.

Sacks, Harvey. 1992. *Lectures on Conversation*. Edited by Gail Jefferson. Oxford: Blackwell.

Saussure, Ferdinand de. [1916] 1959. *A Course in General Linguistics*. Translated by Wade Baskin. New York: McGraw-Hill.

Schutz, Alfred. 1966. *Collected Papers*. Vol. 3: *Studies in Phenomenological Philosophy*. The Hague: Martinus Nijhoff.

Scott, James C. 1985. *Weapons of the Weak: Everyday Forms of Peasant Resistance*. New Haven, Conn.: Yale University Press.

Searle, John R. 1969. *Speech Acts: An Essay in the Philosophy of Language*. Cambridge: Cambridge University Press.

Sherzer, Joel. 1982. The Interplay of Structure and Function in Kuna Narrative, or: How to Grab a Snake in the Darien. In *Analyzing Discourse: Text and Talk*, ed. Deborah Tannen, pp. 306–322. Washington, D.C.: Georgetown University Press.

———. 1983. *Kuna Ways of Speaking: An Ethnographic Perspective.* Austin: University of Texas Press.

Shuman, Amy. 1986. *Storytelling Rights: The Uses of Oral and Written Texts by Urban Adolescents.* Cambridge: Cambridge University Press.

Silverstein, Michael. 1976. Shifters, Linguistic Categories, and Cultural Description. In *Meaning in Anthropology*, ed. Keith Basso and Henry A. Selby, pp. 11–55. Albuquerque: University of New Mexico Press.

———. 1979. Language Structure and Linguistic Ideology. In *The Elements: A Parasession on Linguistic Units and Levels*, ed. Paul R. Clyne, William Hanks, and Carol L. Hofbauer, pp. 193–247. Chicago: Chicago Linguistic Society.

———. 1985. Language and the Culture of Gender: At the Intersection of Structure, Usage, and Ideology. In *Semiotic Mediation: Sociocultural and Psychological Perspectives*, ed. Elizabeth Mertz and Richard J. Parmentier, pp. 219–259. Orlando, Fla.: Academic Press.

———. 1987. The Monoglot "Standard" in America. Working Papers and Proceedings of the Center for Psychosocial Studies 13. Chicago: Center for Psychosocial Studies.

———. 1993. Metapragmatic Discourse and Metapragmatic Function. In *Reflexive Language: Reported Speech and Metapragmatics*, ed. John A. Lucy, pp. 33–58. Cambridge: Cambridge University Press.

Silverstein, Michael, and Greg Urban, eds. 1996. *Natural Histories of Discourse.* Chicago: University of Chicago Press.

Szwed, John F. 1966. Gossip, Drinking and Social Control in a Newfoundland Parish. *Ethnology* 5:434–441.

Taussig, Michael. 1980. *The Devil and Commodity Fetishism in South America.* Chapel Hill: University of North Carolina Press.

———. 1987. *Shamanism, Colonialism, and the Wild Man: A Study in Terror and Healing.* Chicago: University of Chicago Press.

———. 1991. *The Nervous System.* New York: Routledge.

Urban, Greg. 1986. Ceremonial Dialogues in South America. *American Anthropologist* 88:371–386.

———. 1988. Ritual Wailing in Amerindian Brazil. *American Anthropologist* 90:385–400.

White, Luise. 1994. Between Gluckman and Foucault: Historicizing Rumor and Gossip. *Social Dynamics* 20:75–92.

———. 1997. Blood and Fire: Rumor and History in East and Central Africa. Unpublished manuscript.

Wilbert, Johannes. 1972. Tobacco and Shamanistic Ecstasy among the Warao of Venezuela. In *Flesh of the Gods: The Ritual Use of Hallucinogens*, ed. Peter Furst, pp. 55–83. New York: Praeger.

Williams, Raymond. 1977. *Marxism and Literature.* London: Oxford University Press.

Woolard, Kathryn A. 1985. Language Variation and Cultural Hegemony: Toward an Integration of Sociolinguistic and Social Theory. *American Ethnologist* 12:738–748.

———. 1989a. *Double Talk: Bilingualism and the Politics of Ethnicity in Catalonia.* Stanford, Calif.: Stanford University Press.

———. 1989b. Sentences in the Language Prison: The Rhetorical Structuring of an American Language Policy Debate. *American Ethnologist* 16:268–278.

12

Our Ideologies and Theirs

JAMES COLLINS

During the controversies over the Columbian Quincentenary, it became common to speak of the relation between European-derived political formations and indigenous societies as "encounters." Much has also been written recently about the dialogue between anthropologists and their consultants and about how this dialogue fruitfully complicates the apparent dichotomy of observer and observed. It is a theme of this book that ideology is generated in particular social sites, often sites of conflictual exchange. This chapter speaks to the various senses of contact, engagement, and intermeshing involved in the study of ideology. I present a case study from native Northern California that focuses on two language encounters: one of an analyst and native speakers during linguistic fieldwork, one of a native community and state credentialing agencies in official language renewal programs. In both encounters we find divergent beliefs about the nature of language as structure, its place in social action, and its relation to such collective orders as family, tribe, and nation-state. These divergences point to a complex, interlinked history of scientific claim, official recognition, and local contestation that involves field linguists and anthropologists, bureaucratic offices, and an Athabaskan-descended people who have come to be known as the Tolowa. Thus, we truly speak of "our ideologies and theirs" as an intertwining, both wanted and unwanted, of academic and Tolowa perspectives, of bureaucratic imperatives and local concerns. What follows is necessarily about us-and-them. Rather than a general definition of language ideology and an analysis of how Tolowa language beliefs and language use relates to their social order, I present a case study of interlinked and often rival assumptions about and interests in language, focusing on the divergent beliefs, and showing how assumptions and interests become authoritative in particular contexts.

The Tolowa are an Athabaskan-speaking people who lived along the Smith River valley and the coastal plain in what is now Del Norte County, California (see Figure 12.1). They were decimated by Anglo conquest, and their language is nearly extinct. However, for the last three decades, various Tolowa have been involved in an ambitious effort to document and maintain their language, as a part of more general efforts to reassert a distinct social and political identity. These efforts have involved local initiatives to document and teach the language, the securing of state and federal monies for native language education, and the articulating of Tolowa claims about language, culture, and tradition that sometimes agree and sometimes disagree with academic accounts.

In the second half of the nineteenth century, the Tolowa were subjected to the same genocidal events and policies suffered by many native peoples in Oregon and Northern California (Norton 1979, Rawls 1984). By the turn of the century an original population of more than two thousand had been reduced to 121, according to the U.S. Census of 1910 (Kroeber 1925, Gould 1978), from which point it slowly rebounded to current figures of between four hundred and five hundred people. The consequences of genocide and cultural disorientation have been emphasized in an anthropological literature that has repeatedly announced the extinction or near extinction of Tolowa culture and language (Drucker 1937, Gould 1978). Indeed, the Tolowa could earnestly remark, "Rumors of our death are greatly exaggerated." They have been reported as nearing extinction for nearly as long as they have been subject to either the gaze of academic scrutiny or the grip of bureaucratic recordkeeping; yet they have managed to survive into the late twentieth century.

In many respects, the Tolowa are similar to the surrounding white, rural working-class population—they perform similar wagework, drive similar vehicles, wear similar clothing, and share musical preferences. But there are also differences. Most Tolowa are dark-haired and dark-eyed, and they spend more time with other Indians, both other Tolowa and Yurok, than they do with whites. They have been parties to a decades-long struggle to claim and exercise aboriginal fishing rights along the Klamath and the Smith rivers, as well as along various beaches north from Crescent City to the Oregon border. This puts them in potential conflict with commercial or tourist fishermen (both non-Indian) as well as state Fish and Game officials. Many Tolowa go to feather dances and salmon bakes, typically sponsored and organized by prominent families—the extended, inclusive, multigenerational kin groups that were historically crucial in securing population stability after the cataclysm of conquest (Thornton 1986). Some Tolowa speak fully or know fragments of "Indian language," which academics and official types and now increasing numbers of local people call Tolowa.[1] Tolowa is recognized as a language course in the local high school, and it has been codified in two editions of a dictionary and grammar (Bommelyn and Humphrey 1984, 1989).

The past thirty years have witnessed a renaissance of cultural activity among the Tolowa, as among many other native peoples in Northwest California.[2] This

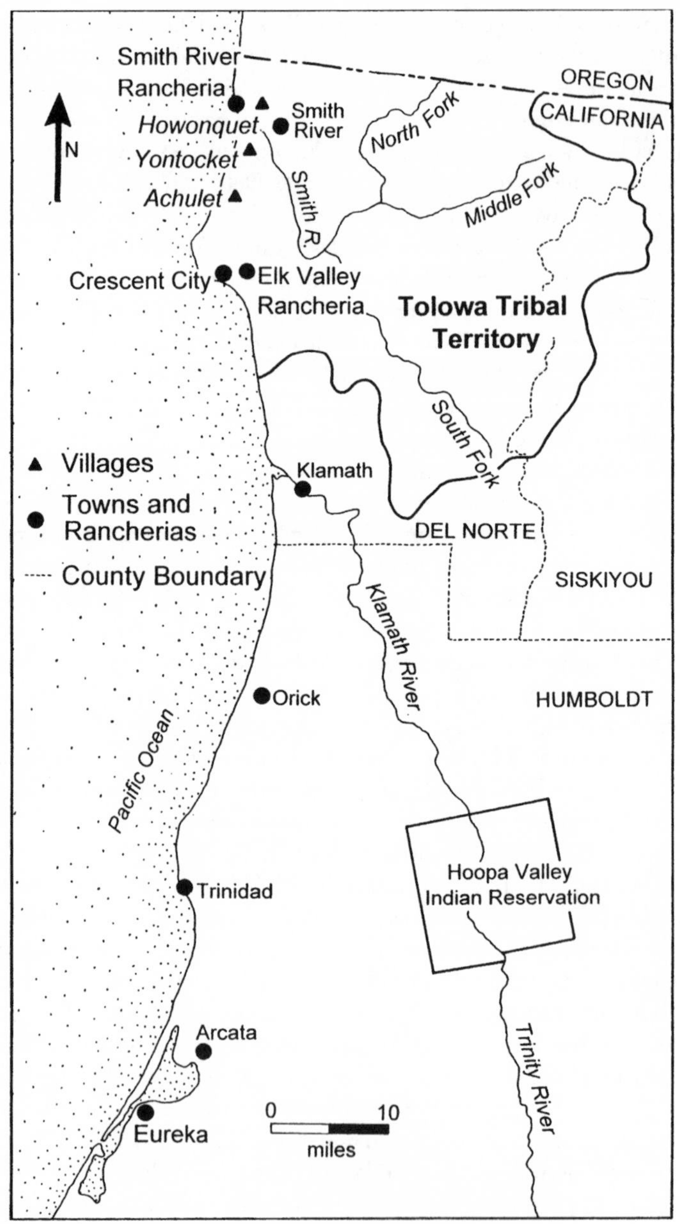

Figure 12.1 Map of pre-contact territory, Del Norte county line, and historical villages and towns. From Collins, *Understanding Tolowa Histories* (1998), with permission from the author.

rebirth has involved political regroupment, cultural assertion, language scholarship, and resource claims. In this multifaceted resurgence and refashioning of a collective identity, various traditional social forms and processes have reemerged in more public arenas: the initiative and rivalry of key extended families in organizing cultural and political activities; the continuing practice of ocean and river fishing, despite ongoing conflicts with state Fish and Game agencies and seafront property developers; and the continously revamped *NedaS*[3] 'dance'. At the same time, their land base has been reduced to a tiny fraction of its original size, and the Tolowa have had to rely on wage labor for survival. Practitioners of cultural/spiritual activities such as dancing have played a game of hide-and-seek with both legal officials and churchmen throughout the century, and now the specialists and organizers are few in number and overextended. The Tolowa language has not been learned as a first language by children since the 1920s. As a result, the linguistic community is moribund.[4]

This chapter is part of a more general effort on my part to understand Tolowa survival and persistence. A more comprehensive analysis is presented in another book (Collins 1998), in which issues of history, politics, and language are more fully developed. For our purposes here, suffice it to say that the effort to understand has required me to challenge disciplinary perspectives—to shift away from a "salvage linguistics" that documents for science another dying language, while trying to understand what losing a language means for those who face that loss; to move away from a "salvage ethnography" that analyzes memory culture, while trying to understand current social dynamics against the backdrop of long-announced and externally perceived cultural death. Such questioning of disciplinary perspectives is also necessary, I believe, when analyzing language ideologies. As academics, our categories of analysis are a part of linguistic practices that characterize social realities, and we inhabit positions as specialists in state-certified institutions that make our statements and our silences unavoidably interest laden.

The two encounters presented and analyzed in this chapter should help flesh out this argument. The first concerns fieldwork exchanges, during which academic categories of analysis are quietly though tellingly resisted by native language consultants. The second encounter concerns certification struggles, during which academics' institutional positions as experts are part of a larger contest to define social and linguistic realities.

Field Encounters

I began fieldwork on Tolowa late in 1981, having been encouraged to do so because it was an Athabaskan language that apparently had never been adequately described and for which there were several living native speakers—the classic charter for "salvage linguistics." Traveling to the Northwest tip of the state of California, I made contact with one of those speakers, who was quite happy to "talk Indian language" with me.

Throughout the next several years of short periods of fieldwork, ranging from three to four days to two months, I concentrated on structural questions in my analysis. I began with a restricted set of syntactic questions derived from earlier work on the evolution of Athabaskan case-marking and verb transitivity. Early on I worked up a short synoptic overview of the grammatical system—the phonology, word-formation processes, and primary syntactic patterns—and spent the next several years writing up expansions of small sections of the overview. These expansions include analyses of historical change in the system of alienably and inalienably possessed nominals (Collins 1985); a fuller description of linked processes of change in vocalic quality, length, and nasalization (Collins 1989); and an analysis of syntactic structure and word formation (Collins 1988). Throughout the interspersed fieldwork and analysis, I had as my primary object of analysis grammatical structure. Phonology and syntax were investigated to establish the grammatical core of the language. Lexicon was analyzed to establish the complex combinatory mechanisms that lay at the heart of the language, at the intersection of word formation and syntax as typically understood. Texts were elicited and analyzed as ways of expanding the analysis of lexicon and syntax.

Throughout this period, I noted the good humor of various language consultants with my focused and narrow elicitations of contrastive alternates and distributional possibilities, whether of sound structure, word structure, or sentence structure. But I also slowly registered a consistently different orientation to language. Simply put, they were interested in words, not grammar.

At the end of a long and wearying elicitation session on phonological contrasts that involved multiple repetitions of the form for 'coyote' */sk'3m'/* (the second consonant of which, */k'/*, is nearly inaudible in this environment), my first language consultant, Ed Richards Jr., launched into a story of how *sk'3m'* fell from the skies. He told the story first in English, then in Tolowa, and followed with laughing yet serious commentary on Coyote's trickster ways and sexual misdoings. After a difficult session on the rarely occurring reciprocal affix */L/*, my second primary consultant, Berneice Humphrey, provided one of her "favorite words" made with this reciprocal form, *LuLte'* 'lovers' (literally: 'they want each other'). Our working sessions often contained a tension between my efforts at focused paradigm elicitation and her presentation of diverse lexical constructions, her questioning of the distinction between whether one "would" and "could" say a given utterance, and her insistence that controlled paradigmatic elaboration was *not* how the "Indian language" operated.

Loren Bommelyn, the current teacher of the Tolowa language course in the local high school and a prime force in the Tolowa effort to document and maintain their own language, has impressed me over the years, both with his interest in structural patterns and, more recently, with his consistent placement of both lexical items and sentences in narrative or conversational contexts. Counterposed to the linguist's presentation and consideration of grammatical patterns in isolation, he always presented a discursive context, and typically a cultural exegesis. Finally, while working with a group of local Tolowa adults whose expertise in the language was self-acknowledged to be limited, I was made curious by the husband of one such consultant, a man in his fifties whose laconic manner, jeans, and pickup made him seem the typical western farmhand. Yet while he, his wife, and I talked about "old words" and their loss, he commented on his memory of the older folks, their continuous stories that he missed, and, most pointedly, the fact that they had names for every feature of geography in the Smith River drainage, as he put it: "a name for every riffle in the creek."

What do we make of these differing orientations, to grammatical regularity versus lexical particularity? It is a familiar contrast, an old story among fieldworkers, and our linguistic discipline gives one explanation. Since Boas (1911), Saussure ([1916]1959), and Sapir ([1925]1949), we have known that grammatical patterns are abstract. Speakers are rarely aware of them explicitly, although those patterns form the cognitive preconditions for their speech behavior. A recent book that celebrates the cognitive riches of human language argues that what speakers know when they know a language is really not knowledge in any normal sense of the term; rather, it is a deeply unconscious feeling for form and pattern, accessible only indirectly (Jackendoff 1993).

Anthropological linguistics has come at the problem of lexicon and grammar slightly differently and has been more preoccupied with the issue of awareness of language. Sapir argued that regular grammatical forms and processes are abstract, part of the "conceptual world of science," while words are practical, the province "of history, of art" (1921:32–33). Whorf argued that word reference is the focus of our beliefs about how language works but that grammatical configurations, of which we are typically unaware, exert a profound influence on our thinking about the everyday world ([1939]1956). Silverstein has analyzed semiotic constraints on language awareness, arguing that it is the continuously segmentable, referring, and contextually presupposing elements of language that are most salient to consciousness (1981). Thus, it is words that stand forth. They are segmentable (relatively identifiable chunks of form/meaning); they are referential (words are most numerously "content words," depicting some thing, event, or state of affairs); and in most uses they are contextually presupposing (the interlingual question "How do you say 'X'" presumes a shared 'X', a preexisting, presupposable reality that words and utterances simply describe or tell about).

In both lines of argument, it is implied that native speakers are aware of and preoccupied with words; only the comparative analyst recovers the grammatical configuration. We need, however, to complicate this received wisdom by asking about the analyst's relation to language. As Briggs notes elsewhere in this volume, and as Silverstein has argued in some detail (1979), we cannot grant sciences of language a special status vis-à-vis ideologies of language. Their fates are linked, and one way to explore that linkage is to pursue some questions. In particular, What are the historical conditions for the production of structuralist knowledge? What might be missed or overlooked when the "history and art" of words is shunted aside in pursuit of grammatical pattern, the "world of science"?

It is widely acknowledged that structuralist abstraction and generality requires detachment, a distance and distancing, between analyst and object of analysis. This distance and distancing have an historical as well as a contemporary dimension. Voloshinov, in *Marxism and the Philosophy of Language*, argued that Saussurean linguistics, "abstract objectivism" as he termed it, resulted from the development of grammatical analysis through "encounters with the alien voice" (1973:65–82): medieval and early modern grammarians analyzing the texts of nonvernacular classic languages; comparative philologists working with the texts of extinct prior stages of national languages; imperial explorers collecting word lists from the languages of a world they so casually subjected to domination and analysis. Bakhtin (1981) also argues that focusing solely on the stable patterns of the "alien voice" leads to neglect of the dynamic, tension-filled heteroglossia and multivocality of language use. Viewing matters from a contemporary, rather than a historical, perspective, we may say that grammatical analysis requires a removal from everyday preoccupations with language use. In anthropology this detachment typically involves an asymmetrical relation between fieldworker and consultants (in which, paradoxically, the learner sets the agenda for what will be learned). Writing of structuralist analysis and this privileged detachment, Bourdieu has put the matter quite sharply: removed from actual engagement in the worlds it studies, structural analysis substitutes "the logic of intelligibility" for "the logic of practice" (1977; see also Fabian 1983 for similar arguments).

But what of this "logic of practice" in the case at hand? What can we say about this orientation to the native, that is, nonalien *word*? First, we may note that the words are indexes of stories and situations; they are embedded within and associated with the art of remembering, a remembering interested in desire and sexual malfeasance and a remembering concerned with a relationship to land. It is a poststructuralist insight, a renovation of the legacy of Freud, that language is intertwined with desire, understood not only as the erotic taproots of humanity's presocial yearning—though Coyote certainly frolics in these shady glens—but also as desire for *sense*, for mastery, for overcoming life's losses, uncertainties, and mortality through names and tales that render the world meaningful (Kristeva 1981, Lacan 1970, Obeyesekere 1990). The words recalled are also often names for places—"every riffle in the creek"—and knowing the words is tied up with knowing what occurred at those places, why they are called by that name. It is a geography that is also a history. As Kari (1986) has argued for the Alaskan Athabaskan peoples, place names are a mnemonic, a "storage and retrieval" system for oral cultures. As Basso (1990) has argued for the Western Apache, place names encode an evaluative stance, a moral tradition tied to a memory of place. For example, *st3ndas3n* is the name for an island in the Smith River that served as one of the few Tolowa villages that survived the 1850s massacres. The island disappeared by 1906, due to erosion; as site name, *st3ndas3n* figures in tales of cultural exuberance and of white trickery and thievery.[5]

Second, we should note that the stories and situations change. The Tolowa have faced the imminent loss of their language for the past several decades; their story traditions are more endangered than those of the Western Apache, their sense of place more embattled than that of the Alaskan Athabaskans. So there is a new story, rendered in English, a tale of collecting words. Two of the most active members of the local language program volunteered accounts of such collecting in a general discussion of the origins of this program. Loren Bommelyn had several stories of "lost words" being recalled, confirmed, or corrected by aunts and uncles, typically hours or days after an initial language query. Berneice Humphrey told of an older neighbor, "an elder," who would often come several days after an initial query, bringing an "old word" for Berneice to write down and include in the language documentation effort. Old words have value, and it is through relations of kinship and other close ties that the collecting occurs. The collecting and passing on of names and tales is part of Tolowa cultural persistence that connects geography, history, and cosmology (Slagle 1987). As Pred (1990) has argued in *Lost Words and Lost Worlds*, his lexicographical and sociological reconstruction of working-class Stockholm at the turn of the century, names for everyday places and everyday things are forms of appropriation and occupation, ways of being in a place and time. This is true, perhaps especially true, when the occupation is threatened, when one's practice of life and names for the practice of life are overrun by dominant discourses and procedures, whether those of the elite classes in working-class Stockholm or those of settlers and their English in the case of the Tolowa.

I have suggested some of what is at issue when an academic concern with systematic regularity leads to a neglect of linguistic practice, its historical situation, and its sociocultural implications. There is, however, another encounter that we should now consider. It is related to the first, though it occurs on a different, more overtly political terrain. The second encounter is between the Tolowa community, more particularly, its language program, and a network of official institutions concerned with legitimating language.

Contesting Tolowa: Community, Academy, and State

Official institutions (in this case, educational credentialing offices and clearinghouses for native language programs) are concerned with the relation between language and culture seen as the rights of officially defined groups, and their concern with the nexus of language, culture, and group raises a basic question: What kind of description of language is to take priority? Is a structuralist analysis of grammatical and lexical resources to be preferred? There are many reasons for assuming so, but the structuralist paradigm leaves unresolved a fundamental question: What is the location, in social or cognitive space, of structural-grammatical knowledge? Is language to be seen as an abstract, asocial knowledge located in the heads of individual speakers, as standard grammatical theory suggests (Chomsky 1988), or is it a "community grammar," an organization or distillation of aggregate linguistic knowledge and practice (Labov 1972, Hymes 1974)? The close linkage of language and social group suggested by the notion of "community grammar" has proven quite problematic (Bauman et al. 1987, Gumperz 1982), and the individual-speaker option simply avoids the issue. Perhaps another sort of description should take priority, for example, the local description and compilation of the language, drawn from years of consultation with speakers but organized on different principles from standard grammatical analysis. If the latter is preferred, then what about claims that this is not a scientific description of the language? Whichever option is chosen, the question remains: How does language map onto social groups?

In the Tolowa case, this question is particularly vexing, for this community has faced linguistic extinction as the last speakers for whom this was a first language have passed away. Formal Western schooling, Christianization, incorporation into a white-dominated wage economy, and a century of pervasive anti-Indian sentiment have tested and transformed Tolowa resource bases, patterns of kinship, forms of ritual celebration, and language learning (Collins 1997, Gould 1978, Slagle 1985). Since the 1920s, ethnic Tolowa children have learned English first and Tolowa only if specially situated and inclined. The result is that today many adults and children know some of the language, but very few speak it fluently or regularly. Social interaction in family or larger social gatherings may involve selective use of Tolowa words and phrases, but English is the shared and dominant medium.

It was awareness of and concern about the trend toward this state of affairs that led a group of Tolowa to begin resisting linguistic extinction some thirty years ago. Those efforts have resulted in a dictionary and grammar and a teaching program, all of which make claims about language and tradition in the past and in the present. Those claims have not gone uncontested. If individual Tolowa speakers have faced dismissal or ignoring of their lexical interests by a field linguist confident in and unselfconscious of his disciplinary assumptions, the Tolowa in their collective efforts to document and preserve their language have faced questioning by academic linguists and management procedures by state offices charged with administering bilingual and bicultural education programs.

Prior to my fieldwork, as well as that of other academic linguists, various Tolowa people had jointly undertaken to document and analyze their language. Working with a local university-affiliated Indian community development funding consortium, they used a non-IPA transcription system, the Unifon Alphabet, and a basic set of English grammatical categories for their descriptive framework. They proposed and initiated a Tolowa language course in the local high school, which they have conducted continuously since 1973, and they published, in 1984, a first edition and, in 1989, a revised and expanded second edition of *Tolowa Language* (Bommelyn and Humphrey 1989). This is a linguistic compendium comprising more than four hundred pages, an English-to-Tolowa dictionary plus various cultural-linguistic sections on genealogies, place names, and so forth.

This local and self-initiated effort at language preservation has proceeded apace, with low-key and continuing controversies over authentic versions of Tolowa. As I began fieldwork more than a decade ago, I was warned to work with "real speakers" and not with those who ran the language program, who had only "limited knowledge of the language," being people who had learned Tolowa as a second language. And as I worked with my first consultant, an elder whose first language was Tolowa, I was told by academic contacts that he was good but did not know the language as well as 'X' and 'Y', who had passed away. Like some linguistic will-o'-the-wisp, the real Tolowa was always just receding on the historical horizon.[6] The local language program efforts at language documentation and teaching have also been questioned for more than a decade, although never, to my knowledge, in print. Since before beginning fieldwork with this group, I have heard dismissive comments about the value of the Unifon script by various prominent Athabaskanists. One derided it as "look[ing] like a batcode," and another warned me in the mid-1980s against lending any academic credibility to the Unifon script as a system for linguistic description.

There is some justification for this academic skepticism. Those native speakers who died in the 1970s were experienced raconteurs and singers, as well as consultants of choice for midcentury linguistic fieldworkers; those who died in the 1980s had felt quite clearly their linguistic isolation. Those who continue the language program have learned the language as a second language, albeit with a singular dedication and impressive results. Similarly, an analysis of either edition of *Tolowa Language* shows that the Unifon script, which is fundamentally based on English orthography and phonetics, fails to make certain consonantal distinctions found in Tolowa, and it overdifferentiates in the vocalic system. The Tolowa Unifon orthography does not have a separate glottal stop [']; instead, it lists a series of vowel-glottal sequences as separate elements: *I'* for /i/+/'/; *E'* for /e/+/'/; *O'* for /a/+/'/. This solution requires a double series of plain and glottalized vowels, and it does not allow for syllable-initial glottals, as in /n'e/ 'land'. In addition, as noted, the grammatical analysis in *Tolowa Language* is based on a simplified English plan, a past-present-future tense scheme, although this Athabaskan language has aspect as its fundamental temporal category, with tense a secondary derivative. Thus, verb paradigms are listed for present and past tense, as in *naYa* 'he walks' or *nasya* 'he walked', with the *s-* perfective, the *Y-* imperfective, and the *n-* repetitive left unexamined. These problems notwithstanding, we should note a double maneuver in the informal academic criticism: locate the real language prior to or away from current speakers, and locate an "adequate description" elsewhere than in the one currently available, a product of local language activists.

This controversy about authentic knowledge and representation is further overlaid with another knowledge interest. The language program has not existed in isolation. From its inception through the late 1980s, it had received financial support from the California State University–affiliated Center for (Indian) Community Development. Teachers in the local high school language course have received special Indian Teacher Education and Eminence credentials from the California state educational system, with the assistance of the Center for Community Development. And if academic linguists have been dismissive of local efforts at language documentation for their failure to achieve descriptive adequacy, the Community Development Center has also had its axe to grind, for it was deeply enmeshed in the business of getting and administering federal and state monies for a variety of Indian-aimed programs, including programs for bilingual and bicultural education.

In the fall of 1987, shortly after a field trip, I was contacted by an associate director of the Community Development Center. Under increasing pressure to legitimate its linguistic efforts, in the wake of "English Only" legislation in California (Adams and Brink 1991), the center wanted to bring in university-affiliated Athabaskan linguists for workshops on Comparative Athabaskan, the structure of the local Athabaskan languages, and the curriculum of the local language programs. But there was a price tag. It wanted not only expertise for workshops but also positive academic evaluation of testing materials for an Indian Teacher Education credential. In my case, it wanted evaluation of the Tolowa section of the test.

The materials were sent to me. They were interesting documents, revealing an official conception of "exotic" language and social life. The Indian Cultures section of the test asked a series of questions about various cultural domains—traditional kinship, flora, fauna, and domestic-food gathering activities—for a variety of Northwest California Indian groups. Students were tested for knowledge of vocabulary drawn from these domains. The Language section presented the Unifon script for each language, a short list of grammatical features, and a story in each language. The Tolowa examples illustrated verbal paradigms in terms of English tense categories, and the syntax of sentences was difficult to determine from the examples given. The discussion of verb tenses listed present, past, distant past, and mythical past, as if these were regular grammatical categories in all four languages, rather than rhetorical options. It said nothing about verb-internal aspect and listed some incorrect forms for Tolowa (e.g., *nasya* 'he walked' was listed as 'he walks'). I checked the roster of consultant linguists and saw listed Algonkianists and Hokanists affiliated with California universities but no one who worked on Athabaskan languages—that is, no one who had worked with the relevant language family.

I wrote back to the associate director, expressing my interest in conducting a workshop and my commitment to working with the Tolowa folks who ran the local language program but also laying out my criticisms of the test as it existed and offering to work on its revision. Shortly thereafter I was phoned by the associate director and told that the center needed a positive evaluation if it was to keep monies for its teacher education program. I said that I had to stand by my criticisms of the existing materials. Shortly after that conversation, I was contacted by the local Tolowa language teacher, who was checking a report from the associate director that I, along with other linguists, was trying to "wreck everything they had done." We talked, I explained my position, and I found out that he had never seen a copy of the teacher's certification test. I sent a copy, and we subsequently discussed some of the Tolowa examples, the oddness and ungrammaticality of which he also found puzzling.[7]

The lesson of this incident is that it is not just the local Tolowa people and distant academic linguists who have a stake in defining an "Indian Language." Local funding consortia also have an interest in such an enterprise, especially as they encounter and interact with the certifying and credentialing operations of state agencies, that is, as a given representation of language is called into question or maintained as legitimate (Bourdieu 1991). In the case just discussed, it did not matter that the treatment of culture was overly simple and the description of language bungled from the perspective of native speaker or linguist. What mattered for ongoing legitimacy was rendering a claim, a representation of cultural and linguistic knowledge of "the Tolowa," in the appropriate, stipulated format of a test and then obtaining expert support, in the form of academics on an advisory board, regardless of their particular linguistic specialization.[8]

We may compare this legitimation effort through professorial and other expert opinion with Tolowa-internal disputes about authority for language. Local Tolowa, both older adults with varying knowledge of the language and their younger kinspeople, do at times question the validity of the *Tolowa Language* compendium and the form of the language learned in the local school. They do not criticize it, however, as academic linguists do, as "not really Tolowa" because it is a violation of a stable structural system that existed prior to current circumstances. Rather, they say, "That is not how we at Smith River [or Achulet or Elk Valley] speak . . .

that is not how my family spoke." Unlike many Americans who assume that cultural chaos reigns unless there is an official standard language (Adams and Brink 1991), Tolowa skeptics question the effort to have a *general* linguistic description for the entire speech community. They call on local definitions of language, as the communicative wherewithal of extended kinship groupings, a view of language and collective order apparently found in much of the aboriginal Pacific Northwest (see Hymes 1981). And, indeed, any inquiry into current cultural and political efforts, whether to preserve fishing rights, to obtain services for a Rancheria, or to initiate language preservation, quickly unveils the importance of local kin groupings, albeit in the name of a larger tribal-national social group (see Collins 1998).

Conclusion

The preceding analysis raises the hoary problem of emic and etic perspectives. Can we study Tolowa language ideology (*their* emic beliefs about language structure and use in relation to collective order) in some neutral, descriptive, etic metalanguage, or must ideological analysis also interrogate our ideologies (*our* beliefs and practices in relation to partially shared social arrangements)? I argue for the latter position. Contemporary American Indian social conditions often involve intricate and volatile connections between local lifeways and state-level processes of a legal and regulatory nature. In such circumstances, academic researchers are never disinterested; they are always tied to interests—local interests, official interests, career interests, perhaps all simultaneously and uneasily.[9] Academic beliefs about language and academic words about language, however well buttressed by accepted theory, are part of the social game that links Indian lives to university careers and both to bureaucratic-legal descriptions and decisions.

Let me review the key encounters discussed in this chapter and what they reveal about contrasting, contested views of, and practices with language. In the field encounter, we have an orientation to words as cultural indices in a situation of enduring alarm about the state of traditional linguistic culture—a culture of stories and dance songs, of names "for every riffle in the creek," of an "Indian language" now spoken by very few. This contrasts with an orientation to grammatical pattern, our structuralist legacy, which bequeaths us both a powerful theory of language description and fundamental ambiguities about the social mooring of linguistic systems. In the local/nonlocal encounter over "authentic" Tolowa we have a multiparty conflict: academic linguists question local efforts in the name of an always earlier, more systematic system; certifying officials seek expert opinion to validate an image of ethnic cultural-linguistic tradition-as-test; and local people question the presumption of a general representation, while recognizing that without efforts at such representation, the language tradition is indeed "lost."

In such encounters, ideology is always present. It reveals itself in basic assumptions about what counts and in practices that build representations (documents, descriptions, images, and stories) that reflect those assumptions. It is present in efforts to authorize one representation and undermine others, efforts rooted in conflicting and complicit institutional, disciplinary, and local-political commitments to define tradition and language. Such assumptions, practices, efforts and commitments define the academic "us" as well as the ethnographic "them."

In terms found elsewhere in this volume, ideology is situated; it is a practice, a producing of language and the social, not an abstracted conceptual grid. Representations of the real are weapons in the struggle to define the real (Bourdieu 1984). Orthographies carry in their train rich histories of conflict, for behind apparently technical questions of representing sound hides a yearning for a fully adequate representation of language; and there is always a politics to this quest (Schieffelin and Doucet this volume). Ideologies of language involve selection, emphasis, and counteremphasis. What is the heart, the core of language? Is it words, as with the Tolowa or with Tewa language purists (Kroskrity this volume)? Is it grammatical structure, as standard theory teaches, or some privileged zone of intentionality, as with Warao shamanistic speech (Briggs this volume)?

Semiotic analyses, especially those developed by Silverstein (1979, this volume), have taught us much about the intricate interweaving of context, language, and intentionality. Such analyses have helped revitalize the study of language ideologies by emphasizing the place of words, situations and practices in the realm of "ideas." But those of us who would describe and analyze this interweaving never fully extricate ourselves from our contexts and interests. We do not escape ideology with a science that studies language use rather than grammar, that considers power as well as context, though we may sharpen our historical appreciation of the interpenetrating, conflicting visions and practice, of language that comprise "our" ideologies and "theirs."

NOTES

Thanks are due to numerous Tolowa people who have extended generous assistance to my studies of their language and life circumstances, especially the late Edward Richards Jr., Fred Moorehead, and Berneice Humphrey and also to Loren Bommelyn, Lila Moorehead, and Joe and Luretta Martin. I have often disagreed with my fellow Athabaskanist Victor Golla, but I appreciate and commend his knowledge and his intellectual honesty. Funds for research have been supplied by various institutions—Temple University, the State University of New York at Albany, the Phillips Fund of the American Philosophical Society, and the Wenner-Gren Foundation. All are gratefully acknowledged. The editors of this volume have provided useful commentary on an earlier draft of this chapter.

1. The Tolowa term for themselves was simply *x3S* 'people' and for their language *x3S weya'* '(the) people speak', or in approximate translation, the current "Indian language." See also fellow Athabaskan usage such as Navajo *dine bizaad* 'the people's language'. The term *Tolowa* appears to be a modification of a Yurok phrase that became the name used in academic and bureaucratic description for Smith River Athabaskans. As noted in the text, "Tolowa" is now part of local Indian and non-Indian usage.

2. For those unfamiliar with this part of the world, a lively and informative discussion and depiction of California Indian cultural life, often by various native artists, activists, and intellectuals, can be found in *News from Native California* (quarterly issues, 1987–), Heyday Press, Berkeley, California.

3. Tolowa examples are in standard IPA transcription except for *S* = alveopalatal fricative (š), *L* = voiceless lateral fricative (ɬ), *Y* = velar fricative (ɣ), and *3* = schwa (ə).

4. This historical process of devastation and regroupment is described in an

acknowledgement petition prepared by the Tolowa Nation group in the mid-1980s (see Slagle 1985). I have analyzed some of the historical and contemporary dilemmas in a separate work (Collins 1998).

5. The last great ten-day dances are said to have been held on *st3ndas3n* just before the island washed away; embattled Tolowa were allowed to settle on the island by U.S. militia, but more land was supposedly promised; later, the papers or deeds were lost (Collins 1998, Gould 1966, Slagle 1987).

6. As I have gathered material from various consultants and assembled, transcribed, and checked tapes that have been collected by various linguistic foraging parties over the past three decades, the historical and sociological, as well as the cognitive, location of "Tolowa grammar" has grown more complicated.

7. Shortly after this, the directorship of the Community Development Center changed hands, and the credentialing program was reorganized.

8. This is not an unusual situation. It is common to Mexico and Australia (John Haviland, personal communication).

9. As Indian scholars such as Vine Deloria Jr. have argued for the past several decades (Deloria 1969).

REFERENCES

Adams, Karen, and Daniel Brink, eds. 1991. *Perspectives on Official English.* New York: Mouton de Gruyter.

Bakhtin, Mikhail. 1981. *The Dialogic Imagination.* Austin: University of Texas Press.

Basso, Keith. 1990. *Western Apache Language and Culture.* Philadelphia: University of Pennsylvania Press.

Bauman, Richard, Judith Irvine, and Susan Philips. 1987. Performance, Speech Community, and Genre. Working Papers and Proceedings 11. Chicago: Center for Psychosocial Studies.

Boas, Franz. 1911. Introduction to *Handbook of American Indian Languages.* Washington, D.C.: Bureau of American Ethnology.

Bommelyn, Loren, and Berneice Humphrey. 1984. *Tolowa Language.* Arcata, Calif.: Tolowa Language Committee and Center for Community Development.

———. 1989. *Xus We-Yo': Tolowa Language*, 2nd ed. Crescent City, Calif.: Tolowa Language Committee.

Bourdieu, Pierre. 1977. *Outline of a Theory of Practice.* New York: Cambridge University Press.

———. 1984. Conclusion: Classes and classifications. In *Distinction*, pp. 466–484. Cambridge, Mass.: Harvard University Press.

———. 1991. The Production and Reproduction of Legitimate Language. In *Language and Symbolic Power*, pp. 43–65. Palo Alto, Calif.: Stanford University Press.

Chomsky, Noam. 1988. *Language and Problems of Knowledge.* Cambridge, Mass.: MIT Press.

Collins, James. 1985. Pronouns, Markedness, and Stem Change in Tolowa. *International Journal of American Linguistics* 51(4):368–372.

———. 1988. Syntactic Structures and Word-formation in Tolowa. Paper presented at Conference on American Indian Linguistics, American Anthropological Association 87th Annual Meeting. Phoenix.

———. 1989. Nasalization, Lengthening, and Phonological Rhyme in Tolowa. *International Journal of American Linguistics* 55(3):326–340.

———. 1998. *Understanding Tolowa Histories.* New York: Routledge.

Deloria, Vine. 1969. *Custer Died for Your Sins.* New York: Macmillan.

Drucker, Philip. 1937. The Tolowa and Their Southwestern Oregon Kin. *University of California Publications in American Archeology and Ethnology* 36:221–300.

Fabian, Johannes. 1983. *Time and the Other: How Anthropology Makes Its Object.* New York: Columbia University Press.

Gould, Richard. 1966. Indian and White Versions of "the Burnt Ranch Massacre": A Study in Comparative Ethnohistory. *Journal of the Folklore Institute* 3(1):30–42.

———. 1978. The Tolowa. In *Handbook of North American Indians.* Vol. 10: *California*, ed. I. Goddard, pp. 128–136. Washington, D.C.: Smithsonian.

Gumperz, John. 1982. Social Network and Language Shift. In *Discourse Strategies*, pp. 38–58. New York: Cambridge University Press.

Hymes, Dell. 1974. Toward Ethnographies of Communication. In *Foundations of Sociolinguistics*, pp. 3–66. Philadelphia: University of Pennsylvania Press.

———. 1981. *"In Vain I Tried to Tell You."* Philadelphia: University of Pennsylvania Press.

Jackendoff, Ray. 1993. *Patterns in the Mind.* New York: Basic Books.

Kari, James. 1989. Some Principles of Alaskan Athabaskan Toponymic Knowledge. In *General and Amerindian Linguistics, in Remembrance of Stanley Newman*, ed. M. Key and H. Hoenigswald, pp. 129–150. Berlin: Mouton de Gruyter.

Kristeva, Julia. 1981. Place Names. In *Desire in Language*, ed. L. Roudiez, pp. 271–294. New York: Columbia University Press.

Kroeber, Alfred. 1925. *Handbook of the Indians of California.* Washington, D.C.: Government Printing Office.

Labov, William. 1972. The Study of Language in Its Social Context. In *Sociolinguistic Patterns*, pp. 183–259. Philadelphia: University of Pennsylvania.

Lacan, Jacques. 1970. The Insistence of the Letter in the Unconscious. In *Structuralism*, ed. J. Ehrmann, pp. 106–136. New York: Anchor Books.

Norton, Jack. 1979. *When Our Worlds Cried.* San Francisco: American Indian Historical Society.

Obeyesekere, Gananath. 1990. *The Work of Culture.* Chicago: University of Chicago Press.

Pred, Alan. 1990. *Lost Words and Lost Worlds.* New York: Cambridge University Press.

Rawls, James. 1984. *Indians of California.* Norman: University of Oklahoma Press.

Sapir, Edward. 1921. *Language.* New York: Harcourt, Brace and World.

———. [1925] 1949. The Psychological Reality of Phonemes. In *Selected Writings of Edward Sapir*, ed. D. Mandelbaum, pp. 46–60. Berkeley: University of California Press.

Saussure, Ferdinand de. [1916] 1959. *Course in General Linguistics.* New York: Philosophical Library.

Silverstein, Michael. 1979. Language Structure and Linguistic Ideology. In *The Elements*, ed. P. Clyne, W. Hanks, and C. Hofbauer, pp. 193–248. Chicago: University of Chicago Linguistics Society.

———. 1981. The Limits of Awareness. Working Papers in Sociolinguistics 84. Austin, Tex.: Southwest Educational Development Laboratory.

Slagle, Allogan. 1985. *Huss: The Tolowa People. A Petition for Status Clarification/Federal Recognition Prepared for Submission to the United States Department of Interior.* Arcata, Calif.: Humboldt State University, Center for Community Development.

———. 1987. The Native American Tradition and Legal Status: Tolowa Tales and Tolowa Places. *Cultural Critique* 7:103–118.

Thornton, Russell. 1986. History, Structure, and Survival: A Comparison of the Yuki (Ukomno'm) and Tolowa (Hush) Indians of Northern California. *Ethnology* 25:119–130.

Voloshinov, V. N. 1973. *Marxism and the Philosophy of Language.* New York: Seminar Press.

Whorf, Benjamin. [1939] 1956. The Relation of Habitual Thought and Behavior to Language. In *Language, Thought, and Reality*, ed. J. Carrol, pp. 134–159. Cambridge, Mass.: MIT Press.

13

Indonesian(’s) Development

On the State of a Language of State

JOSEPH ERRINGTON

Prior to the end of the Cold War, development theory and practice in the Third World had already come under considerable critical scrutiny, and since the demise of the Soviet Union it has become more difficult than ever to “[t]alk about development . . . with the same confidence and encompassing scope with which intellectuals and activists spoke . . . in our most recent past” (Escobar 1992:20). Emergent, bloody ethnonationalisms have thrown into sharp question Development’s presuppositions, goals, and overall fit with emerging political and cultural dynamics of new nation-states.

As a subfield in or object of development, languages came to the fore at the peak of the development era in a theoretical and policy-oriented literature represented most influentially, perhaps, by the 1968 collection *Language Problems of Developing Nations* (Fishman et al.). “Language development” may then have seemed to nonspecialists a bit marginal in comparison with “core” problems of technological, political, and economic modernization. Now, that situation seems reversed. Language-linked identities have come to the fore in diverse struggles for ethnic autonomy, as images of “pure” forms of native languages figure in nativist narratives of primordial ethnic origins. Resurgent concerns for “national character” bespeak fears of what Herder called “state-machines . . . wholly devoid of inner life” with “no sentiment, no sympathy of any kind linking [their] component parts” (quoted in Barnard 1965:59). Insofar as such fears are instigated by international development and ideas of modernity, so too can images of quasi-sacred language take on new salience as evidence and symbols of the kind of authentic, natural-seeming "inner life" that Herder famously propounded in his treatise on the origin of languages.

Notwithstanding this crisis of confidence, the idea of Development is not now a residue of postcolonial Cold War politics, nor is it receding on the rear horizon of history in a new, still inchoate international era. It has, instead, engendered a quandary: "despite the recognition of its demise, the imaginary of development—still without viable alternatives although somewhat weakened by the recent crisis—continues to hold sway" (Escobar 1992:21). "Development," indispensable yet problematic, is considered here in relation to one developing country where it seems to have had real, continuing salience for socioeconomic, cultural, and linguistic change.

I present here a few particulars of the practice and "imaginary" of Indonesian language development. Indonesian is apposite as a "miraculous" instance of language development, at least in the eyes of the foremost figure in that field (Fishman 1978:332). At the end of World War II it was an artificial administrative dialect of Malay, spoken by a few million native speakers and, in various pidginized and creolized forms, by a few million residents of the Dutch East Indies colonial empire. Now it is the fully viable and universally acknowledged language of the Indonesian nation and citizenship, over and against the native languages of about 190 million members of four hundred or so ethnolinguistic groups. Notwithstanding difficulties in evaluating the results of censuses, which include questions about language, there seems to be broad evidence and consensus among Indonesians and interested non-Indonesians alike that Indonesia is well on its way to solving "the national language problem" and enhancing its status as "the envy of the multilingual world" (Lowenberg 1983:3).[1]

Because Indonesian is conspicuously unattached to any politically salient ethnic native-speaking community, it is quite transparently related to the institutional infrastructure of the Indonesian state. As such, it is an index both of Indonesia's derivativeness of a Dutch colonial project (see Chatterjee 1983) and of the effectiveness of ongoing state-sponsored, state-legitimizing programs of national development (*pembangunan nasional*). Put differently, the absence of any plausible appeal to a primordial, originary Indonesian (speaking) community makes apparent Indonesian's crucial role and support in what Abrams called the state-system: "a palpable nexus of practice and institutional structure centered in government," at once "extensive, unified, and dominant" (1988:58).

But Indonesian is not just a vehicle of state discourse; it is also a mode of talk between Indonesians. As it enters the give-and-take of everyday life, it informs new, national ways of mediating face-to-face interaction and becomes a new medium for common, intersubjective social experience. In this respect, Indonesian is also a vehicle for what Roland Barthes might call a *doxa* of national development, a general "public opinion"—"diffuse, full, complete, 'natural'" and "a diffused . . . osmotic discourse which *impregnates* . . . the socio-symbolic field" (1989:121). Put alternately, it is both vehicle and symbol of what Abrams calls a "state-idea: projected, purveyed, and variously believed in different societies at different times" (1988:58).

My purpose here is to locate Indonesian, however sketchily, within its "state-system" and as mediator of a "state-idea" of development. In both respects, it is presented as a "*project* for the assumption of 'modernity' within the modalities of an autonomous and autochthonous social-political tradition" (Anderson 1966:89). I try at the same time to develop by example an approach to "the imaginary of Development" that is strategically relativized. On one hand, then, it is organized to critique figurings of "language" in an (ideo)logic of "Development"; on the other hand, that critique is relativized to sociohistorical specificities of Indonesian, a developing language which is entering local communities as it mediates the power of Indonesian state institutions.

My strategy is to contextualize and consider a single, diagnostic event during which agents of the Indonesian "state system" gathered to explicate and act on a "state idea" of language and identity, ethnic and national. At a well-publicized state-sponsored Javanese Language Congress in the summer of 1991, the largest and dominant ethnolinguistic group of Indonesia came to be figured, through Javanese language, within the broader state discourse of development. By reading through that event, and against its institutional grain, I try to adduce some of its enabling presuppositions and to explicate emergent understandings of language, ethnicity, and nationality in an era of (national) development.

From Colonialism to Modernism

Like other languages, Indonesian has no date of birth. But it does have an identifiable baptismal event: the celebrated 'meeting of youth' (*Rapat pemuda*) on October 28, 1928, in Batavia, then capital of the Dutch East Indies. There, an ethnically diverse group of Dutch educated native intelligentsia jointly adopted a nationalistic program and renamed Malay (*bahasa Melayu*) Indonesian (*bahasa Indonesia*), the language of their nation-to-be. Their 'oath of the youth' (*sumpah pemuda*), repeated on its anniversary every year across the country, conferred public, formal recognition on the project of 'one homeland' (*satu nusa*), 'one people' (*satu bangsa*), and 'one language' (*satu bahasa*). It does not now ring hollow, as Indonesian has become far more widely known than its antecedent, a variety of Malay first standardized and propagated by Dutch colonialists and later propriated to the nationalist cause.

Ambiguities of the label 'Indonesian' (*bahasa Indonesia*) tacitly enable a double vision of Indonesian's origins and development, as well as the double allusion made to it in popular accounts of nationalism. On one hand, its baptismal event evokes a vision of a nationalist future and modern, supraethnic lingua franca imbued with modernism and progress. On the other hand, it is invocable transhistorically as a kind of protonational Malay-yet-Indonesian speaking ur-community, not unlike those that figure in primordialist national narratives. Slippage between these two senses is easy enough to allow even the most famous and outspoken of Indonesian modernist ideologues, S. T. Alisjahbana, to write that "Chinese had at the beginning of the Christian era come to Indonesia [*sic*] and encountered a kind of Indonesian [*sic*] lingua franca in these islands, which they called Kwenlun" (1956:6).[2] Allusions to an "*Indonesian* lingua franca" resonate broadly with Romanticist visions of protonational communities and invoke without explicitly claiming a kind of interstitial primordial language community.[3]

This same slippage helps to elide the political and cultural salience of native Malay-speaking communities in Sumatra and (in creolized forms) on coasts of other Indonesian islands. It also elides the institutional history that made Malay not just desirable but feasible as a vehicle of nationalism. Prior to 1928, the national language-to-be was a variety of Malay fashioned by and for Dutch colonial administrators and disseminated through colonial institutions.

So there has been a double distancing of Indonesian: from antehistorical communities of native speakers and from a proximal colonial history. This double break with the past, and Indonesian's symbolic value as language of nation-state, rests squarely in a strongly modernist rhetoric of national development, or *pembangunan*:

> The Indonesia yearned for by the new generation is no continuation of [the precolonial kingdom of] Mataram, no continuation of the kingdom of Banten, no continuation of the kingdom of Minangkabau or Banjarmasin. In their thoughts, Indonesian culture is likewise in no way a continuation of Javanese culture, of Malay culture, of Sundanese culture or any other. (Alisjahbana 1977:42)[4]

Pembangunan justifies a wide range of top-down governmental policy decisions, many with massively disruptive effects on local communities. As Alisjahbana's formulation suggests, it figures ethnic diversity less as a problem to be solved than as a condition to be abandoned or allowed to recede on the historical horizon as Indonesians advance into a modern national future.[5]

Pembangunan has also been a keyword in the discourse that has for three decades been propagated to legitimize Indonesia's self-dubbed New Order state, which succeeded Sukarno's regime following the bloody conflict of 1965. President Suharto, for instance, has acceded to the title 'Father of Development' (*Bapak Pembangunan*, as opposed to Sukarno, self-styled 'voice of the people'). Development rhetoric can be 'development communication' (*komunikasi pembangunan*) and, in fulfilling its national duty the press—under more or less overt but always effective government surveillance—operates as a proper 'development press' (*pers pembangunan*). General Benny Moerdani, a central figure in the New Order military and political elite, periodized Indonesian history into the revolutionary period (*periode perang kemerdekaan*) and development period (*periode pembangunan*), effectively eliding the historical salience of Sukarno and his era. However questionable its status elsewhere in the post–Cold War era, 'development' is an ongoingly crucial legitimizing rubric for New Order social, political, and economic policy and for its moves to subdue opposition and resistance to its decisions.

New Order development is likewise intimately bound up with the fortunes of Indonesian, as is obvious from one of Suharto's earliest unilateral decisions (a Presidential Instruction) after gaining power. In 1965 he mandated the government-supervised building and staffing of elementary schools throughout the country, particularly in rural areas. These have been a primary institutional means to the end of disseminating standard Indonesian to the citizenry. As part of *pembangunan*, state language policy has long been framed in terms consonant if not identical with those used in other spheres of modernization. Issues of Indonesian usage are regularly framed as issues in language development (*pembangunan bahasa*) in papers by state employees at state-sponsored conferences on the 'Politics of the national language' (*Politik bahasa nasional*). Repeatedly emphasized there are the needs of political integration: "The concept of national community cannot be fully realized if there is not one national language. . . . A state that has one common language known by its entire populace will be more progressive in development, and its political ideology will be safer and stabler" (Burhan 1989:77).[6] Tacitly assumed in such self-evidently policy-oriented, state-sponsored venues is the status of Indonesian as one among several "targets" or "objects" of institutional treatment, an institution that will "develop" through conscious, rational, policy-oriented actions by the state and its agents.

In all crucial respects the Indonesian language project fits the broad developmentalist profile often associated with the work of language development experts like Joshua Fishman. Indonesian is considered, as the quotation suggests, as part of the nation-state's infrastructure, promoting homogeneity among citizens across national territory and so facilitating the modernization of the economy and the stabilization of social configurations. It is likewise derivative of a state-supervised, "top-down" process, through which Indonesian is superimposed on otherwise diverse communities through a bureaucratically hierarchized system of state-sponsored or state-supervised schools. It resonates with the vision of bounded but socially and linguistically homogeneous space characteristic of national forms of territoriality. Something of the tenor of the New Order rhetoric of development (language and otherwise) can be conveyed in contrast with its Old Order antecedents. Such a critical analysis of tropes of "development" before and during the New Order period has been carried out by Ariel Heryanto, who has demonstrated a shift from broadly organic to mechanical conceptions of change and, more directly relevant here, of "language development."

Heryanto reads from thirty years of discourse on development a broad transition from a specifically organic metaphor of development (*perkembangan*) to the architectonic or mechanical rhetoric of *pembangunan*. *Kembang*, glossable most readily as 'flower' or 'blossom', and *perkembangan*, its derived nominal form glossable as 'flowering' or 'growth', were central in much prenational and pre–New Order discourse. They were constitutive of a discourse of development that, as Heryanto suggests, was a "NATURAL PROCESS of change, which is motivated primarily by some INTERNAL necessity, enforced primarily by its own INTERNAL energy, its pace and extent being PROPORTIONAL to its own nature" (1985:49–50). This version of "development," redolent of Romanticist visions of language and nation, had its earliest and most eloquent expression in Alisjahbana's Western-influenced writings.[7]

In the 1950s the discourse of organic *perkembangan* interarticulated with the more mechanistic, instrumental discourse of *pembangunan*. As Heryanto writes:

> In essence, *pembangunan* does not refer to things in nature or natural processes. On the contrary, it refers to an exploitation of nature, as of human beings. In essence, it denotes CRAFTMANSHIP as well as ENGINEERING, with the chief emphasis on yielding MAXIMAL PRODUCT, in the most EFFICIENT pace and manner possible, by bringing EXTERNAL forces to bear upon the object, *bangunan*. (1985:50–51)

Heryanto reads the ascendance of the discourse of *pembangunan* over *perkembangan* from a variety of writings on New Order programs. This newer, progressively dominant vision of development affords a vision of social change as basically agentive, instrumentalist, and rational: constructing from parts a new whole "like," in Suharto's (1971) own words explaining *pembangunan*, "a person building a house."[8]

This shift to an instrumentalist, highly agentive rhetoric of means and ends lends a new, legitimating accent to the state's self-assumed role as primary sponsor of engineered socioeconomic change. As the practice and rhetoric of *pembangunan* have been progressively restricted to the economic sphere of development, so, too, the term has become increasingly linked with technocratic metrics for gauging the success of development projects. In this respect, New Order language policies may be called language engineering, a phrase that more fully captures the state's ideological positioning as backer, author, and executor of this and other aspects of nation building.

Theories of Nationalism, Ideologies of Development

If organic imagings of an Indonesian community appear to be losing salience on the contemporary scene, the Indonesian language still figures as crucial medium and proof for appeals to specifically Indonesian allegiances and identities. But the Indonesian "linguistic miracle" is less important here as part of the critique of language development I am trying to develop than as apparent confirmation for functionalist visions of national development, particularly Ernest Gellner's broader account (1983) of national languages. These transparent institutional relations between language and state fit well Gellner's state-focused account of nations and nationalism, which assimilates issues of national language and culture into an economistic account of state-supervised development. In these and other respects, Indonesia's success with Indonesian seems a paradigmatic example of what Gellner calls "the general imposition of a high [here, Indonesian] culture on society, where previously low cultures had taken up the lives of the majority . . . of the population." Thirty years of New Order government have yielded what Gellner calls "a . . . school-mediated, academy-supervised idiom, codified for the requirements of reasonably precise bureaucratic and technological communication" (1983:57).

Any convergence between New Order practice and functionalist theory hardly confirms the latter's general validity, as evidenced by widespread ethnonationalist upheaval in the post–Cold War period. Rather, Gellner explicates the epistemological or cognitive dimension of language development within a broader account of nationalism, one that resonates well with New Order visions of a developed, modern, Indonesian language. In this respect, Gellner's aperspectival, transcontextual image of modern national languages offers an explication of New Order language ideology.

Pembangunan appears from this angle to be part of what Gellner calls the "deception and self-deception" of nationalism, obscuring the "mechanisms" of development and (as Gellner has it) what "*really* happens" in nation building. Gellner thus reads ideas and sentiments of nationalism as covertly subordinate and instrumental to a national society's institutional and socioeconomic development. He argues, in a manner quite consistent with Fishman's vision of language development, that nationalism is a specifically modern form of collective representation; through it, he asserts, the state worships itself in particularly naked form, presupposing and promoting cultural and linguistic homogeneity among its members.

The national language is thus derivative of and symbiotically related to modern state infrastructures[9] as a means for the state-supervised industrial division of labor. In this respect, Gellner critiques and extends Durkheim's thesis on the division of labor by arguing that industrial societies (unlike what he calls advanced agrarian societies) require distinctively *generic* training,[10] with specifically secular literacy in a homogeneous language achieved through a process of "exo-socialization [and] exo-education outside the local intimate unit. . . . [This] makes the link of state and culture necessary" (1983:38). Gellner's account could certainly charter the New Order's efforts to foster both an industrial infrastructure and universal competence and literacy in Indonesian through its state school system. Whether or not Indonesia's technocratic elite, the architects of development, would accept Gellner's characterization of nationalism as a necessary (self-)deception, they clearly recognize the utility for development (*pembangunan*) of what he calls a "high culture."

But Gellner the philosopher develops a cognitive extension to this relatively straightforward functionalist argument by arguing that modern, national languages are also infrastructural for broadly rational modes of thought. To this end he invokes Weber's theorization of rationality, arguing that social and linguistic homogeneity makes a modern language unrestricted for topic, user, or use-context. Standard languages are for Gellner exoteric, contextually uninflected instruments of thought in two respects. One of these devolves from those languages' "coherence or consistency, [for] the like treatment of like cases, regularity, what might be called the very soul and honor of the bureaucrat. The other is efficiency, the cool, rational selection of the best available means to given, clearly formulated, and isolated ends; . . . the spirit of the ideal enterpreneur" (Gellner 1983:20). In these paired respects, Gellner goes on to argue, the modern national language counts as

> a single conceptual currency. . . . All facts are located within a single continuous logical space, [such] that statements reporting them can be conjoined and generally related to each other, and so that in principle one single language describes the world and is internally unitary. . . . In our society it is assumed that all referential uses of language ultimately refer to one coherent world, and can be reduced to a unitary idiom; and that it is legitimate to relate them to each other. (1983:21)

National languages, unrestricted in context of use or sphere of application, furnish a cognitive style and rational stance that enables aperspectival objective thought, a "view from nowhere" (Nagel 1986).

Gellner's argument cannot be taken as describing an endpoint in a process that we (post)moderns have completed—the end, as Sartre's definition of progress has it, of "a long hard road that leads to us." It is, rather, a kind of teleological metric for evaluating progress in the development of exosocialized citizenries. Construed as a charter for Indonesian development, Gellner's covertly prescriptive account can be thought of as ideological in Karl Mannheim's sense; it constructs a discursive object that is "alien to reality" and "transcend[s] actual existence" but is "effective in the realization and the maintenance of the existing order of things" (1936:192). So, too, it has much in common with the Indonesian development ideology that it so usefully complements and supplements.

Pembangunan incorporates the same teleological appeal and legitimizes the sort of state action that Gellner apparently describes and tacitly prescribes. So, too, Gellner's argument provides a highly suggestive explication of development ideology's epistemological correlates, a kind of ideological derivative of a program focused on economic advancement and social control.

Standardism and Ethnicity: The Javanese Language Congress

Such developments have occasioned little sustained commentary in the Indonesian state and media, notwithstanding occasional programmatic observations like Alisjahbana's. But not long ago the Indonesian mass media focused much attention on another aspect of state language development: a concerted, institutional effort to mitigate putatively pernicious side effects of Indonesia's successful development on Javanese linguistic and cultural heritage. In 1991 high-level Indonesian officials were convened in Semarang, capital of Central Java, for a Javanese Language Congress (*Kongres Bahasa Jawa*), which was opened by President Suharto (himself Javanese). Six hundred Indonesian technocrats, politicians, and intellectuals (mostly Javanese) met to discuss (mostly in Indonesian) the current state of their nation's dominant ethnic language (their native language) in the dynamic of national development.

The congress served, in one observer's words, "to focus on complaints from many parties about the decline and retreat of Javanese" (*Kompas* 1996).[11] But the topic of this conference was less "the Javanese language" (in Indonesian, *bahasa Jawa*) in any general, received sense than the distinctively elite, esoteric registers of spoken and written Javanese that have long been associated with a colonial noble elite, the *priyayi*. Members of the courtly circles in formerly royal polities of Jogjakarta and Surakarta now participate in political and economic power only insofar as they have been assimilated into the new, national society and political system. In Indonesia, they figure not as an ethnic threat in need of neutralization but as a source of reinvented ethnic tradition and legitimacy and a target for appropriation by the Javanese-dominated New Order.

Suharto opened the conference by urging the various language experts in attendance to discuss ways that Javanese philosophy, especially as contained in the Javanese orthography, could be used to develop and disseminate Javanese character.[12] Claiming rather disingenuously to speak not as president of the Republic but as a Javanese, he expressed his hope for the Indonesian people to possess the "noble spirit" necessary for "proper relations" between people and between people and the environment, as well as between people and God. In fact, few Indonesian functionaries take seriously the notion that in the foreseeable future, "ordinary" Javanese will be threatened by extinction through massive language shift to Indonesian. Suharto's fond hope and the institutional logic of the conference presuppose, rather, that Javanese stands in need not of development like Indonesian but rehabilitation and preservation as an exemplary ethnic tradition. This appropriative focus on traditionally prestigious, ostensibly moribund forms of "high" Javanese[13] is part of the ongoing construction by the New Order of a newly invented Javanese tradition—well described by Florida (1987) as a lofty, monolithic, ineffable 'noble sublime' (*adhiluhung*)—of which the state is itself custodian.

Much attention at the conference was given to the complex system of Javanese verbal etiquette, the correct forms of which (several papergivers argued) are disappearing from use by younger speakers. Largely ignored by such arguments is the fact that control of these most refined forms of usage has never extended widely beyond traditional elite circles (Errington 1985, 1989, 1991). So, too, much was made of ignorance of Javanese literacy and literature, traditionally an esoteric, distinctive sphere of knowledge in a cult of royal exemplary centers.

After suitable deliberation, participants recommended that Javanese language (*bahasa*) and tradition (*budaya*) be placed under the custodial aegis of the state—specifically, the Department of Education and Culture—which was authorized to establish (so, standardize) a version of Javanese to be taught in state schools. In this way, a formerly esoteric tradition can be assimilated into a modern institutional framework and disseminated in newly exoteric form to the nation's Javanese/Indonesian constituency. As Javanese enters schools in Central and East Java, it takes on the status of 'local content' (*muatan lokal*) in a translocal, state-established curriculum. Tacitly but effectively detached in this way from its present-day exemplary loci, and reframed as exoteric subjects of instruction in state institutions, Javanese traditions are being rendered homogeneous and uniform across those provincial parts of Indonesian national space that happen to count as Javanese. Assimilated into and subordinated to the institutions and ideologic of the nation-state, exemplary language becomes an object in and for a standard, public culture.

The "Javanese language" constructed at the Javanese language conference represents, then, just the sort of "not properly united . . . hierarchically related sub-world" and sphere of "special privileged facts, sacralized and exempt from ordinary treatment" that Gellner identifies with prenational (and, implicitly, prerational) polities. Under the aegis of the New Order, that "sub-world" seems destined for assimilation to a standard, exoteric emblem of Javanese-Indonesian ethnicity and for a new symbolic role as neotraditional source of legitimacy for New Order goals and decisions.

The cartoon in Figure 13.1 suggests something of the conflicted intent and effect of this congress, at least in the eyes of one shrewd Javanese Indonesian observer.[14] It depicts what I presume to be an anonymous government official reciting the Javanese syllabary—represented in the cartoon along with its Roman alphabet equivalents—as he holds up a puppet from the shadow play (*wayang kulit*), a traditional Javanese performance genre closely associated with courtly culture.

To one side stands a young boy dressed in modern, not to say well-to-do clothes, who, like the vast majority of young Javanese Indonesians, is illiterate in the *hanacaraka* orthography being recited. At once audience and commentator, he says to his father, in idiomatic Indonesian, "Well, if you, Dad, of Javanese descent, don't understand it . . . all the more for me . . ." In this way, he notes in puzzled

Figure 13.1 One Javanese Indonesian's view of the language congress.

tone what conference participants chose to ignore: that this orthography was not widely known among Javanese of his father's generation, either. Interestingly, the boy attributes Javanese-ness to his father's ancestry (*keturunan*), rather than to his social identity per se, as would have been true had he called him "a Javanese" (*orang Jawa*). Whether or not this youth has affirmed his own ethnic descent, the cartoon suggests, the associated ethnic tradition is as little known to his own father as to himself, and seemingly irrelevant to the lives of either.

Even if Suharto's language project falls short of imbuing Indonesian students with the ethos of their new-yet-old "ethnic tradition," it will not by that token be a failure. To the degree it impresses on young Javanese Indonesians the simple fact of that ineffable, state-sponsored ethnic past, it will propagate a conception of state as custodian of and successor to that tradition and provide a reference for a territorialized ethnic identity. This newly exotericised body of knowledge can then be overtly and publicly invoked as a means for "enriching" development with Javanese content in a national frame. In this way, too, the New Order can valorize as "nonnative" perceivedly uncongenial side effects of development. As symbols of what Herder might have called "national character," Javanese language/literacy mediates long-standing ambiguities of ethnic and national identity for the New Order, in New Order terms. "Reduced" to the "unitary idiom" (in Gellner's words), which is Indonesian, formerly esoteric, now exoteric Javanese transposes the ambiguities of collective identity into more manageable, state-constituted discourses and contexts.

Conclusions

If Indonesia and Indonesian seem exceptionally successful stories of Third World development, an event like the Javanese Language Congress may take on broader salience and multiple construability. On one hand, it might be diagnosed as symptomatic of the survival and ongoing relevance of "the imaginary of development" in the production and management of knowledge. Development, following Foucault and Said, is then a discourse formation that constitutes and has the Third World for an effect, a population of targets for "new mechanisms of power . . . economies, societies, and cultures . . . offered up as new objects of knowledge"(Escobar 1992:28). But this discourse appears, in light of the Congress, to have been internalized and reproduced within more local spheres of dominance. Cynically or "naturally," agents of a developing state in this way apply a standardist logic to symbols of identity, and so assimilate them into the institutional logic of the state system.

Read with an eye to Gellner's functionalist charter for development policy generally, and language development particularly, the Javanese Language Congress appears a necessarily self-deceiving step on the road to a modern, nationally reinvented version of standard, exoterically symbolized ethnicity. An ethnic elite heritage, now assumed by a national elite, seems to have already been assimilated into the state-idea, and made to subserve the "development" of progressively homogenized sociosymbolic subparts of Indonesian territory.

The former critique already responds to Gellner's argument and the avowedly objectivist claims it both presupposes and purports to explicate. Professor Ernest

Gellner locates educational institutions at the crux of the state's sociosymbolic power (1982:34), identifies the professoriate as its secular priesthood, and so acknowledges his own highly situated, interested authorial position as high priest of the cult of the state. But the obverse point can be made with Escobar, who notes the broadly similar dilemma faced by critical theorists of Development. To the degree that their goal is a global critique, they must have some recourse, albeit tacit, to what Gellner calls a "universal conceptual currency." They, then, seem less apostates from a faith of reason than secret sharers in a belief in autonomous theory and thought.

Faced with this dilemma, Escobar correctly identifies situatedness as a major need in and impetus for relativized understandings of social development. So he promotes the importance of localized understandings, citing Jelin's characterization (1987:11, translated in Escobar 1992:29) of "the intermediate space between individualized, familiar, habitual, micro-climactic daily life, on the one hand, and socio-political processes *writ* large, of the State and the solemn and higher institutions, on the other." It is such a space, shot through with language as interactional medium and ideological construct, that I have tried to sketch here for "the Indonesian case."

The Javanese Language Congress is salient, I suggest, because it occupies and constitutes just such an intermediate space, mediating between the "individualized, habitual" sphere of talk, on one hand, and "solemn and higher institutions" of the New Order state, on the other. If it offers a convincing *entrée* to broader issues of Development, writ small and large, then it suggests the salience of "language" for understandings of "discourse" and the critical study of the ideological framings through which global forces called Development or Modernization impinge on and are mediated in communities and lives.

NOTES

1. The 1971 national census shows that some 40 percent of the national population of 118 million then knew Indonesian; the 1981 census placed that number at almost half of 150 million Indonesians; projections by Abas (1987) (from whom these figures are adapted) are that 60 percent of approximately 190 million know Indonesian as of 1991. By 2001 that percentage is projected to rise to slightly less than 70 percent of a projected population of 240 million. At a recent international conference on the teaching of Indonesian, the Indonesian Minister of Education and Culture asserted that in 1990, 131 million (83 percent) of citizens over the age of five knew Indonesian and that by the year 2010, all of Indonesia's 215 million citizens will be speakers of the national language.

2. ". . . orang-orang Tionghoa jang pada permulaan kurun Masehi datang ke Indonesia telah menemui sedjenis lingua franca Indonesia de kepulauan ini jang dinamakannya Kwenlun."

3. Certainly more detailed invocations of protonational past would unavoidably lead to the naming of one or another of several empires or monuments now perceived as being Javanese, and so as foreshadowers of the current dominant position of Javanese in the Indonesian state apparatus.

4. "Indonesia yang dicita-citakan oleh generasi baru bukan sambungan Mataram, bukan sambungan kerajaan Banten, bukan kerajaan Minangkabau atau Banjarmasin. Menurut susunan pikiran ini, maka kebudayaan Indonesia pun tiadalah mungkin

sambungan kebudayaan Jawa, sambungan kebudayaan Melayu, sambungan kebudayaan Sunda atau kebudayaan yang lain."

5. This does not mean that even the highest and most "modern" of Indonesia's predominantly Javanese political elite has left an ethnic politics of culture behind; for extensive discussion see Pemberton 1994 and, in its linguistic refraction, Errington 1986.

6. "Gagasan tentang masyarakat bangsa tidak akan dipahami dengan baik oleh masyarakyat bila satu bahasa nasional . . . tidak ada. Negara yang mempunyai satu bahasa umum yang dikenal oleh seluruh rakyatnya kan lebih maju dalam pembangunan, dan ideologi politiknya akan lebih aman dan stabil."

7. For example: "A culture begins to bud, when there grows up within a society a conviction of the truth of a certain system of values . . . the ability of a culture to develop is not unlimited, for every culture contains within itself the dialectic of all growth. As the papaya seed, which sprouts in the fertile soil and joyfully thrusts up through it to greet the beneficent rays of the sun, must experience, the further it rises up out of the earth, an increasing remoteness from the soil, from which its roots suck up the sap, that makes it grow, so every culture that gives expression to a definite system of values, must eventually experience the limits to the possibilities of its further development" (Alisjahbana 1961:3).

8. "Ibarat orang mendirikan gedung besar."

9. "Not only is our definition of nationalism parasitic on a prior and assumed definition of the state: . . . nationalism emerges only in milieux in which the existence of the state [and] politically centralized units . . . are taken for granted and are treated as normative" (Gellner 1983:4).

10. "Industrial society['s] . . . educational system is unquestionably the *least* specialized, the most universally standardized, that has ever existed. . . . The kind of specialization found in industrial society rests precisely on a common foundation of unspecialized and standardized training" (Gellner 1983:27).

11. ". . . menyoroti keluhan berbagai pihak atas kemerosotan dan kemunduran bahasa Jawa."

12. Because at the time of writing I was unable to gain access to copies of papers read at the conference, or minutes of its proceedings, I have been obliged to draw on accounts in the mass media. For present purposes these general reports suffice.

13. Far from verging on extinction, these forms now appear to be alive and well in the formal, public speech of Indonesian functionaries in official Indonesian venues; on this topic see Errington 1995.

14. My thanks to its author, Bapak Pramono R. Pramoedjo, for permission to include his cartoon in this chapter.

REFERENCES

Abas, H. 1987. *Indonesian as a Unifying Language of Wider Communication: A Historical and Sociolinguistic Perspective.* Pacific Linguistics Series D, No. 73. Canberra: Research School of Pacific Studies, Australian National University.

Abrams, Philip. 1988. Notes on the Difficulty of Studying the State (1977). *Journal of Historical Sociology* 1(1):58–89.

Alisjahbana, Sutan Takdir. 1956. *Sedjarah Bahasa Indonesia* [History of Indonesian]. Djakarta: P. T. Pustaka Rakjat.

———. 1977. *Polemik kebudayaan* [Cultural polemic]. Edited by Achdiat Mihardja. Jakarta: P. T. Dunia Pustaka Jaya.

Anderson, Benedict O'G. 1966. The Languages of Indonesian Politics. *Indonesia* 1:89–116.

Barnard, Frederick M. 1965. *Herder's Social and Political Thought.* Oxford: Clarendon Press.

Barthes, Roland. 1989. The Division of Languages. In *The Rustle of Language*, pp. 111–124. Translated by Richard Howard. Berkeley: University of California Press.

Burhan, Jazir. 1989. Politik bahasa nasional dan pengajaran bahasa. In *Politik bahasa nasional* [Politics of the national language], ed. Amran Halim, pp. 65–83. Jakarta: Balai Pustaka.

Chatterjee, Partha. 1983. *Nationalist Thought and the Colonial World: A Derivative Discourse?* Totowa, N.J.: Zed Books for the United Nations University.

Errington, Joseph. 1985. *Language and Social Change in Java: Linguistic Reflexes of Modernization in a Traditional Royal Polity.* Athens: Ohio University, Center for International Studies.

———. 1986. Continuity and Discontinuity in Indonesian Language Development. *Journal of Asian Studies* 45(2):329–53.

———. 1989. Exemplary Centers, Urban Centers, and Language Change in Java. Working Papers and Proceedings of the Center for Psychosocial Studies 30. Chicago: Center for Psychosocial Studies.

———. 1991. A Muddle for the Model: Diglossia and the Case of Javanese. *Southwestern Journal of Linguistics* (special issue on diglossia) 10(1):189–213.

———. 1995. State Speech for Peripheral Publics in Java. *Pragmatics* 5(2):213–24.

Escobar, Arturo. 1992. Imagining a Post-development Era? Critical Thought, Development and Social Movements. *Social Text* 31/32:20–56.

Fishman, Joshua. 1978. The Indonesian Language Planning Experience: What Does It Teach Us? In *Spectrum: Essays Presented to Sutan Takdir Alisjahbana on His Seventieth Birthday*, ed. S. Udin, pp. 332–339. Jakarta: Dian Rakyat.

Fishman, Joshua, Charles Ferguson, and Jyotindra Das Gupta, eds. 1968. *Language Problems of Developing Nations.* New York: Wiley.

Florida, Nancy. 1987. Reading the Unread in Traditional Javanese Literature. *Indonesia* 44:1–16.

Gellner, Ernest. 1983. *Nations and Nationalism.* Ithaca, N.Y.: Cornell University Press.

Heryanto, Ariel. 1985. The Language of Development and the Development of Language. *Indonesia* 40:35–60.

Jelin, Elizabeth. 1987. *Movimíentos sociales y democracia emergente.* Buenos Aires: Centro Editor de América Latina.

Kompas. 1996. Kongres Bahasa Jawa II 22–26 Oktober di Malang [Javanese Language Congress II, October 22–26 in Malang].

Lowenburg, Peter. 1983. Lexical Modernization in Bahasa Indonesia: Functional Allocation and Variation in Borrowing. *Studies in Linguistic Sciences* 13(2):73–86.

Mannheim, Karl. 1936. *Ideology and Utopia: An Introduction to the Sociology of Knowledge.* Translated by Louis Wirth and Edward Shils. London: Kegan Paul, Trench, Trubner.

Nagel, Thomas. 1986.. *The View from Nowhere.* New York: Oxford University Press.

Pemberton, John. 1994. *On the Subject of "Java."* Ithaca, N.Y.: Cornell University Press.

Suharto 1971. *Kumpulan Kata-kata Presiden Soeharto 1967–1971* [Words of President Suharto, 1967–1971]. Djakarta: Sekretariat Kabinet R.I.

14

The "Real" Haitian Creole

Ideology, Metalinguistics, and Orthographic Choice

BAMBI B. SCHIEFFELIN AND

RACHELLE CHARLIER DOUCET

In this essay, we examine the cultural categories and the conceptual logic that underlie the orthography debates about kreyòl that have taken place over the past fifty years.[1] In Haiti, as in many countries concerned with nation-building, the development of an orthography for vernacular literacy has been neither a neutral activity nor simply a search for a way to mechanically reduce a spoken language to written form. The processes of transforming a spoken language to written form have often been viewed as scientific, arbitrary, or unproblematic.[2] However, the creation of supposedly arbitrary sound/sign (signifier/signified) relationships that constitute an orthography always involves choices based on someone's idea of what is important. This process of representing the sounds of language in written form is thus an activity deeply grounded in frameworks of value.

We suggest that arguments about orthography reflect competing concerns about representations of Haitianness at the national and international level—that is, how speakers wish to define themselves to each other, as well as to represent themselves as a nation. Because acceptance of an orthography is based more often on political and social considerations than on linguistic or pedagogical factors, orthographic debates are rich sites for investigating competing nationalist discourses. To draw on Anderson's (1983) evocative notion, orthographic choice is really about "imagining" the past and the future of a community.

To understand the symbolic importance of the decisions taken in standardizing kreyòl orthography, we have focused on the interconnectedness of speech practices, language ideologies, and nationalist agendas. We draw on Silverstein's notion of linguistic ideologies, which are "sets of beliefs about language articulated by users as a rationalization or justification of perceived language structure and use" (1979:193). Language ideology is the mediated link between social structures and forms of talk, standing in dialectical relation with, and thus significantly influencing, social, discursive, and linguistic practices. Research on language ideology is a bridge between language structure and language politics, as well as between linguistic and social theory (Woolard 1992:235–236). Language ideologies are likely places to find images of "self/other" or "us/them," as, for example, in the recent debates about the English Only movement and American language policies (Silverstein 1987, Woolard 1989).

Language ideology often determines which linguistic features get selected for cultural attention and for social marking, that is, which ones are important and which ones are not. In countries where "nation-ness" (Anderson 1983:4) is being negotiated, every aspect of language—from its phonological features to lexical items to stylistic alternatives to multilingualism—can be contested, and often is. Similarly, in such situations, there is rarely a single ideology of language. Rather, one finds multiple, competing, and contradictory ideologies of language that are offered as the "logic" for which features may be contested.[3] Such logics are often claimed to be strictly scientific, when, in fact, they are culturally constructed and represent particular political and social interests. Not surprisingly, these discourses, as part of nationalist discourses, often use oppositions as important rhetorical devices.

Gal's exemplary analysis of Bartók's funeral, for example, points out how sets of oppositions frame the continuing debate in Hungary about how the future of that nation should be shaped—in some native, eastern, Magyar way or in a European way. The two terms "Europe" and "Hungary" are enmeshed in a dual classification system that, in spite of changing valences depending on context of use, expresses profound contradictory and enduring oppositions, such as alienation: community, civilized: backward, to name but two (1991:443–444). In these "dichotomizing discourses" (444), the opposition between authenticity and modernity often receives elaboration, as it is deeply tied to the question of what social stratum is to represent the nation. The nature of these symbolically loaded oppositions ensures that any commentary on them is sharply contested and assigned membership in one or another opposition camp.

The orthography debates about kreyòl share these and other structural and symbolic properties of dichotomizing discourses. Critical to the debates is the question of who counts and who does not, who is "us" and who is "them." In terms of nation-building, these oppositions often point to serious social divisions and ambivalences that have deep historical roots. The debates draw on language ideologies that are also contradictory and dichotomizing, articulated by metalinguistic terms demarcating kreyòl speech varieties—varieties that mark social divisions that have affected national identity formation. The discourse of these debates also engages with critical historical events, as evidenced in arguments about whether or not to represent French, the colonial language, in the kreyòl orthography. The logic employed in Haiti's orthography debates is not limited to local or national considerations. Because of the Haitian diaspora, arguments about orthography have repercussions for the representation of Haitian identities transnationally. It is significant that many Haitians who reside in the United States refuse to become American citizens and give up their Haitian passports. Furthermore, orthographic choice here is a statement about a nation's potential connections to other communities; given Haiti's historical connections to France, there are international implications, at least at the symbolic level.

Anderson makes the point that "communities are to be distinguished . . . by the style in which they are imagined" (1983:6). For Anderson, one of the most important manifestations of how communities are imagined is their shared signs, that is, literacy—its practices and its texts. In order to get to print capitalism, literature, and newspapers, however, there has to be a standardized orthography. There should also be a literate readership. For some nations, these two factors are not unproblematic, and the achievement of both involves complex political as well as social decisions.

Sounds and spoken languages are not at the center of the political issues in Anderson's imagined communities. Sounds, however, are at the center of Haiti's orthography debates. The single cultural practice that all Haitians share is speaking kreyòl, yet the *image* of this language, its representation in ideology, is itself deeply contested. To make our argument about why kreyòl orthographies have been the subject of debates that have gone beyond linguistic and pedagogical issues, we start with an overview of Haiti's sociolinguistic situation and describe aspects of kreyòl dialects, in particular the contested front rounded vowels. This is followed by an analysis of metalinguistic terms refering to kreyòl speech varieties that encode critical social distinctions. We offer comparative material drawn from other French Creole–speaking nations to show similarities among pairs of metalinguistic terms and suggest that the oppositions articulated are part of similar dichotomizing discourses. After a brief history of the writing of kreyòl, we present the main proposals for a systematic orthography. This is followed by a consideration of contested orthographies as sites of contested identity as we examine the social, symbolic, and political values of the sounds and the look of the kreyòl orthographies.

The Sociolinguistics of Haiti

For Haitians, the history and ideology associated with kreyòl and French have social and political implications that are played out in all social relationships. The appropriate use of those languages in educational, religious, and political contexts is widely discussed in public fora. Examining the complex and often paradoxical values associated with these debates is critical to understanding the ways in which Haitians evaluate each other and think about themselves. Kreyòl, like other creole languages, still pays the price of its origins. By-products of European colonization of the New World, creole languages developed on plantations from the forced contacts between the European masters and their African slaves. According to most creolists, West African languages are the substrate and French the superstrate for kreyòl. What this means is that many elements of the grammatical structure of kreyòl were contributed by the dominated West African slaves, while the lexical base came largely from the dominating French colonizers (Koopman 1986, Singler 1993). Like many other creole languages, kreyòl continues to exist in a complex political and social relationship to a "standard" language, in this case French, which has been used in government since 1804 when Haiti won its independence, but was not legally recognized as the "official" language of the nation until 1918. Haiti was the first of the Caribbean countries to give its vernacular the status of an "official language."[4] In 1964 kreyòl was mentioned for the first time in a Haitian constitution: the law now permitted the use of kreyòl in specific circumstances where the use of French could be detrimental to monolinguals, for example, in legal courts. An educational reform sponsored by the government was approved in 1979, and kreyòl was officially introduced into the schools. In 1980 one orthography was made official. Kreyòl was recognized as a "national" language, together with French, in 1983; nonetheless, French still played the role of the "official" language.[5] Finally, in 1987, Haiti officially became a "bilingual" country with two official languages, French and kreyòl, in spite of the fact that only 7 percent of the population is bilingual. But, as the anthropologist Michel-Rolph Trouillot has pointed out, "most linguists have stopped calling Haiti bilingual" (1990:115). These distinctions and shifts between what is the "official" language and what is the "national" language are linked significantly to definitions and redefinitions of Haitian identity through the respective status of French and kreyòl, as is discussed later in this chapter.

Formerly, sociolinguists described the relationship between Haitian French and kreyòl as diglossic: both were considered varieties of the same language, used by speakers in different social contexts for different functions.[6] Haitian French was viewed as the high-prestige form and kreyòl as the low-prestige form. However, Haiti is better described as a nation predominantly composed of two linguistic communities, the minority kreyòl/French bilingual elite (7 percent) and the monolingual kreyòl urban and rural masses, with varying degrees of linguistic interaction between the two, depending on domains of contact (Valdman 1984). Currently, most creolists no longer accept the view that Haitian French and kreyòl are varieties of the same language but regard them as two distinct languages.

For most of its history, kreyòl has been a language of oral expression, while Haitian French has a literate tradition. Currently, there are approximately 6 million speakers of kreyòl, including those in the Haitian diaspora, located largely in New York, Miami, Boston, and Montreal. Many are literate in English and/or French, and while there are no reliable statistics available, it is likely that less than 10 percent are literate in kreyòl.

Kreyòl Dialects and Metalinguistics

The Haitian linguist Sylvain published the first serious study of kreyòl in 1936, *Le Créole Haïtien, Morphologie et Syntaxe*. Her view was that Haitian grammar derives largely from Ewe, a West African language. Later studies by Haitians as well as by foreign linguists focused on issues of origin, phonetics, phonology, morphology, syntax, lexicography, and semantics.[7] Despite their work, the perception about kreyòl as a variety of French still persists outside Haiti in both scholarly and popular works.

One area in which there is little consensus concerns the phonology of kreyòl, specifically the status of four front rounded vowels: /ü/, /ö/, /œ/, /œ̃/. (Curiously, the nasal front rounded /œ̃/ is not given much consideration in the discussions.) The debates center on whether the four front rounded vowels should be included in the description of kreyòl and, consequently, whether they should be represented in the writing system. These debates focus essentially on critical features that differentiate sociolinguistic variants of kreyòl.

Both geographical and social dialects exist in Haiti. The Haitian linguist Michelson P. Hyppolite (1949) was the first to analyze three regional dialects, a northern variety, a western variety, and a southern variety. These are marked by minimal phonetic, lexical, and syntactic differences.[8] In contrast to these regional differences, the social dialects not only are relevant to the description of kreyòl but are central in the debates about various orthographies. *Kreyòl fransize* (Frenchified kreyòl), *gwo kreyòl* (vulgar kreyòl), *kreyòl swa* (smooth kreyòl), and *kreyòl rèk* (rough kreyòl) are used both popularly and scientifically to describe varieties of kreyòl.

While some linguists disagree about the importance of variation in kreyòl in terms of both geographical and social dialects (Déjean 1980a, 1993; Fattier 1993; Valdman 1984:85), there seems to be agreement about the existence of a rural variety (*créole rural*) and an urban variety (*créole urbain*) of kreyòl (Lofficial 1979:41). The kreyòl spoken by the urban and rural masses, called *gwo kreyòl* (rough/popular/vulgar kreyòl) (Férère 1974:28, Hall 1953:12, Pressoir 1947:66), refers to a variety spoken by the *gros peuple* (masses) (Hall 1953:214), as opposed to the *kreyòl fransize* (Frenchified kreyòl) of the educated bilingual minority. The Haitian linguist Vernet (1989:20) notes the existence of the variety called *kreyòl fransize*, a term used to refer to the variety of kreyòl spoken by educated urban bilinguals.[9] They contrast their *kreyòl fransize* with *gwo kreyòl* (rough, vulgar kreyòl), which they say is spoken by uneducated urban people and peasants. Both terms refer not only to the phonology, vocabulary, and intonational contours of the speech itself but also to the nonverbal gestures used by speakers of each variety. Uneducated speakers, however, prefer the term *bon kreyòl* (good kreyòl) to refer to the variety that they themselves use, though they know the other terms. However, speakers often cannot spontaneously switch between these varieties. Depending on their own language socialization experiences and social networks, educated speakers can recognize *kreyòl rèk* but are not always able to produce it, and uneducated speakers can recognize the other variety but not speak it spontaneously.

The French sociolinguist Dominique Fattier-Thomas distinguishes between *kreyòl swa* (smooth kreyòl), the sociolect of the bilingual educated minority, and *kreyòl rèk* (rough kreyòl), the variety spoken by the monolingual masses (1984:39). Lofficial also uses the term *kreyòl rèk*, which he describes as "le niveau ressenti comme le plus rude de la langue" (1979:118) (the level felt to be the roughest of the language). While these metalinguistic terms are noted in the sociolinguistic literature on kreyòl (Fattier-Thomas 1984; Valdman 1988, 1989a, 1989b, 1991) and are commonly known by Haitians in a variety of social classes, the words *rèk* (not ripe), *swa* (smooth), and *gwo* (large or rough as in *gwo pèp* [the people (of the lower classes)]) are not listed in the various kreyòl dictionaries in their metalinguistic usage. It is informative for later discussions of the orthography to elaborate on the semantics of these expressions because they carry important cultural meanings.

Swa (smooth, French *soie* [silk]) as a single lexical item is primarily used as an adjectival modifier of *cheve* (hair) and refers to fine, straight hair. The opposite of *cheve swa* in this referential sense is *cheve grenn* (tightly curled, kinky; French *crépu*). Men are also said to be *swa* (smooth) if they are well mannered, educated, emotionally even, and pleasing to women (*nèg sa a swa* [that guy is smooth]), a positive description. *Swa* as an adverbial modifier refers to the smooth manner in which some action is carried out. For example, one says of a car that runs smoothly and is problem free, *machin sa a mache swa*. Yet another example, *pale swa* (speak smoothly and persuasively), describes speech that is flowing, regardless of the social or educational background of the speaker.

Kreyòl rèk, another speech variety, is not strictly opposed to *kreyòl swa*, though these two terms are reportedly contrasted (Fattier-Thomas 1984; Valdman 1989a, 1989b, 1991). Outside of its reference to speech, the primary meaning of the word *rèk* is agricultural, where it refers to fruit or vegetables that are not yet ripe but ready to pick.[10] When referring to persons, *rèk* is often applied to children in the sense of precocious physical maturity, as *ti moun sa a rèk* (this child looks older than he/she really is). In addition, *rèk* refers to strength, particularly in men.

Unlike *swa*, which can modify a range of actions, *rèk* is used only to describe a manner of speaking: *pale rèk* (speak roughly) is the opposite of *pale swa* (speak smoothly). *Pale rèk* also indexes a verbal style of directness, in opposition to the more indirect style of *pale swa*. Yet another way to refer to styles of indirection is the kreyòl expression *pale franse* (lit. "speaking French"). The cultural meaning of this expression is somewhat different from *pale swa*. *Pale franse* emphasizes speaking indirectly (in either French or kreyòl), with the implication of tricking someone through the use of beautiful sounds, obfuscated speech, or irrelevant arguments. The result may be confusion for the listener. Depending on the speakers and the context, what sounds good (*pale swa* or *pale franse*) can be viewed as potentially deceptive.[11]

The differences between *kreyòl swa* (similar to the *fransize* variety) and *kreyòl rèk* (similar to *gwo kreyòl*) lie in the various degrees of similarities to French (phonetic as well as lexical traits, but also intonation, comportment) of the *fransize* or the *swa* varieties. The main characteristics of *kreyòl swa* (all pertaining to surface structure) can be listed as follows and include phonetic, lexical, and discourse features:

use of front rounded vowels /ö/, /œ/, /ü/ where *kreyòl rèk* would use the nonrounded vowels /e/, /ɛ/, and /i/

use of the postvocalic /r/ at the end of words[12]

use of lexemes closer to French

use of code-switching between kreyòl and French

use of "quasi-lexified" French idiomatic expressions (kreyòl: *predventen*; French: *près de vingt ans* [about twenty years ago])

vocabulary differences due to particular domains and stylistics (Fattier-Thomas 1984:41–42)

Relevant to the orthography debate is the prevocalic Haitian /r/ and its possible realization as a more labialized /w/ in four main contexts: /ɔ̃/, /o/, /ɔ/, /u/. While Haitian linguists agree about this distribution at the phonetic level, there is much debate about the labialized form /w/ when we examine its representation in written form (Déjean 1980a:97, Vernet 1989:18).[13]

Since 1986, with the liberation of the press and the increased access of the masses to the media, there has been a shift in values associated with these speech varieties. Fattier-Thomas (1987) remarks that some bilinguals, in particular politicians, try to modify their usual *kreyòl swa* to sound more like the popular variety *kreyòl rèk* in an attempt to identify with the masses. Monolinguals try to imitate the prestigious form *kreyòl swa*. Both categories of speakers meet with little success. *Kreyòl rèk* and *gwo kreyòl* are now given value in some progressive circles where claims of authenticity and rootedness in cultural identity are asserted. As this is happening, the term *bon kreyòl* is becoming an alternative to *kreyòl rèk* and *gwo kreyòl*, because the latter two have long-standing negative connotations for the bilinguals. *Bon kreyòl* is currently the term used in Haiti to refer to the kreyòl spoken by the masses.[14]

While these metalinguistic terms from Haiti are worth considering on their own, by expanding the frame of reference for a moment to other French lexicon-based creoles spoken in the Caribbean (Martinique and Guadeloupe) as well as in the Indian Ocean region, we see that particular ideas about the superiority of the French language (Swiggers 1990) and the creoles that are in relationship to it have originated in France.[15] The languages of Haiti, Martinique, Guadeloupe, the Seychelles, and Mauritius share a wide range of lexical and syntactic structures due to their historical commonalities. These islands were colonized by the French in the seventeenth, eighteenth, and early nineteenth centuries and during their early history had slavery-based plantation economies and a population that consisted preponderantly of African slaves (Goodman 1964:14). Their creole languages developed under similar social and economic circumstances, where varieties of French were in contact with different African languages. This colonial experience provided not only the medium in which similar linguistic structures and vocabularies evolved but also the socioeconomic foundation for the development of a set of attitudes and ideologies about the languages and their speakers. In all of these countries, Haiti included, a small group of French speakers occupied positions of authority over a large, dominated population. French was the prestige language, and the creoles were assigned a range of lower social values.

It is not surprising, therefore, to find that when speakers in Martinique, Guadeloupe, the Seychelles, and Mauritius, for example, refer to the different varieties of creole language spoken within their speech communities, they use metalinguistic terms quite similar to those found in Haiti. These terms not only express a set of complex relationships to French but also assign hierarchical values to the varieties of creole themselves, as social strata are viewed as having their own named varieties of creole. For example, in the Seychelles two varieties are distinguished: *gros créole* and *créole de la bourgeoisie* (Bollée 1989:185–186). In Martinique the term *kréyòl rèk* is used by the intellectuals to refer to the variety of kréyòl that is the furthest and most differentiated variety from French. While the characteristics of this "basilectal" creole is its *déviance maximale* with regards to French (Bernabé 1985:12), it is also assigned values of authenticity and purity (Prudent 1989:71). *Kréyòl rèk* is used in opposition to the term *langue tjòlòlò*, which is the Frenchified variety of creole. The term *tjòlòlò* (watery, diluted, without taste or substance) refers to liquids as well as language. Here it is the creole that is diluted with particular foreign elements: French words, sounds, and culture. The contrast *rèk-tjòlòlo* is authenticity versus acculturation and alienation. Thus, not only did France leave its language in its colonies, but French colonists transmitted broadly shared social and linguistic ideologies that have had similar repercussions regarding attitudes toward varieties of the languages spoken there, including the creoles. The same language ideology has had an impact on choices concerning the development of orthographies of these creole languages.

Before addressing the specifics of the different kreyòl orthographies, we offer one further observation about attitudes held towards creole languages. Today, even in scientific spheres, a persistent stigma is attached to creole languages.[16] Because their formative period, the seventeenth and eighteenth centuries, was relatively recent, they are often seen as not yet fully formed, complex languages. The descriptions of creole languages in some linguistic circles are similar to the attitudes of many creole speakers toward their languages. These languages are described as "reduced," simple, and easy to learn; lacking in abstract terms, they are inadequate for scientific, philosophical, and logical operations. For most of their histories, creole languages have not been considered adequate for government, schooling, or Western religious services.

The effects of pseudoscientific arguments or preconceived emotional ideas are evident in the negative attitudes lay persons generally hold toward creole languages and their speakers and are revealed by the many pejorative terms used by native and nonnative speakers alike. Folk terminologies describe the French-lexicon creoles as "broken French," "patois," "dialects," or "jargons," and many assume that creole languages are "diminished," "reduced," "deformed," "impoverished," "vitiated," "bastard" forms of the European standard languages that contributed to their birth.[17] Many educated middle-class Haitians, members of the petite bourgeoisie, as well as Haitian elites, view kreyòl as derived from a simplified form of French with African and Arawak inputs. Many claim it is not a real language at all but a mixture of languages without a grammar. The different varieties of kreyòl are viewed by Haitians of those social categories with a great deal of ambivalence. *Kreyòl rèk* and *gwo kreyòl* are often associated with pejorative connotations regarding the sounds (harsh, not harmonious, guttural, deformed), the grammatical features (debased, corrupt, elementary, lacking complexity), and the social origin of the speakers (rural, lower class) and defects usually attributed to the speakers themselves (coarse, clumsy, stupid, illiterate, uneducated). On the positive side, the same varieties have been associated with national identity, authenticity, independence, sincerity, and trustworthiness. Much of this is connected to romantic notions about rural people—rough, coarse, but also authentic, real.

These ideas about kreyòl not only have had important repercussions for the ways in which monolingual kreyòl speakers have been viewed but have also had important consequences for the codification and functions of written kreyòl. As we will see, the question of the nature and meaning of these language varieties in Haiti and who speaks them is at the core of the orthography debate that has been going on in Haiti for more than fifty years and which, despite the claims of many linguists that the question is closed, still provokes reactions among linguists and educators both in Haiti and in New York today. The debate on the use of kreyòl itself, and particularly on the use of kreyòl in schools, is broader and is taken up by parents and teachers in addition to writers and media people. But the issues of orthography and use, we argue, are connected through broader ideological issues.

Writing kreyòl: A Brief History

Historical evidence suggests that while Haiti was under French colonial rule (1695–1803), kreyòl was widely spoken among both masters and slaves as well as among the *affranchis* (freed slaves). Written kreyòl, however, was quite rare (Fouchard 1955, 1972; Hoffman 1989). The first accounts of written kreyòl date to the late eighteenth century when kreyòl was used for both official and literary purposes.[18] While a few official documents for political purposes were prepared in kreyòl during these early periods, they were read to the nonliterate population and did not circulate as written documents. The use of written documents in kreyòl for political or administrative purposes did not appear again until two hundred years later, in the late twentieth century. During the eighteenth and nineteenth centuries, the few writers who attempted to write in kreyòl applied French orthographic rules, which resulted in different *étymologisantes* (more or less etymological) spellings.[19] We cannot talk of a spelling system for kreyòl before the twentieth century.

Only a few written texts in kreyòl dating from the early part of the twentieth century can be found. It is not surprising that they are mostly written versions of Haitian folktales, which are part of a rich oral tradition. There is, for example, Georges Sylvain's *Cric? Crac!* (1901) and translations or adaptations (from the French) of La Fontaine's fables for children, such as Doret's *Pour amuser nos tous petits: Fables de la Fontaine traduites en prose créole* (1924). Written kreyòl was thus limited to minor genres (poems, folktales, *saynètes* [playlets]) and aimed at entertaining specific audiences: children or a condescending elite. These writers, as those before them, continued to use nonconventionalized orthographies based on French etymologies and the stylistic conventions and punctuation of written French. Furthermore, it is important to note that the use of kreyòl for these limited genres can be linked to ideas still held by many today: that kreyòl cannot be used for serious matters, such as education, science, or major literary genres, and is best for jokes and light entertainment.

Following the American occupation of Haiti (1915–1934), a different consciousness emerged. Dr. Jean Price-Mars, whose work laid a foundation for *Négritude*, denounced in *Ainsi parla l'oncle* ([1928] 1973) the prevailing scornful attitude among Haitian elites toward Haitian culture and their indiscriminate adoption of the European lifestyle, which they judged superior. This was later echoed by members of the Indigenist Movement (late 1930–1970s) who promoted a broader use of genuinely

Haitian themes in literature and an acceptance of popular culture in Haitian society (Pompilus 1977). Despite the nationalist agenda, production of written kreyòl texts was still rare. Most Indigenist writers still used French, a French mingled with kreyòl locutions and phrases for local color, which gave it a Haitian touch. None of them produced a body of work written entirely in kreyòl, since their target was precisely those members of Haitian society who, most of the time, used spoken and written French in their everyday life and rejected the use of kreyòl.[20]

The few members of the Indigenist School or other writers *engagés* (militant) who used kreyòl employed an orthography *étymologisante* (etymologizing) for kreyòl, that is, an orthography very close to French.[21] While there was strong support for indigenous cultural practices and their integration into artistic spheres, especially literary productions, an "indigenous" orthography was not contemplated at that time. Orthography was simply not viewed as a symbolic domain in which Haitian identity could be affirmed.

In the 1960s, new developments in kreyòl literature took place. The first literary "landmarks" were translations of French and Greek "literary monuments" into kreyòl, such as Corneille's *Le Cid* by Numa (1975), and Sophocle's *Antigone* by Morisseau-Leroy (1953b). These translations were different from the earlier translations of La Fontaine because the audience was an adult readership (not children), and, unlike fables, which were considered a nonserious genre, these works showed that kreyòl was able to handle sophisticated masterpieces as a *langue de culture* (cultured language, a language that can carry culture or introduce culture). This phase was followed by the creation of new literary works in kreyòl. *Dézafi*, the first novel in kreyòl, was written by Frankétienne in 1975, and the appearance of Trouillot's *Ti difé boulé sou istoua ayiti* (1977) (Controversies about Haitian history) demonstrated that written kreyòl could be used not only for literary genres but also for serious scientific essays.

Developing an Orthographic System for kreyòl

Since the mid-1920s, the proposals for a systematic orthography for written kreyòl have undergone different phases that can be summarized as follows:

1925–1940	The pioneers (Doret, Beaulieu)
1940–1951	The first technical orthographies (McConnell-Laubach and Pressoir)
1953–1979	The contested reign of Pressoir-ONAAC (Office National d'Alphabétisation et d'Action Communautaire)
1980–present	The reign of the official orthography (with isolated rebellions)

The development of these different orthographies is elaborated later in this chapter. Since the promulgation of the official orthography in January 1980, some of the debate has diminished, but arguments for and against the official orthography are still aired in a variety of arenas, including educational circles, the Haitian press, and elsewhere.[22] There were, however, almost as many proposals as there were participants in the debates. As of 1980, Déjean (1980a:162) identified a total of eleven proposed spelling systems. Nonetheless, despite the apparent diversity, three main types of proposals can be identified:

1. Those that support a pro-phonemic approach
2. those that take a pro-etymological or anti-phonemic perspective
3. those in an intermediary camp that propose a phonemic orthography but with some concessions to French spelling.[23]

The earliest systematic orthography for kreyòl was proposed in 1924 by Frédéric Doret, an engineer interested in teaching methods for monolingual kreyòl speakers, especially children (Doret 1924). Later, in 1939, Christian Beaulieu, a Haitian educator, undertook the task (Beaulieu 1939). Their efforts remained essentially unnoticed.

In 1940 the development of an orthography for writing kreyòl became a serious issue. At that time, an Irish Protestant missionary, Ormonde McConnell, who had done work in adult literacy in rural southern and western areas of Haiti, devised the first technical orthography. It used thirty-three symbols and was phonemic:

oral vowels:	a é è i o ò u
nasal vowels:	â ê ô
semivowels:	i/y w u (in the dipthong ui)
consonants:	b d f g h j k l m n p r s t v z
digraphs:	sh gn (Déjean 1980a:19–20)

In 1943 McConnell was joined by an American literacy expert, Frank Laubach, who was not familiar with kreyòl, and together they revised McConnell's original spelling system. The second version was called McConnell-Laubach, or *òtograf Laubach*, and was also a phonemic orthography. It used the same alphabet as McConnell's, with the following differences: the letters *ou* instead of *u* to represent the sound /u/ as in kreyòl *dou* (French *doux*); and the letters *ch* instead of *sh* to represent the sound /š/ as in kreyòl *chante* (French *chanter*). This spelling system was used in the literacy campaign sponsored by the government of Elie Lescot. The materials, almost all inspired from Protestant religious texts, were designed to bring salvation and light to the Haitian rural masses.

The Haitian scholar Charles Fernand Pressoir (1947) strongly criticized the McConnell-Laubach orthography mainly because of (1) the absence of the front rounded vowels /ü/, /ö/, /œ/, /œ̃/; (2) the broad use of the "Anglo-Saxon" letters *w* and *y*; and (3) the use of the circumflex accent to mark the nasalized vowels (â, ê, and ô), thus using a French diacritic but with a different application (French uses the letter *n* to indicate nasalization). Some called this system *kréyòl bwa-nan-nen* (kreyòl with a wooden stick on the nose) because of the abundance of circumflexes.

This refers both to the way the words look in their written form and to how they were to be pronounced when read.[24] Pressoir claimed (1947) that this new orthography was good for "savages" who spoke a *gros créole* (rough creole).

The literacy campaign, however, failed for political and cultural reasons. It was closely associated with the unpopular government of President Elie Lescot and coincided with an infamous "antisuperstition campaign" geared towards the suppression of the "barbarous" practices of vodou, which resulted in the destruction of many temples and sacred objects (Déjean 1963:23–44).

Although systematic, the McConnell-Laubach orthography was contested by many educated Haitians because of its association with Protestantism and its "American" look—a sensitive political issue, since Americans had occupied Haiti from 1915 to 1934 (Pressoir 1947). Those Haitians did not want any reminders of the American presence, not even in the writing system. They were not happy about the novel representation of nasalized vowels through the use of the circumflex, which treated these nasal sounds differently from the ways in which they are represented in French. This made the representation of kreyòl appear strange and foreign and, in particular, far from French. Arguments were made that this orthography would inhibit learning French, a goal in educational circles.

Pressoir, who led the opposition to McConnell-Laubach's system but was himself in favor of a pro-phonemic orthography, introduced a number of changes. He eliminated the circumflex to indicate nasalization and introduced the letter *n* in its place. In spite of the fact that the "Anglo-Saxon" letters *k*, *y*, and *w* looked "too American," he nonetheless retained the letter *k* instead of choosing the letter *c* (as in French) to represent the sound /k/ and also kept the letter *y* together with the letter *i* to represent the semiconsonant /j/ (Déjean 1980a:185), as in for example, *ayè* (yesterday). Instead of the letter *w*, however, he used the digraph *ou* to represent both the vocalic sound /u/ and the semivocalic sound /w/, thus adopting the French orthographic convention for representing those sounds.

Pressoir's system used the following alphabet of thirty symbols:

oral vowels:	a é è i o ò u	digraph: ou
nasal vowels:	an in on	
semivowels:	i/y ou u (in the dipthong ui)	
consonants:	b d f g j k l m n p r s t v z	digraphs: ch gn

(Déjean 1980a:183)

Pressoir also introduced the hyphen to distinguish between the nasalized vowels as in /pãtã/ (kreyòl *pantan* [surprise]) and (nonnasalized) vowels that are followed by the nasal consonant /n/, as for example in *pa-n* (French *panne* [mechanical breakdown]).

The Pressoir orthography was adopted with some modifications. For example, some users introduced the apostrophe instead of the hyphen (Déjean 1980a:194). The Pressoir orthography has been used, primarily by government agencies, for more than thirty years in adult literacy programs and has been considered quite satisfactory (Déjean 1980a:182, Férère 1977:59, Pompilus 1985:163). American missionaries, however, used a modified McConnell-Laubach orthography for Bible translation and instruction. In literary circles, independent writers who wished to write in kreyòl created their own orthographic systems, more or less close to French etymology and orthography, thus contesting the Pressoir system. There was thus no consensus about orthography.

Discussions regarding the appropriate orthography were based on the premise that literacy in kreyòl was exclusively targeted at the large nonliterate adult population. This changed in the 1970s as a result of social and political pressures to change the social order of the country, including the educational system. Before 1946, the educational system was elitist in both content and clientele, and French was the only medium of instruction. After the revolution of 1946, education became a real possibility for the lower classes, whose offspring progressively outnumbered those of the elite. The schools could not respond to the needs of this growing heterogeneous student body, and, as a consequence, by the 1970s the educational system faced a crisis. While other factors, such as economic and social dimensions, were involved, the poor academic achievement of the majority of lower-class students was explained primarily by those students' ignorance of the language of instruction, that is, French. It was suggested by the Ministry of Education that kreyòl should become the new language of instruction. This radical proposal was met by passionate reactions among the public regarding, first, the use of kreyòl itself and, subsequently, the choice of an orthography for kreyòl. The debates mainly involved writers, educators, and linguists. During 1972 and 1973 the media were used for much animated discussion. Many proposals were made, too numerous to detail here.[25]

Once kreyòl was officially introduced by law in the schools in September 1979, it was vital that the Haitian government unify kreyòl orthography. To do so, it established as the official orthography a system developed by Haitian linguists from the Institut Pédagogique National in collaboration with French linguists from the Université René Descartes. The official orthography has an alphabet of thirty-two symbols:

oral vowels: a e è i o ò ou

nasalized vowels: an en on oun

semivowels: w y u (in the dipthong ui)

consonants: b ch d f g h j k l m n ng p r s t v z

The official orthography, called *òtograf IPN* (after the Institut Pédagogique National) or *òtograf ofisyel* or, more simply, *òtograf kreyòl*, was made official on a trial basis by a communiqué of the Ministry of Education on January 30, 1980. After four years of experimentation, the government was supposed to take a definitive decision. The four years have long since passed, but no official document has, as yet, either endorsed or discredited the official orthography. The system is still contested by some linguists and provokes passionate reactions among the public for reasons to be discussed in the following section.

In this orthography the sound /ɛ̃/ is represented by *en*. Only one accent mark has been retained, the grave, as in *ò* to represent the sound /ɔ/ and *è* to represent the sound /ɛ/. The use of the hyphen and apostrophe are optional. (For example, in New

York Haitian educational circles, one never sees hyphens or apostrophes, and suggestions that they be used meet with a negative response). Another option concerns the representation of the prevocalic /w/ as either the letter *w* or *r* before /o/, /õ/, /ɔ/, or /u/ (for example, *gwo* or *gro*), and the use of the letter *y* is used to represent the sound /j/. For the back-rounded vowel /u/ the graphic representation is *ou*.

One of the major goals of the McConnell-Laubach orthography was that it be easy for the monolingual masses to learn and use and thus make it possible for them to quickly become literate in French, the goal at the time. For Pressoir, the major ideological concerns were that the orthography not look American and that it function as a bridge to literacy in French. When the *òtograf kreyòl* was introduced in 1979, the linguistic ideology regarding kreyòl itself had changed significantly, and this factor affected the attitudes people held toward the orthography as a representational system. Unlike the earlier periods of adult literacy campaigns, in which kreyòl was treated simply as a transitional tool or medium to be used for the achievement of other goals, by 1979 kreyòl was thought about not only in the context of literacy but more generally as the *language of instruction* as well as an *object of instruction*. The image of kreyòl, both spoken and written, and, consequently, its role in social and political life had changed.

Pro-phonemicists, Pro-etymologists, Intermediaries: What and Whom Are They Representing?

Why is the issue of the kreyòl orthography so important to Haitians? The matter is not simply whether to write, for example, the kreyòl word for bread (/pɛ̃/) with *e* (*pen*) or *i* (*pin*) or *ain* (*pain*) as in the French *pain*. The underlying issue is about representations of self ("Haitianness") and representations of the nation.

Pro-phonemicists insist that kreyòl must be written in a coherent, systematic, and logical way. Even though some anti-French feeling can be noticed in some representatives of the group (for example, Déjean 1975a, 1975b, 1980a, 1980b, 1980c), the first criterion they consider is that a kreyòl orthography be easy to learn as well as completely independent from the French orthographic system. For them, the target groups are monolingual kreyòl speakers who do not read French and theoretically can learn any orthography. The most straightforward kreyòl system is the easiest for the not-yet-literate monolinguals because the only relevant facts are kreyòl facts. The orthography should represent the sounds of *their* kreyòl. The pro-phonemicists comprise those who have adopted and used, even if with slight variations, Pressoir's orthographic system and, since 1980, the *òtograf kreyòl*. Most who adopt this approach are people involved in adult literacy and/or children's literacy programs in Haiti and in the United States. Representatives of this camp are the Haitian government (Office National d'Alphabétisation et d'Action Communautaire, Institut Pédagogique National, and the Ministry of Education); the Catholic and Protestant churches; linguists, including Vernet, Déjean, and Bayardel; and independent writers and nonlinguists. The opinions of this group are not homogeneous; Déjean, for example, explains that he accepted the official orthography, though with reservations, in order to put an end to "useless" discussions (1980a, 1980b,1980c).

Pro-etymologists, on the other hand, argue that kreyòl must stay as close as possible to the French orthographic system. The reasoning that underlies this position is that French and kreyòl will always coexist in Haiti, and thus it is logical to facilitate the learning of French through kreyòl. This idea is usually expressed by the image of an "orthographic bridge" that will help avoid the confusion that might result for kreyòl monolinguals as well as for bilinguals from the use of two totally different systems for languages that, they think, are quite similar. Kreyòl orthography, the pro-etymologists assert, must also reflect kreyòl's origin, which, for them, is predominantly the French language. Those who align themselves with the pro-etymologist position include mainly literary people and members of the intelligentsia (for example, Archer 1987, Labuchin 1973, Métellus 1990, Roumer 1973), primary and secondary school teachers, and many parents from both the middle classes and the lower classes who are concerned about the introduction of kreyòl into schools.

A third position, which advocates an intermediate solution, is represented by the Haitian linguists and educators Pompilus (1973) and Lofficial (1979). From their perspective, the orthography should be phonemic but whenever possible should use the same conventions as the French orthography to represent sounds similar in French and kreyòl. Their reasoning is that French and kreyòl coexist in Haiti; one day, they believe, the country will be totally bilingual. Their first suggestion is to include the front rounded vowels (usually associated with the speech of bilinguals) in the phonetic description of kreyòl and to provide a graphic representation for each of them. Pompilus gives two reasons for this: (1) many noneducated people also pronounce those vowels in their everyday speech, and (2) eliminating the vowels will have as a consequence the rejection by many people of the orthography itself and of the use of kreyòl for instruction (1973:30).[26]

It is difficult to reconcile Pompilus's proposal for an intermediate orthography that would integrate the front rounded vowels with his declaration that it would be illusory to take the variety of kreyòl spoken by the urban educated as the standard (cited by Déjean 1980a:170). This contradiction reveals the tension inherent in creating a bridge between the past (etymology) and the future (when Haiti will be totally bilingual) when the present itself is so full of conflict. Lofficial argues that it is better to prevent potential problems, since it is likely that, with the influence of schools and the media, the occurrence of the front rounded vowels will increase (1979:118). Thus, it is better to anticipate the difficulties that could arise from two totally different systems and integrate the front rounded vowels now. The Haitian linguist Gérard Férère advocates something quite similar with his proposal of an "ethno-orthography" (1974:23), that is, an orthography culturally and socially acceptable—an orthography that must include the front rounded vowels, which are not just marginal sounds (Férère 1974:50).

Orthography as Representation: How the Language Sounds and Looks

The question of the status of kreyòl and the orthographic debates is deeply tied to issues of representation at both the national and the international levels. Orthographic debates when situated within the broader framework of language ideology—the cultural beliefs that underlie language practices, choices, and attitudes of a people—can be seen as articulating historically grounded tensions between groups that do not hold equal shares in the social and political system. Often these inequalities developed during colonial encounters and were maintained after the original colonists were no longer present.

The notion that the French language is superior to all others was transmitted to the French colonies and survived in the minds and practices of both the former colonizers and the formerly colonized. Most of the discussions that took place in Haiti between 1930 and 1990 about language choice and orthographic representation can be traced to a prevailing ideology about the inherent superiority of the French language. This is connected to ideologies about the superiority and refinement of French culture based on the achievements of the great French writers of two past centuries: the Century of Reason (seventeenth century) and the Century of the Enlightenment (eighteenth century). Ideas of the clarity, exactness, logic, rationality, natural order, and richness of the French language as contributing to the greatness of French civilization have been defended by many Haitian writers.[27]

Schools in Haiti, particularly the private ones (which, for the most part, until recently remained exclusively in the hands of the French clergy), played an important role in keeping these ideas strong. After its independence, Haiti rejected anything that was reminiscent of France. Although many French colonists were killed, nonetheless the new nation kept the French language among its *butin de guerre* (war booty) (Dorin 1973:9). Independent Haiti also copied French administrative and organizational structures in order to survive.[28] Since the beginning, the new ruling classes maintained two contradictory positions in their relationship to Europe, particularly to France: hatred and fear at one pole, admiration and emulation at the opposite pole.

The same ambivalence is reflected in Haitians' attitudes toward French and kreyòl, and it is in this light that the importance given to the issue of kreyòl orthography can be best understood. If we look carefully, we will see that the debate is not only about how to write kreyòl, that is, how to represent graphically the sounds of kreyòl. It is about the conception of kreyòl itself as a language and as an element of Haitian national identity, about how Haitians situate themselves through languages at the national and international levels, and about the notions of Haitianness, authenticity, nationalism, and legitimacy. The battle over the orthography cannot be understood if we do not situate it in its social context. The dual linguistic system is a manifestation of the dual cultural system that exists in Haiti. We focus on two specific issues: the question of the "sounds" and the question of the "look" of kreyòl from the perspective of the different camps, all of which have social, political, cultural, and symbolic implications.

The Sounds of kreyòl

The first disagreement is about the sounds that the alphabet should represent, particularly about the existence or nonexistence in kreyòl of four front rounded vowels, /ü/ as in French *tu*; /ö/ as in French *peu*; /œ/ as in French *boeuf*; /œ̃/ as in

French *un*. The existence or nonexistence of the front rounded vowels is viewed by many (including Déjean and Lofficial) as the dividing line between the educated minority and the masses, between rural and urban. But to this is linked more profound questions of representation and legitimacy. Which variety of the language should be standardized and codified? This "technical" question has its counterpart in the sociopolitical arena: which variety constitutes the "real," "authentic" kreyòl? This question leads to others, such as: Who is the "real" Haitian, and whose interests must be taken into account and served? Not surprising to anyone, these questions refer to the struggles for power that have gone on between Noirs and Mulâtres since colonial times and the struggles for upward social mobility by the masses.

Whether the front rounded vowels are the "*apanage*" (exclusive domain) of a minority of educated bilinguals, as Déjean argues, or whether they are also used by monolinguals, as Férère, Pompilus, and Lofficial assert, what interests us in the debate is the role of prestige marker ascribed to them by the population. Déjean himself documents many cases of hypercorrection in the speech of monolingual kreyòl speakers (1980a: 124–125). Fattier-Thomas also notes the use of hypercorrections (related to the front rounded vowels) in commercial advertisements to establish a kind of complicity with the public (1984: 41). This is to say that, for both bilinguals and monolinguals, the front rounded vowels have a highly marked and symbolic value. For the educated and noneducated urban dwellers, the front rounded vowels are associated with the front unrounded vowels, which are considered their antithesis, and function as prestige markers (the front rounded ones being the prestigious forms). For example, consider the following pairs:

	kreyòl		*French*	*English*
OPPOSITION	FRONT ROUNDED	FRONT UNROUNDED	FRONT ROUNDED	
/ü/ - /i/	duri	diri	du riz	rice
	suk	sik	sucre	sugar
/ö/ - /e/	bleu	ble	bleu	blue
	meuzu	mezi	mesure	measure
/œ/ - /ɛ/	pèu	pè	peur	fear
	bèu	bè	beurre	butter
/œ̃/ - /ɛ̃/	lundi	lendi	lundi	Monday
	pafun	pafen	parfum	perfume

These pairs are not minimal pairs. They are variants that are found in social dialects, and they function as social markers. The use of the front rounded series is associated with educated classes, good manners, and harmonious sounds, whereas the second series is associated with popular usage, rough manners, and strident and even vulgar sounds. Metalinguistic terms are used to qualify the second series, the unrounded vowels, and reflect the low esteem associated with these sounds.[29] To pronounce an unrounded vowel when a rounded vowel is expected is to make a mistake, and when one makes this error, Haitians will say that one has a *bouch su* or *bouch si* (sour/acidic mouth) or, more elegantly, a *bouch surette* (puckered mouth).[30] This is related to the idea that these unrounded vowels have intrinsically disagreeable sounds, and these are labled *su* or *si* (sour/acidic). Other meanings of *si* or *su* in kreyòl refer to the taste of lemons and other acidic or unripe fruits and of milk or other kinds of food that can turn sour. When they go bad, one says, "lèt la si" (the milk is sour) or "manje a si" (the food is sour). When food smells rotten, one says, "manje a santi si" (this food smells sour). When someone has indigestion (acidic or upset stomach), one says, "manje a rete si sou lestomak mwen" (I did not digest that food). People can also have a disagreable sour smell, expressed as *nèg sa a santi si* (that man smells sweaty). These examples show the connection of the words *su/si* with the idea of something that has turned disagreeable, sour, rotten.

The negative attitudes toward the unrounded vowels also explain the hypercorrections often made by noneducated speakers when they try to affect a certain degree of education and good manners by avoiding the marked sounds even in cases where there are no alternates. The expressions *bouch su* and *bouch si* as well as *bèk su/si* and *djòl su/si*, of which *bèk si* and *djòl si* are the *rèk* variety and have the pejorative sense of "disgusting trap," are used to describe what speakers do and how they sound when they hypercorrect these vowels in their speech. Those ideas are internalized, it must be stressed, by members at both ends of the social ladder, who react with equal vigor against the official decision to eliminate the front rounded vowels and to generalize the use of the *su/si* sounds. They want their children not to acquire "bad habits" (i.e., *bouch su*) but rather to speak elegantly and as close to French as possible (Jean-Charles 1987, Zéphir 1990). As Lofficial argues "un parti-pris pour les formes marquées peut heurter le sentiment populaire" (a deliberate choice for the marked forms may hurt popular feelings) (1979:118). From this it is reasonable to suggest that an important assumption underlying the rounded-unrounded vowel question is that kreyòl is a deformation of French and that French is the model to imitate.

Both the linguists who designed the official orthography and the government that implemented it consider the front rounded vowels as "marginal sounds." No graphic representation of them is included in the alphabet because, says Vernet, for example, "Il ne faut pas apprendre à l'enfant des sons qu'il ne prononce pas quotidiennement dans sa langue maternelle" (One need not teach a child sounds that he does not pronounce in his mother tongue everyday) (1980:43–44). Déjean has expressed a similar idea: "Choisir un système graphique qui intègre les voyelles antérieures arrondies, c'est augmenter sa difficulté d'apprentissage pour l'immense majorité des Haïtiens" (To choose a graphic system that includes the front rounded vowels is to increase the difficulty of its learning for the majority of Haitians) (1980a:172–173). This suggests another important assumption—that the front rounded vowel sounds are difficult for monolinguals to learn to use (Déjean 1980a:171–173). Thus, those sounds should not figure in the alphabet, in order not to embarrass and marginalize the majority of speakers. By advocating the use of the front unrounded vowels, Déjean expresses his sociopolitical militantism: anyone who proposes to include the four front rounded vowels is *réactionnaire et élitiste* (reactionary and elitist) and aims at promulgating a class and cultural imperialism (1980a:175).[31]

To a lesser extent, the same prestige issue holds for the use of certain nasalized forms. For many words, there is a choice between a less nasalized form and a more nasalized form. In the more nasalized form, a vowel preceding a nasal consonant is itself highly nasalized. In the example, *agronòm agronnonm* (agronomist), *agronòm* has nasal consonants but the vowels are not highly nasalized, whereas *agronnonm* has both nasal consonants and nasalized vowels. "Excessive nasalization" is considered a characteristic of rural speech and is felt to be vulgar (*rèk*) (Lofficial 1979:118). Thus, we have the equation: nasalization = rural = vulgar. The team that developed the *Ti Diksyonnè Kreyòl-Franse* (under the direction of A. Bentolila) chose the nasalized forms as "characteristic" of kreyòl, as indicated by the spelling of the word *diksyonnè* (dictionary). The double *n* marks the pronounciation as extended nasalization, which has rural connotations. Thus, another equation can be stated: rural = authentic = Haitianness. The *Ti Diksyonnè* has been quite controversial in Haiti and New York.[32]

A set of implicit oppositions and contradictions emerges from the debates about the sociolects and standardization of kreyòl. Characteristics of the educated are that they are from higher social classes, use *kreyòl swa*, and are urban, elegant, agreeable, and civilized, all desirable traits for both bilinguals and monolinguals. Characteristics of the uneducated are that they are from the lower classes, are rural (*habitan*), speak *kreyòl rèk*, and have *bouch su/si*, all of which are undesirable for both bilinguals and urban monolinguals but desirable for many nationalists and progressives (linguists, thinkers, and politicians).

The sound system leads directly into the core of the debate about social classes, legitimacy, and authenticity. If we push the idea of authenticity to its limits, the following questions emerge: What sounds are those of the real, authentic kreyòl? What is the real, authentic kreyòl? Thus, who is the real, authentic Haitian—the dominated "Africanized" masses or the dominant "Frenchified" elites? Is there a "pure" kreyòl? We see that the ideological basis of such questions can lead to a vicious circle.

The question of the sounds of kreyòl, particularly when examined in the context of the question of front rounded vowels, led us to issues of legitimacy, social prestige, and social mobility, and also to issues of representation in the local arena. The question of the look of kreyòl can be placed at a different ideological level, involving mainly the relationship of Haiti to other countries, and is centered around the issues of nationality, independence, and autonomy.

The Look of kreyòl

The pro-etymologists center their arguments around the issue of the roots of kreyòl. According to them, kreyòl, derived from French, must reflect its origin and should be easily classified on the basis of its appearance as belonging to a particular world language family, that of the romance languages (Archer 1987). An etymologic orthography will be helpful for learning French later, they argue, since French will always be spoken in Haiti. Haiti must not forget its membership in the *francophonie* (French-speaking community). To adopt an "Anglo-Saxon look," represented by the "non-Latin" letters *w*, *k*, and *y*, is to deny that membership (Archer 1987). According to the most fervent pro-etymologists, the use of the three letters mentioned gives kreyòl a weird look and, even worse, prevents the easy learning of French for both bilinguals and monolinguals. The most zealous pro-etymologists, who also present themselves as zealous nationalists, think that the Anglo-Saxon orthography has been imposed on the Haitian people by imperialist powers. This idea, expressed in 1947, pointed to McConnell and Laubach as agents of the United States, the first imperialist power. This idea was later echoed by Archer (1987). According to her, the purpose of the United States was clear: to eliminate French in order to introduce English, a task that would be accomplished through the anglicization of kreyòl. She believes that the United States also wanted to substitute the Protestant religion for the Catholic faith and vodou religions and that the U.S. interest in Haitian literacy is based only on its desire to sell Bibles and convert Haitians to Protestantism.

Still according to Archer, the aim of the French—the second imperialist power—in this endeavor is not very clear, but it is still worthwhile to raise the question: Why the sudden interest of the Western powers in the vernaculars, in the Caribbean as well as in other parts of the world? Why this insistence on using the vernaculars in education? Archer calls for vigilance and the retention of French and an etymological kreyòl system. Not everyone who is pro-etymological expresses such extreme ideas as Archer, but there is certainly a defensive reaction against or a discomfort with foreign intervention in matters that Haitians consider strictly domestic (Métellus 1990). The same rejection or mistrust is also found in the other two camps (Déjean [1980a] and Lofficial [1979]).

Among the most contested letters is *k*, which not only represents the danger of U.S. imperialism but also has even been claimed to represent the threat of communism.[33] Déjean (1980a) reports that the literacy activists have been accused of being disguised communist agents by a government official under François Duvalier's regime. Here is revealed a fear of a sudden "wakeup" of the masses. Dejéan also reports that a militant communist accused the same orthography of being "bourgeois, réactionnaire et macoute" (1980a:55).

The underlying assumption of the pro-etymologists is that the orthographic system of the language must be linked to a literate culture, to a literary tradition. Kreyòl orthography must follow a sound tradition. The most extreme assumption is that kreyòl needs French to rely on and that French must be given credit for its contribution. On the contrary, answers the opposite pro-phonemic group, no nationality, religion, culture, or political allegiance can be ascribed to single letters like *w*, *k*, and *y*. An orthography is just an arbitrary and conventional system, and, from a linguistic point of view, a writing system should be neutral (Déjean 1980a). Thus, the pro-phonemic group advocates an orthography totally new and independent for kreyòl. From their perspective, the choice of a phonemic system is scientifically justified; it is the more rational and the simpler way of writing kreyòl, which should avoid the errors and aberrations of the French orthography. It is just a conventional system, and the use of *w*, *k*, *y* has nothing to do with being Anglo-Saxon or Protestant, Russian or communist. The underlying assumption is that kreyòl is a language that can stand by itself and does not need to rely on someone else's tradition. Consequently, the pro-phonemic group argues that the teaching of kreyòl must be independent from the teaching of French. For the militants of that group who are the most involved in literacy (for example, Déjean and Vernet), the target is the monolingual masses, not the educated elites.

It is interesting to note that the two most extreme camps, the pro-phonemic and the pro-etymologists, invoke the authority and the neutrality of "science" for their arguments. But we have seen that there are no neutral positions, only ideological stances. One more example of the deeply ideological character of the debate is the silence regarding the simplification of many final consonant clusters involving stops and liquids (both *r* and *l*) and the clusters *sm* and *st*, as in:

/bl /	as in /posib/	French: /posibl/	possible
/pl/	as in /poep/	French: /poepl/	people
/br/	as in /lib/	French: /libr/	free
/pr/	as in /prɔp/	French: /prɔ pr/	clean
/sm/	as in /komunis/	French: /komunism/	communism
/st/	as in /komunis/	French: /komunist/	communist

These final consonant cluster simplifications are not discussed—maybe because they are a general pronounciation feature common to all Haitians, educated and noneducated, present whenever they speak kreyòl or French. Where there is no difference, there is no possibility of marking prestige and social distance through these consonant clusters.[34] Another question unrelated to pronounciation but relevant to writing concerns the use of punctuation, particularly the use of hyphens and apostrophes. Their use is advocated by the pro-etymologists to show contractions (apostrophe) or grammatical relationships (hyphen). Even though the *òtograf kreyòl* allows the use of both signs, many pro-phonemicists reject their use.[35]

Conclusions

These arguments reveal the complexity and the ambivalence of cultural definitions of Haitianness. Since Haiti is still in the process of integrating its dual African/European heritage, there are numerous arenas where cultural duality is continually negotiated. Religion (vodou and western religion) is one important locus of this negotiation process, and language (French and kreyòl) is another. The debates about language also illustrate the extent to which an issue—in this case, orthography—can be politicized when intolerance is the dominant note.

With few exceptions, throughout the nineteenth century, the elites defined themselves as "colored French" and spoke of Haiti as the *fille ainée de la France* (the oldest daughter of France) or as *France Noire* (Black France). Although acknowledging their African roots, the elites also claimed their affiliation with Latin culture. The Indigenist School and the Haitian Ethnology School affirmed that Haitian culture was Afro-Latin but with a predominance of African elements. African elements are associated with blackness, vodou, and the masses. Kreyòl, the only element that the educated claim to share with the masses, is the enduring symbol of Haitian identity. But we have seen an ambivalence in the values attached to kreyòl: the *rèk* variety is used for nationalist discourse on authenticity and pride but at the same time carries negative connotations about these same masses. This ambivalence is reflected in the orthography quarrels themselves, as well as in the wish on the part of the pro-etymological camp for a kreyòl orthographic "bridge" that links the past (French) and the future (when French and kreyòl will coexist peacefully) but that has no solid foundation in an ever-changing present.

It is noteworthy that Haiti is not the only country where language issues and orthography issues in particular provoke emotional reactions. Examples abound of orthographic quarrels in industrialized societies as well as in the so-called third and fourth worlds.[36] The recent arguments regarding the implementation of the reform of the French orthography are a good example of how a country can stick to its orthographic icons as symbols of its identity.[37] When a language is codified and an orthography is officially adopted, this is usually interpreted to mean that there is one correct way to spell and write the language and that all others are simply wrong. To design and implement an orthography is neither a simple nor a neutral endeavor. It establishes norms of pronunciation as well as norms for writing. Because of its prescriptive character, an orthography can be perceived in different ways. The main reason for reaction is that the elaboration of an orthography implies the choice and standardization of one dialect over the others. And when a variety, through its officialization, is given the status of a standard, the users of the other varieties sometimes react with a surprising virulence because they feel that their language variety and its speakers are denied representation.

The latest *òtograf kreyòl* is implicitly positioning the kreyòl spoken by the masses as the standard. This has created resistance both to the adoption of the orthography and to the use of kreyòl as a medium of instruction in school. The double resistance comes from both the masses and the educated elite minority. The masses see the officialization of written and spoken kreyòl in school as limiting their access to French and, consequently, their social and economic mobility. The elites, who already know kreyòl, do not see the point of teaching it, in any form, in school. They also hold the view that *kreyòl rèk* and *gwo kreyòl* are directed toward the lowest common denominator, bringing them down instead of elevating the masses.

As we have seen, the debate around the orthography takes on issues of legitimacy and authenticity. Who is meant to be represented by this *òtograf kreyòl*, whose speech, values, cultural identity? Which version of kreyòl can be said to be genuinely Haitian? Is it the *kreyòl swa* or *kreyòl fransize* of the educated minority, or the *kreyòl rèk*, the *gwo kreyòl*, or the *bon kreyòl*, the "real kreyòl" of the masses? What is the real kreyòl? These rhetorical question have an implicit corollary: "Who is the real Haitian?"

This essay is a reflection on metalinguistic terms used by kreyòl speakers and their relationships to the debate on the elaboration of an orthography for writing kreyòl. We have seen how the metalinguistic terms and the orthography debate are deeply rooted in symbolic systems of representation and in the different and ambivalent meanings ascribed to Haitianness, whether it refers to the national level (issues of identity, authenticity, and legitimacy) or to the international level (issues of sovereignty and self-determination). We hope that this exploration of the terms *rèk*, *swa*, *gwo kreyòl*, *kreyòl fransize*, and *bouch su/si* will be extended by further research that will evaluate the extent and frequency of their use and their relative weight in the sociocultural, economic, and political scenes in Haiti.

Any linguistic policy based exclusively on "purely linguistic facts" takes the risk of going the wrong way, because language not only is an instrument of communication but also carries symbolic values that condition social, political, and economic spheres. The main question to raise, in the Haitian case, is how to give the currently stigmatized variety of kreyòl spoken by the majority of the population, as well as that majority itself, the effective means to reverse the present situation. Such means are not limited to the linguistic sphere but necessarily overlap and have consequences for the economic, social, and political domains, as well.

NOTES

We would like to thank the many Haitians in New York and Port-au-Prince who participated in our research project and freely shared their views about kreyòl with us; the Spencer Foundation and New York University (Research Challenge Fund) for supporting this research; and Michel DeGraff, Susan Gal, Paul Garrett, Fred Myers, Gillian Sankoff, John Singler, Lucien Smarth, and Kathryn Woolard, all of whom generously provided helpful suggestions and encouragement when they were most needed. This chapter was previously published in *American Ethnologist* 21(1), © 1994 American Anthropological Association, reprinted by permission.

1. We refer to the language in the title of the article in the form that is most familiar to an English-speaking audience, Haitian Creole. However, in the body of the text we refer to the language as kreyòl, the way it is referred to by Haitians, and we have chosen to write it and our own transcriptions using the *òtograf ofisyel* (official orthography). We have, of course, maintained the original orthographies used in published sources.

This collaborative project grew out of an investigation of kreyòl language use in New York City, which was then extended to Port-au-Prince. Participants were from diverse social and educational backgrounds and varied in terms of linguistic repertoires, migration history, and age. During the course of transcribing audiotaped family interaction data with native speakers, the issue of orthographic conventions arose frequently. We realized that the very transcription conventions we chose indicated an ideological stance. This, in conjunction with native speakers' metalinguistic commentaries about other participants' speech, led us to investigate the relationships between varieties of speaking and orthography. Our research methods include the use of historical, literary, sociolinguistic, and ethnographic data.

2. According to Saussure, "the signs used in writing are arbitrary; there is no connection, for example, between the letter *t* and the sounds that it designates. . . . Since the graphic sign is arbitrary, its form matters little or rather matters only within the limitations imposed by the system" ([1916]1966:119–120). In the orthography debates about kreyòl, the forms/signs themselves have symbolic value and, therefore, matter.

3. Research investigations of language ideology have pointed out the prevalence of competing ideologies in different types of communities. See, for example, the papers in this volume, and Gal and Woolard 1995.

4. Both Duvalier the father and Duvalier the son adopted a "vanguard" position in comparison with the majority of their constituents' attitudes towards kreyòl and French in Haiti.

5. Ironically, as both Duvaliers based their power on a nationalistic ideology, kreyòl benefited from their policies from a linguistic point of view. Official standardization, how-

ever, cannot by itself change the social and cultural assumptions about the kreyòl language prevalent in Haitian society. For a sociopolitical perspective on the status and functions of several Creole languages in the Caribbean, see Devonish 1986.

6. The use of the term "diglossia" has been the subject of often emotional debates. First used in 1928 by the French Hellenist Jean Psichari (cited in Fattier-Thomas 1987:100), Ferguson 1959 refined the concept to signify two varieties of a language that are functionally distributed and applied it to several cases, incuding Haiti. Ferguson's statements about the relationship between French and kreyòl, though eventually shown to be inaccurate, dominated the way in which many linguists viewed the relationship between the two languages, both structurally and functionally. For various perspectives on this issue see Déjean 1980a, 1983, 1988; Férère 1977; Fishman 1967; Fleischman 1984; Prudent 1980, 1981; Racine 1970; Tabouret-Keller 1982; Valdman 1968, 1976, 1978, 1987; and Winford 1985. Even now, however, one still finds textbooks that refer to Haiti as an example of "classical diglossia" (Fasold 1984:53).

7. See, for example, d'Ans 1968; Bentolila et al. 1976; Carden and Stewart 1988; Déjean 1980a, 1983; Holm 1989; Koopman 1986; Lefebvre 1986, 1990; Lefebvre et al. 1982; Spears 1990; Valdman et al.1983.

8. The main syntactic differences between the southern variety and the other two is the form of the nonpunctual aspect marker *pe* instead of *ap* or *ape*. The distinctive morphosyntactic feature of the northern dialect is the use of the particles *a* and *an* to mark possession, while the other dialects rely on word order alone. At the phonetic level, the northern dialect displays the use of post-vocalic /r/, whereas the other two varieties do not.

9. The term *kreyòl fransize* is not used by the bilinguals themselves to qualify their speech. It is confined to the linguistic literature, according to Pompilus 1990, Lofficial 1992, and others.

10. Used in this way, it is part of a continuum of ripeness, beginning with *vèt* (unripe, green) and ending with *mi* (ripe/ready). These terms, however, are not applied to speech.

11. For a related point see Efron 1954.

12. The exception is in the northern dialect, which has this postvocalic feature throughout (Hyppolite 1949, Orjala 1970).

13. The debate about written forms *wo, wõ, wò*, and *wou* is not about whether they are *rèk* or *swa* but about the pedagogical usefulness of *w* versus *r*. The official orthography gives a choice between *w* and *r*.

14. We have reason to believe that for many Haitians living in New York and Boston where knowledge of French is not necessary to function in society, *kreyòl swa* and *kreyòl fransize* remain the prestige varieties associated with the educated upper social classes.

15. Bourdieu's ideas (1975, 1977, 1979, 1982) concerning prestige language, and symbolic capital illuminate this argument. Bourdieu 1975 argues that through the *langue légitime* (legitimate language)—the language elaborated by the writers and grammarians—the dominant classes establish a distance between themselves and the rest of the speakers. Thus, the language functions not only to communicate but at the same time to set the boundaries between elite and masses, boundaries that are well accepted by all classes, consciously and unconsciously. One of the main characteristic of the legitimate language, "correctness," is a privilege of the dominant classes.

16. Diamond's 1991 article in *Natural History*, titled "Reinventions of Human Languages: Children Forced to Reevolve Grammar Thereby Reveal Our Brain's Blueprint for Language," includes the following:

> Between human languages and the vocalizations of any animal lies a seemingly unbridgeable gulf. . . . One approach to bridging this gulf is to ask whether some people,

deprived of the opportunity to hear any of our fully evolved modern languages, ever spontaneously invented a primitive language. . . . Children . . . [placed in a situation comparable to that of the wolf-boy] . . . hearing adults around them speaking a grossly simplified and variable form of language somewhat similar to what children themselves usually speak around the age of two . . . proceeded unconsciously to evolve their own language, far advanced over vervet communication but simpler than *normal* languages. These new languages were the ones commonly known as creoles. (p. 23; emphasis added)

17. Auguste Brun, a French scholar who wrote in the early part of the twentieth century, claimed that "une langue est un dialecte qui a réussi. Un patois est un langue qui s'est dégradée" (A language is a dialect that has been successful. A patois is a language that has deteriorated) (quoted in Pressoir 1958:27). Such a view is still held by some educated Haitians today.

18. The first official written documents in kreyòl are the proclamations of the Commissaires Sonthonax and Polverel to the slaves (May 26, 1793); the proclamations of the Commissaire Sonthonax to the slaves abolishing slavery (29 August 1793); the proclamation of the First Consul Napoleon Bonaparte to the slaves of Haiti, dated 17 Brumaire, Year Tenth, urging them to warmly receive the French expedition of General Leclerc in 1802 (Fouchard 1972, cited by Jean-Baptiste 1984:17–18.)

19. The first example of literary efforts in kreyòl is a poem called "Lisette quitté la plaine" by Duvivier de la Mahautière (1757), cited in Sylvain 1936:8. Two texts have been located from the early part of the nineteenth century: *Idylles et Chansons ou Essais de Poésie Créole* (1811), cited in Charles 1984:155, and a play by the Haitian author Juste Chanlatte, *Compte des Rosiers* (1818), reproduced in *Le Nouvelliste*, 19 août 1979.

20. The most famous works from that period are written in French mixed with Haitian "creolisms." An example is *Gouverneurs de la Rosée* (Masters of the Dew) by Jacques Roumain, published in 1944 and translated into fourteen languages. It is considered a masterpiece of Haitian literature. A second is *Compère Général Soleil* (Comrade General Sun) by Jacques Stephen Alexis (1955). Both are peasant fiction novels in which one cannot find a single dialogue totally in kreyòl.

21. See, for example, Rigaud's *Tassos* (1933), Morisseau-Leroy's *Diacoute* (1953a), or Pressoir's *Sèt-Poe-M Ki So-T Nan Mo-N* (1954b).

22. For example, Archer 1987, Maysonnave 1991, Métellus 1990, and Michel 1990, to cite but a few.

23. Debates regarding orthography in Mauritius (Robillard 1989) and Martinique (Prudent 1989) show similar divisions between those advocating a phonemic basis and those arguing for an etymological one.

24. The term *bwa-nan-nen* refers to the practice of putting a small wooden pincer, like a clothes pin, on the face or ear of someone who loses at each round of dominoes or cards and is still done in urban as well as rural areas. Pompilus 1973:25 suggested that the appellation *bwa-nan-nen* (wooden stick on the nose) was suggested by the literacy instructors to help their students remember that the circumflex represented nasalization. One characteristic generally admitted of rural kreyòl is extended nasalization (Lofficial 1979:118).

25. For example, Manigat (1970, 1972) suggested that the digraph *sh* instead of *ch* represent the sound /s/. Pompilus 1973 proposed that the letters *c* and *qu* instead of *k* represent the sound /k/; the digraph *ou* instead of the letter *w* represent the semiconsonant /w/; the digraph *oi*, closer to French, represent the dipthong /wa/; the letter *i* instead of *y* represent the sound /j/; the four front rounded vowels already mentioned. Lofficial 1979:120–122 proposed using the ONAAC orthography (the government's adaptation of Pressoir's

orthography) but adding "Pressoir's front rounded vowels" (which, in fact, were not part of Pressoir's orthography) and McConnell-Laubach's representation of nasals (i.e., the circumflex). Other proposals, including those made by Hall 1951a, 1951b, 1953; Churchill 1957; Berry 1964, 1975; and Valdman 1974, received little attention in Haiti.

26. Pompilus 1990 now accepts the official orthography but with reservations regarding the "overuse" of the letters *y* and *w*.

27. For example, Dantès Bellegarde, a prominent thinker of the first half of the twentieth century, wrote:

> La langue française . . . est sans conteste l'idiome dont la connaissance importe le plus au gens cultivés de tous les pays. Par la richesse de son vocabulaire (philosophie, science, médecine, droit, théologie, critique), par ses qualités supérieures de clarté, de précision, et de souplesse, elle mérite bien le nom de langue de civilisation. (The French language is undisputably the idiom of which knowledge is the most important to learned people of all countries. By the richness of its vocabulary [philosophy, science, medicine, law, theology, criticism] by its superior qualities of clarity, precision, and flexibility, it well deserves the name of language of civilization.) (quoted in Garrett 1990:58)

For more details concerning similar views about the French language see Grillo 1989 and Swiggers 1990.

28. Hoffman explains that the Haitians were aware of the paradox inherent in their conscious imitation of those who had caused them so much suffering, the French. "[They] attempted to resolve it by asserting that they had been oppressed in colonial times not by the French, but by the *colons*, a disreputable minority of adventurers recruited from the dregs of French society" (1984:59). These were not the same French of the metropole who epitomized culture and civilization. We thank Paul Garrett for pointing this out.

29. An extremist and nonscientific view associates the unrounded vowels with the African slaves, who were thought to have a congenital incapacity to pronounce sounds properly and consequently had a loose and free pronunciation. Archer has stated, for example, "Les Noirs remplacent toujours *u* par *i*, *eu* par *é*, *un* par *in*, ils rejettent le *r* final; ils ont un parler lâche et libre" (1987:129) (Black people always replace *u* with *i*, *eu* with *é*, *un* with *in*, they drop the final *r*; they have a way of speaking loosely and freely). Interestingly enough, the dropping of the *r* is seen by the French philologist Albert Dauzat as characteristic of the French regional dialects of Normandy and Picardy (Dauzat, cited by Churchill 1957:5).

30. One possible explanation of the origin of this term locates its metaphoric origins in the sounds produced when speaking while sucking a hard candy called a *surette*. Indeed, if one were to speak with a surette in the front of the mouth, all vowels would be rounded (DeGraff 1992).

31. Dejéan states: "L'adoption de graphèmes pour représenter les quatre voyelles antérieures arrondies est une manoeuvre illusoire et trompeuse" (1980a:173) (The adoption of graphemes to represent the four front rounded vowels is but an illusory and tricky maneuver).

32. According to Lofficial,

> Le Dictionnaire Elémentaire Créole-Français privilégie, probablement par souci d'authenticité, des formes qui sont ressenties comme rudes par les Haïtiens. Ainsi chaque fois qu'il y a un choix entre une forme très nasalisée et une autre (*agronnonm* et *agronom*, par example), c'est la première qui est présentée comme forme de base,

l'autre n'étant présentée qu' à titre de variante" (1979:118). (*The Basic Kreyòl-French Dictionary*, probably concerned with authenticity, prefers forms that are considered rough by Haitians. Each time there is a choice between a form very nasalized (*agronnonm* and *agronom* for example), the first is presented as a basic form, the other one just as a variant.)

The dictionary being referred to by Lofficial prints the forms as *agronnòm* var. *agrónòm* (French *agronome* [agronomist]) (Bentolila 1976:21).

33. It is interesting to note that another value is ascribed to the letter *k* in the development of Papiamentu, the creole language spoken in Aruba, Bonnaire, and Curacao, to mark "African ancestry" (Winer 1990:266 fn. 1). In the United States, it is used by black power movements and other groups as a marker of social protest against undemocratic practices, as in "Amerika." Similar symbolic analyses have been carried out concerning the letter *ç* in Catalan and the letter *k* in the creole of Réunion (Neu-Altenheimer et al. 1987).

34. Labov's 1966, 1972 research on hypercorrection and variable norms among socially stratified speakers in New York City is the model for this social variation. While kreyòl does not show variation in the final consonant clusters, there is social variation in initial consonant clusters /sp/ and /st/. The *rèk* variety adds /e/ before the cluster, for example, /espor/ (*rèk*) : /spor/ (*swa*) 'sport'; /estad/ (*rèk*) : /stad/ (*swa*) 'stadium'. This variation has not been discussed in the literature.

35. Our purpose is not to discuss whether the different positions are right or wrong but to see their ideological implications and connections. Déjean, for example, argued that there were too many inconsistencies and difficulties in their use (1980a, 1980b, 1980c), but it may be also that they are viewed as looking "too French."

36. For a discussion of other contested orthographies see, for example, Bernabé et al. 1983, Coulmas 1990, Fodor and Hagège 1982–1990, GEREC 1982, Graves 1991, Hellinger 1986, Jaffe 1990, Ludwig 1989, and Winer 1990.

37. As a postscript, we would like to add the following: As reported by Coles 1990, a French commission made recommendations, approved by the Académie Française, to partially suppress the circumflex (eliminating its use with the letters *i* and *u* but not *o*, *e* and *a*) and also "to remove the hyphen whenever possible." But after much debate, which sometimes took a very aggressive tone, the French Academy decided (by a vote of twenty-three to six) that "pour rien au monde!" the French would not give up their beloved circumflex and hyphens.

However, accents are also being added, especially to foreign words to make them appear more French. At the same time, the spellings of the English words are adapted to French pronunciations and orthography. Since French orthography has always been a major subject of debate, the claim is that these simplifications are meant to improve general spelling skills. It should be noted, however, that the Education Minister hopes that these simplification of spelling will also stop the French language from being overrun by *anglais*. Signs of *la résistance* to these changes are already emerging (Greenhouse 1991; see also *Economist* 1992:43).

REFERENCES

Alexis, Jacques Stephen. 1955. *Compère général soleil* (Comrade General Sun). Paris: Gallinard.

Anderson, Benedict. 1983. *Imagined Communities*. London: Verso.

Archer, Marie Thérèse. 1987. *La créolologie haïtienne: Latinité du créole d'Haïti*. Port-au-Prince: Le Natal.

Beaulieu, Christian. 1939. Pour écrire le créole. *Les Griots* 4:589–598.

Bellegarde, Dantès. 1949. La langue française et le créole haïtien. *Conjonction*, 19.

Bentolila, Alain, Pierre Nougayrol, Pierre Vernet, Charles Alexandre, and Henry Tourneux. 1976. *Ti diksyonnè kreyòl-franse: Dictionnaire élémentaire créole haïtien-français*. Paris: Editions Caribes/Hatier.

Bernabé, Jean. 1985. Créole et code de communication scolaire. *Antilla-Kréyòl* 4:9–13.

Bernabé, Jean, Lawrence D. Carrington, Pat Charles, Félix Henderson, K. Hippolyte, and Pearlette Louisy. 1983. The Development of Antillean Creole. a Report of the Second Creole Orthography Workshop held in St. Lucia, September 16–19, 1982. Castries.

Berry, Paul. 1964. *Research and Development in Applied Psychology and Linguistics for Mass Education in Haitian Creole*. Croton on Hudson, N.Y.: Hudson Institute.

———. 1975. Literacy and the Question of Creole. In *The Haitian Potential: Research and Resources of Haiti*, ed. Vera Rubin and Richard P. Schaedel, pp. 83–113. New York: Teachers College Press.

Bollée, Annegret. 1989. Le développement du créole écrit aux Seychelles. In *Les créoles français entre l'oral et l'écrit*, ed. Ralph Ludwig, pp. 183–200. Tübingen: Günter Narr Verlag.

Bourdieu, Pierre. 1975. Le fétichisme de la langue. *Actes de la Recherche en Sciences Sociales* 4:2–32.

———. 1977. The Economics of Linguistic Exchanges. *Social Sciences Information* 16: 645–668.

———. 1979. *La distinction: Critique sociale du jugement*. Paris: Les Editions de Minuit.

———. 1982. *Ce que parler veut dire*. Paris: Librarie Arthème Fayard.

Carden, Guy, and William Stewart. 1988. Binding Theory, Bioprogram and Creolization: Evidence from Haitian Creole. *Journal of Pidgin and Creole Languages* 5(3):1–67.

Charles, Christophe. 1984. Les pionniers de la littérature haïtienne d'expression créole. *Conjonction* 161–162:151–158.

Churchill, Margareth Anne. 1957. Haitian Creole: Linguistic Analysis and Proposed Orthography. M.S. thesis, Georgetown University.

Coles, Peter. 1990. The French Used to Have a Word for It. *Nature* 347:323.

Coulmas, Florian. 1990. Language Adaptation in Meiji Japan. In *Language Policy and Political Development*, ed. Brian Weinstein, pp. 69–86. Norwood, N.J.: Ablex.

d'Ans, André Marcel. 1968. *Le créole français d'Haïti*. The Hague: Mouton.

DeGraff, Michel. 1992. E-mail message to B. Schieffelin, March 20.

Déjean, Paul. 1963. Problèmes d'alphabétisation en Haïti. Mémoire pour l'obtention de la licence en sciences sociales, dactylographié, Institut d'Etudes Sociales, Institut Catholique de Paris.

Déjean, Yves. 1975a. *Dilemme en Haïti: Français en péril ou péril français?* New York: Les Editions Connaissance d'Haïti.

———. 1975b. Franse se danje. *Sèl* 23–24:32–39.

———. 1980a. *Comment écrire le créole d'Haïti*. Québec: Collectif Paroles.

———. 1980b. Ann kase koub otograf la. *Sèl* 8(48–49):4–5.

———. 1980c. Iv Dejan ap reponn keksyon sèl sou nouvo otograf kreyòl la. *Sèl* 8(48–49):25–35.

———. 1983. Diglossia Revisited: French and Creole in Haiti. *Word* 34:189–213.

———. 1988. Diglossia in Haiti. In *Geolinguistic Perspectives*, ed. J. Levitt, L. Ashley, and K. Rogers. Lanham, Md.: University Press of America.

———. 1993. An Overview of the Language Situation of Haiti. *International Journal of Sociology* 102:73–83.

Devonish, Hubert. 1986. *Language and Liberation: Creole Language Politics in the Caribbean*. London: Karia Press.

Diamond, Jared. 1991. Reinventions of Human Language. *Natural History* (May):22–28.

Doret, Frédéric. 1924. *Pour amuser nos tous petits: Fables de La Fontaine traduites en prose créole.* Paris: Imprimerie des Orphelins-appprentis.

Dorin, Bernard. 1973. La fausse querelle du créole et du français. *Conjonction* 120:9–12.

Economist. 1991. "Comme vous étiez." January 26:43.

Efron, Edith. 1954. French and Creole Patois in Haiti. *Caribbean Quarterly* 3:199–214.

Fasold, Ralph. 1984. *The Sociolinguistics of Society.* Oxford: Basil Blackwell.

Fattier, Dominique. 1987. Portraits de bilingues francophones haïtiens. *Conjonction* 176:97–125.

———. 1993. L'haïtien: Fragments de géographie linguistique. In *La République Haïtienne. Etats des lieux et perspectives,* ed. G. Barthélemy and C. Girault, pp 75–89. Paris: Karthala.

Fattier-Thomas, Dominique. 1984. De la variété rèk à la variété swa: Pratiques vivantes de la langue en Haïti. *Conjonction* 161–162:39–51.

Férère, Gérard A. 1974. Haitian Creole Sound-System, Form-classes, Texts. Ph.D. diss., University of Pennsylvania.

———. 1977. Diglossia in Haiti: A Comparison with Paraguayan Bilingualism. *Caribbean Quarterly* 23(1):50–60.

Ferguson, Charles A. 1959. Diglossia. *Word* 15:325–40.

Fishman, Joshua A. 1967. Bilingualism with and without Diglossia; Diglossia with and without Bilingualism. *Journal of Social Issues* 23(2):29–38.

Fleischmann, Ulrich. 1984. Language, Literacy and Underdevelopment. In *Haiti Today and Tomorrow: An Interdisciplinary Study,* ed. Charles Foster and Albert Valdman, pp. 101–117. New York: University Press of America.

Fodor, Istvan and Claude Hagège, eds. 1982–90. *Language Reform: History and Future.* 5 vols. Hamburg: Buske Verlag.

Fouchard, Jean. 1955. *Le théâtre à Saint-Domingue.* Port-au-Prince: Imprimerie de l'Etat.

———. 1972. *Les marrons de la liberté.* Paris: L'Ecole.

Frankétienne. 1975. *Dézafi.* Port-au-Prince: Edition Fardin.

Gal, Susan. 1991. Bartók's Funeral: Representations of Europe in Hungarian Political Rhetoric. *American Ethnologist* 18(3):440–458.

Gal, Susan, and Kathryn Woolard, eds. 1995. Constructing Languages and Publics. *Pragmatics* 5(2):129–282.

Garrett, Paul Brian. 1990. Spoken Identity: The Social Implications of Language for Haitians. Senior Essay, Department of Sociology, Yale University.

GEREC (Groupe d'Etudes et de Recherches en Espace Créolophone). 1982. *Charte culturelle créole: Se pwan douvan avan douvan pwan non!* Fort-de-France: Centre Universitaire Antilles-Guyane.

Goodman, Morris F. 1964. *A Comparative Study of Creole French Dialects.* The Hague: Mouton.

Graves, William. 1991. Orthographies and Identities: The Politics of Writing in an American Indian Community. Paper presented at the annual meeting of the American Ethnological Society, Charleston, S.C.

Greenhouse, Steven. 1991. A Question of Spelling Turns the French Testy. *New York Times,* January 2:2.

Grillo, Ralph D. 1989. *Dominant Languages: Language and Hierarchy in Britain and France.* Cambridge: Cambridge University Press.

Hall, Robert A., Jr. 1951a. A la recherche d'une orthographe créole. In *Vers une orthographe créole,* ed. Lélio Faublas, pp. 24–27. Port-au-Prince: Imprimerie de l'Etat.

———. 1951b. Le créole et l'orthographe française. In *Vers une orthographe créole,* ed. Lélio Faublas, pp. 28–31. Port-au-Prince: Imprimerie de l'Etat.

———. 1953. *Haitian Creole, Grammar, Texts, Vocabulary*. Washington, D.C.: American Anthropological Association.

Hazaël-Massieux, Marie-Christine. 1991. *Bibliographie des études créoles: Langues, cultures, sociétés*. Paris: Didier-Erudition.

Hellinger, Marlis. 1986. On Writing English-related Creoles in the Caribbean. In *Focus on the Caribbean*, ed. Manfred Görlach and John Holm, pp. 53–70. Amsterdam: John Benjamins.

Hoffman, Léon-François. 1984. Francophilia and Cultural Nationalism. In *Haiti Today and Tomorrow: An Interdisciplinary Study*, ed. Charles Foster and Albert Valdman, pp. 101–117. New York: University Press of America.

———. 1989. *Haïti: Couleurs, croyances, créole*. Montréal: Editions du CIDIHCA (Le Centre International de Documentation et d'Information Haïtienne, Caraïbéene et Afro-Canadienne).

Holm, John. 1989. *Pidgins and Creoles*. Vols. 1–2. Cambridge: Cambridge University Press.

Hornberger, Nancy H. 1995. Five Vowels or Three? Linguistics and Politics in Quechua Language Planning in Peru. In *Power and Inequality in Language Education*, ed. James W. Tollefson, pp. 187–205. Cambridge: Cambridge University Press.

Hyppolite, Michelson P. 1949. *Les origines des variations du créole haïtien*. Port-au-Prince: Imprimerie de l'Etat.

Jaffe, Alexandra. 1990. Language, Identity and Resistance on Corsica. Ph.D. diss., Indiana University, Bloomington.

Jean-Baptiste, Pauris. 1984. Kreyòl nan literati politik ak literati ofisyèl. *Conjonction* 161–162:15–22.

Jean-Charles, Hervé Louis. 1987. Attitudes of Teachers and Parents toward French and Creole in Haiti, Ph.D. diss., Stanford University.

Koopman, Hilda. 1986. The Genesis of Haitian: Implications of a Comparison of Some Features of the Syntax of Haitian, French, and West African Languages. In *Substrata versus Universals in Creole Genesis*, ed. Pieter Muysken and Norval Smith, pp. 231–258. Amsterdam: John Benjamins.

Labov, William. 1966. *The Social Stratification of English in New York City*. Washington, D.C.: Center for Applied Linguistics.

———. 1972. *Sociolinguistic Patterns*. Philadelphia: University of Pennsylvania Press.

Labuchin, Rassoul. 1973. Graphie du créole, point de vue. *Conjonction* 120:40–44.

Lefebvre, Claire. 1986. Relexification in Creole Genesis Revisited. In *Substrata versus Universals in Creole Genesis*, ed. Pieter Muysken and Norval Smith, pp. 279–300. Amsterdam: John Benjamins.

———. 1990. La genèse du créole haïtien. *Interface* 2(5):27–33.

Lefebvre, Claire, Hélène Magloire-Holly, and Nanie Piou, eds. 1982. *Syntaxe de l'haïtien*. Ann Arbor, Mich.: Karoma.

Lofficial, Frantz. 1979. *Créole, français: Une fausse querelle*. Montreal: Collectif Paroles.

Ludwig, Ralph, ed. 1989. *Les créoles français entre l'oral et l'écrit*. Tübingen: Günter Narr Verlag.

Manigat, Max. 1970. Alphabet "Jé Kléré," une nouvelle méthode de transcription du créole haïtien. Unpublished manuscript.

———. 1972. Kèk lidé sou òtograf kréyòl la. *Sèl* (December):30–32.

Maysonnave, Georges Edouard. 1991. Lettre au Dr. Georges Michel. *Le Nouvelliste* (March 12):5.

Métellus, Jean. 1990. Simplification de la langue. Réforme de l'orthographe. Enjeux linguistiques. Poétique et technologie. *Le Nouvelliste* (July 6–8):1, 8, 10.

Michel, Georges. 1990. *Lettre à Lucien Montas à propos de la réforme éducative*. Port-au-Prince: Editions Fardin.

Morisseau-Leroy, Félix. 1953a. *Diacoute*. Port-au-Prince: Imprimerie Deschamps.

———. 1953b. *Antigone en Créole*. Port-au-Prince: Le Centre de Production de Materiel Educatif.

Neu-Altenheimer, Irmela, J. Carpanin Marimoutou, and Daniel Baggioni 1987. Névrose diglossique et choix graphiques: <<ç>> in catalan et <<k>> en créole de la Réunion. *Lengas* 22:33–57.

Numa, St. Arnaud. 1975. *Jénéral Rodrig. Adaptation Le Cid*. Port-au-Prince.

Orjala, Paul. 1970. A Dialect Survey of Haitian Creole. Ph.D. diss., Hartford Seminary Foundation.

Pompilus, Pradel. 1973. De l'orthographe du créole. *Conjonction* 120:15–34.

———. 1977. *Histoire de la littérature haïtienne illustrée par les textes*, 3. Port-au-Prince: Editions Caraïbes.

———. 1985. *Le problème linguistique haïtien*. Port-au-Prince: Imprimerie Deschamps.

———. 1990. Conversation with Rachelle Doucet, August 28.

Pressoir, Charles Fernand. 1947. *Débats sur le créole et le folklore*. Port-au-Prince: Imprimerie de l'Etat.

———. 1954a. Méthode de français oral: Passage du créole au français. Port-au-Prince: Imprimerie de l'Etat.

———. 1954b. *Sèt-Poe-m Ki So-T Nan Mo-N*. Port-au-Prince: Imprimerie de l'Etat.

———. 1958. L'avenir du créole dans notre petit pays. *Bulletin du Bureau d'Ethnologie* III, 16:26–31. Port-au-Prince: Imprimerie de l'Etat.

Price-Mars, Jean. 1973. *Ainsi parla l'oncle*. new ed. Montreal: Lemeac.

Prudent, Lambert-Félix. 1980. *Des baragouins à la langue antillaise*. Paris: Editions Caraïbéennes.

———. 1981. Diglossie et interlecte. *Langages* 61:13–38.

———. 1989. Ecrire le créole à la Martinique: Norme et conflit sociolinguistique. In *Les créoles français entre l'oral et l'écrit*, ed. Ralph Ludwig, pp. 65–80. Tübingen: Günter Narr Verlag.

Racine, Marie-Marcelle Buteau. 1970. French and Creole Lexico-Semantic Conflict: A Contribution to the Study of Languages in Contact in the Haitian Diglossic Situation. Ph.D diss., Georgetown University, Washington, D.C.

Rigaud, Emile. 1933. *Tassos*. Haiti.

Robillard, Didier de. 1989. Le processus d'accession à l'écriture: Etude de la dimension sociolinguistique à travers le cas du créole mauricien. In *Les créoles français entre l'oral et l'écrit*, ed. Ralph Ludwig, pp. 81–107. Tübingen: Günter Narr Verlag.

Roumain, Jacques. 1944. *Gouverneurs de la roseé*. Port-au-Prince: Imprimerie de l'Etat.

Roumer, Emile. 1973. Graphie du créole, point de vue. *Conjonction* 120:39–40.

Saussure, Ferdinand de. [1916]1966. *Course in General Linguistics*. New York: McGraw-Hill.

Silverstein, Michael. 1979. Language Structure and Linguistic Ideology. In *The Elements: A Parasession on Linguistic Units and Levels*, ed. Paul Clyne, William Hanks, and Carol Hofbauer, pp. 193–247. Chicago: Chicago Linguistic Society.

———. 1987. Monoglot "Standard" in America. Working Papers and Proceedings 13. Chicago: Center for Psychosocial Studies.

Singler, John. 1993. African Influence upon Afro-American Language Varieties: A Consideration of Sociohistorical Factors. In *Africanisms in Afro-American Language Varieties*, ed. Salikoko Mufwene, pp. 235–253. Athens: University of Georgia Press.

Spears, Arthur. 1990. Tense, Mood and Aspect in the Haitian Creole Preverbal Marker System. In *Pidgin/Creole Tense, Modality, Aspect Systems*, ed. John V. Singler, pp. 119–142. Amsterdam: John Benjamins.

Swiggers, Pierre. 1990. Ideology and the "Clarity" of French. In *Ideologies of Language*, ed. John E. Joseph and Talbot J. Taylor, pp. 112–130. New York: Routledge.

Sylvain, Georges. 1901. *Cric? Crac! Fables de la Fontaine racontées par un Montagnard haïtien et transmises en vers créoles*. Paris: Ateliers Haïtiens.

Sylvain, Suzanne. 1936. *Le créole haïtien, morphologie et syntaxe*. Port-au-Prince: Wetteren.

Tabouret-Keller, Andrée. 1982. Entre bilinguisme et diglossie. *Le Linguistique* 18:17–44.

Trouillot, Michel-Rolph. 1979. *Ti difé boulé sou istoua Ayiti*. New York: Koléksion Lansièl.

———. 1990. *Haiti: State against Nation: The Origins and Legacy of Duvalierism*. New York: Monthly Review Press.

Valdman, Albert. 1968. Language Standardization in a Diglossia Situation. In *Language Problems in Developing Nations*, ed. Joshua A. Fishman, Charles A. Ferguson, and Jyotirindra Das Gupta, pp. 313–326. New York:Wiley.

———. 1974. L'élaboration d'une orthographe. *Revue de la Faculté d'Ethnologie* 24:5–14.

———. 1976. Vers la standardisation du créole en Haïti. In *Identité culturelle et francophonie dans les Amériques*, ed. Emile Snyder and Albert Valdman, pp. 166–201. Quebec: Les Presses de l'Université.

———. 1978. *Le créole*. Paris: Klincksieck.

———. 1984. The Linguistic Situation of Haiti. In *Haiti: Today and Tomorrow*, ed. Charles Foster and Albert Valdman, pp. 77–100. New York: University Press of America.

———. 1987. Le cycle vital créole et la standardisation du créole haïtien. *Etudes Créoles* 10(2):107–125.

———. 1988. Diglossia and Language Conflict in Haiti. *International Journal of the Sociology of Language* 71:67–80.

———. 1989a. Aspects sociolinguistiques de l'élaboration d'une norme écrite pour le créole haïtien. In *Les créoles français entre l'oral et l'écrit*, ed. Ralph Ludwig, pp. 43–63. Tübingen: Günter Narr Verlag.

———. 1989b. Vers la déminorisation des créoles. In *Actes du symposium organisé par l'Association Internationale de Linguistique Appliquée et la Commission Interuniversitaire Suisse de Linguistique Appliquée*. Neuchâtel, September 16–18, 1987, pp. 187–206. Geneva: Librarie Droz SA.

———. 1991. Decreolization or Dialect Contact in Haiti. In *Development and Structures of Creole Languages*, ed. Frank Byrne and Tom Huebner, pp. 75–88. Philadelphia: John Benjamins.

Valdman, Albert, Robert Chaudenson, and Marie-Christine Hazaël-Massieux, eds. 1983. *Bibliographie des etudes créoles, langues et littératures*. Bloomington: Indiana University Creole Institute.

Vernet, Pierre. 1980. *Techniques d'écriture du créole haïtien*. Port-au-Prince: Le Natal.

———. 1989. Alphabétisation en Haïti. Aspects Linguistiques. *In Hommages au Dr. Pradel Pompilus*, ed. Centre de Linguistique Appliquée, pp. 17–36. Port-au-Prince: Imprimerie Deschamps.

Winer, Lise. 1990. Orthographic Standardisation for Trinidad and Tobago: Linguistic and Sociopolitical Consideration in an English Creole Community. *Language Problems and Language Planning* 14:237–268.

Winford, Donald. 1985. The Concept of Diglossia in Caribbean Creole Situations. *Language in Society* 14:345–356.

Woolard, Kathryn. 1989. Sentences in the Language Prison. *American Ethnologist* 16:268–278.

———. 1992. Language Ideology: Issues and Approaches. *Pragmatics* 2(3):235–250.

Zéphir, Flore. 1990. Language Choice, Language Use and Language Attitude of the Haitian Bilingual Community. Ph.D. diss., Indiana University.

15

Multiplicity and Contention among Language Ideologies

A Commentary

SUSAN GAL

The phenomena brought together in this volume as "language ideologies" would have been examined, some years ago, under several different rubrics. For example, the ethnography of speaking was from its beginnings concerned with cultural conceptions about the role of speaking in social life. Linguists and philosophers of language have pondered the implications for linguistic structure and use of the provocative fact that ordinary language is always and unavoidably its own metalanguage. Many students of interaction have noted that, to understand interaction, one has to have cultural categories for "what is going on," and what can possibly be going on, in any strip of talk. Scholars of multilingualism and language contact, no less than the makers of language policy, have understood that choice of a language has political implications exactly because of speakers' commonsense convictions about what a language is and what the use of a language is assumed to imply about political loyalty and identity. And historians of ideas have noted the important influence that linguistic theories and social movements have often had on each other. The studies in this volume suggest that reframing such apparently diverse yet familiar problems as all questions of "language ideology" will produce a Nekker cube effect: a switch in perception and perspective that will allow neglected, yet related, aspects of these phenomena to become newly visible.

Several important consequences of this change in perspective are suggested by the contributions gathered here, especially when they are read in the context of related work. I highlight four related issues and the directions for further research that these imply: matters of scale; the "semiotics of dominance"; the relationship between local ideas about language and other conceptual systems; and representations of sociolinguistic difference and their sociopolitical effects. In each of these four areas, the case studies make provocative contributions by emphasizing the widespread multiplicity of linguistic ideologies and the social contestations that occur around them.

Matters of Scale

Despite the diversity of its definitions, the notion of language ideology allows an integrated study of social phenomena usually taken to be of different *scales* of analysis, and therefore too rarely discussed together in social approaches to language. Detailed studies of face-to-face interaction, for instance, have demonstrated the means by which some interactants in meetings are silenced while others gain credibility, or the ways in which responsibility and intentionality are assigned to speakers in different cultural contexts (see Brenneis and Myers 1984, Duranti 1990, Hill and Irvine 1993). Yet, despite the evident relevance of ideas about authority and responsibility to state politics, it has seemed difficult to bring these understandings from the study of interaction to bear on the imposition of national languages and orthographies, for instance, or to bring them into the same theoretical framework as the study of large-scale political movements formed around language. It is therefore instructive that the notion of linguistic ideology allows for the integration of what, in more traditional terms, would seem to be different "levels" of social phenomena (e.g. macropolitical and microinteractional). To the degree that the implicit assumption of a micro/macro split has determined, in practice, the researcher's choice of field site and method, a switch in focus encourages multisite and multimethod research, a trend that converges with developments in other corners of social science. In both these ways, the focus on linguistic ideology puts aside the overly familiar separation of phenomena into levels and fruitfully suggests dissections of social life along different lines.

For instance, for middle-class Americans, ideas that make "transparency" in language an index of personal honesty and responsibility are arguably as important in constituting civil society as they are in mediating expectations about the nature of friendship in routine, everyday conversation. The papers in Part III—in contrast to many earlier studies in linguistic anthropology—exemplify this important movement along the dimension of scale. A focus on ideology allows James Collins (chapter 12) to reveal both the bases of conflict and the intimate connections between actors who seem to share an interest in language maintenance but are located in social organizations of quite different scale: informally linked speakers of Tolowa, professional linguists in university settings, and managers in state-sponsored programs of language teaching. Similarly, Charles Briggs (chapter 11) is able to make the presence of the nation-state visible within his analysis of the verbal contests among local elites by showing how the linguistic skills of the younger contenders (literacy, competence in Spanish) can compete with the quite different skills of older leaders only because the younger men's skills are made valuable through institutions based on the nation-state's linguistic ideology. Joseph Errington, too (chapter 13), ranges across institutions, showing that in different sites, Indonesian is both the language through which the state and its officials communicate with a distant populace and also a medium for a new kind of common, intersubjective experience within that populace. In their consideration of Haitian attitudes towards orthography, Bambi Schieffelin and Rachelle Doucet (chapter 14) are able to discuss the prestige-effects of particular sounds and letters in local interaction, but also their symbolic implications for national imagery and international relations.

If the notion of "language ideology" encourages analysis to emcompass both social interaction on the one hand and, say, state policy on the other, this is in part because it can be understood both as verbalized, thematized discussion and as the implicit understandings and unspoken assumptions embedded and reproduced in the structure of institutions and their everyday practices. While language ideology always refers to matters of human understanding—ideas, consciousness, and beliefs about the relation of language and talk to social life—different traditions in the analysis of ideology have staked out diverse stances on the question of how explicit such understandings are and where one might look for evidence of them. Woolard here calls this the different "sitings" of ideology. Put another way, some theories have assumed that signification is fundamentally separate from materiality, while others, in contrast, assume ideational matters to be inscribed in the lived relations of everyday life.[1] In these latter approaches, language and signification are inseparable from materiality and action. The general question of the "siting" of ideology involves basic assumptions about the efficacy of language and its relation to action and thought. Therefore, this question is itself an aspect of linguistic ideology in our current scholarly life.

Because social organizations and institutions that differ significantly in size, spatial dispersion, and duration (consider, for instance, the differences between states, NGOs, schools, political movements, professional societies, town meetings, friendships, and market interactions) can all nevertheless be constituted around cultural principles about the relation of language to social life, while also enacting implicit understandings of such a relation, a focus on language ideologies can enable analyses to range across social arrangements of different extent and temporality. By starting with linguistic ideologies, one can highlight unexpected links, contestations, and contradictions among such organizations, thereby bringing them within a single theoretical purview.

Multiplicity and the Semiotics of Dominance

Whatever analytic advantages are gained by ranging across different scales of social institutions, these are not usually considered the major theoretical issues invoked by the term 'ideology'. More usually attended to, as the contributions in this book remind us, are the varying links among social position, knowledge, and power. Reflecting on these matters, the papers in Part III implicitly reject the position that linguistic ideology is a politically neutral cultural construction, no different from a "worldview" about language. But they equally reject the notion that ideas about the role of language in social life are merely distortions of a separately knowable (perhaps scientifically knowable) reality. Instead, they assume that social life and its materiality are constituted through signifying practices. Thus, different ideologies construct alternate, even opposing realities; they create differing views arising from and often constituting different social positions and subjectivities within a single social formation.

This emphasis on multiplicity in the analysis of linguistic ideologies within a social formation is an important theoretical departure, when seen against earlier studies. Recall that the ethnography of speaking usually attributed to each social group a single, patterned worldview about language. Even in variationist studies, which otherwise celebrated heterogeneity, the speech community was defined as the locus of shared evaluations and attitudes toward varieties (Labov 1972). This explicitly excluded variation from the realm of what we here would call ideology. Less expected, perhaps, is that an assumption of ideological uniformity persists, though in diluted form, in more recent studies that discuss linguistic variation in terms of symbolic domination. For in these works there has been a tendency to identify a single, monolithic, and firmly entrenched "dominant" ideology—often linked to the state (as in Bourdieu) or to an economically dominant class—which is then seen to be in conflict with oppositional views implicity built around a single cultural principle encoded in linguistic practices (e.g., local solidarity, human dignity). The work of J. Scott on the linguistic "arts of resistance" is perhaps the best example of this genre (see Gal 1995).

Yet, if we understand dominant ideology, for the moment, to be the ideology of dominant groups, there is ample evidence that, like the social makeup of dominant groups themselves, their ideologies are rarely monolithic, nor always stable. Schieffelin and Doucet show that discursive battles about kreyòl orthography have long been common among Haitian elites. And, as Collins demonstates, there are "multiparty conflicts" among actors in Californian institutions that are all dominant—state-supported schools, scholarly disciplines—but are nevertheless built around importantly different language ideologies. Lest one think that smaller social formations are more likely to be homogeneous in this respect, Briggs shows that among the Warao, leaders' ideas about language are various and sometimes contradictory.

This empirical evidence for multiplicity, however, suggests only a linkage between ideologies and diverse (elite) social positions. As Woolard notes, this is analytically distinct from the role of ideologies in the acquisition or maintenance of social, economic, and political power. It is useful, in this connection, to focus for a moment on concepts of power. Recall that in recent years there have been several successive conceptualizations of the way in which linguistic practices contribute to the attainment of positions in a social formation, with each formulation implicitly relying on a different understanding of power (Lukes 1974). Most familiar is the notion that linguistic skills—expertise in particular linguistic practices—provide access to material resources and leadership positions through institutions like schools, literary production, or performance genres such as verbal dueling. Second, knowledge of linguistic practices can provide the means for effectively participating in decision-making events that require culturally recognized skill in speech, such as oratory or debate.

But, it is the third definition that ultimately undergirds the other two and is our central focus here: ideas and signifying practices provide (enacted) representations of the social world. A diverse set of social theorists has argued that the power of such signifying practices resides not only in their ability to constitute social groups and subjects (positionality), but also in their ability to valorize one position, one group, and its practices or knowledge over that of others; to formulate—but also to elide, preclude, or disable—possible forms of action. Power resides as well in the ability of some ideologies to gain the assent or agreement even of those whose social identities, characteristics, and practices they do *not* valorize or even recognize. This is an insight shared by otherwise quite diverse conceptualizations of ideological phenomena: "symbolic domination," "cultural hegemony," and Foucauldian "discourse." In this sense, some ideas and practices are "dominant," not simply because they are produced or held by dominant groups, but because their evaluations are recognized and accepted by, indeed partially constitute, the lived reality of a much broader range of groups.[2]

The various theorists who have formulated notions of such a dominant ideology vary a great deal in how open and vulnerable to opposition they conceive these ideas to be. Perhaps most mobile and flexible, in this respect, is the tradition surrounding the Gramscian notion of hegemony. Many interpreters of Gramsci emphasize that dominant ideas achieve a "saturation of the whole process of living" (Williams 1977:110) and may be all the more powerful because they are the taken-for-granted aspects of a larger field of more explicit ideological phenomena. Yet there is general agreement that such hegemony is never absolute or total. Rather, it is a process, constantly being made, partial, productive of contradictory consciousness in subordinate populations, therefore fragile, unstable, vulnerable to the making of counterhegemonies. For this very reason, dominant ideas are susceptible to defeat by alternative ideologies, new hegemonies built out of activities in economic interactions and civil society (Bocock 1986:98; see also Woolard 1985).[3]

Given this conceptualization, the focus on multiplicity and contention among linguistic ideologies leads to a deeper question: In the contestation among ideologies, by what processes does any ideology become dominant, that is, more authoritative or credible than others, if only temporarily and partially? The making of hegemony no doubt requires the assertion of social control over various modes of symbolic production. But how is such control turned into cultural effectiveness? It is a commonplace that successful ideologies routinely render their view of the world "natural," "essential," "universal," "ahistorical," "commonsensical" (Eagleton 1991:56–59). What has not been noted is that naturalization and essentialization are semiotic transformations or effects. In the analysis of how such effects are achieved, it is crucial to understand that semiotic processes themselves require interpretation through linguistic ideologies. That is, in order to achieve their effects, semiotic devices must be filtered through cultural assumptions about how language works in social life. Thus, language ideologies are doubly significant. Clearly, their logic and relation to other ideas warrant attention, just as do ideas in any cultural domain. But because they participate in the semiotic processes through which ideas become naturalized, essentialized, universalized, or commonsensical, ideas about language are implicated in the process by which *any* cultural ideas gain the discursive authority to become dominant.

Bakhtin's famous discussion of the "authoritative word" raised exactly this issue. Whereas much of ordinary interaction, as well as novelistic discourse, consists of the heteroglossic quoting, reporting, and interpenetration of our own words with those of numerous others, he argued that "authoritative" speech is resistant to being creatively assimilated, penetrated, or subverted by another speaker or author (Bakhtin 1981:342; see also Voloshinov 1973). In a more limited domain, Bloch (1975) tried to capture the same sort of insight by characterizing "traditional" oratory as powerful because it required the use of fixed, formulaic, apparently unchangeable utterances attributed to ancestors. In contrast, more recent discussions have argued that a crucial device in the creation of authoritative discourse is not rigidity of form but rather the metapragmatic practice of reported speech itself. But, like any other such formal device, reported speech gains its social significance within the diverse range of linguistic ideologies that define how speakers should "hear" or interpret it. More broadly, this points to linguistic ideology as a guide to speakers for how they should understand the (metapragmatic) cues that relate linguistic signals to their contexts of use and that provide information about the 'what is going on here' of interaction (Silverstein 1993; for an earlier, related sense of "cues" see Gumperz 1982).

For example, in varying cultural contexts it is possible to create or evoke, through reported speech, authorizing realms such as that of the gods, ancestors, nature, or the collective social unit, which can then be heard as speaking through the utterers. Moreover, through the diverse ways of framing another's utterance within one's own, speakers are able to distance themselves from responsiblity for the opinions expressed or, contrarily, to associate themselves more closely with the quoted speaker or entity. The impressive ability of reported speech to construct authority, and the sorts of authority it creates, depend on the ideological formation and historical moment in which reported speech occurs: what is more highly valued and how, the individual or the collective voice? What are the implications of acting in accordance with the wishes of the gods, ancestors, science, the "people," or the public will? Who or what is understood to have agency, intentionality, and, hence, voice in regard to the matter at issue: individual actors, fate, distant officials, an anonymous public? Indeed, through close study of devices such as reported speech and their ideological loading, it is possible to discern the real-time construction of timelessness, naturalness, and social normativity in interaction. It is possible to see how agency is attributed to realms and speakers invoked by reported speech and how it is artfully attached to the goals and positions of actual speakers (see, e.g., Lucy 1993, Hill and Irvine 1992).

In his contribution to this volume, Briggs presents a rich description of Warao linguistic ideologies surrounding reported speech, through which cultural ideas about inequality are authorized and particular "misrecognitions" are invited. This is an excellent example of the doubled interest in linguistic ideology: through a single metapragmatic device, interpreted within quite different linguistic ideologies, actors contest each others' attempts to create discursive authority, not only concerning language, but also in other domains. For instance, women's ritual wailing is heard not as the opinion of any one or even many different individuals but, rather, through one local ideological interpretation of reported speech, as the unimpeachable voice of the collectivity. But gossip, another local genre, is not heard as the voice of the group, although it too is a form of reported speech. Instead, senior male curers who are criticized by subaltern gossip can devalue it by invoking another linguistic ideology according to which only curers have true access to the 'beginnings' of things and, thus, to the sort of knowledge that gossip is supposed to provide. Elder curers try to deflect all challenges by assimilating them to the category of "gossip." Because the linguistic ideology that valorizes the specialized knowledge of curers overrides all others in gossip events, the validity of other sources of knowledge is thereby suppressed, and the curers' version of truth telling—an important aspect of the social status quo—is authorized above others.

Although I have been discussing reported speech, there are other metapragmatic devices around which linguistic ideologies form and that can somtimes achieve the semiotic effects so closely linked to dominance. For instance, Caton's (1990) study of politics among Yemeni tribesmen highlights not reported speech and invocations of outside authority but, rather, the use of poetic parallelism in political persuasion. The recent exploration of decontextualization and recontextualization of genres, chunks of speech, and text also promises to reveal some of the ways in which recounted events and replayed performances can be made to appear—within specific linguistic ideologies and historical contexts—as timeless, ahistorical, and even universal phenomena (see Briggs and Bauman 1992, Silverstein and Urban 1996).

It is the recognition that hegemony is never complete and that, in any social formation, ideologies—including linguistic ideologies—are multiple and at odds that renders the achievement of domination problematic, often fragile, and makes the semiotic aspects of its constant construction important to explore.[4]

Linguistic Ideologies and Other Conceptual Systems

I have been discussing the ways in which linguistic ideologies shape the interpretation of talk. Viewed from another perspective, however, the importance of linguistic ideologies for social research lies exactly in the fact that they are not only about talk. They envision and enact connections between aspects of language and other arenas of social life. Ultimately, any analysis of language ideologies will want to understand the social institutions that create and enact these links and the effects of the social relationships produced. However, a first important task is to specify the cultural logic by which different populations make connections between ideas about language and such apparently diverse categories as morality, emotions, aesthetics, authenticity, epistemology, identity, nationhood, development, or tradition.

A double analytical strategy is apparent in many studies of language ideology: ideologies that appear to be about language, when carefully reread, are revealed to be coded stories about political, religious, or scientific conflicts; ideologies that seem to be about, say, religion, political theory, human subjectivity, or science invite reinterpretation as implicit entailments of language ideologies or as the precipitates of widespread linguistic practices (e.g., Gal and Woolard 1995a). The contributions in Part III deftly show exactly such interconnections, with a focus on the political. Indeed, it appears that images of linguistic phenomena gain credibility when they create ties with culturally salient aesthetic, moral, scientific, or political arguments. And, conversely, ideas about language often contribute to legitimation (or, in Bourdieu's term, misrecognition) of political arrangements.

A familiar example will illustrate this point. In the course of the nineteenth century, European philosophy and political practice did the ideological work of making the connection between the categories of "language" and "nation" appear a necessary, natural, and self-evident one, used as much in everyday political discourse as in scholarly arguments. This occurred in part through the establishment, by the end of the eighteenth century, of a science of language that, in contrast to well-established earlier views, defined its object of study as a natural entity, out there to be discovered. While understood to be a product of human nature, language was nevertheless widely seen as independent of individual voluntary acts and as therefore not the creation of any self-conscious human will or intervention (see, e.g., Taylor 1990). In linguistics, as in the creation of other European sciences over the same lengthy period, what is now meant by "objectivity" was constituted in part through a series of steps that attempted to deny or extirpate the "personal" and the "willed" from the project of scientific observation and analysis (Daston and Galison 1992). And, exactly because the formation and characteristics of languages were thought to be objective in this sense, hence prior to intentional human political activity, they could be called on to justify political actions, such as the formation of states for populations putatively linked through shared linguistic origins.

Thus, scientific epistemology undergirded linguistic debates about nationhood, which themselves had political consequences. But aesthetic arguments were also involved. For example, while linguistic unity provided one legitimation of nationhood in Europe, another version of the European national idea understood uniformity of language throughout the nation-state to be important for other reasons. It was thought indispensable to ensuring free communication among a rational and mobile citizenry that could thereby achieve modernity and the exercise of its political rights (Hobsbawm 1990). The infamous French debates on this subject credited the aesthetic qualities of the French language—its supposedly exceptional clarity, simplicity, exactness, referential adequacy—with the ability to ensure rational discourse among citizens. In this way they justified policies that subordinated and eliminated other, supposedly less well-endowed, languages spoken on French territory (Weber 1979, Swiggers 1990).

Although later generations of scholars have repeatedly tried to dissolve the cultural link among language, race, and social group (e.g., Boas 1940, Hymes [1968] 1984), these connections have remained powerful as part of the traveling discourse of the nation-state, with varied repercussions in diverse regions. The contributions by Errington and by Schieffelin and Doucet examine the play of these ideas in two postcolonial situations. Errington's subtle analysis notes the irony of the highly successful Indonesian language, which indexes not any primordial ethnic group but the rationalizing and modernizing plans of the state and its rhetoric of "development." Yet the vision of ethnolinguistic nationhood is not absent. It is evoked through a double historical elision. The rhetoric of linguistic development erases the particularity of the colonial populations that spoke a precursor of Indonesian, projecting instead the tradition of an earlier, spurious, unified ethnicity. It allows, as well, a backgrounding of colonialism, to which an earlier form of Indonesian (colonial Malay) would otherwise have to be linked. Thus, Indonesian language, like the state, can be planned and improved in the future but in the past has no embarrassing precedents. Given this implicit equation, arguments about the development, planning, and instruction of Indonesian are always also about policies and images of the current Indonesian state.

Similarly, Schieffelin and Doucet, in their carefully nuanced exploration of a highly sensitive debate, note that intellectuals' long-standing discussions about the beauty of Haitian sounds and orthography are hardly concerned simply with writing or even with metalinguistic judgments. They are coded arguments about a dual national identity, internal social stratification, and international relations. In choice of sounds to represent orthographically, it is the ethnic definition of nationhood that is most clearly at issue: whose pronunciation is to be represented, hence, what part of the stratified population is to count as the most authentic speakers of kreyòl? But the modernizing or rationalizing discourse of nation is also in evidence: some question whether "authenticity" should count at all, rather than education, civility, sophistication, and instrumental questions of upward mobility.

Intricate arguments such as these, intertwining local aesthetics, political theories, and epistemological commitments with images and ideas about language, appear to be widespread, occurring in quite different cultural and political systems and under varying political economies. They must lead us to complicate considerably Anderson's (1983) influential proposals about the relationship between language and nationhood. First, it is clear that not only communities but also languages must be imagined before their unity can be socially accomplished. They are not the self-evident natural facts that Anderson assumes. Further, contestation occurs around definitions of language as much as around community. Second, it seems evident that culturally embedded ideas about language are involved in processes of political legitimation well beyond the by now notorious case of imagined primordial ethnicity in the modern nation-state.

For instance, nineteenth-century Yemeni society, ruled by the traditional Islamic law-code *shariʿa*, has been described as a "calligraphic state" (Messick 1993) because political power accrued to scholars trained to memorize and interpret sacred written texts in locally specific ways. The legitimacy of leaders depended on their place in a chain of oral apprenticeships, ideally reaching back to Mohammed and the model of his own memorization of the word of God. This "textual domination," creating authority through practices that produced the effect of oral continuity, contrasts interestingly with the linguistic practices of radicals in the years of the French Revolution. Here, too, local theories of language seem to have been key. But these were put in the service of making discontinuity out of the materials of the past: a practice of politics for what was claimed to be a wholly new kind of government. Among the French, politicized groups at all levels were obsessed with renaming the entire social world and with oaths that performatively constituted speakers as members of the new category "citizen" (Hunt 1984). In both these cases one could fruitfully explore the precise mechanisms for discursively creating continuity, as opposed to social rupture, by either eliding or highlighting intertextual gaps (Briggs and Bauman 1992).

Finally, we might add to these examples Habermas's ([1962]1989) analysis of the European public sphere as a form of politics that, he claims, provided the early legitimation for liberal democracy against absolutist monarchy. Habermas points to the way a rising bourgeoisie imagined an ideal of politics as a novel communication process: groups of private individuals who gather to discuss matters of common concern bearing on state authority and whose debates are decided on the basis of reason, rather than by the relative statuses and particular identities of the interactants. The point is not whether such communication ever actually existed, a matter about which there is considerable doubt among historians (Calhoun 1992). A reanalysis of Habermas suggests, rather, the notion of a "public" depends on the image of a sociolinguistic process. It evokes a kind of conversation—either face-to-face or mediated by anonymous print—conceived to be both emblem and legitimator of a democratic political order that proposed to include "everyone" by being no-one-in-particular (Gal and Woolard 1995b).

The effect of impersonality and print mediation required to produce a "public" is worth discussing in the same theoretical framework as the authority emanating from distant realms believed to be accessible only through reported speech. Both of these are invocations of "absence" and, hence, contrast suggestively with the necessity of "co-presence" and the centrality of script characteristic of the linguistic ideology that constructed Yemeni textual domination. However, the more general point is that language ideologies, when intertwined with the formation of states and with cultural conceptions about matters that we might roughly gloss as power, beauty, and truth, deserve not only explication but considerably more comparative attention.

Representations of Sociolinguistic Difference

But the question of comparison immediately raises more fundamental and reflexive concerns. First, a crucial issue for the study of language ideology is how local theories define what is "linguistic" at all, and, second, how they conceive of the connection between people and the linguistic forms they use. For instance, different ideologies recognize or highlight different units of language as salient and as indicative of speakers' identities. There are doubtless perceptual constraints on the sorts of linguistic units that tend to be noticed by speakers (Silverstein 1981, Errington 1985). But there is clearly a range of variation, even within such constraints, that is not totally arbitrary and deserves further explication. Thus, a central task in the study of linguistic ideologies is to understand the semiotic processes by which "chunks" of linguistic material gain significance as linked to, or representative of, socially recognized categories of people and activities. In attempting such an analysis, one needs to attend to the ideas of linguists, linguistic anthropologists, and other professional observers whose positioned, interest-laden views of such linkages are as worthy of ideological analysis as are any other of the many perspectives likely to coexist in a social formation.

Concerning the first question, discursive battles about what constitutes a language or what counts as linguistic knowledge are evident in several of the contributions to Part III. A memorable set of vignettes enables Collins to show how Tolowa speakers are alert to lexicon and to the connection of words to landscape, memory, and desire. Structuralist linguistics provides a familiar contrast to this view, since it devalues such lexical and contextual focus in favor of attention to grammatical patterning in isolation from ongoing discourse. Both are different from a bureaucratic understanding in which knowledge is equated with lexical domains perceived as exotic and testable. As Collins notes, linguistic assumptions and the representations of language that emerge from them define the academic "us" as well as the ethnographic "them." Similarly, Schieffelin and Doucet reveal a wide range of professional opinion about what kreyòl "really" is or should be.

Significantly, conflicts arise not only about what a language is but also how linguistic forms map onto social groups. While Athabaskanist linguists argue about who speaks "real Tolowa," Tolowa speakers themselves resist this implicitly standardizing position, conceiving of Tolowa as the resource of extended kinship groupings. They question the effort to have a general linguistic description for the entire valley, let alone all possible speakers. Similarly, the Javanese cartoonist cited by Errington is questioning exactly whose knowledge is depicted by the official representation of Javanese.

The ubiquity of arguments among speakers and professional observers about the mapping of linguistic forms onto social groups indicates a need for further conceptualization of the way such links are formed. Rather than seeking the elusive correlations that will definitively reveal who really speaks what language "on the ground," I suggest the entire "mapping" problem is most productively approached as a question of language ideology. How are linguistic differences noticed and understood by speakers and observers in different social positions? How are linguistic differences connected to culturally salient images of social groups and activities? Whatever correlations are empirically found will be, in part, a complex result of such conceptualizations.

Several current approaches to these questions draw on Peirce's important distinction among indexical, iconic and other sign forms. I would like to focus on a conceptual scheme that Judith T. Irvine and I are currently developing (Gal and Irvine 1995; Irvine and Gal, forthcoming) and briefly explore its relevance to the studies collected here.

It is by now a commonplace of sociolinguistics that linguistic forms become indexes of the social groups that regularly use them. Such connections between speakers and linguistic forms often enough arise out of contingent circumstances, historical accidents. But, however they arise, we have observed that both the system of linguistic contrasts and the system of social categories are usually noticed by speakers and are elaborated, systematized, and rationalized.

These elaborations are, in effect, ideologies of linguistic differentiation that have at least three semiotic properties. First, in numerous examples we have noticed that the sign relationship between linguistic features and the social images to which they are linked is transformed; linguistic differences that index social contrasts are reinterpreted as *icons* of the social contrasts. In this process of *iconization*, the ideological representation fuses some quality of the linguistic feature and a supposedly parallel quality of the social group and understands one as the cause or the inherent, essential, explanation of the other. As Irvine (1989) has argued, linguistic features are assumed to be expressions of broader cultural images of people and activities. Participants' ideologies about language locate—and sometimes even generate—linguistic phenomena as part of, and as evidence for, what they believe to be systematic behavioral, aesthetic, affective, and moral contrasts among the social groups indexed. Schieffelin and Doucet's description of *kreyòl rèk* provides an excellent example. The perceived quality of the sounds and grammatical features associated with *kreyòl rèk* (harsh, deformed, debased, simple) are "usually attributed to the speakers themselves . . . ," thereby illustrating exactly the process of iconization.

A second semiotic process that appears to be closely linked to iconization in ideologies of linguistic differentiation is *recursiveness*. This involves the projection of an opposition salient at one level of relationship onto some other level. Thus, the dichotomizing and partitioning process that was involved in some understood opposition (between groups or identities) recurs in distinctions made within the group, creating subcategories that mimic the original contrast. In this way, intragroup distinctions can be projected onto intergroup relations, or vice versa. Once again, Schieffelin and Doucet's nuanced descriptions might be reread in this way. For example, the iconically linked characteristics of people and varieties apparent in the opposition between *kreyòl rèk* and *kreyòl swa* appear to be partially replicated in debates about how kreyòl and its speakers contrast with French and francophones. Intranational contrasts are projected onto international relations, and vice versa. In Errington's case, the "ethnicization" of Javanese seems to proceed by an attempted recursive projection in which Javanese, however esoteric in actual practice and thus inappropriate to the role, is nevertheless reframed by New Order ideologues to be a monolithic, subordinated, ethnic language, parallel to other ethnic languages within Indonesia, just as Indonesian is seen as a homogeneous, standardized, national language among the other such languages of the world.

This immediately highlights *erasure*, the third semiotic process common in ideologies of linguistic differentiation. Erasure occurs when an ideology simplifies a sociolinguistic field, forcing attention on only one part or dimension of it, thereby rendering some linguistic forms or groups invisible or recasting the image of their presence and practices to better fit the ideology. Recursiveness itself often leads to the erasure of inconvenient elements. New Order linguists attempting to subordinate and ethnicize Javanese systematically elide the esoteric and hierarchized nature of its literature and verbal etiquette. They bemoan the loss of this esoteric register but ignore the fact that control of the most refined forms was never common beyond elite circles. As Errington notes, this double erasure is exactly what is involved in ethnicizing Javanese, refiguring its earlier image as highly stratified (socially and linguistically) into a new image of homogeneity that makes Javanese more bendable to the New Order's legitimating purposes. He also provocatively suggests that the institutionalization of this erasure might well hasten the linguistic effect of leveling that it projects. As another illustration, we might turn to Collins. The academic insistence that the real Tolowa was "always just receding on the historical horizon" could well be understood as an erasure that makes invisible the current usage patterns of Tolowa speakers that do not fit the scholarly ideology of regular structural principles.

Operating together in a particular historical context, iconization, recursiveness, and erasure are semiotic processes that can produce the kind of naturalization—this time of sociolinguistic differentiation—that I noted earlier as the effect of linguistic ideology in the making of discursive authority and in the achievement of political legitimation through images of sociolinguistic process. Furthermore, it appears that the processes of iconization, recursiveness, and erasure can themselves sometimes become the object of attention, debate, and ideological contestation. These papers alert us to the fact that we must carefully attend to the specific historical and political processes through which some representations of language are made to "stick," thereby excluding or debasing alternate images.

Conclusions

The strength of these contributions is their subtle, precise disentangling of the multiple ideologies of language that coexist in a single social formation. They vividly document how such simultaneous representations and assumptions vie and articulate with each other within social institutions of varying scale and temporality. By taking semiosis seriously, it is possible to show exactly how linguistic ideologies create discursive authority through processes of naturalization, detemporalization, and essentialization and thus to give substance and analytic bite to broad concepts such as misrecognition, hegemony, and legitimation. The task is to explicate how linguistic forms, when interpreted through particular linguistic ideologies, come to be seen as evidence of the moral, intellectual, and aesthetic qualities of speakers and to demonstrate that, when linked to ideas about knowledge, identity, groupness, and beauty, linguistic ideologies provide the justification for widely varying political arrangements.

NOTES

1. On the one hand, cultural analysis in anthropology has often assumed that salient terms and metaphors, folk theories, and local exegesis are the primary sources for investigating cultural conceptions, including ideas about language. Similarly, in the Marxist tradition, work inspired by *The German Ideology*'s concern with the ruling ideas of the ruling class focused on ideas that are verbalized, thematized, and often codified. On the other hand, a hermeneutic tradition in ethnography focuses on the implicit meanings that can be inferred from rituals and other events. Similarly, in scholarship inspired by Marx's discussion of commodity fetishism, (mis)understandings of social causation are analyzed as a result of ideas implicitly inscribed in a set of social relations. On this second view, ideology is enacted in the structured social practices through which humans act on the world. They must be inferred from action (including, often, linguistic action) and are not always easily accessible to conscious reflection. Such otherwise distinct approaches as Althusser's

notion of "subjectivity," Bourdieu's "symbolic domination," Gramsci's always contested "hegemony," Bakhtin's "voice," and Foucault's "disciplines" of everyday life share this quality of being understood as inscribed in lived relations.

2. There are, of course, theorists who claim that dominant ideas are not usually "accepted" by subaltern groups but, rather, that such groups lack the unity or wherewithal to oppose them (Abercrombie et al. 1980). Such theories reject the centrality of ideology in the maintenance of social formations.

3. Indeed, some readings of Gramsci emphasize a similarity to Max Weber, in that consent to dominant ideologies is understood to be built not so much on unspoken practices but on intellectual and moral leadership (see Bocock 1986).

4. The focus on the multiplicity of linguistic ideologies also suggests some methodological priorities. Arguments and debates about language, by a variety of social actors, are particularly fertile sites for determining what ideologies are in play and how they articulate. Furthermore, such ideologies are often most explicitly declaimed and implictly enacted within public performances of various kinds. Frequently, these are political and religious festivals, rituals, mass-mediated celebrations, and debates inscribed in texts. It is not coincidental, then, that Errington finds effective the strategy of focusing on a single well-publicized event. He infers the enabling presuppositions of a state-sponsored Javanese Language Congress, in which agents of the Indonesian state gathered to explain, and performatively enact, a redefinition of Javanese identity within Indonesia. Schieffelin and Doucet unravel the meaning and fate of kreyòl orthography through critical readings of several generations of scholarly argument. By suggesting that such empirical materials and venues deserve special scholarly attention, the focus on linguistic ideologies has had the salutary result of expanding and extending a long-standing methodological preference in linguistic anthropology to focus primarily on the structuredness of face-to-face talk.

REFERENCES

Abercrombie, Nicholas S., Stephen Hill, and Bryan S. Turner. 1980. *The Dominant Ideology Thesis.* London: George Allen and Unwin.

Anderson, Benedict. 1983. *Imagined Communities.* London: Verso.

Bakhtin, Mikhail M. 1981. *The Dialogic Imagination.* Austin: University of Texas Press.

Bloch, Maurice. 1975. Introduction to *Political Language and Oratory in Traditional Society.* London: Academic Press.

Boas, Franz. 1940. *Race, Language and Culture.* New York: Free Press.

Bocock, Robert. 1986. *Hegemony.* London: Tavistock.

Bourdieu, Pierre. 1991. *Language and Symbolic Power.* Cambridge, Mass.: Harvard University Press.

Brenneis, Don L., and Fred R. Myers, eds. 1984. *Dangerous Words.* New York: New York University Press.

Briggs, Charles L., and Richard Bauman. 1992. Genre, Intertextuality and Social Power. *Journal of Linguistic Anthropology* 2(2):131–172.

Calhoun, Craig, ed. 1992. *Habermas and the Public Sphere.* Cambridge Mass.: MIT Press.

Caton, Steven. 1990. "*Peaks of Yemen I Summon.*" Berkeley: University of California Press.

Daston, Lorraine, and Peter Galison. 1992. The Image of Objectivity. *Representations* 40:81–128.

Duranti, Alessandro. 1990. Politics and Grammar: Agency in Samoan Political Discourse. *American Ethnologist* 17:646–666.

Eagleton, Terry. 1991. *Ideology.* London: Verso.

Errington, Joseph. 1985. On the Nature of the Sociolinguistic Sign: Describing the Javanese

Speech Levels. In *Semiotic Mediation*, ed. Elizabeth Mertz and Richard Parmentier, pp. 287–310. Orlando, Fla.: Academic Press.

Gal, Susan. 1995. Language and the "Arts of Resistance." *Cultural Anthropology* 10(3): 407–424.

Gal, Susan, and Judith T. Irvine. 1995. The Boundaries of Languages and Disciplines: How Ideologies Construct Difference. *Social Research* 62(4):967–1001.

Gal, Susan, and Kathryn A. Woolard, eds. 1995a. Constructing Languages and Publics. *Pragmatics* (special issue) 5(2):129–282.

Gal, Susan, and Kathryn A. Woolard. 1995b. Constructing Languages and Publics: Authority and Representation. *Pragmatics* 5(2):129–138.

Gumperz, John J. 1982. *Discourse Strategies*. New York: Cambridge University Press.

Habermas, Jürgen. [1962] 1989. *Structural Transformation of the Public Sphere*. Cambridge, Mass.: MIT Press.

Hill, Jane, and Judith T. Irvine, eds. 1993. *Responsibility and Evidence in Oral Discourse*. New York: Cambridge University Press.

Hobsbawm, Eric. 1990. *Nations and Nationalism since 1780*. New York: Cambridge University Press.

Hunt, Lynn. 1984. *Politics, Culture and Class in the French Revolution*. Berkeley: University of California Press.

Hymes, Dell. [1968] 1984. Linguistic Problems in Defining the Concept of "Tribe." In *Language in Use*, ed. John Baugh and Joel Sherzer, pp. 7–27. Englewood Cliffs, N.J.: Prentice Hall.

Irvine, Judith T. 1989. When Talk Isn't Cheap: Language and Political Economy. *American Ethnologist* 16:248–267.

Irvine, Judith T., and Susan Gal. Forthcoming. Language Ideology and Linguistic Differentiation. In *Regimes of Language*, ed. Paul Kroskrity. Santa Fe, N.M.: School of American Research.

Labov, William. 1972. *Sociolinguistic Patterns*. Philadelphia: University of Pennsylvania Press.

Lucy, John, ed. 1993. *Reflexive Language*. Cambridge: Cambridge University Press.

Lukes, Steven. 1974. *Power: A Radical View*. New York: Macmillan.

Messick, Brinkley. 1993. *The Calligraphic State*. Berkeley: University of California Press.

Silverstein, Michael. 1981. The Limits of Awareness. Working Papers in Sociolinguistics 84. Austin, Tex.: Southwest Educational Development Laboratory.

———. 1993. Metapragmatic Discourse and Metapragmatic Function. In *Reflexive Language*, ed. John Lucy, pp. 33–58. Cambridge: Cambridge University Press.

Silverstein, Michael, and Greg Urban, eds. 1996. *Natural Histories of Discourse*. Chicago: University of Chicago Press.

Swiggers, Pierre. 1990. Ideology and the "Clarity" of French. In *Ideologies of Language*, ed. John E. Joseph and Talbot J. Taylor, pp. 112–130. New York: Routledge.

Taylor, Talbot J. 1990. Which Is to Be Master?: Institutionalization of Authority in the Science of Language. In *Ideologies of Language*, ed. John E. Joseph and Talbot J. Taylor, pp. 9–26. New York: Routledge.

Voloshinov, V. N. 1973. *Marxism and the Philosophy of Language*. Cambridge, Mass.: Harvard University Press.

Weber, Eugen. 1979. *Peasants into Frenchmen*. Stanford, Calif.: Stanford University Press.

Williams, Raymond. 1977. *Marxism and Literature*. Oxford: Oxford University Press.

Woolard, Kathryn A. 1985. Language Variation and Cultural Hegemony. *American Ethnologist* 12:738–748.

INDEX